Cultu

Around the World

An Ethnographic Reader

Paul V. McDowell

Kendall Hunt
publishing company

Cover image © Shutterstock, Inc.

Kendall Hunt
publishing company

www.kendallhunt.com
Send all inquiries to:
4050 Westmark Drive
Dubuque, IA 52004-1840

Printed in the United States of America
10 9 8 7 6 5 4 3 2 1

Contents

CHAPTER 1

Introduction to the Case Studies

Introduction

This collection of ethnographies was inspired by the presence of several existing ethnographic anthologies that have one element in common: they each take one theoretical theme or another. As readers, we are invited to focus on a cultural materialist perspective, or a postmodern one, or one of symbolic interactionism. To present a straight ethnography is, well, so Boasian, so last century.

Yet implicit in this collection is the argument that the first step to a scientific anthropology is to generate information that is as accurate as conditions will allow. The conditions should involve an ethnographer whose observations and recordings are as free of bias—any bias—as possible, a difficult task but not impossible. The conditions should also involve reliance on key and non-key informants who are sincerely committed to having their culture as faithfully represented as possible. Both require careful provision and recording of information and taking critical pains to ensure that such information is accurate.

This selection is not exactly a "back to the Bible" screed but to suggest that the time has come to represent each case study as is reflected in the ethnographies. There is no conscious axe to grind in this collection. No doubt there will be questions as to whether the ethnography is accurate or not. But we have to start from somewhere. Corrections may be in order in some instances, but no amount of adversarial comment will clarify unless it originates from solid observation and research of the culture and its people themselves.

For example, Napoleon Chagnon's study of the Yanomamö of southern Venezuela has been the target of acrimonious debate (Borofsky 2005). The accounts of the Yanomamö as originally presented form the core of the case study, but I also mention in the selected literature section some of the critiques of that ethnography. As a viewing of *Secrets of the Tribe* demonstrates, the debates resemble something of a soap opera. Was Kenneth Good's marriage to, and subsequent divorce from, a young Yanomamö woman an instance of pedophilia for which he could have been indicted in his home state of Pennsylvania? Did a French ethnographer obtain his data by successfully propositioning a passel of Yanomamö males to engage in homosexual acts with him? Did Chagnon and his team actually infect his informants with a deadly strain of measles? These issues are referenced in both a video and two books.

The approach I will take to the Chagnon et al. study is to present the most updated ethnography of Chagnon's work and provide references that will lead the careful or determined researcher to competing interpretations. Borofsky's review cited in the Amazonian chapter is the most comprehensive review of these issues. Other videos and literature are cited for all the chapters in this work.

To conclude, the collection is presented in the spirit of Jack Webb's famous quote through Dragnet's Sgt. Friday: "Just the facts, ma'am" (or sir, if you prefer). I leave interpretation to others and the references at the end of each chapter serve as leads to the available range of interpretations.

Strategy of this Collection

The purpose of this collection is to provide a starting point for 20 cultures, all of which originated in a college course titled, like this book, "Cultures Around the World." The descriptions are a first start for the reader, and each chapter ends with some recommended videos and literatures that will lead to further resources. The references are generative rather than comprehensive; each reference will lead to others not listed here. The aim is to provide the raw material for understanding human behavior: the diverse ways of making a living, the cooperation necessary to organize work, how exchanges of goods and services take place, the various concepts of ownership and property (or lack thereof), the means of social control through governance and law (or lawlike customs), the various beliefs in the supernatural, and how different cultures have come to terms with economic and political globalization which, at present, is dominated by a corporate power elite.

This book attempts to represent different cultures around the world with different degrees of complexity. Thus, we include the foraging bands (Inuit and the !Kung or the more accurate Ju/'hoansi), the tribal peoples (the cattle herders of Kenya, the peoples of Amazonia/Orinoco in South America, and those of Papua New Guinea), the chiefdoms (the Northwest Coast, the Trobriand Islands, the Afghans), and the state level societies ranging from the agrarian (West Africa—the Aztecs, Mayan, and Inca and their descendants) to the empires (Egypt, Mesopotamia/Iraq) to the states of contemporary times (Bali, Tibet, China, India). Throughout, the question repeats itself—can we in twenty-first century Britain or the United States or Europe learn from these peoples how to handle our own affairs? The main continents are represented—the Americas, Africa, the Middle East, and Central, Southern, and East Asia.

To save time, the next chapter covers the elements common to several cultures. What is culture anyway and how is it acquired? How do peoples around the world make a living, exploit and distribute their resources, products, and services? How do they organize themselves into family and larger family-derived units? What kind of social control do they exercise? Finally, how do the different cultures view the supernatural and what practices involving the unseen are observed?

CHAPTER 2

Cultural Anthropology: A Reference Guide

Introduction

Many of the terms you will encounter in the case studies involve technical concepts that become repetitive as you move from one ethnography to another. Several cultures observe patrilineal descent, practice cross-cultural marriage, or rely on foraging for survival. Therefore, it seems appropriate to put into one chapter the basic ethnographic concepts that you will encounter in the case studies that follow. These concepts are defined and explained.

The concepts include basic elements of culture: subsistence systems—how people make a living worldwide—kinship, marriage, and family types along with their extensions; economic and political organization, which are often fused together; religion and magic; and broad trends in cultural change and globalization. For all of these, the commonalities are described and explained in this chapter. The case studies will look at how these concepts fit within their ethnic contexts.

Culture: Their Salient Features

The word *anthropology* is derived from two Greek words: *anthropos,* which means "man" or "human," and *logos,* which means "the science of," or "the study of," or "the logic of." There are hundreds, if not thousands, of definitions of anthropology. We'll stick to one definition to which most of the others would agree: **Anthropology is the comparative and holistic study of humankind.** That means that anthropology is the study of human groups taken as a whole and involving comparison of such groups throughout the world, and that is our concern in this collection of ethnographies.

One of the first anthropologists to define culture was Edward Burnett Tylor, the gentleman who founded anthropology at Oxford University in England. Before going to the next topic, read this definition carefully. Can you see that it involves a holistic approach: "That complex whole"? It gives a sampler of what anthropologists look at: knowledge, belief, arts (which includes basic skills like making tools), and so on. Then notice that these are "acquired," namely by learning. Last, man is a "member of society." That anticipates the next discussion.

3

Anthropologically, then, culture concerns human behavior as guided by rules of the society of which they are a part; it is not just about individuals or even groups, but of entire societies. Such societies may be small, such as the Chumash of coastal California, with a hundred or so people making up a group in precontact times. They may comprise entire nations, as Japan does with its millions sharing the same language and culture. Culture has at least five attributes that separate human groups from nonhuman ones.

a. **Culture is learned.** Culture entails learning rather than genetic transmission. Ants, fish, and termites all acquire their behavior through the genes. That does not mean that nonhuman animals lack learning. For example, dogs do learn, but their behavior is the product of conditioning, or repeated training with rewards. Humans, on the other hand, apply their learning to new situations. In anthropology, *enculturation* refers to the transmission of a society's culture from one generation to the next.

b. **Culture is based on symbolism.** *Symbolism* is the capacity to bestow a meaning to a thing or event (e.g., speech) which has no inherent relationship to the thing itself. Symbols can be reflected in a stop sign, or a cross, or a Star of David; there can be negative associations, such as the hammer and sickle in the now-disintegrated Soviet Union or the swastika in Nazi Germany. These are commonplace meanings of symbols.

From a cultural standpoint, the most important form of symbolism is language. As you can see and hear for yourself, there is no meaning to the letters [k] or *c* or a or [æ] or [t] or *t*. Puzzled by the letters in the square brackets? These are letters from the **International Phonetic Alphabet,** or IPA, used to standardize spoken sounds on paper. Language acquires meaning only when these letters are strung together to form words. By themselves, *c*, *a*, and *t* mean nothing. Strung together, *cat* means something in English—a feline creature, or perhaps a make of bulldozer. Strung together another way, *act* means performance on the stage. Tack [tæk] is what you pin on a bulletin board. Although this seems a trivial example, language is the basis of culture. Without language, there is no culture. Picture symbolism as water, and we're the fish. Without the water, we are nothing, and we have nothing. The same applies to language: no language, no culture.

c. **Culture is shared.** A culture may be shared among a group of people who speak a common language and share a common set of customs. Such groups may be as small as 50 persons in a !Kung San (Ju/'hoansi) band or a dispersed assemblage of Inuit families—or as numerous as 117 million people in Japan, which is probably the least ethnically diverse nation in the world. (The largest indigenous minority in Japan are the northern Ainu.)

d. **Culture is patterned or integrated.** One aspect of a culture reflects other aspects of society as well. For example, the !Kung (now also known by their own name Ju/'hoansi) observe a sharing ethic that reflects the changing fortunes of the hunt. Because of their hunting technology—bows and arrows tipped with a weak poison—game is hard to come by. If you share your game today, someone else will share his tomorrow. The "owner of the arrow" that first penetrated the animal "owns" the animal—but only to give it away. Elderly may "own" the arrow and play that role of distribution. Sharing is king when it comes to game. Meantime, women provide most of the food (via gathering roots, nuts, and berries), and, partly for that reason, they have a large say as to where the band should move to next.

Of course, all societies have some aspects that make them somewhat less than integrated, and there may be internal conflicts. Consider our own, which, despite its self-concept as the land of the free and the home of the brave, there are institutions which deny freedom to our own, let alone the peoples of other countries of the world. And many would consider the current president as lacking the quality of bravery. Edgerton in his 1992 *Sick Societies* documents many societies similarly less than integrated.

e. **Culture is generally adaptive.** !Kung are in a relatively impoverished environment that could not sustain anything more complex than hunting and gathering; private ownership, legally known as fee simple, would militate against survival. In one instance, the attempt by one band of !Kung to herd goats proved disastrous as the animals exhausted a limited water supply.

As you can surmise, we cannot see culture. An axe is a product of culture, but it is not culture. This intangible blueprint is what guides our behavior as cultural beings. This is what enables the five characteristics of culture we just reviewed: learning, sharing, integration, adaptation, and symbolism—to become evident in behavior and its products. We have a physical architecture and a cognitive architecture—and they come in both sexes and, culturally speaking, two genders. We will return to that point in gender relations.

Finally, as you read the ethnographies in this collection, note that each culture is within a specific time frame. Hoebel's description of the Cheyenne, for example, is set in the 1840s though he describes them as if their features were the present. This describes the principle of the **ethnographic present.** Indeed, as change is taking place rapidly among all cultures in today's globalizing world, the ethnographer has no choice but to describe a culture in terms of its ethnographic present. The !Kung San of Nyae Nyae district in South West Africa were described by the Marshall Family through three time frames. The ethnographic present of this band as hunters and gatherers was the 1950s; that for their period in a South African internment camp was 1960–1990; and that for their cattle ranching was 1990 to the present under the new nation-state of Namibia. The ethnographic present will be specified for each culture and culture area in this collection.

Kinship: The Superstructure of Non-Western Culture

Most preindustrial societies, except those with large populations (mostly states, but with a few exceptions), are based on primary, or face-to-face relations. Of these, the most important is kinship, or human relations based on the facts of birth, marriage, and death. It is perhaps the first organization known to humankind because it is closest to the biological functions affecting all human groups: copulation, reproduction, maturation, and death.

Why Kinship?   Kin groups, or groups based on marriage and family, are often the unit of property ownership; you cannot know anything about property ownership until you know who is included and is excluded from the property-owning group, and to know that, you need to know the principles of descent. Kin groups are often the unit of economic cooperation. They also govern the political units of a culture and society; for example, in **chiefdoms** or **states,** descent determines who will be chief or king, and it may rank nobles to each other, as is the case among Northwest Coast Indians. Certainly, with the widely reported practice of ancestor worship, kinship has some bearing on supernatural beliefs, as we will see in many cultures. Finally, kinship affiliation may even determine whom one fights, as is the case among the pastoralist Nuer of Ethiopia and the Sudan.

Constants of Kinship

Based in part on Robin Fox's *Kinship and Marriage,* one might identify six constants—four biological and two sociopsychological—that underlie kinship affiliation and its uses. They are as follows:

Biological Constants
a. Women bear the children
b. Men impregnate the women
c. Children are dependent on adults for a long period (15 years, more or less)
d. Death comes to all and demands a replacement

Psychological and Social Constants
a. Primary kin may not mate with each other (the incest tabu)
b. Men exercise the authority in households and wider social groups

Biological Constants. No human population is free from sex, reproduction, child rearing, or death, so these four qualify as constants, functions that kinship must fulfill. The first two constants—male procreation and female childbearing—involve at least minimum cooperation between the sexes. The third constant recognizes the long period of the mother's nurturance of her child, followed by a long period of **enculturation,** or child rearing, whereby the child acquires the skills, values, and norms of the society necessary to become a full participant in the affairs of the band, village, or other society. Finally, death takes away a member and demands a replacement. The member's property must be inherited or otherwise disposed of, the household headship must be filled by a survivor, and the vacated kingship demands a successor. As we shall see, each of these constants generates a role that kinship must play.

Psychological and Social Constants. Although neither the incest tabu nor male dominance is entirely universal, they are statistical equivalents of constants. Almost all cultures, according to pre-vailing assumptions in anthropology prohibit sexual behavior between **primary kin:** father-daughter, mother-son, brother-sister. (The main exception is royal incest; Egypt in ancient times will cover that practice.) Others prohibit sexual behavior among **secondary kin** as well; those who are related by **consanguineal** or blood ties. They may range from cousins to any two persons related by a distant ancestor whose identity may not even be known.

As for male dominance, the question is less certain from a statistical standpoint. Many house-holds are female dominated. Among the Iroquois or Haudenosaunee, women owned the long-houses and the gardens, and had enough influence to initiate a divorce by placing their husbands' belongings outside the doorway. Women's status vary from complete subordination among the Masai and Chinese to equal partnership among the !Kung to strong influence among the Iroquois and Hopi. Nevertheless, some kinship roles assume male dominance in many societies, if not all.

Kinship as a Social Reckoning of Biological Fact.
It must be remembered that biology alone does not determine kinship. If this were true, the Romans would not have to write into family law,

as they in fact wrote, that "the father of the child is the husband of the mother"; that would have been understood. In many societies, the father is not always the husband of the mother, nor in some societies does it matter.

We could also point out that our own system of **reckoning** kin, or recognizing persons as one's relatives, goes along the lines of biology. We do recognize kin on our father's side as equal to those on our mother's side. This assumption, however, overlooks our forgetfulness. Try to recall the first names of all the siblings of your four grandparents or the first name of all eight of your great grandparents. For most readers, point made. In other cultures, there are rules of eligibility that eliminate some of the bilateral kin for certain purposes, such as land ownership or community decision making rights.

Defining Rules of Descent

The term **descent** refers to the rules that affiliate individuals with particular sets of kin because of known or presumed common ancestry. More prosaically, descent concerns those rules by which individuals are placed into the category "kin" or "relative" because of known or presumed ancestry. Descent implies rights and obligations. They may involve certain rights, such as inheritance, or access to use of cattle or land, or rights of political succession. They also involve duties, such as hospitality, or cattle herding, or defense of the homestead against invaders.

Taken at a broad perspective, there are two major kinds of descent: **bilateral** and **unilineal.** Note the Latin etymology, or origins, of the two words. "Bilateral" comes from *bi–* or "both" and *–lateral,* which means "side"; that means that bilateral descent emphasizes both sides of a person's descent affiliation. "Unilineal" comes from *uni–* or "one" (more precisely, "one, and only one") and *–lineal,* which means "line." Therefore, the term emphasizes a line of males or females that links a person to his or her ancestor. The meanings of bilateral and unilineal involve two referents— *two* versus *one* and *side* versus *line*—and not just one referent (*two* versus *one*). This point is important and will be repeated throughout our discussion; kinship will not make sense without this understanding.

But first things first. Let's start with the basics of kinship diagrams, using Figure 2.1 on bilateral descent to illustrate. Every kinship chart starts with ego, namely you. All the males are triangles, all the females are circles, and those of either sex are squares. The horizontal line connecting the figure (triangles, circles, or squares) from above links siblings of either sex and so is called a **sibling link.** A vertical line connects one generation to the next and is therefore called a **generational link.** An equal sign connects two spouses and so is called an **affinal link.** If the spouses are drawn too far from each other on a chart for an equal sign, they are connected by a horizontal line drawn *below* the two figures, and is likewise called an affinal link. Ego is always drawn in black. These preliminaries done, we can get down to business.

Bilateral Descent. **Bilateral descent** refers to the rule of descent whereby kinsmen are reckoned (recognized) through both male and female kin equally; distance between kin is used to mark off different kinds of kin. Emphasized here are the sides, or lateral aspect, as well as the two sides of one's family (namely, the "father's side" and the "mother's side").

One example of bilateral descent is our own (i.e., Euroamericans of North America). First, we consider that our mother's family and relatives are no less related to ourselves than those of our father's family and relatives. Furthermore, under the laws of most states and provinces, sons and

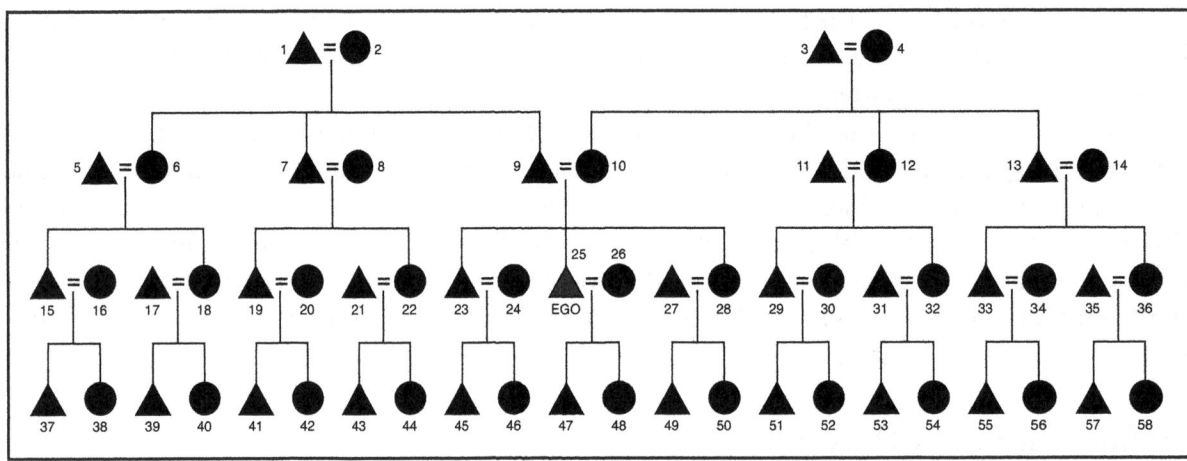

FIGURE 2.1
Bilateral descent. Can you exclude *anyone?*

daughters whose parents die intestate (without a will) have equal inheritance rights; legally and often in practice. If we mention our "grandmother," others might ask "which one?" since she could be our father's mother or mother's mother or, to express it in common language, my "grandmother on my father's side" or our "grandmother on my mother's side."

So far, then, we cannot really speak of ancestors. Which ancestor would you choose two generations back? Your father's father? Your mother's mother? How about your father's mother, or mother's father? As you can see, bilateral descent means that you could have four ancestors two generations back, eight ancestors three generations back, sixteen ancestors four generations back—the possibilities are endless and, without rules of exclusion, useless. (Actually, cultures with a bilateral rule of descent do reckon ancestors, but only by rules of exclusion that make their relationships manageable.)

Therefore, it is not surprising that everyone on the diagram is related to everyone else. All the **consanguineal** kin are related to each other, and all the **affinal** kin are tied together by their children. By definition, affiliation through bilateral reckoning is limited only by biological ties, and only socially derived rules can limit these ties.

Unilineal Descent. **Unilineal descent** refers to the descent rule whereby kin is **reckoned** (recognized) through one line of descent only, either through males or females, but not both. Here, the lineal, not lateral, aspect is emphasized. **Patrilineal descent** is the rule of affiliation through descent lines of males only.

To see how this works, refer to the next chart on patrilineal descent.

The first order of business is to learn the rules of descent. We westerners reckon, that is recognize, our kin through the male and female sides of the family equally. Our mother's brother's children, mother's sister's children, father's sister's children, and father's brother's children are all the same to us: cousins. This is bilateral reckoning, as you have seen above.

But other cultures do things differently. Take the patrilineal Yanomamö, for example. They reckon only one side of the family as their own and that expression "one side of the family" is not

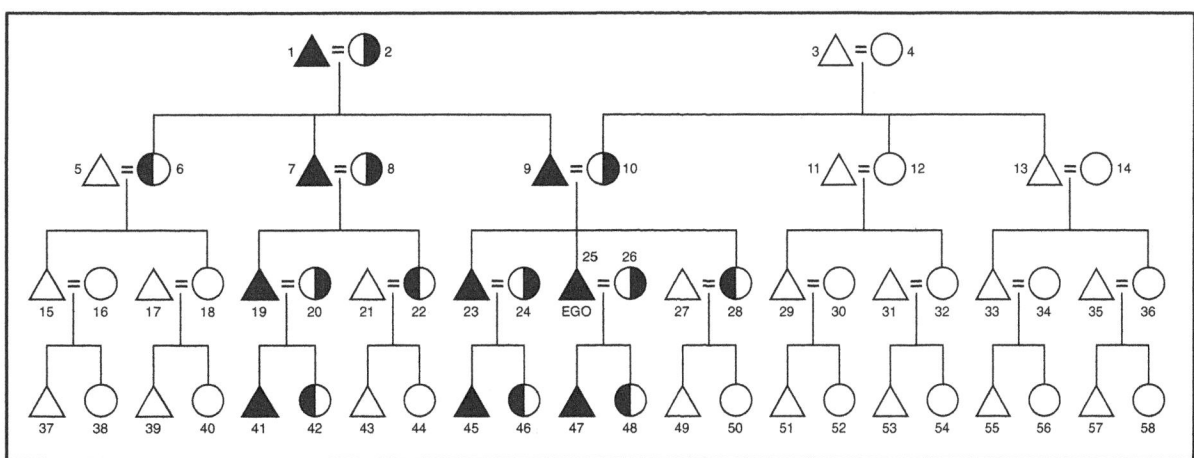

FIGURE 2.2
Patrilineal descent. Note relations among consanguineal males that include No. 25.

quite accurate. They reckon only a *line,* not side, of males as kin: father, father's father, father's father's father, and so on. Our system of surnames is that way.

In patrilineal descent, all the males (triangles) are shaded black, denoting the fact that a man gets his patrilineal affiliation from his father and passes it down to his son. A woman obtains her affiliation from her father, but she does not pass her affiliation either to her son or to her daughter. In other words, the patrilineal buck stops with her, and with all female kin. This means that the males only are connected to a patrilineal group, provided that the male line is unbroken by a female. Women who marry *out* of Ego's group are denoted with the left half of the circle shaded black. Women who marry *into* Ego's group are shaded in black to the right half of the circle.

For fun, practice with your own last name. Give Ego your last name. (If you are a married woman, use your maiden name). Then trace those with your name. From whom did your name come from? Your father? Your father's father? To whom will you pass your name? Make your own chart. Then, who will be born with your last name but will lose it when she marries? Your sister, right, or your father's sister? Now who will get your name upon marriage? Your wife? Your father's wife (also known as your mother)? Once you have filled out a chart of your own, it will look like the chart in Figure 2.2. Your naming system is patrilineal!

In contrast with **patrilineal descent,** the term **matrilineal descent** refers to the rule of descent whereby kin affiliation is through the line of females only. The principles that govern patrilineal descent apply, in reverse, to matrilineal descent.

From Figure 2.3, you can see that Ego's (No. 26, who is female) linking kin are all females and they are all direct descendants of No. 4. Not a single male is to be found in those lines (see for yourself).

Again, notice the following: First, exclusion is automatic; this time it is the males who cut off affiliation of any female to her ancestor. Second, it is as easy to discern the line of females to their female ancestor as it was to discern the line of males in the patrilineal case. Third, matrilineal descent is a virtual mirror image of patrilineal descent, and if you put your diagrams side by side, they are indeed mirror images.

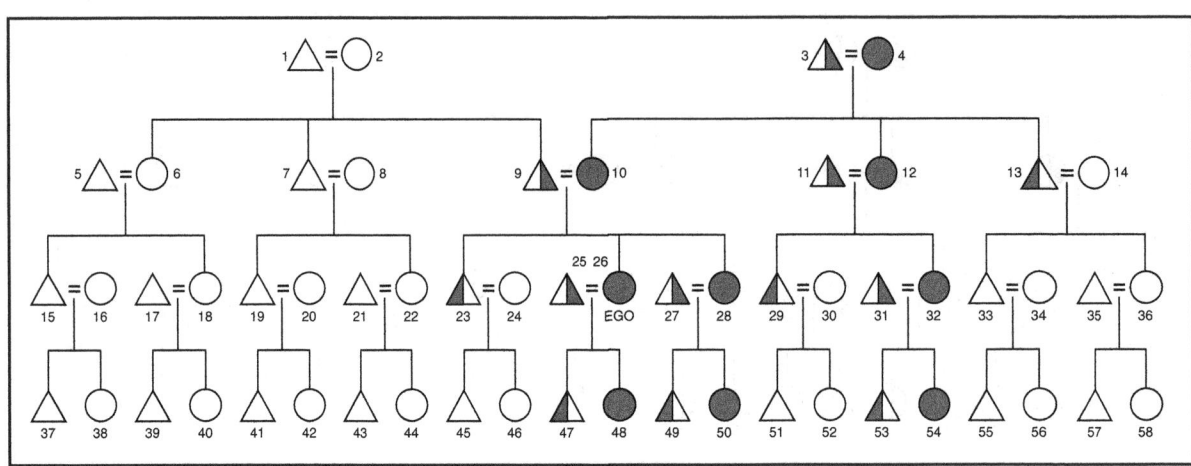

FIGURE 2.3
Matrilineal descent. Note relations among consanguineal females that include No. 26.

There is one caveat to note, however. Even in at least some matrilineal societies, men play an important, even dominant role. But if matrilineal groups are units of inheritance of, say, "Male" property, or do have some estate it owns or defends, they are not mirror images of patrilineal groups. In those instances, property would be inherited by a man's sister's son, as would be chieftainships or other important offices, such as among the Trobriand Islanders of Melanesia or the Haida of northern British Columbia.

It is worth noting, too, that multiple descent principles can exist in the same society. Our own example is the coexistence of bilateral descent for kin reckoning and disposal of inherited property with patrilineal descent for our system of surname assignment. The Yakö of southeastern Nigeria have a **double unilineal descent** system (known in shorthand as **double descent**). Immoveable property is inherited patrilineally and movable property is inherited matrilineally; male moveable property is inherited from mother's brother to sister's son.

Sex and Gender

Defining Sex and Gender. To begin with, we need to examine two concepts that are often confused with each other: sex and gender. **Sex,** in its broadest sense denotes the physical characteristics of men and women. These include **primary sex characteristics,** or the reproductive systems of the two sexes: the penis, testicles, and associated genital parts of men; and the vagina, fallopian tubes, and uterus of women.

They also include **secondary characteristics** that comprise the **sexual dimorphism,** or marked differences in size and appearance of the males and females of any sexually reproducing species. For humans, several attributes contribute to sexual dimorphism. There are average differentials in physical size. Some women may be heavier or taller than some men, but overall, men are heavier and taller than women. Men also have greater average grip strength than women, proportionately larger hearts and lungs, and greater maximum uptake of oxygen. Turning to females, women have the pendulous breasts that men lack. Women also have greater portions of body fat than men, and wider pelvises to accommodate childbirth.

Derivative of sex in the physical sense, **gender** comprises the elaborations and meanings assigned by cultures to the biological differentiations of the sexes. In other words, **sex** refers to the biology of differences; whereas **gender** refers to the cultural facts that arise from sex differences.

The notion that men (until recently) were the breadwinners and women the homemakers reflects gender, the roles that society assigned to the sexes, at least in the United States. Now this is changed, but other gender characteristics haven't changed: that men should shave and women should put on make-up is gender-based; that men are supposed to be the assertive partner in a sexual encounter is gender-based; that emotion should be openly expressed in women but not in men is gender-based. Gender roles vary from society to society, as the case studies will show.

Incest Tabu

Of the modes of control over sex, the most widespread is the prohibition of sexual relations between **primary kin,** that is, between parents and child (i.e., father-daughter and mother-son), and between siblings (brother-sister). This is one form of the **incest tabu,** which refers to cultural prohibitions against copulation between close relatives. Although this tabu has been found widely among primary kin, it often extends to **secondary kin** or all other kin for whom the tabu applies; these vary widely across cultures.

There are, as in everything else in the social sciences, exceptions to this tabu. In state-level societies, the royal lineage may allow marriage between close relatives. The ancient Egyptian, Inca, and Hawaiian states actually prescribed brother-sister marriage (and of course mating).

Incest Tabu and Exogamy.   One indication of sloppy thinking about the subject is the distinction many anthropologists fail to make between the **incest tabu** and **exogamy,** or a rule that one must marry outside a group. The first rule forbids sexual behavior between close kin; the second forbids marriage between close kin.

There are reasons for making a sharp distinction between incest tabus and rules of exogamy. In some societies, couples may mate but may not marry, as is the case for the Arunta of Australia. More important, there are theoretical reasons for the distinction. Explanations for incest tabus center around biological or psychological explanations. Explanations for rules of exogamy focus on alliance formation.

Explanations of Incest Tabus.   Why are incest tabus widespread, if not universal? The short answer is that no one really knows. Three explanations are commonly cited: fear of inbreeding, sibling indifference, and intrafamilial jealousy. There are inadequacies of each one.

Explanations of Inbreeding. One truism among geneticists is that most, if not all, deleterious alleles of a gene—those that are harmful to the organism—survive because they are recessive and usually are "hidden" when matched with a nonlethal allele of the same gene. Inbreeding would pass parents' deleterious alleles to offspring. Children of inbreeding are likely to develop hemophilia, have intellectual or emotional defects, or show other anomalies.

A major objection to the inbreeding explanation involves the assumption that the connection between copulation and childbearing is known within a given culture, yet there are cultures in which the connection is not made. Trobriand Islanders of Melanesia believe pregnancy is induced by ancestral water spirits who enter the woman when she bathes in a stream or lagoon. Males merely "open the way" (through copulation) for the child to be born. The matrilineal Trobrianders, "stuck with fathers, eliminate their procreative role," as Fox puts it in his *Kinship and Marriage.*

Even if we assume that peoples of a culture have their facts of life straight, birth defects may be explained by other reasons: witchcraft, or entry of some evil spirit in the womb. A defect may not show up for many generations.

Childhood Familiarity. According to another genre of explanations, developed by Edward Westermarck, close kin do not mate either because of instinctive revulsion over the idea or because opposite-sex kin reared together from birth are uninterested in each other—familiarity either breeds contempt or lack of interest. For example, in separate studies of Israeli kibbutzim, the anthropologists Melford Spiro and Yonina Talmon both found that children growing up in the same kibbutz tended not to marry within it. Talmon particularly points out that, despite parental encouragement to do so, there "was not one instance in which both mates were reared from birth in the same peer group."

This prima facie evidence becomes problematic when one recognizes the existence of military conscription—the draft—of all men and women when they reach the age of 18, just about the time they are thinking of finding a mate. Thus, by the time they are discharged from the armed forces two years later, the children of the kibbutz are likely to have selected their mates from outside their own—or any—kibbutz. Then there is the nagging question: if siblings lack mutual sexual desire, why have any incest tabu?

Sexual Competition. Several explanations have been advanced arguing that incest would lead to sexual competition among consanguineal kin and so disrupt the family. One is psychoanalyst Sigmund Freud's Oedipus complex, which posits that the son, at age five, desires the mother and is willing to kill the father in order to possess her. This follows the Greek myth in which Oedipus the King unwittingly murders his father and marries his mother.

Yet, many cultures around the world practice **polygyny,** or the marriage of one man to two or more women. A few practice **polyandry,** or the marriage of one woman to two or more men. Brothers often marry the same wife. Yet there is little evidence that either marriage type disrupts households in which they are practiced. Nor is there evidence that the brother-sister marriage within royal lineages of the Egyptians, Inca, or Hawaiians disrupted the royal families. Indeed, where siblings marry the same person, evidence indicates the families are more stable, not less.

Marriage and the Family

On this note, we start the series on marriage, family formation, and ultimately larger kin groups. First, we define the concept in a number of ways and note such variants as sambandham, woman marriage, and homosexual partnerships. Second, we examine marriages involving only two spouses and those with more than two at the same time, and we show how they play out structurally. Third, we examine **postmarital residence** and discuss their implications for various types of **extended families.** We also talk about divorce. We then reserve for the next chapter the implications they represent for larger kin units, **lineages, clans,** and **ambilineal descent groups.**

Marriage: Toward a Definition

The term **marriage** has been defined numerous ways, and reams have been written on the subject. Rather than review more than the hundreds of definitions offered over the years, we cover two definitions that reflect standard views of marriage and one that covers all, or almost all, types of marriage: standard and nonstandard.

Notes and Queries Definition. Probably as good a starting point as any is the *Notes and Queries* definition, published in a newsletter by that name in 1951 under the auspices of the Royal Anthropological Institute of Great Britain and Northern Ireland. The definition, "A union between a man and a woman such that children born to the woman are recognized legitimate offspring of both sexes," emphasizes heterosexuality and the assumption that bearing and rearing children is an important function.

The key term in this definition is **legitimate offspring.** Children born of male-female unions that are culturally approved are allowed full membership in the culture in which they are a part, have a right to inherit, and have other rights that pertain to their birth. We must emphasize that what defines **legitimate** are the norms and mores of the culture in which the marriage takes place, not those defined in the United States or any other Western country.

On Legitimacy. One of the recurring themes of relationships that involve the birth and rearing of children is legitimacy, the recognition that children born to and reared by a couple has all the birth-related rights of the society at large and of their status in society. One practice that incorporates legitimacy is the Nayar practice of **sambandham.** The Nayar are located in the present state of Kerala in southwest India on the Malabar Coast. The Nayar household is a matrilineal group called the *taravad.* Brother and sister live in this compound and cannot mate because of the incest tabu against sibling mating. Where do the children come from? They come from the sexual relationship between the woman and a lover—in fact, up to twelve of them—who is a nonmember of her *taravad.*

Is this a legitimate arrangement? Glad you asked. It is legitimate among the Nayar if, and only if, the liaison meets three criteria: (1) the two partners both have to be Hindu, leaving out the Muslims and Christians who also reside in the region; (2) they are not members of the same *taravad;* and (3) they belong to the same warrior caste (there is some allowance for the man to be a member of the Brahmin, or priestly, caste). The child's birth is legitimated if, and only if, one of her lovers presents a small gift to the midwife who delivers the baby. If none steps forward, the child is deemed illegitimate, as is the liaison. Consequences range from selling into slavery of the mother and child to their murder by her kinspersons. The Masuo, or Na, of southern China have a similar practice.

The child was reared in the household of the woman and her brothers, who functioned as the child's **pater** or social father; the role of **genitor,** or biological father, was played by the woman's lovers. Families of this type are known as **consanguine families,** of which more is discussed below.

There are other arrangements. In Africa, for example, barren women are often divorced for their infertility and often wind up without either husband or natal kin. However, the Nuer of Ethiopia and the Sudan have an institutional solution to this plight. A barren woman arranges to marry a fertile woman, who is impregnated and bears more than one child. They form a household, rendering the barren woman the status of "female husband" and her mate as "wife." A similar practice has been described for the Nandi, also a pastoralist tribe like the Nuer. Other practices have been described for other cultures in Nigeria, and the arrangement does not involve female homosexuality.

In light of the Nayar practice and African woman marriages, Gough attempted a more comprehensive definition: "a relationship established between a woman and one or more persons, which provides that a child born of the woman under circumstances not prohibited by the rules of the relationship, is accorded full birth-status rights common to members of its society or social stratum."

Even this convoluted definition does not anticipate homosexual marriage now becoming widespread in the United States and elsewhere, today part of the political debates between Republicans and Democrats. A similar practice is described for the Kwakiutl of British Columbia, and a marriage-like relationship, involving the *berdache,* or men who assume women's roles among the Plains peoples, has been extensively reported and analyzed. Both are represented in this collection.

Single and Multiple Marriages. Assuming that monogamy stands alone, and is not embedded in extended or polygamous families, families developing out of monogamy are typically **nuclear families,** or families comprising a man, a woman, and children. Again, homosexual couples are likely to find ways to create a family by nontraditional means.

Polygamy refers to marriage of one person to two or more spouses at the same time. This is a generic term. Often, this term is confused with one of its subtypes, **polygyny,** which refers to the marriage of a man to two or more women at the same time. Although this practice is reported for around 80% of the world's cultures, most men probably cannot afford more than one wife, even where polygyny is the norm. Often, a man may marry two or more women who are sisters to each other; this is known as **sororal polygyny.**

Correspondingly, the marriage of a woman to two or more men who are brothers to each other is known as **fraternal polyandry.** Fraternal polyandry occurs even in the classic East Indian epic poem, the *Mahabhrata,* which portrays the marriage of five sons of the deceased king Pandu to one woman, Draupadi. This practice has been described for the Toda of Northern India and also for many Tibetan peoples.

Group marriage, or the marriage of two or more men to two or more women, is extremely rare; only the Caingang of Brazil appear in Murdock's World Ethnographic Sample as consistently practicing group marriage, and it is not the dominant marriage form there. This practice has also been described for the chiefly families on the Marquesas of the South Pacific. On the assumption held by many anthropologists that group marriage develops from polygynous and polyandrous unions, the term **polygynandry** is also used.

Postmarital Residence

When a couple marries, they need a place to stay. In most societies, the choices are already made for them. They may live in an entirely new home, move in with the groom's or bride's family, or make other arrangements. We describe six basic rules of **postmarital residence,** and each type has structural implications for **extended families,** or families with three generations of married consanguineal kin, which we discuss in the next and final section of this chapter. Throughout this discussion, the suffix *–local* for each term means "the place of."

The most common form among the world's cultures is **patrilocal residence,** in which the couple lives with or near the groom's kinsmen. **Virilocal residence** (from the Latin *vir* meaning "man") usually means the same thing, although where a distinction is made, patrilocal means to live with the groom's parents, and virilocal means to live near them. A moment's reflection will indicate that the men stay with their parents and the women leave theirs, while the daughters of the paternal household also leave when they marry.

Matrilocal residence is the pattern of residence whereby the couple lives with or near the bride's kin. **Uxorilocal residence** (from the Latin *uxor* meaning "woman") means the same thing, although a finer distinction may define as matrilocal residence with the bride's parents, and as uxorilocal residence near them. In this instance, the women are the ones who stay with their parents, the men leave theirs, and the sons of the maternal household also leave when they marry.

Another type of residence is usually found in association with **matrilineal descent.** This is **avunculocal residence** (from the Latin *avunculus* or "maternal uncle"), in which the couple moves in with the groom's mother's brother. This reflects the practice among many societies, the Trobriand Islanders for one, in which a boy lives with his mother and father until he reaches the age of five or six.

He then moves in with his mother's brother, because of his matrilineal affiliation, namely through his mother. Though his father is the **genitor,** his **pater** is his mother's brother. In other words, it is his mother's brother, not his father, who will rear the boy. Some societies stipulate that the girl also moves in with her mother's brother, whereas others stipulate that she stays with her own mother. When the boy reaches maturity, he brings his wife with him to his mother's brother's residence. As they say, this is a long story, and we take some of it up in the section on extended families below. The logical opposite, **amitilocal residence,** whereby the couple would move in with the wife's father's sister, is unknown among the world's culture and is a theoretical construct only.

Duolocal residence refers to the pattern of residence whereby the bride stays with her kin and the husband stays with his. The Nayar represent one example of this arrangement. This form of residence is the most infrequent in the world's cultures; indeed, the *World Ethnographic Sample* lists only 8 out of roughly 400 cultures around the world. This would fit in well with societies in which the sister and brother stay together, but only four are matrilineal like the Nayar; the other four are patrilineal.

Ambilocal residence (sometimes known as **bilocal residence**) refers to the pattern of residence whereby the groom and bride have a choice between living with the groom's kin and the bride's kin. This form of residence is usually found in association with bilateral descent, and choice of residence is usually, if not always, the determinant whereby one chooses with which kin of the bilateral group the individual will affiliate. The implications of this choice are discussed below under "Extended Families"; we examine the Gilbertese *kainga* as an illustration.

Neolocal residence, the arrangement most familiar to North Americans, refers to the pattern of residence in which the couple forms their own household. This form is generally associated with industrialized societies, such as our own. In urban areas, there are not enough resources to support an extended family, only a nuclear one; hence it makes little sense for the couple to reside with the kin of either bride or groom on any but a temporary basis. Only five percent of the world's societies are neolocal; a preindustrial example is the Inuit ("Eskimo").

Family and Households

Marriage types and postmarital residence gives rise to the kinds of family structures, and this is where we encounter one basic question. Are families residential units only, or can one have non-residential families as well? In our own society, households containing nuclear families are the norm (although the presence of divorce, remarriage, homosexuality, and single parenthood has given rise to a plethora of family arrangements), but does that mean that grandparents, aunts and uncles, cousins, and nephews and nieces are not also part of one's family, though they may be hundreds of miles away?

Therefore, we may define as a **family** a group of consanguineally related and/or adopted kin consisting minimally of a parent and child who usually, but not always, shares the same residence. We may define a **household** or **domestic group** as that part of a family that shares a common residence; families and households may be one and the same or they may not be. Households are classified by family type; thus, nuclear family household, extended family household, polygynous family, and so on.

Extended Families. How a family is defined hinges in part on its longevity. A **nuclear family,** defined as one comprising a man, woman, and their children, lasts no longer than the maturity and departure of the children. Sometimes, however, married children may remain with their parents temporarily until they acquire enough assets to form their own household. Therefore, we need some kind of yardstick to determine whether a household with two or more generations of married kin is extended or nuclear. Also adding to the problem of definition is the phase in the household's **domestic cycle,** or a series of phases whereby the household develops, from formation to advanced phase to termination.

One rule of thumb is the number of generations of married kin. Most definitions set the minimum number at three. Two generations could constitute a temporary arrangement. For that reason, **extended family household** refers to a household containing three or more generations of coresident married kin. By this measurement, one is reasonably sure that we are dealing with permanently rather than temporarily multigenerational households.

Extended families are structured by the postmarital residential patterns of newly married couples over the generations. **Patrilocal residence** generates household composition that is distinct from **matrilocal residence,** with the compositions created by both very different from **ambilocal residence.** We discuss the varieties of household composition in turn.

Patrilocal Extended Family Households. A subtype of extended family is the **patrilocal extended family,** a group comprising at least three generations of married consanguineal males, their wives, and unmarried kin. Daughters will leave upon marriage; sons will stay. Taken over the generations, we see a core of males forming the household, together with in-marrying wives and unmarried women.

What explains the presence of patrilocal extended family households? There is no completely accepted answer; for every answer advanced, there have been exceptions. One explanation, for example, is of male cooperation in subsistence activities (such as herding large animals or intensive cultivation) or in defending these assets. Other explanations center around male control of large amounts of property, particularly when it is valuable, and the practice of polygyny, which is often related to property. Thus, it is unsurprising to find patrilocal extended families among the

Masai, whose *laibon* ("wise men") own hundreds of cattle, may marry up to a dozen or so women, and who required a retinue of warriors to defend their herds.

Matrilocal Extended Family Households. Among other cultures, **matrilocal extended family households** are the norm. This time, it's the consanguineally related females who form the core group. Such households seem to arise where female cooperation is important, such as in horticultural societies where women do the work, or in which political organization is relatively simple and uncentralized. Often, men do not move far from their natal homes. The Embers have also suggested that matrilocal households are likely to predominate where warfare is either nonexistent or external when women do most of the subsistence work, such as horticulture.

Avunculocal Extended Family Households. When fully developed, the **avunculocal extended family household** comprises the mother's brother and his sister's son, together with their wives, sons under five years of age, and unmarried daughters (or mother's sister's daughters where they also move in with the mother's brother). It seems to be a compromise between the demands of a patrilineal society and the constraints of matrilineal descent. This form of household seems likely by factors that favor patrilocal residence, but in which descent through women is considered crucial for transmission of rights and property. One possibility is that women were the cooperating gender in gardening at one time. Warfare and long-distance trade, both of which involve male cooperation, may explain the shift from matrilocal toward avunculocal residence and corresponding change in type of extended family. There are other explanations.

Ambilocal Extended Family Households: Ambilocal residence is compatible with bilateral descent, inasmuch as both sexes bear equal weight in the choice of one household or the other. **Ambilocal extended family households,** based as they are on the aggregate choices generations of couples have made, are not so predictable as the other types of extended family cooperation. We can predict with reasonable accuracy who will dwell with whom in patrilocal or matrilocal extended family households; if outcomes differ from the expected, they are the product of situational variables.

Here, the couple chooses one of two possible residences, and the problem turns on the considerations that underlie the couple's choice. The situational trumps the logical. One consideration may be the relative attractiveness of the two residences in some way. Ambilocal residence is usually found in relatively circumscribed terrain, such as mountainous regions or islands. In Scotland, the clan was actually a kin group founded on ambilocal extended families. We find similar situations in many Pacific islands such as the Gilberts. If one household had more land than people as compared with the other; the couple would move to the first household. The Gilbertese land-holding groups *kainga* is one example, according to Fox.

Neolocal Residence and Extended Families. Neolocal residence is the one residential pattern that militates against extended family households. By definition, couples select their own residence apart from either of their parents', and when their children mature, they move away to another residence. This does not prevent the formation of extended families, however, if the term *family* is defined as nonresidential. Parents who live separately from their married children remain in the same family, as do grandparents; they simply do not live under the same roof.

Extended families are further modified by terms indicating residence. You may live in a nuclear family with neolocal residence, yet chances are you have an extended family—just that not all of them live with you. Extended families are often residential. Therefore, there are extended family households that are patrilocal, others that are matrilocal, and still others that are avunculocal. As noted above, brother-sister households observed among the Nayar (and Na/Masuo) are consanguineal households, because they are formed around the siblings.

Other Family Types. There are other family types. One is the **matrifocal family household,** in which the mother and her children reside. This was characteristic of many households in the Caribbean in marginal economic conditions, and has become increasingly common as the feminization of poverty becomes more widespread. A less common pattern is the **patrifocal family household.** The sexual revolution, deliberate choice to live without a spouse, and divorce have all contributed to the households of these two types. As divorce and remarriage has soared, more and more **blended families,** comprising couples and children of previous marriages, have become commonplace as well. Finally, with the removal of stigma toward homosexuals, **homosexual households** have also developed, some legally recognized as marriage (although in the U.S. election of 2004, voters rejected the gay rights amendment in 11 states). Children may be adopted, the offspring of previous marriage, or, in the case of female homosexuals, reproduced through sexual relations with outside males. Though more widespread than ever in history, none of these developments is new. Homosexuality, divorce, and remarriage have gone on for centuries, perhaps millennia.

Descent Units and Groups

Sooner or later, extended families will divide into two, sometimes more. Households become crowded and everyone gets into everyone else's way. Does that mean that the new households will have nothing further to do with each other? Hardly. There are functions to be fulfilled beyond the household. Perhaps there are larger herds of cattle to manage, or some households may put distant kin up for the night. In most instances, if not all, larger descent units form, and have done so for centuries.

To identify such groups, you need to know two terms before proceeding to the study of descent units and groups. First, some groups involve the ability to trace, male by linking male, to the founding ancestor. This is known as **demonstrated descent.** The groups formed by demonstrated descent are called **lineages.** Others assume that they are descended from an ancestor, but can't identify just how they are related. That assumption is known as **stipulated descent.** The groups formed by stipulated descent are known as **clans.**

The process of lineage formation can be surmised from the diagram on the following page.

As this diagram illustrates, every member of Ego's group can trace their descent to the founder of the entire lineage. And lineages don't stop with this diagram. In some societies, a man can trace his ancestry not just at a local lineage, but through larger ones. In groups like the Nuer of Ethiopia, every member belongs to a minimal segment, a minor but larger segment, and a major and even larger segment. *These are all lineages.* So it is possible to be a member of a small lineage and at the same time be a member of a larger lineage that includes this small lineage. And so it goes up to the last known traceable ancestor. These are known as **segmentary lineages.**

If we included clans, they would include smaller lineages. Clans are those groups whose ancestry is stipulated, that is, assumed. This diagram shows how extended families can build up to become lineages, and how several lineages could develop into a clan.

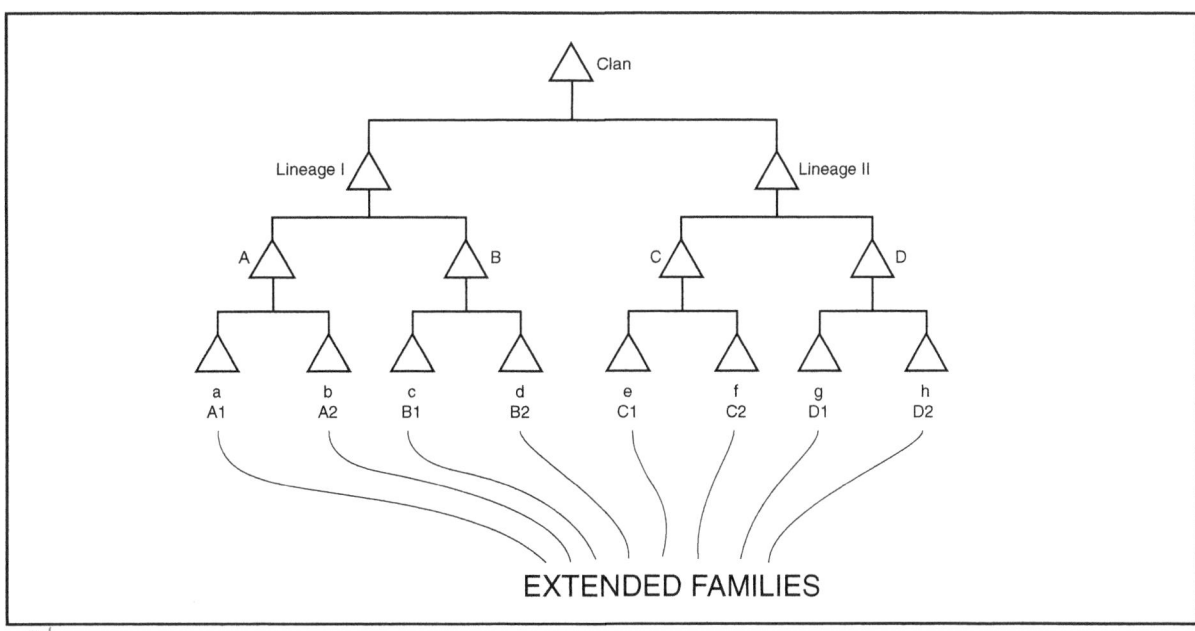

FIGURE 2.4
How extended families form lineages and lineages form clans.

If you focus on clan, you notice that it comprises several lineages. Members of the lineage can demonstrate their ancestry, but as clan members, they can only stipulate their relationship to the founder. Each of the lineages arose from the extended families.

Linking Families and Unilineal Groups: Marriage and Exchange

As mentioned in our discussion of the incest tabu versus rules of exogamy, different sets of explanations account for each one of these. Incest tabu explanations center around biological or psychological factors. Exogamy explanations rely on questions alliance. This section discusses how alliances are formed by marriage.

Many exchange marriages—those involving **cousin marriage**—are predicated on two issues: group size and the reproductive power of women. Preindustrial societies are very small. Foragers number anywhere between 40 or 50 and 100 persons. Pastoralists and horticulturalists number up to 1000. Therefore, the very survival of a band or tribe is dependent on women and their fertility. Viewed in this light, it is not surprising that barrenness is one frequent cause of divorce among African societies.

When marriage takes place, therefore, the bride-giving group is at risk. The incest tabu in most societies precludes brother-sister mating and thus marriage. Therefore, it is giving up a member who could have borne members of the next generation for this kin group. In one way or another, she must be replaced with another woman capable of childbearing. It is unsurprising that we find bridewealth in many preindustrial societies and cousin marriage in others.

They form a kind of preindustrial insurance policy that the group will continue into the next generation.

It is also important that the group one marries the daughter into is a good group: the daughter will not be mistreated or live in poverty, the husband and his group are good producers, and the husband's group will not attack that of the daughter and bride. Indeed, the husband's group will come to the aid of the bride's group if the latter is attacked or loses its cattle or crops to disease. Viewed in this light, mother-in-law jokes become somewhat less humorous.

There is, therefore, a logic behind marriages involving exchange. First, we examine the transfer of labor and assets: what, after all, is **bride labor** for, and how about **bridewealth** (often called, somewhat erroneously, **bride price**)? Often, the transfer of persons substitutes for (or supplements), transfer of assets, and so entails **parallel cousin** and, more often, **cross-cousin** marriage. In other cultures, the **dowry,** in which the bride's group transfers some of its assets to the groom's group is provided. These transactions are discussed wherever appropriate in the case studies.

Kinship Terminology

Often the student groans when, after learning about marriage types, the family types they produce, the finer aspects of descent groups and—ye gods!—cross-cousin marriage, that there's the little matter of kinship terminology. But then, kinship terms are something that a six-year-old Australian aboriginal or Masai or Yanomamö kids know already—why shouldn't we?

Generally speaking, kinship terminology has a more or less direct relationship with rules of descent and patterns of marriage. Some are easy to grasp—the Hawaiian, Eskimo (Inuit), and even the Iroquois come to mind. The Sudanese system is more difficult for the layperson and the Crow and Omaha systems are the most difficult of all. First, however, we need to discuss some preliminary concepts of terms: **descriptive** versus **classificatory** terms and the aunt-uncle terms **bifurcate merging, bifurcate collateral, lineal,** and **generational.**

Principles of Classification.   Several principles are used in classifying kin. First, **descriptive terms** refer to terms that refer to one or at most two kinds of relatives. In the United States *mother* refers to only one person; an adult female with her own children. At the opposite end of the spectrum are **classificatory terms,** those whose term covers a wide range of relatives. Thus, in the United States, the term **cousin** covers parents' siblings' offspring without further distinction. In Mexico, France, Germany, and many other countries, the terms make only one distinction: by gender. In actuality, there are varying degrees between descriptive and classificatory kin.

Next are other principles that govern assignment of kinship terms. The first is **generation,** which distinguish **ascending** (parental, grandparental, and so on) and **descending** (children's, grandchildren's, and so on) kin from ego's own generation. The second is **relative age,** in which older siblings are distinguished from younger ones. English terms make no such distinctions. The third is **gender,** in which females are distinguished from males.

The next set of principles are somewhat more complex, because many of these do not apply in our own society. The first set is **lineality** versus **collaterality. Lineal** kin are related in a single line, such as grandfather-father-son (patrilineal in this instance). **Collateral kin** are descended from a common ancestor with ego, but are not ego's direct ascendants or descendants. Brothers and sisters are collateral kin, as are cousins, aunts, and uncles. This is an important distinction in our own society.

Another set of principles concerns **consanguineality** versus **affinity.** Persons related to ego by blood (parent-child, siblings) are known as **consanguineal kin;** whereas those related to ego by marriage (husband-wife, parents-in-law) are known as **affinal kin.** Again, this distinction is important to our society.

Less familiar to Anglo-American societies are the terms based on **sex of linking kin.** To us, it does not matter whether your cousin is related to you through your father's brother or mother's brother; to the Yanomamö, it matters a great deal. A male must avoid his father's brother's daughter, but may—indeed has an obligation to—marry his mother's brother's daughter. To most cultures of the world, this principle is essential.

Also unfamiliar to Anglo-Americans are the terms based on **bifurcation** or **merging. Bifurcation** refers to the practice of distinguishing relatives on the father's side from the mother's side. **Merging** entails no such distinction. Apart from the distinction between father and mother, American terminology is merging: aunts and uncles are not distinguished by side of kin.

Cousin Terminology.   Although somewhat oversimplified, anthropologists recognize six systems of terminology. Some are consistent with bilateral descent; others with one or the other form of unilineal descent. In addition, type of cousin marriage may influence the terminology.

Our own terminology, **Inuit** or **Eskimo,** distinguishes Ego's siblings from his/her cousins. In the **Hawaiian** system, siblings are not distinguished from cousins. In the **Iroquois** system, brothers and sisters are merged with parallel cousins, but distinguished from cross-cousins. In the **Sudanese** system, siblings, parallel cousins, and cross-cousins are all distinguished from each other. The last two are distinguished by rule of descent: maternal kin are distinguished in detail in the matrilineal Crow system; paternal kin are distinguished in the patrilineal Omaha system. Individual terminologies are discussed where appropriate in the relevant case studies.

Conclusion

As one can see, kinship regulates not only family and marriage, but also other aspects of preindustrial societies as well. For that reason, learning the types of descent affiliation, descent groups, marriage types, family types, and even types of marital alliances are essential to understanding other aspects of society. To understand cultures without understanding the principles of kinship (even societies that do not rely on complex kinship relations, such as the Inuit, and of course industrial ones) is akin to learning chemistry without the periodic tables or physics without the theories of relativity or the laws of thermodynamics.

Nor have you left the principles of kinship just yet. In economic anthropology, the logic behind exchange marriages are discussed in reviewing Mauss's three obligations of the gift, and in political anthropology, the alliance patterns formed by bilateral and matrilateral cross-cousin marriage will be discussed. As stated, you cannot understand preindustrial cultures without understanding kinship. Have a nice day.

Subsistence Systems

Subsistence Systems: Making a Living Cross-Culturally

People of every culture around the world have to eat, and cultures differ by how their people make their living. One we find around the world, and definitely among Native Americans, is foraging or hunting and gathering. The Inuit and !Kung are classic example that we will see in this course. Another is horticulture, and we find examples of those among the Iroquois and many of the Plains peoples before they took up buffalo hunting—the Crow for examples. A third is intensive cultivation, and we find that among the civilizations from the Inca to the Egyptians and Mesopotamians. Then there is pastoralism, or living exclusively on herding animals like cattle and horses. The East Africans were cattle herders and the fabled Mongols before and under Genghis Khan were horse herders. Then there are equestrian hunters, of which North American Plains peoples are almost the sole example. The Plains Indians (long known by that rubric) invented this strategy once they obtained some stray horses from the Spaniards.

Foraging. Foraging, or hunting and gathering, involves a total reliance on nature for food. It is worldwide, as you will see among the !Kung, a classic example of foragers. Most foragers rely more on gathering plant foods than hunting game. But the Inuit are a major exception. The Inuit (formerly known as "Eskimo") rely strictly on meat; except for the Arctic summers, the climate is too cold for vegetation.

Until about 10,000 years ago, all our ancestors were hunters and gatherers. Then, first in the Near East and Egypt, and later elsewhere, plants and animals became domesticated and eventually this invention has affected us all. In the Near East, Emmer and Einkorn wheat set the Neolithic Revolution, as this domestication of plants and animals came to be called. Elsewhere, corn and rice were the staples. With this invention, we could now control our food productions and didn't have to rely on the kindness of nature to support us. Settled communities formed, and in the long term, state level societies formed.

Horticulture. Horticulture—planting and harvesting using hand tools—were characteristic among many peoples who practiced agriculture. Slash and burn cultivation, widely known among South American peoples in Amazonia and elsewhere, such as parts of Southeast Asia and Melanesia, was an ecologically sound practice. Trees and brush are cleared at the beginning of the dry season, and then burned at the end of the season. Crops are then planted as the rains begin and harvested as they ripen. Cultivated sites are then abandoned as they lose their fertility and revert back to the forest. If the population is below the area's carrying capacity, the forest restores the fertility of the site, and it can be planted anew.

Intensive Cultivation. Intensive cultivation was found among more complex societies, such as Mesopotamia, Egypt, much of East and South Asia, and Central and Andean America. The Embers define intensive cultivation as the permanent cultivation of fields, reflecting most definitions of the practice. Irrigation was practiced in most regions; use of the plow is one variation of intensive agriculture. Staple or mainstay crops varied: wheat in the Near East, Europe, and parts of South Asia, rice in most of Asia, corn (maize) in Mesoamerica, and potatoes in Andean America and later in Europe. Relatively few crops are cultivated and, though highly productive, require large inputs of pesticides, fertilizer (often artificial), and, where mechanized, fuel. Famine remains a perennial risk, of which the Irish potato famine of the 1840s was an example. It generated mass migrations to North America and Australia.

Pastoralism and Equestrian Hunting. Two other subsistence systems entail total or predominant reliance on larger (draft) animals. Pastoralism involves reliance on domesticated cattle, as in East Africa; horses, as in Central Asia; and sheep, goats, and camels, as in the Near East. This means that plant foods have to be imported or obtained in trade from settled communities, and often the symbiotic relationship between tribe and community can turn hostile; trade can easily turn to raid. Often, warfare and heavy tasks of herding tend to favor male cooperation and dominance. Pastoralists are more adaptive to grasslands, which produce a tough sod that horticulturalists cannot penetrate with their hand tools. Pastoralists migrate according to the seasons.

The adaptive features of pastoralism tend also to favor equestrian hunting because of the grassland environment, and such was the case with North American Native peoples of the Great Plains. The grasslands of the plains supported massive heads of bison, which unlike cattle could not be domesticated, and so were hunted. Until the horse was introduced through the Spanish invasion of the American Southwest, native peoples hunted by foot; the horse transformed local native cultures to equestrian hunters throughout the North American plains. The stereotype of the Plains "Indians" encompassed all North American Native peoples in popular conceptions.

Environmental Potential and Limitation

All subsistence systems involve the transfer of energy from the environment to members of every culture. How food is obtained may often determine how a culture is organized. Frequently, foraging supports only small nomadic groups called bands. Often, high-yield foraging may support complex societies, as was the case of the Native Peoples of the Pacific Northwest Coast. Horticulture, including slash and burn cultivation, places upper limits to the number of people it can support, as we will see for Amazonia and Papua New Guinea. Pastoralism and equestrian hunting are limiting in another sense; grasslands can support these two systems, and often that is all they can support. This limitation is removed where cultures have the plow, which breaks the sod. This is one variation of intensive cultivation, which allows a small portion to farm and support populations in nonfarm occupations and also support large populations—and complex societies such as the state. Energy is what makes the human world go around, and you are not only what you eat. Your culture is what it produces and how.

The upper limit of group size is established by the carrying capacity of the environment. Game could be limited, there may be a shortage of the much-favored mongongo nuts, but the efficient limit is the scarcest resource. According to Liebig's Law of the Minimum, the population may not increase beyond the level of that resource, which in a desert like the Kalahari is water (see Chapter 22). Justus von Liebig, an Austrian agronomist who lived in the nineteenth century, came up with this principle to analyze the availability of nutrients in a field of crops when deciding what fertilizer to use. The least plentiful nutrient—potash or nitrogen or iron, say—sets absolute limits to the fertility of the soil. He illustrated the principle using a hypothetical barrel with uneven staves. The barrel cannot hold more water than the level of the lowest stave. Extension of this metaphor suggests that the lowest resource limits the carrying capacity of a given environment.

Economic Anthropology

Introduction

We all fret about "the economy." Will the stock market continue to plummet? Will the unemployment rate ever go down? Will my job be shipped off to Bangladesh or Bangalore next year? All of these questions refer to a capitalist, market-driven economy under which we live—and all too often we think and behave as if ours were the only economy in the world. We might recall that Russia, once upon a time known as the Soviet Union, had a "communist" economy, more accurately a **command economy.** But that is as far as we go.

In fact, there have been economies in the world's cultures, some of them containing markets but not dominated by one. The !Kung until about 60 years ago had no market and no money and no use for either. The Northwest Coast Indians traded, but used no currency, nor was the trade primarily for economic gain. There are (or at least until roughly 60 years ago) many economies that do not (1) have stock markets, (2) have markets at all, (3) have money as we know it, (4) have businesses, and (5) have corporations. This is where our ethnocentrism and culture-bound notions dominate our conscious and even unconscious thinking.

So what, then, is an economy? Let's look at the roots of the word. Economy is derived from the Greek *oikonomia,* which means "household manager," which are further derived from *oikos,* house, and *nemein,* to manage. Metaphorically, then, a band, a tribe, a nation-state are comparable to a house that is to be managed. One manages a household by keeping it clean and uncluttered, making best use of the food, clothing, furniture, and so on. In this light, I leave to you to evaluate how well we the people are managing our household, our nation-state.

So now, in given its derivation from Greek, **economy** might best be defined as the production, distribution, and distribution of goods and services in a society. All societies have the need to produce, to exchange, and to consume, so that is about as universalistic a definition we can get. However, there is another aspect to economics that also plays a role in many societies. This is the need to **economize,** or to make the best use of the goods and services to which one has access. That, too, is the essence of good house management.

We have compared five basic subsistence systems, or food-getting techniques. Often, however, the literature speaks of a "herding economy" or a "hunting-and-gathering" economy. These are technological matters, not economic ones. The techniques of hunting, or clearing forests, or irrigating fields are related to technology, not economy. The focus shifts to the economic when we ask how work is organized, whether in a Yanomamö village or in a factory. When we ask who owns the hunting territory or the plots of ground being irrigated or the water used for irrigation, we are also asking questions pertaining to economics.

Thus, we begin by discussing approaches to economic anthropology, including the relationship to economics and society. We address the notion of scarcity, which forms the foundation of Western economic science and contrast the substantive with the formalist approaches. We then turn to the kinds of property ownership in the world's culture—where there is such a thing, that is. Organization of production is addressed next, and you may be surprised that the notion of "company time" is foreign to most cultures. We then look at exchange systems to show that market exchange is but one of many. Finally, we look at consumption, including the rights and privileges attached thereto.

Economy and Society

To begin, we need to take up the fundamental assumption of Western economics. If you are taking, or have taken, economics, you know about the **scarcity postulate,** which holds that, inasmuch as human wants (the focus of economics is on wants, not needs) are infinite and the means for satisfying them are finite, we must deal with the reality that all goods and services are **scarce.** Lionel Robbins set forth a concise definition of economics in this light: "the science which studies human behaviour as a relationship between ends and scarce means which have alternative uses" (1937). Any scarce good is therefore an **economic good;** any good that is infinite in quality (say air—let's ignore air quality for a moment) is a **free good.** Once upon a time, water was considered a free good—but have you looked at your water bill lately? Case closed!

In light of the scarcity question, about 40 years ago an acrimonious debate erupted among economic anthropologists as to the best cross-cultural treatment of a topic we call economy. On the one hand were those who held that **substantivism** is the most appropriate framework. Scarcity, the substantivists argued, was not present in all places for all goods. To assume otherwise was to apply ethnocentrically models of supply and demand or other economic models to societies where neither property nor scarcity was an issue.

Therefore, we must question how each society goes about providing goods and services to meet its people's needs. Moreover, economies are embedded in society. You cannot understand bridewealth without also understanding the relations between families which it bonds. The economy, wrote Karl Polanyi, himself an economic historian, is an "instituted process" (1944, 1971). Why else does the Trobriand Islander canoe with his fellows from one island to another, braving storm, reefs, cannibalistic enemies, and sharks, just to trade a white armshell for a red necklace? Why do Northwest coastal peoples hold potlatches offering one another valuable gifts just to validate the status of the next chief?

In rebuttal, another school advanced the notion of **formalism.** In every society, they argued, there is scarcity in every society in some respect. The !Kung, they might argue, might have all the building material they need, perhaps plenty of food of all kinds, but what about large game? Aren't giraffes or wildebeests hard to come by? As for the Northwest Coast Indians, isn't the prestige of a chief a scarce commodity? And if the New Guinea tribesmen have enough sweet potatoes to eat, why then do they go into all the effort and expense to raise pigs to give away and consume at the next big moka (feast) every ten years or so?

Therefore, we have no choice but to recognize that every society has unlimited wants of some sort for which limited quantities of goods and services are available. Do we want prestige for a New Guinea big man? Then he must spend his waking hours mobilizing his followers to marshal the necessary pigs. Do you want your daughter to marry well? Then you must entice a well-regarded family with large numbers of healthy cattle as bridewealth. Scarcity is everywhere, even in noneconomic sectors. The question, then, is how does one economize? How does one make the best use of one's resources? That is the economic question from the formalist perspective.

This debate went on for years without resolution. In part, this was because every argument was met with a counterargument from either side. Mainly, however, a tune by Bob Dylan sums up the issue: "You were right from your side; I was right from mine." There is something to viewing economies from a relativistic standpoint: Not all societies are market societies and people do not behave rationally according to the rules of the marketplace. From the other side, something is scarce in every society, even if the thing that is scarce is time or prestige.

Property

One of the fundamental questions of economic anthropology is property ownership and its allocation. At first glance, we might assume that property is not a major issue to, say, foragers. Many foragers define their territory loosely, and property rights, where they exist, tend not to be exclusionary. As populations increase and assets like land and animals become more valuable, exclusionary property rights are likely to emerge.

Thus, we may develop a typology of ownership types. First is **communalism,** the property arrangements whereby everyone has access to its assets. Foragers range in more or less defined territories, though theirs may overlap with the territory of others, as will be shown for the !Kung and the Inuit. Such rights—the communal right of property access but the individual right of use—is known in legal terms as **usufruct.** Men who hunt down the animals "own" it, but only to give its meat away—in other words, ownership means only stewardship.

Yet even exclusive property rights may be found among foragers. Among the Owens Valley Paiute of the Nevada Basin in the Western United States, piñon nut trees were particularly valued, so that families and band claimed exclusive rights to territory containing these stands and defended it against all intruders. Generally, most scholars find that the greater the predictability and concentration of resources within a territory, the more pronounced the conception of exclusive property rights. Generally speaking, however, the main norm involves rights to all to common property for individual exploitation.

In societies with more complex technologies, it is likely that control of resources tends to be **joint ownership,** or ownership by an extended family, lineage, or clan. In this case, the entity owns land, cattle, or other resources, or may exercise some regulative or protective function while the family actually exercises ownership. Thus, the property becomes an **estate,** a defining feature of corporate **kin groups,** as discussed above.

When assets—land, cattle, or other resources—become scarce, then more restrictive forms of ownership apply. Elite clans may continue to exercise joint control, or the assets may be held in **fee simple,** that is, owned privately. Garden land may be claimed and owned by the chief, lord, or monarch, who allocates land for their use in exchange for taxes, labor, or tribute to support the institution of the chiefdom or state. A society may be based on a **feudal** or **patrimonial** arrangement, whereby the peasant or serf provides a portion of his product and labor to his lord, who in turn provides tribute to a superior lord, and so on up a hierarchy, such as those found in sub-Saharan Africa, Japan before the Meiji restoration in 1868, or medieval Europe. Finally, there is **capitalism,** whereby production for use is displaced by production for profit. When this occurs, the products become transformed into **commodities,** goods and services offered not so much for use as for sale on the market. Ours is a commodity-based, market-driven economy, so that even labor is a commodity. It is significant, perhaps, that ultraconservatives would substitute the phrase "life, liberty, and the pursuit of happiness" with "life, liberty, and the pursuit of property."

Division of Labor

Often tied in with property arrangements (or lack thereof) is the division of labor. In most preindustrial societies not based on intensive cultivation, the division of labor is based on **gender** and **age.** The gender division of labor varies considerably from one society to another. The only exceptions that seem to be universal are that men engage in warfare and women attend to child-care tasks. Men tend to do the heavy work, but women attend to strenuous tasks as well. No matter what generalization one makes on the gender division of labor, there are always exceptions.

Age also plays a role in differentiating tasks of society. The young engage in play, which in many respects prepare them for adult work. Yanomamö boys may shoot arrows at iguanas or insects, preparing them for hunting porcupines or tapir five or ten years hence. As the young reach adolescence, they take on increasingly important tasks until they reach the status of adults as locally defined. As adults, they do all the hunting and gathering or cultivation or herding on which their band or village or nomadic tribe depends. The aged do less in the way of productive work, but they draw on their experience to advise the younger members.

Whatever the rules governing division of labor, pre-agricultural peoples engage in the primary sector of their economy full time. Everyone, in the end, hunts or gathers, tends to the herds, or gardens. More important, the households produce for themselves and secondarily, if at all, for exchange for products they cannot produce themselves. This is known as the **domestic mode of production,** or production for the household. When the needs are met, labor usually ceases.

With the advent of intensive cultivation, the division of labor shifts from the primary sector of cultivation to the rise of full-time artisans or craftspersons. In due course, villages transform into cities, or are absorbed by them. Guilds may arise to assure the quality of footwear, or clothing, or metal products. Some cities may specialize, as well, so that trade gradually arises. Productive resources become **capital,** resources or products that are used in further production. In due course, nonfarm workers take up a significant part of the economy. At that point, the domestic mode of production becomes displaced by any of a variety of systems whereby the peasant or craftsperson must produce for exchange, not merely for the household.

As fossil fuels displace animals as an important source of power, the division of labor again undergoes a transformation. Though high energy inputs and machinery are crucial to industrial production as we know it, equally important is the rise of **detail labor.** Up to now, the craftsperson handled all aspects of his or her craft. Industrial labor now demands that these aspects be broken down to their constituent labor process. Whereas the shoemaker tanned the leather, cut it, sewed the parts to form a shoe, and nailed on the soles and heels, now these tasks are broken up and assigned to different workers. In his classic work *Wealth of Nations,* written in 1776, the Scottish philosopher Adam Smith illustrated the point using pin manufacture. Which is more efficient, he asked: five men, each cutting the wire, pointing each pin, putting a head on each, adding whiting (a preservative), and putting them on lengths of paper to be sold; or the same five men doing a single task each? The answer was clear; the second alternative is more productive. It was this assignment of specialized tasks that the assembly line was born and society becomes industrialized.

Distribution and Exchange

Once a good is produced or a service made available, the product or service must reach the consumer in some way, who in the meantime has a good or service to offer that she or he has produced. At that point, some form of **exchange** or **transaction** is about to take place. In anthropology, however, the issue is not as simple as that. We started this chapter by pointing out the embedding economy in society. Nowhere is this as evident as in preindustrial societies.

In this section, we first discuss Mauss's three obligations of the gift, then move on to describe three principal types of exchange: **reciprocity** (which subsumes three subtypes, **generalized, balanced,** and **negative**), redistribution, and **market exchange.** Then we show how these exchanges become part of what Polanyi called "an institutionalized process"—in other words, how they are embedded in society.

The Gift and Its Obligations.   What, then, is the rationale of all exchange: goods, services, marriage, or otherwise? One explanation is that, in the absence of the modern state and its laws, the act of gift giving, acceptance, and repayment is imperative, although enforced by no police or army. No one puts the matter more clearly than the French sociologist Marcel Mauss.

Mauss, nephew and student of the eminent French sociologist Emile Durkheim, attempted in 1925 a cross-cultural explanation of gift giving and its attendant obligations in his book titled *The Gift: Forms and Functions of Exchange in Archaic Societies (Essai sur le don).* His starts with the assumption that two groups (band, tribe, chiefdoms, perhaps even agricultural states) have the imperative to establish a relationship of some kind. There are three options that the two groups have when they meet for the first time. They may pass each other by and never see each other again. They may resort to arms with an uncertain outcome; one could wipe the other out or, more likely, win at great cost of men and property or fight to a draw. The third option is to what he calls "come to terms" with each other. In other words, they find ways to establish a more or less permanent relationship.

Groups deciding on the third option can cement relations by exchanging gifts. However, unlike our own views of making gifts, such exchanges are obligatory in societies that do not have central governments, formal law enforcement organizations, or collection agencies. The obligations, which he called "total prestations," have the force of law in the absence of law. No Dun and Bradstreet will come to collect, but the presence of conflict that could break out at any time reinforces these obligations.

The obligation to give is the first obligation, one that must be met if a group is to extend social ties to others. The second obligation is to receive; refusal constitutes rejection of an offer to friendship as well. Conflicts can well arise from the perceived insult of a rejected offer. The third obligation is to repay. One who fails to make a gift in return is soon perceived as being in debt, being, in essence, a beggar. Mauss offers several ethnographic cases to illustrate these obligations. Every gift confers power to the giver, expressed by the Polynesian terms *mana* (an intangible supernatural force) and *hau* (among the Maori, the spirit of the gift, which must be returned to its owner).

Reciprocity and Its Variations.   Stripped to its essentials, **reciprocity** refers to the direct exchange of goods and services between individuals but, more commonly, between groups of individuals (bands, families, kin groups, villages, or any other). Typically, they are economic goods and services—but their functions go well beyond the confines of an economy. There are three varieties of reciprocity: generalized, balanced, and negative.

Generalized reciprocity refers to the kind of exchange in which the receiving party (individual, family, lineage, et al.) does not repay immediately, nor is it expected to do so. Generalized reciprocity may involve the pooling of resources within a household. It may involve meeting the needs of children, with the understanding that the children will care for their parents in old age.

A similar case arises among the !Kung when a hunter may fail to kill large game for several months or longer; he receives meat during that time until he finally bags an animal. Overall, we find generalized reciprocity within families, or between closely related kin. Generalized reciprocity serves as a kind of social insurance; in the case of game, it ensures that the animal, which could neither be consumed by a family nor stored, will not be wasted.

Balanced reciprocity refers to the exchange of goods of nearly equal value with the obligation to make a return within a definite period of time. This type of exchange is familiar to us all; we give and receive gifts at weddings, birthdays, and religious holidays such as Christmas or Hanukkah. We take turns buying rounds at the pub. The kula ring, described in the module on the Trobriand Islands in the western Pacific, near Papua New Guinea, is a classic example of balanced reciprocity.

Balanced reciprocity generally takes place among more distant kin or villagers who have known each other for a long time. It helps cement relationships between traders who live long distances from each other.

When such confidences are betrayed, or expected, then relations are characterized by **negative reciprocity,** or exchange conducted for the aim of gaining material advantage and the aim to get something for nothing. Tribal and agrarian societies often distinguish between the insider, whom it is morally wrong to cheat, and the outsider, from whom every advantage may be gained. These include horse raids among Plains Indians as an extreme example of negative reciprocity, and a similar example might be taken of the Masai, who view their neighbor's cattle as given to them by God—hence the raids. A joke about the second U.S.-Iraq war asks "What is our oil doing in the sands of Iraq?"

One type of exchange that falls somewhere between balanced and negative reciprocity is **silent trade.** Conducted usually between mutually hostile groups, this trade is one way for each group to provide goods the other group needs. For example, the foraging Mbuti of the Ituri Forest, Congo, exist in a state of **hostile symbiosis** with their Bantu agricultural neighbors. Yet the Mbuti need the Bantus' crafted and garden products, and the Bantu need game animals and hides that the Mbuti can provide. Thus, a Mbuti may leave, say, some hide and meat at a designated site and retires into the forest. The Bantu come, inspect the goods, and if they like what they see, they take them and leave their own product for the Mbuti, who then takes it if it meets with their approval. Either party rejects the product simply by leaving it in place (Turnbull 1961, 1965). This is a common form of exchange among soldiers on opposite sides of a war.

Redistribution. The second major type of distribution and exchange is **redistribution,** or one in which goods (and services) are collected from or contributed by members of a group and then distributed to the group in forms ranging from ceremonial feast to public services. Redistribution is often found in complex societies, ranging from the Kwakiutl and other native peoples of the Northwest Coast through agricultural states to industrial societies. In the United States, April 15 of every year is a stark reminder that, through the personal income tax, we have a system of redistributive exchange, the use of whose revenue is not necessarily to everyone's liking. (Note: It may help to donate to a favorite charity.)

The **potlatch,** a major feast held during an important occasion, such as the coronation of a new chief, is held throughout the Pacific Northwest among the Kwakiutl, Tlingit, Haida, Tsimshian and other societies that are rich enough to support chiefs and their privileges. These are all **complex foraging** societies, based principally on a plentiful supply of salmon, which are preserved by smoking, and on other abundant food sources, further descriptions may be found in the module on the peoples of the Pacific Northwest Coast.

Other more complex societies also rely on redistribution. Among the Inca of the preconquest Andes of South America, a classic example of a **command economy,** the emperor controlled much of the land in the Andes cordillera and the adjacent coastal region stretching from modern day Peru to northern Chile. Peasants of the empire were obliged both to provide **tribute**—goods in kind—and **corvée labor,** or a labor tax; they were paid in textiles of cotton and llama wool, particularly valuable in a cold climate, in chicha (a kind of corn beer), and other necessities in life. Markets were underdeveloped, and virtually all goods and services were distributed under the Inca administrators. This model is also referred to as a **tributary mode of production,** in which an elite exacts services and goods from agrarian workers. The efficacy of economic planning, therefore, needs to be evaluated not only in light of the recently collapsed socialist states of the Soviet Union and Eastern Europe, but also what can be reconstructed of the Inca Empire. All of these are examples of economies dominated by **redistribution.**

Market. The third major type of distribution and exchange is the market. The market pervades our own societies, not to mention the former socialist countries such as the Soviet Union or the modified socialist economies such as China and even Vietnam and Cuba. We buy and sell food, clothing, houses, even labor. Your success in this economy hinges on your labor skills which some employer is willing to buy—we call that hiring. If you turn out to be less than useful, the employer takes his business elsewhere and you are fired.

The term **market** refers to the exchanges in which prices (usually in monetary terms) are set by supply and demand, whether or not the transaction actually occurs in a marketplace. Those familiar with eBay and other sites on the internet know you don't necessarily need to be at a store or supermarket to be involved in market transactions. The same is true for those who buy and sell stocks and bonds online.

The "pure" market hinges on several assumptions, serving as the "invisible hand," as Adam Smith put it in *Wealth of Nations* (1776) in regulating exchange. First, unlike reciprocity, which involves two individuals or groups, market contains two "crowds," the buyers who are able and willing to make purchases (summarized by the term **demand**) and sellers who have goods and services they are willing to part with at a price (summarized by the term **supply**). Under this assumption, no one individual has control or influence over the number of buyers making their demand nor the number of sellers hawking their wares. Therefore, the greater the demand, the higher the price. The buyer can go to the next vendor for apples or oranges if the price charged by the first vendor is too high. The greater the supply, the lower the price. If there are too many oranges on the market, sellers have no choice but to charge less. Demand and supply continue to fluctuate until these two countervailing forces cancel each other out—in other words, reach an equilibrium.

There are other assumptions. One is that the government or other third party does not intervene, such as impose a tax, fix prices, grant subsidies to sellers or buyers, or something of the sort. The second is that information about any price changes is available immediately. Still another is that buyers and sellers are free to enter and exit the market.

Probably the best ethnographic illustrations are the open air markets one finds around the world: Nigeria, Haiti, and our primary focus, Guatemala, with primary emphasis on Panajachel. Sol Tax argued that the Panajachel market showed most of the attributes of free markets as **ideal types.** There are many buyers and sellers. Entry into the market is free for buyers; sellers have to pay a small plaza tax, which is negligible. See "The Maya Culture Area" for more details.

The title of Sol Tax's book, *Penny Capitalism,* written in 1952, is no accident. The market is adaptive in a location where money is scarce and exchange might often be direct, that is made through **barter** (direct exchange of one good or service for another, rather than through cash payment). For most market participants, the aim is to exchange what one produces to obtain what one cannot produce, or produce with difficulty. Indeed, in highland Mesoamerica, regional markets encompass contiguous villages. They may be **rotating markets,** whereby markets move daily from location to location within a region. Larger towns may hold daily **solar markets,** such as that in Quezaltenango, the second city of Guatemala, or Guatemala City itself.

In such markets, villages and their hinterlands tend to specialize—exercise a semi-monopoly over—a particular product. Such is the case of Nahualá and Santa Catarina, which specialize in pitch pine for lighting fires, Momostenango, known for its woolen products such as chaquetes (jackets), blankets, and woven bags; Zunil and Almolonga for fresh produce; San Cristóbal for broadcloth for women's skirts; Santa Catarina Ixtahuacán for sugar cakes; and Salcajá for its alcoholic *caldo de fruta* of questionable legal status. Such semi-monopolies ensure some kind of a market for each product. The market, thereby, is an extension of the **domestic mode of production,** as discussed above. Transactions can be summarized by the formula $C \rightarrow M \rightarrow C$, in which C represents "commodity" and M represents "money." The main goal is to exchange commodity for money and to use the money to obtain other commodities.

Other market participants are known as **resgatones,** or resellers, whose aim it is to sell manufactured products in regional market for a profit; such objects include plastic containers, factory-made clothing, metal utensils—all the products no rural village can manufacture. The reseller buys his products at a warehouse in a city or market town at a discount and sells them at a higher price in the villages. The reseller's aim is represented by the formula $M \rightarrow C \rightarrow M'$, whereby M represents the initial outlay of money, C represents commodity, and M' (M-prime) represents increased amounts of money, that is, a profit. It is when we see this formula pervading society, particularly an industrialized society like our own, that the formula $M \rightarrow C \rightarrow M'$ dominates all transactions, major and in most cases minor. Then we enter the **capitalist mode of production,** where, combined with private ownership of the **factors of production** (land, labor, and capital), the productive process is oriented toward profit. **Capital** simply comprises manufactured goods involved in further production, or the claims (stocks or bonds) for such goods.

What makes the world go around—or drive exchange further—is **money.** This refers to a durable medium of exchange, based on a standard value that is used to purchase goods and services. The dominant type of money in today's society is **general-purpose money,** which can be used for all economic transactions. There are several attributes. First, it is portable; you can carry it around. Second, it facilitates exchange; you do not have to carry, say, a canoe to buy potatoes and figure out how many potatoes it costs, then lug the potatoes about to exchange for, say, tomatoes, and figure out their relative value. All you need to do is find out how many dollars and cents a sack of potatoes is and make the purchase. Third, money is a store of value. It retains its value to some extent. Finally, it is usually standardized by government fiat, making counterfeiting impossible or at least difficult.

Special purpose money, in contrast, is used only for specific transactions within different **spheres of exchange,** whereby money fungible in one part of an economy cannot be used in another. Modern bus tokens are one example; you can use it only for bus fare. The Trobriand Islands give two examples of special purpose money in the case study, plus a further example of 21 types of money on nearby Rossel Island. In east Africa, cattle are another example of special purpose money, used primarily for bridewealth, if not exclusively.

Conclusion

As we have seen already in this section, the economy is embedded in society or, in Polanyi's words, an "institutionalized process." The kula exchange system is as much social as it is economic, though it may facilitate trade in utilitarian economic goods. Money cements ties between two kin groups or villages through bridewealth, though the wealth itself (cattle in traditional East Africa; money in recent years) has economic uses. The potlatch may involve blankets and other utilitarian objects, but its use is to validate a chiefly status, as we will see in Chapter 13. Only in modern society does the economy become increasingly divorced from society in modern society. I buy a motor vehicle from you, pay for it, and that's the end of our relationship. Even so, we still have social distinctions between "old money," the traditional elite whose names appear every year in the *Social Register,* and the **nouveau riche,** the newly wealthy who are yet to be accepted in circles of the "right people." Even in modern society, the economy is not entirely unembedded in society.

Sociopolitical Anthropology

Introduction

One of the major questions in anthropology, as in social science generally, is how societies retain social control among its constituent populations. In this connection, political anthropology is concerned with the generation and distribution of power in the social sense.

Anthropology is especially relevant here, inasmuch as Western concepts that attend government—the legitimacy underlying the right to rule, the control of the sovereign state over the lives and death of its constituents—is often inappropriate in stateless societies.

We start this section by discussing some of the political concepts that have some bearing on all cultures and societies, simple or complex. We then shift attention to the concept **levels of integration** and its role in understanding the relatively simple and complex systems of control through social class, use of force or threat of such use, and law—and functional equivalents of societies lacking formal institutions to implement these processes. In this section and the next, we discuss in alternating fashion the types of societies with or without social class—**egalitarian societies, ranked societies,** and **stratified societies**—then discuss their corresponding levels of integration, namely **band, tribes, chiefdoms,** and **states.** Throughout, we provide examples of their integrating mechanism, such as **age grades** and **age sets, secret societies, segmentary lineages,** and even **marriage alliances.** We then round out our discussion with **law,** describing the difference between informal law and **codified law** and between **restorative justice** versus **retributive justice.**

Political Concepts

A dual intangible force governs the workings of politics: **power,** or the ability to induce the behavior of others in specified ways by means of coercion, or the use or threat of use of physical force; and **authority,** or the ability to induce the behavior of others by persuasion (Fried 1967). An extreme example of power in practice are the *gulags* (prison camps) in Stalinist Russia, the death camps under Nazi rule in Germany and Eastern Europe, and the prisons in Guantanamo Bay, occupied Cuba, in which "suspected" persons may be snatched off the streets, detained without the right to a fair trial, and incarcerated indefinitely. At the other extreme, in most forager societies, the group complies with the wishes of the most persuasive member—though decision is usually reached by consensus.

In actuality, the two concepts form poles of a continuum. Even Hitler had to hold the Nuremberg rallies to persuade the German population that his leadership was the way to national salvation, and the Soviet leadership felt the need to hold mass parades and rallies every May Day. At the other end of the spectrum, coercive force is not absent, as indicated by homicide among the Inuit of any character that (to them) is obnoxious in the extreme.

A related concept in both politics and law is **legitimacy,** the right of individuals to leadership in whatever form of government or law. This is particularly applicable to complex societies, those that require centralized decision making. Historically, the rights to rule have been based on varied principles. In agricultural states, such as Mesopotamia, the Aztec, or the Inca, justification has been based on rules of succession, usually of the eldest son of the ruler.

Often, supernatural beliefs or their functional equivalent are invoked to justify rule by an elite. The Inca emperors derived their right to rule from the Sun God; the Aztecs monarchs had Huitzilopochtli (Hummingbird-to-the-Left) to thank for their power. European monarchs invoked the divine right to rule, reinforced by the Church of England (Britain) or the Roman Catholic Church (other countries prior to the Reformation). In India, **karma,** or the cumulative forces created by good and evil deeds in past lives, serves to justify the dominance of the Brahmin elite over the other **castes.** Secular equivalents also serve to justify rule by the elite. In the Soviet Union, legitimacy rested in the promise of a worker's utopia once the state no longer proved necessary to defend the revolution. In Nazi Germany, it rested on the promise of a master Aryan race. In the United States and other democratic forms of government, legitimacy rests on the consent of the governed in periodical elections—even though the incoming president is sworn in using a Christian Bible, despite the stated separation of church from state.

At the opposite end of the political spectrum, legitimacy for an elite is absent, and even antithetical. To describe forager nonrecognition of political legitimacy, Christopher Boehm develops the concept of reverse **dominance** in his book *Hierarchy in the Forest* (2001). Reverse dominance occurs when a group exercises control over anyone who tries to assert power over them. The group achieves this aim by ridicule, criticism, disobedience, strong disapproval, or even informal execution of offenders or extremely offensive males.

Even at that level, decisions have to be made. Sometimes a headman may make them, particularly among some foragers, horticulturalists, many pastoralists, and equestrian hunters. Even in that event, he is not free to take decisions without coming to a **consensus** with his fellows, that is, one in which everyone is in general agreement. So in a backhanded way, legitimacy characterizes even societies without institutionalized leadership.

Another set of concepts refers to the reinforcements for compliance with the directive and laws in complex society. **Positive reinforcements** are the rewards for compliance: medals, financial incentives, other forms of public recognition. **Negative reinforcements** are the punishment for noncompliance with the directives or laws of a power elite: fines, imprisonment, death sentences. These reinforcements can be identified even among foragers, such as increased influence for the best hunters or ridicule or even homicide for the nonconforming. Reverse dominance is one form of negative reinforcement.

Levels of Sociocultural Integration

If cultures at various levels are to be compared regardless of organizational simplicity or complexity, there must be some common base for comparison; in other words, all cultures must have something in common. One such basis is the concept of **levels of sociocultural integration.** This notion refers to the levels of organization in cultures, ranging from one or two among foragers—the household and the larger **band,** which we will define momentarily—to several levels in **state** societies, starting again with the household and moving through the village or nomadic tribe, the administrative subunit equivalent to U.S. states or Canadian provinces, and finally the empire or nation-state.

Whether among such cultures as the Nevada Basin Shoshone performed all functions at the family level or were part of a larger group, we do see many functions of the family being pre-empted by larger organizations as societies become more complex. The resources, for example, become pre-empted in the form of tribute, the educational functions are taken over by schools, and the authority structure in the family is assumed by the state. Therefore, we need to categorize the levels of sociocultural integration.

In so doing, we develop two concepts that mesh with each other. On the one hand, we conceptualize a society based on **social classes** or lack thereof. These are **egalitarian, ranked,** and **stratified** societies. On the other hand, we mesh these concepts with four **levels of sociocultural integration,** which consist of the **band,** the **tribe,** the **chiefdom,** and the **state.** It should be emphasized that these are **ideal types,** designed to identify the essential characteristics of societies "out there: in the so-called real world." This discussion is based on two sources: Morton Fried's *The Evolution of Political Society* (1967) and Elman Service's *Origins of the State and Society* (1975).

Egalitarian Societies

In complex society, it may seem that like death and taxes, **social class** is inevitable. Clearly one is born into wealth, poverty, or somewhere in-between, and one has no say in the matter, at least at the start of life. In other words, social class is an ascribed and involuntary position in society. Is it, however, universal? This is one of the rationales of anthropology; only by a cross-cultural test can one determine if social class is everywhere found.

There are, of course, problems of definition. We humans are not equal in all things. As shown above, the status of women is low compared to men in many societies, if not most. There is also the matter of age. In traditional societies, the aged enjoy greater prestige than the young; in modern society, the aged are subjects of discrimination in employment and other areas. Finally, not all of us have the same abilities, naturally acquired or achieved through effort. Some of us are more eloquent than others; some are expert craftspersons while others are not; some are excellent at conceptual thought, whereas for the rest of us, there's always the *Dummies* series, whether in computers, computer software, or even wine and sex.

Apart from these differences, are there social classes everywhere in the world? As they say, let's look at the record we call ethnographies. We find that among foragers, there is no advantage to hoarding game; in most climates, the meat will rot before your eyes. Nor is there any particular advantage to hoarding other foods. Leadership is informal, if it exists at all.

If this is the case, then perhaps there is such a thing as societies without social classes after all. Foragers such as the !Kung, the Inuit, and the aboriginal Australians can better be described as **egalitarian** societies, or societies in which there are as many valued status positions as there are individuals capable of filling them. Good and poor hunters do not belong to different strata in the way that the captains of industry do from you and me. Poor hunters still receive a share of the meat; they have a right to be heard on important decisions. As for the more complex horticulturalist, pastoralist, and equestrian hunting peoples, the egalitarian definition still applies. Headmen emerge by consensus of the entire polity: village or nomadic tribe.

Therefore, we are looking at societies that lack a government or centralized leadership. They include not only **foragers,** but also **horticulturalists,** many **pastoralists,** and **equestrian hunters.** There are two levels of integration that coexist with egalitarian society: the **band** or **band level of integration** and the **tribe** or **tribal level of integration.** First, we discuss each in turn. We show how each retain their egalitarian characteristics, the classic example of which is the New Guinean **big man.** Then we discuss some of the mechanisms whereby societies can function without a state. For bands, they are virtually nonexistent. For tribes there are integrative mechanisms based both on kin-based and on nonkin-based organizations, and we discuss them in connections with this level of integration.

Band Level of Integration

It is probably more precise to say what bands are not than what they are. Usually, they comprise **simple foragers,** who rely on hunting and gathering, are nomadic for that reason, involve low populations (rarely exceeding 100 persons), and form informal groups with a few families and shifting population. They lack formal leadership and some might go so far as to say that the Dobe !Kung, at least, have no leaders. To quote one informant, "Of course we have headmen. . . . Each one of us is headman over himself." At most, leaders are *primus inter pares* or first among equals—assuming anyone is first at all. Modesty is a valued trait; arrogance and competitiveness are not. We have already described **reverse dominance.**

Leadership is also transient. Informal leadership often shifts with the circumstances. For example, "rabbit bosses" coordinate rabbit drives during the rutting season, but play no leadership role otherwise. Some leaders may be excellent mediators whenever two individuals dispute over some issue, while others might be better at coordinating a hunt. Still other individuals may be perceived as good shamans or prophets. There are no formal offices, nor are there rules of succession.

In resolving disputes, informal means of resolution also apply. There are neither formal mediators nor any organizational equivalent of courts of law. A good mediator may emerge—or the parties may just resolve the issue face-to-face. Sometimes, duels are employed. Among the Inuit, for example, the disputants engage in a song duel where, drum in hand, they chant insults at each other before an audience. The audience selects the better chanter, and thereby the winner of the dispute. Ridicule is reported among the Mbuti, in which even children berate an adult for laziness, quarreling, or selfishness. If ridicule fails, the elders try to evaluate the dispute carefully, show why things went wrong, and, in extreme cases, walk to the center of the camp and criticize individuals by name; using humor softens the criticism—the group, after all, does have to get along with each other.

Nevertheless, conflict does break out into war between bands and, sometimes, within them. Usually, warfare is sporadic and extended conflict is rare. There is not the formal leadership, let alone the manpower, to sustain conflict for long. Most of the conflict arises from interpersonal arguments.

Tribal Level of Integration

The next level involves not one but two or more groups, known as **segments,** and usually consisting of lineages, clans, ambilineal descent groups, or other organization. A second characteristic involves some integrative device binding them together. Some of the ethnographies in this section provide different types of such integration. Integration may be achieved through bilateral **cross-cousin marriage,** as among the Yanomamö of Venezuela and Brazil. A kin-based alliance such as a **segmentary lineage,** as among the Nuer of Sudan and Ethiopia, may perform that integrative function. They may involve pan-**tribal sodalities,** or organizations not based on kinship ties, such as **age grades** and **age sets** in Eastern Africa, **men's houses** in New Guinea, or **secret societies** such as the *poro* and *sande* among related tribes in Liberia and other countries in West Africa.

Whereas bands involve small populations without structure, **tribal societies** involve at least two well-defined groups linked together in some way and often range in population from 100 to as many as 5,000. Despite social institutions that can become fairly complex, there is no centralized political structure nor are there offices in the strict sense of the term. There may be headmen, but there is no rule of succession, nor do sons necessarily follow in the footsteps of their father.

Leadership roles are open to any male, particularly elder males, on the basis of their personal abilities and qualities. Like bands, they do not have the means for coercing others nor do they have formal powers associated with the position. They must persuade others to take any action they feel is needed to be taken.

Like bands, tribes are egalitarian societies. First, property may or may not be accumulated by individuals, but not to the extent whereby others are deprived. Second, every male has a chance to become headman, and like bands, one's leadership position may be situational. One man may be a good mediator, another a great war leader, and a third capable of leading a hunt or finding a more ideal area for cultivation or grazing herds. Thus, a tribe may be defined as an **egalitarian society** as one in which there are as many valued status positions as there are persons capable of filling them.

There are several examples in the ethnographies. The leadership of Papua New Guinea illustrates the role of the big man, more accurately translated as a man of influence. Several subtypes of tribes are illustrated in this collection. The big man can coordinate events, such as a pig feast or war, but he does not have the coercive power of a chief or king.

Kin-Based Systems of Integration. In addition to two or more segments, some anthropologists define tribal societies in terms of sodalities, or associations. For example, the Yanomamö have no association to consolidate the two intermarrying lineages, yet when villages fission, subgroups of intermarrying lineages stay together. The integrative factor is **bilateral cross-cousin marriage.**

Bilateral Cross-Cousin Marriage. The Yanomamö practice of **bilateral cross-cousin marriage** serves as an example of such an integrative mechanism. This is the arrangement whereby a man marries his cross-cousin related to him through both links: his father's sister and his mother's brother.

This alliance can be appreciated from the diagram in Figure 2.5. Here, let X refer to all the males of Lineage X and Y refer to all the males of Lineage Y; correspondingly, let *x* refer to all the females of Lineage X and *y* refer to all the females of Lineage Y. Let's take a third-generation example from this diagram. X has married *y*.

Now trace the relationship between X3 and y3 through their *matrilateral* links. Notice that the marriage link is *below* the two figures because on the diagram this couple is at the opposite extremes of this chart for this generation. Try linking *them* with an equal sign! Note that his mother is *x2*. Her brother is Y2, whose daughter is *y3*. Therefore, *y3* is X3's mother's brother's daughter. *Review this paragraph several times and refer it to the diagram.*

Now trace the *patrilateral* links of this couple. X3's father is X2, X2's sister is *x2*, she has married Y2, which makes her daughter *y3*—therefore his father's sister's daughter. Again, review this description several times and compare it against the diagram.

Now do the same thing with Y3. Trace his *matrilateral ties* with his wife *x3*. Notice that his mother is x2, her brother is X2 and so his mother's brother daughter is *x3*. Now trace Y3's *patrilateral* ties with his wife *x3*. His father is Y2, his sister is *y2* who has married X2, making his daughter *x3*. Again, concentrate on these two descriptions and compare them with the diagram.

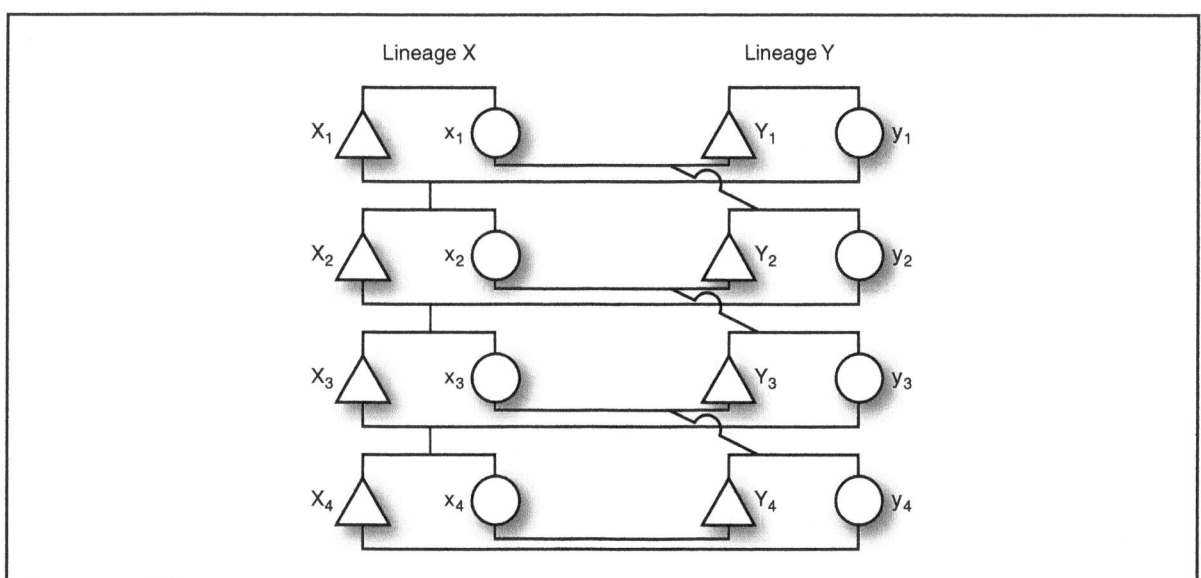

FIGURE 2.5
Bilateral cross-cousin marriage. Follow the figures of this diagram carefully. When a tribe fissions, can you see why both lineages would break away?

As you can see, the **ideal type** of **bilateral cross-cousin marriage** is that a man can marry a woman who is *both* his mother's brother's daughter and his father's sister's daughter. In other words, the man's matrilateral cross-cousin and patrilateral cross-cousin is one and the same woman! Retrace both links until you grasp the workings of this arrangement.

In real life, it is plain that not all marriages can conform to this idea. Often, the patrilateral cross-cousin is not one and the same person, there may be two or more persons. Furthermore, a man may marry either a matrilateral or patrilateral cross-cousin, but not both.

The function of ideal types is to explain the logical outcome of cross-cousin marriage. Villages tend to remain in two sets, even though bilateral cross-cousin marriage is more the ideal than the real.

Segmentary Lineages. Another type of kin-based integrative mechanism is a **segmentary lineage.** Because all lineages do **segment,** or divide into two or more daughter lineages, this may seem a redundancy. Conventional use, however, assigns a distinct meaning to this term.

A **segmentary lineage** is a hierarchy of lineages that exists for a limited purpose. At the base are several **minimal lineages** whose members trace their descent from their founder back to two or three generations. At the apex is the founder of all the lineages, of which there may be two or more **maximal lineages** derived from the lineage of the founder. There are several **intermediate lineages** at various levels between the maximal and minimal lineages. For purposes of simplicity, we will include in this discussion only the maximal and minimal lineages.

One characteristic of segmentary lineages is **complementary opposition.** To illustrate, consider the following chart (Figure 2.6). Here, we represent two maximal lineages A and B, with two minimal lineages each: A1 and A2 for A and B1 and B2 for B.

Suppose that A1 starts a feud with A2, say, for cattle theft. Being of the same maximal lineage A, it is likely that the feud will be contained within it. B1 and B2 ignore the conflict; it is no concern of theirs. Now suppose A2 attacks B1 for cattle theft. Now A1 unites with A2 to feud with B1, which whom B2 joins in defense. The feud, in other words, involves everyone in maximal lineage A against everyone in maximal lineage B. Finally, suppose an outside tribe attacks, say, A1. Now everyone, A and B included, rise up to defend A1.

Segmentary lineages occur but rarely in the world's cultures, usually among pastoralists; classic examples include the Nuer, the Tiv, and the Bedouin. They often develop in an environment of other tribes, whose hostility induces its members to retain their ties, mobilizing their kin as external conflicts arise, such as the Nuer against the Dinka. When the conflict is over, the segmentary lineage dissolves back to its constituent units. This also maintains another attribute of

A		B	
A1	A2	B1	B2

FIGURE 2.6
Note that territoriality is tied to genealogy.

segmentary lineages, **local-genealogical segmentation,** in which closer lineages also dwell more closely with each other, serving as a physical reminder of their genealogy. A Bedouin proverb summarizing the philosophy behind segmentary lineages runs as follows:

> I against my brother
> I and my brother against my cousin
> I, my brother, and my cousin against the world

Although segmentary lineages function to regulate warfare, it also serves to regulate inheritance and property rights. Often the population of tribes with segmentary lineages may approach 100,000 persons, as have been reported for the Nuer.

Nonkin Systems of Integration.

Sometimes known as **sodalities,** these systems function to cut across kinship ties to maintain a larger group. In a way, they represent a transition from localistic kin to wider societies. Among age grades, for example, men's loyalty to their own clans is tempered by their loyalty to their fellows of the same age, regardless of kin affiliation. In this section, we discuss several cross-cutting sodalities (age-based organizations, single-sex associations, and secret societies) and their role in maintaining societies that are not centralized, at least as yet.

Age Grades and Age Sets. In one sense, all societies are divided into age categories. In the U.S. educational system, the age of every child is matched with the grade he or she is placed—or should be placed according to education planners. If a child is six years of age, she or he should be in grade 1; if 13 years, grade 8.

However, the herders of most East African cultures support a more or less dual age-based structure: permanent **age grades,** to which all males are assigned, and **age sets,** movable categories to which men of a certain age grade are assigned. The age grades often have duties and age-related assigns to them, and as age sets advance, the men assume these roles. Age grades and age sets are common among East African societies, such as the Tiriki of Kenya as an ideal type. Other well-known examples are the Masai and the Jie, also of East Africa.

Bachelor Associations and Men's Houses. Among most tribes of New Guinea, if not all, men's houses serve to cut across the clans that comprise each village. Typically horticulture is combined with pig raising. New Guineans are decentralized, but the households are not autonomous. An ideal type of men's houses is described for the Mae-Enga or Enga of New Guinea. By various devices, the boys of each clan are induced to be loyal more to the men's house than the clan to which they were born. Men's houses represent the center of male-centered activity. It is in the men's houses that warfare is planned and strategies drawn. It is the seat of ritual activity, where magic is performed and ancestral spirits honored. It is also the place where the periodic pig feasts are planned and rituals rehearsed.

Tribal Law

Tribal societies generally lack **codified law,** a system of law whereby damages or crimes are specified and the remedies or punishments are spelled out. Only the state (see below) can determine, usually by writing, which behavior is permissible and which is not, and this we discuss below. Nor is there a system of **law enforcement,** whereby some agency—police, sheriff, army—can enforce a law enacted by some appropriate authority. As already shown, no headman nor big man can force his will on others.

In tribal society, as in any society, conflicts arise between individuals. In tribal society, the aim is not so much to determine guilt or innocence or criminal or civil responsibility as it is to resolve a conflict. There are several ways in tribal society to resolve a conflict. Two individuals or parties may choose to avoid each other. Indeed, bands, tribes, or kin groups often move away from each other, and it is much easier for them to do so than for people living in a complex society.

Guilt or Innocence: Oaths and Ordeals.   One issue in tribal societies, as in all societies, is guilt or innocence. Often, the offense was committed in the absence or unreliability of witnesses. In the absence of forensic technology—fingerprint, blood-type, or DNA matches—tribal societies may rely on supernatural means. An **oath** is the act of calling on a deity to bear witness to the truth of what one says; we see the oath in court as a holdover from this practice. An **ordeal** is a means used to determine guilt or innocence by submitting the accused to dangerous, painful, or risky tests believed to be under supernatural control. One example is the poison oracle used among the Azande of the Congo Democratic Republic and Sudan, who assume that most misfortunes are induced by witchcraft (which in this case does not involve ritual but rather ill feeling of one person toward another).

Negotiation and Mediation.   A more commonly exercised option is to find ways to resolve the dispute. In small groups, any unresolved question quickly escalates to violence and to disruption of the group. The first step is often **negotiation,** whereby the parties attempt to resolve the conflict by direct discussion in the hope of arriving at an agreement. Sometimes the offender, particularly if he or she is sensitive to community opinion, will make a **ritual apology.** In Fiji, for example, the offender will make a ceremonial apology called *i soro,* one of the meanings of which is "I surrender." An intermediary speaks, offers a token gift to the offended party, and asks for forgiveness. The request is rarely rejected.

If negotiation or ritual apology fails, often the next step is to recruit a third party and engage in **mediation,** whereby the third party tries to bring about a settlement in the absence of an official who has the power to enforce a settlement. One classical example in the anthropological literature is the **leopard skin chief** among the Nuer, who is identified by wearing a leopard skin wrap about his shoulders. The leopard skin chief cannot force a settlement, nor enforce the settlement if it is reached. The source of his influence is the desire for the parties to avoid a feud, which could well escalate to an ever-widening conflict involving kin descended from different ancestors.

This discussion largely reflects the preference of other societies to mediate, given the alternative of a long-term feud. Even in state societies, mediation is often preferred. In the agrarian town of Talea, Mexico, even serious crimes are mediated in the interest of preserving some degree of local harmony. Often the national authorities will tolerate local settlement if it maintains the peace.

Tribal Warfare

What happens, then, if mediation doesn't work and the leopard skin chief cannot convince the aggrieved clan to accept 40 or 50 cattle in place of their loved one? You go to war. In tribal society, war varies in causes, competence, and duration, but in the absence of large populations and technology, they tend to be less deadly than those run by the state, as we shall see.

Compared to bands, tribal societies engage in warfare more often, both within (internal) and between (external) tribes. Causes vary. Among pastoralists, theft of cattle or attempts thereof may spark conflict, and it is the pastoralists who have the reputation to be most warlike among prestate societies. Horticulturalists, however, also engage in warfare, as the film *Dead Birds* about warfare among the highland Dani of west New Guinea (Irian Jaya) attests. Here, revenge killing occurs after revenge killing, and so it goes on ad infinitum.

Tribal wars vary in duration. A frequent type of war is the **raid,** involving a short-term use of physical force that is planned and organized to achieve a limited objective, such as the acquisition of cattle (pastoralists), other forms of wealth, and often the abduction of women, usually from neighboring communities. Longer in duration is the **feud,** a state of recurring hostilities between families, lineages, or other kin groups. The responsibility to avenge is the responsibility of the entire group, and the murder of any kin member is considered appropriate, because the kin group as a whole is considered responsible. Among the Dani, for example, vengeance is an obligation; spirits are said to dog the victim's clan until its members murder the perpetrator's clan.

Ranked Societies.   Unlike **egalitarian societies, ranked societies** (sometimes called "rank societies") involve greater differentiation between individuals and the kin groups of which they are a part. These differences may be inherited and often are. Nevertheless, there are no significant restrictions on access to basic resources, and all individuals can meet their basic needs through membership in kinship groups. Rather, the differences are based on **sumptuary rules,** or norms that permit persons of higher rank to wear distinctive clothing, jewelry, and decorations denied those of lower rank. One may therefore define a ranked society as one in which there are fewer valued status positions than persons capable of filling them.

Chiefdoms.   This definition leads us directly to the characteristics of **chiefdoms.** The position of **chief** is, unlike the position of **headman,** an **office,** that is, a permanent political status that demands a successor when a given chief dies. Put another way, there are two concepts of **chief,** the man himself (women rarely occupy these posts) and the office. Thus, the expression "The king is dead; long live the king" reflects the dual meaning of both *king* and *chief.* If one contrasts this with the New Guinean **big man,** we see at once that the death of the big man is also the end of his status; other big men will arise to take his place, and there is no rule that stipulates his eldest son—or any son—must succeed him. For the post of chief, however, there *must* be a successor and there must be a rule of succession.

Usually, the exchange system known as **redistribution** accompanies political centralization, which begins with chiefdoms. As noted above, redistribution entails the flow of goods and services from the population at large to the central authority, represented by the chief. It then becomes the task of the central authority to return the flow of goods in another form. The system of taxation in state from agrarian-based kingdom to modern society fits this pattern. The discussion of the potlatch discussed for the cultures of the Pacific Northwest is a classic example of a chiefdom, in connection to the form of redistribution known as the **potlatch,** and so discussion is reserved for this culture area.

Kin-Based Integrative Mechanisms: Conical Clans.   With the centralization of society, kinship is most likely to continue playing a role, albeit a new one. Among Northwest Coast peoples, for example, the ranking model has every lineage ranked, one above the other, siblings ranked in order of birth, and even villages in a ranking scale. The farther north one goes, the more rigid the ranking scheme is. The most northerly of these coastal peoples trace their descent matrilineally; indeed, the Haida consist of four clans. Those further south tend to be patrilineal, and some show characteristics of an ambilineal descent group. It is still unclear, for example, whether the Kwakiutl *numaym* are patrilineal clans or ambilineal descent groups.

Non-Kin Integrative Mechanisms: Associations. Chiefdoms, lacking the means to enforce their power by resource control or by monopoly over the use of force, rely on the integrative mechanisms similar to non-kin associations that cut across kinship groups. Secret societies are one means of integration, such as the men's Poro and women's Sande of the Mande-speaking peoples of Liberia, Sierra Leone, and elsewhere in West Africa. Another is the *kachina* societies of the Hopi in the Southwestern United States.

Stratified Societies

Opposite from the **egalitarian society** in the social class spectrum is the **stratified society,** which may be defined as one in which a minority controls the strategic resources that sustain life. The Kpelle of Liberia are the closest of ranked societies that fall short of being stratified, and one might argue that it is a transitional society. By **strategic resources,** we refer to such resources as water in states that are dependent on irrigation agriculture, land in the **feudal mode of production** or patrimonial society, and oil in industrial society. **Capital,** or products and resources used for further production, is a **mode of production** that, in industrial society, is reliant on oil and other fossil fuels, such as natural gas.

Caste Systems. Operationally, **stratification** is, as the term implies, the structure of society that involves two or more largely mutually exclusive layers of population. An extreme example is the **caste** system of traditional East Indian society that draws for its legitimation **Hinduism,** of which more is said in the case study of India. A **caste** is a form of social class in which membership is determined by birth and remains fixed for life. **Social mobility,** or movement from one social class, either upward or downward, within a lifetime is not an option. Nor can a person of one caste marry another person of a different caste; they are **endogamous** in which marriage is allowed only within a caste. Although efforts have been made to abolish castes since India achieved its independence in 1947, they still predominate Indian society, especially in rural areas. Further details are spelled out of the caste system in the modules of India and Bali.

Although the most extreme, India is not the only society with a caste system. In Japan, a caste known as *Burakumin* is similar in status to the *Dalits,* or "untouchables" described in the module for India. Although no different in physical appearance from other Japanese, this population has been forced to live in ghettos for centuries. They are descendants of peoples who worked in the leather-tanning industry, a low-status occupation, and still work in leather industries, such as shoemaking. Marriage between *Burakumin* and other Japanese is restricted at most, and their children are excluded from public schools. These are further described for the module on Japan.

Social mobility of a greater or lesser extent characterizes all societies, but even the so-called **open-class societies** are not quite so mobile as one might think. In the United States, despite the

Horatio Alger and rags-to-riches myths, actual movement up the social ladder is rare. Stories of individuals "making it" through hard work ignore the majority of persons whose hard work does not pay off or who actually experience downward mobility. The current Occupy Wall Street movement is a reaction to this reality. On the other hand, in India, a **closed-class society,** there are exceptions to the caste system in the ideal sense. In Rajasthan, for example, those who own and control most land are not of the warrior caste, as one might expect, but of the lowest caste; their tenants and laborers are, by contrast, Brahmins.

State Level of Integration

The **state** is the most formal of the four levels of integration under study here. In the state, political power is centralized in a government that exercises a monopoly over the legitimate use of force. It is important to understand that such exercise constitutes a last resort; indeed, one hallmark of a weak state is the frequent use of physical force to maintain order. States exist in societies with large populations—hundreds of thousands or more—a complex economy, either a command economy or a market driven one; social stratification; often an ethnically diverse population, and at base an intensive agricultural or industrial base.

Several characteristics accompany the monopoly over the use of legitimate force in a state. First, like tribes and chiefdoms, states occupy a more or less clearly defined **territory,** or land enclosed by boundaries that mark it off from other political entities that may or not be a state. Egypt was a state bounded to the west by desert and possibly foraging or tribal nomadic peoples. Mesopotamia was a series of city-states competing for territory with other city-states.

Second, there are heads of states, who may be individuals known as kings, emperors, or monarchs with other names. Others may be democratically elected, in fact or in name—even military dictators may be known as presidents. Usually there is some board or councilors (the cabinet in the United States, the politburo in the former Soviet Union). Often the council may be supplemented by a legislative assembly and sometimes two. Rome, an empire, had a senate (which originated as a body of councilors) and up to four assemblies that combined patrician (elite) and plebian (general population) influences. Today, almost all countries have some sort of an assembly, however often they may rubber-stamp the decision of the executive branch.

Third, there is an administrative apparatus, a bureaucracy that handles the public functions provided for by executive order or legislation or both. Formally, the offices are typically arranged in a hierarchy, with the top offices delegating specific functions to lower ones. The arrangement of personnel within any branch mirrors the hierarchy of offices in general. Generally speaking, the relations tend to rely on interpersonal relations in agricultural states, and principles of rational hierarchical organization in industrial ones.

Fourth, there is the power to tax, adding power to the system of **redistribution** whereby everyone from proletarian or plebe to peasant has no choice but to participate. This power comes in various guises, from the *mitá* or labor tax of the Inca to the tributary systems of Mesopotamia to the monetary tax known to us and to many other subjects throughout the history of the state. Control over others' resources is another mechanism undergirding the power of the state.

Fifth, there is the presence of ideology, designed to reinforce the powerholders' right to rule. Ideology may manifest itself in philosophical forms—the Divine Right of Kings in preindustrial Europe, *karma* and the caste system in India, the consent of the governed in the United States, the metaphorical Confucian family in Imperial China. More often, ideology is more indirect, less perceptible as propaganda. We may watch the Super Bowl or follow the latest Martha Stewart interior designs, oblivious that both are diversions from the reality of power in this society. Recruits may be lulled into the Iraq war, as their parents were into the Vietnam War, in the belief that military life is a way out of unemployment (or underemployment at Wal-Mart). In thousands of ways and across different cultures, Plato's parable of the shadows in the cave—that watchers misperceived the shadows as reality—have served to reinforce political ideologies.

Finally, there is the delegation of the coercive power itself. The necessity to use power betrays an important weakness—that a wide portion of the subjects or citizens do not recognize the powerholders' right to rule. Even where the legitimacy of power is not questioned, force serves to maintain the state, and the functions are delegated. The police force serves to maintain the internal order of the country, whereas the army and its military cohorts are defending the country against enemies, perceived or real, or often expanding the country's borders.

State and Nation.   The frequent interchangeability of **state** and **nation** often obscures the distinction between a coercive institution and an ethnic population. Statistically, there are about 200 states in the world, many of which did not exist before World War II. In contrast, there are possibly 5,000 nations, each with a language, territorial base, history, and political organization. Few states are conterminous with a nation. Even in Japan, whose millions of people are of one ethnicity, there is a significant indigenous minority known as the **Ainu,** at one time a distinct biological breeding population as well as an ethnic group. Only recently has Japanese society included migrant minorities such as the Koreans and Taiwanese. Otherwise, most states comprise multiethnic societies, including the United States.

Nor do all ethnicities have their own states. The Kurds are a nation without their own country, located as they are in adjacent areas of Turkey, Syria, Iraq, and Iran. In the colonial era, the Mende-speaking peoples range across at least four West African countries, and the borders were drawn without respect to the tribal identity of its population. In addition, there are **Diasporas**—peoples of one ethnicity scattered across the globe. Ashkenazi and Sephardic Jews are classic examples, but others include Armenians, various African nations uprooted by slavery, overseas Chinese, and, in recent years, many others as refugees are forced to flee their homelands.

Formation of States.   States fall into two categories according to how they are formed. The **pristine states** are those that develop where none has existed before so that causal factors do not include modeling after, or adapting to the presence of, existing states. Historically, there are no recorded or well-documented examples of states forming where none existed before. **Secondary states** are those that develop amid other states, which do serve as models and may exert pressure for a society to develop a government of its own, partly to prevent being conquered.

How do states form? One precondition is the presence of a **stratified society,** one with an elite minority controlling life-sustaining strategic resources. Another is the increased productivity of agriculture which, in turn, is capable of supporting a larger population. Nevertheless, neither is a sufficient cause. One group, dissatisfied with conditions in the home region, has the motivation to move someplace else—unless there is no place to move to.

This is where **circumscription** enters the picture. The region may be hemmed in by mountains or desert, and any migrant community would have to change its subsistence strategies from agriculture back to foraging, herding, or horticulture. Indeed, the Inca Empire never colonized on a massive scale beyond northern Chile to the south or into the Amazon, because the indigenous people there simply picked up and moved elsewhere. Even so, the majority of the Inca population did not have this option. Circumscription also results when an adjacent desirable region is already taken by other states or chiefdoms.

The State and Peasantry.   Who, then, are the subjects of the state? One short answer is **peasants.** Derived from the French *paysan,* which means "countryman," one thinks of a landed yeomanry who have long constituted the foundation of an agricultural state. Yet peasantry has entered relatively late in the anthropological literature. In his 800-word tome *Anthropology,* written in 1948, Alfred L. Kroeber defined peasantry as "part societies with part cultures." Other anthropologists have defined the term in various other ways.

One commonality is that virtually all anthropologists define "peasant" in reference to some larger society, usually an empire or a state or a civilization. In light of this development, Wolf in his definitive work *Peasants* seeks to place the definition on a structural footing. Using a funding metaphor, he compares peasants with what he calls "primitive cultivators." First, both primitive cultivators and peasants have to provide for a caloric fund: grow food and, by extension, provide for clothing, shelter, and all other necessities of life. Second, both must provide for a replacement fund, that is, not only reserve seed for next year's crop, but also make repairs on the house, replace a broken pot, rebuild a fence, and all the rest. Third, both primitive cultivator and peasant must provide for a ceremonial fund, whether a rite of passage for the *poro* rites or the fiesta for a Mesoamerican village.

Where peasant and primitive cultivator part ways is that the one lives within a state and the other does not. The state exercises a domain over the peasant's resources for which he must provide a fund of rent. The fund of rent comes in many guises—tribute in kind, taxation in money, or *corvée* labor to some empire or lord. The primitive cultivator, in Wolf's conception, is free of these obligations.

The State and the Landless.   Not all subjects, however, are landed. Indeed, landless populations have a long history. To begin with, **slavery** has long coexisted with the state. Forced labor without compensation is a long tradition that reaches back to chiefdoms—the Kwakiutl had slaves. Long before Portuguese, Spanish, and English seafarers added slaves to their trading along the west coast of Africa, Arab slavers took Africans both west and east of the continent. The module on West Africa has more to say on this topic.

Among peasantry, loss of land, known as proletarianization, has been a continuous process. The **enclosures** of England and Western Europe, whereby the last of the landed gentry found sheep herding more profitable than the tributes of peasants, illustrate this point. This process is described for Guatemala in the module on the Mayan Culture Area.

Law and Order

At the level of the chiefdom, and particularly the state, law becomes increasingly a formal process. Procedures become more and more regularly defined, and categories of breaches in civil law and of crime emerge, together with their remedies. Agricultural states came to formalize legal decision and punishments through legal codes, formal courts of law, police, and legal specialists such as lawyers and judges. Mediation may still be practiced, but often they are supplanted by **adjudication,** where the judge's decision is binding on all parties. The decision may be appealed to a higher judge, but any final decision must be accepted by all concerned.

The first known system of codified law was enacted under the warrior king Hammurabi in Babylon located in the present state of Iraq. This law was based on standardized procedures for dealing with civil and criminal offenses, and subsequent decisions were based on precedent, or previous decisions. Crimes became offenses not only against other parties but also against the state. Other states developed similar codes of law in China, Southeast Asia, and even in the state-level societies of the Aztec and Inca.

Two interpretations, not necessarily mutually exclusive, have arisen about codified law. One school of thought argues from analyses of the Hammurabi codes that these laws reinforced a system of inequality by protecting the rights of an elite class while keeping the peasants in a subordinate status. This is consistent with a stratified society as already defined. Another interpretation has it that the maintenance of social and political order is crucial for agricultural states. Any disruption within the state would lead to neglect of agricultural production, which would prove deleterious to all members, regardless of social status. Civil law ensures, at least in theory, that all disputing parties will get a hearing—assuming that high legal expenses and bureaucratic logjams do not cancel out this process—and criminal law ensures protection of all citizens from offenses ranging from theft to homicide.

However valid the ideal of formal procedural law, there are circumstances in which such law fails to realize its aims. For example, the United States has one of the highest crime rates in the industrial world. Although the violent crime rate declined during the mid-1990s, this was possible only with the construction of more prisons per capita (in California) than of schools. Nationwide, there are more than one million prisoners in state and federal correctional institutions, making this country one of the highest imprisoned populations in the industrial world.

Warfare

Warfare occurs in all societies, even among foragers, but at no level of integration does it involve as widespread a population as at the state level of integration. Indeed, warfare was integral to the formation of the agricultural state. As governing elites accumulated more resources, warfare came to be one of the major means of increasing their surpluses. Often, as the wealth of states themselves became the target of nomadic pastoralists, the primary motivation for warfare shifted from control over resources to control over neighboring populations.

A further shift comes with the advent of industrial society; industrial technologies, driven by fossil fuels, enabled countries to invade distant countries. One of the primary motivations for these wars has been to establish economic and political hegemony over foreign populations. Wars of the past century, particularly World War I, World War II, and the lesser wars that have taken place since then, have generated ever higher levels of war-related technology, such as wireless communication devices, tanks, stealth aircraft, nuclear weapons and, since 2011, unmanned missiles called drones. Competition among nations has led to the emergence of the United States as the militarily most powerful nation in the world.

This has not come without costs. All nation-states have involved civilians in military adventures, and almost everyone has been involved in some way in their countries' wars—if not as military, then as members of the civilian workforce in the military industries. World War II created an unprecedented armaments industry in the United States, Britain, Germany, and Japan, among others, and the aerospace industry underwent expansion in the so-called Cold War that followed.

Stability and Duration of States

It should be noted that states show a clear and long-term tendency toward instability, despite trappings designed to induce awe in the wide population. Few states have lasted as long as 1,000 years. The American state is 230 years old, yet the increase in extremes of wealth and poverty, escalating budgetary and trade deficit, a war initiated under false pretenses, and escalating social problems are indications that it could collapse before long. Jared Diamond's recently released book *Collapse* (2004) draws parallels between complex societies such as Easter Island, Chaco Canyon, and the Maya with contemporary societies such as our own, and finds that overtaxing the environment has been an efficient cause in all these societies. More recently, Morris Berman has written a trilogy arguing that the United States is already in decline, spelled out especially in his last book *Why America Failed* (2012).

Why states decline in due course is not hard to fathom. The extreme disparities in wealth, the use of force to keep the population in line, the stripping of people from their resources (such as the enclosures in England), the harshness of most laws all should create a general animosity toward the elite. The Occupy Wall Street movement is the latest manifestation of this content.

Yet why have Occupy Wall Street and the earlier Arab Spring taken so long to break out? Here is the paradox: though widespread, this animosity does not automatically lead to the dissolution of the state nor the overthrow of the power elite; this is yet to occur even with the events of the past two years. Thomas Frank addresses this issue in *What's the Matter with Kansas?*, which shows that, despite the fact that jobs have been shipped abroad, that once-vibrant cities like Wichita are virtual ghost towns, and that both Congress and the state legislature have voted against social programs time and again, Kansans continue to voting into office the very Republicans who are responsible for these conditions in the first place. Nor is this confined to Kansas or the United States. That slaves themselves—blacks, and many before them—tolerated slavery for hundreds of years (despite periodical revolts), that workers tolerated extreme conditions in the factories and the mines long before unionization, that there was no peasant revolt strong enough to reverse the enclosures—all of these demand an explanation. Frank himself discusses reinforcing variables—the propaganda of televangelists and Rush Limbaugh, for example—but offers little explanation besides them. In fact, the electoral success of the Tea Party and the evangelical right in the state and federal election of 2010 eludes explanation. Why do Americans—and many other peoples of the world—continue to vote against their own interests?

Anthropology of the Supernatural: Religion and Magic

Introduction

Belief in the **supernatural,** or beings, objects, and forces that occur beyond nature, or the range of the five senses and their extensions, exists in all cultures. We cannot see an entity called God, or *mana* believed to exist among the Polynesians, or the being *di* among the Trobriand Islands, but people somewhere in the world believe that they are there. Americans, or at least some of them, separate the supernatural from the natural as handily as the U.S. Constitution separates church from state; but there are many peoples around the world who treat the supernatural as real as the tree in front of their house or the pigs they tend or the sun in the sky.

In point of fact, there is much we do not know. We have no idea where we "came from" (other than a woman's womb and a man's sperm), nor do we know where we go after death (if we go anywhere, that is) or what happens to us (if anything other than becoming a feast for the worms).

Defining the Supernatural

One of the fundamental distinctions in the supernatural involves that between magic and religions, a distinction that Sir James George Frazer made in his classic work *The Golden Bough: A Study in Magic and Religion* (1890).

The World View of the Supernatural. Taking his categories, we may define **magic** as a religious ritual involving manipulative means to induce spirits or forces to produce the effect desired by the practitioner. One may define **religion** as a social process that orders the relationship between humankind and the supernatural world, whether dominated by a single God, multiple gods, spirits, forces, ghosts, demons, or some combination thereof. The module on Bali will show that these categories can and do overlap. How many devout Catholics—religious that they are—ask St. Jude, the Saint of Lost Causes, for favors and thank him in newspaper advertisements for favors rendered—an example of magic?

Magic has its subtypes, and in some instances may have its evil side. **Sorcery** refers to the manipulation of supernatural beings and forces to bring harm to others. **Witchcraft** refers to the ability to harm others by harboring malevolent thoughts about them, but without the ritual. **Shamans** are individuals who are perceived as intermediaries between the material and spirit world, but who themselves are not recognized officials of any organized religion.

Religion, too, has its subtypes. One of the earliest recognized forms of religion is **animism,** the belief that there is a spirit world populated by spirits, demons, ghosts, and other beings. According to E. B. Tyler, dreams represent an entry point into this world; one leaves the body while sleeping and wanders in a space whereby every natural object—trees, rocks, sun, sky, water—has a conscious being. A second interpretation, known as **animatism,** holds that forces rather than beings are behind the natural objects and events. The Polynesian concept of mana is one such example. This comprises tabu, which infests objects that are forbidden to most people as too dangerous to handle, much like electricity, which is something that most of us shouldn't handle.

At the other end of the social spectrum stand highly structured, formal, and organized religions, which become increasingly intertwined with stratification and the state. The religious traditions that develop in agricultural states are known as **ecclesiastical religions,** whereby no distinctions are drawn between religion and state, as is the case of the Jewish state of Israel or the Islamic Republic of Iran. Also developing in agricultural states are **universalistic religions,** those purporting to represent all of humankind rather than a specific nation-state or empire. Two major branches emerged: one emerged in the Middle East and spawned the historically related religions of Judaism, Christianity, and Islam; the other arose in southern Asia and spawned Hinduism and Buddhism.

Denizens of the Supernatural. Cutting across the societies are gods, spirits, and ghosts, who themselves are often dichotomized as benevolent or malevolent. **Gods** refer to beings that are divine in origin, that is, not of the earth, who display human attributes. In **polytheistic religions,** they may specialize in different realms of human existence, such as the chief executive (Zeus or Jove in Greek and Roman mythology, or Brahman in Hinduism), wealth (Mammon in Greek and Roman mythology or Ganesh in Hindu society), and many others. In **monotheistic** religion, there is one god, the shared perception of which he (rarely she) is omniscient (all-knowing) and omnipotent (all-powerful).

The gods (or god) of morality or creation have their antithetical beings, of which Satan is a well-known example in all three universalistic religions of the West—Christianity, Judaism, and Islam. Among the Balinese, as in other religions originating in southern Asia, the demons are perceived not so much the purveyors of evil as of dissolution. To the Balinese, the task is not so much to eradicate evil as to maintain the balance between the forces of creation versus the forces of decay. Even the demons have their place.

Other supernatural beings have their origins on earth, as deceased humans. The term **ghost** applies generically to all spirits of human origin. There are ancestral spirits, who are the objects of veneration in many societies. The Day of the Dead, held throughout Latin America at or toward the beginning of November every year, welcome their (not so) departed relatives with their favorite food, drink, and ornaments.

Often ghosts turn malevolent. Sometimes, their malevolence is the product of neglect. Among Mexican Nahuatl-speakers, departed spirits may bring misfortune on kin who do not erect shrines or make offerings on the Day of the Dead. Ill will also may arise over some issue in life that has remained unresolved.

Coexistence or No Existence: Gods and the Spirits. Even the monotheistic gods coexist with other supernatural beings in most societies, if not all. Spirits, or more local beings, also usually of nonhuman origin, are found everywhere. Even in post conquest Latin America, one finds local spirits hiding behind the names and images of saints. The Virgin of Guadalupe, the national patron saint of Mexico, has shades of a fertility goddess, Tenanting or Coatlicue. This process of combining supernatural beliefs from two or more different belief systems is known as **syncretism.**

Explaining the Supernatural

Studying questions of religions often inspires skepticism from a scientific standpoint. We are dealing, after all, with attributes of things and events whose very existence cannot be tested. In Bali, did the volcanic Mount Agung erupt in 1963 because the Balinese priesthood, under pressure from the then-Indonesian president Achmed Sukarno, attempted to conduct the Eka Desa Rudra ceremony before the proper time had arrived—or would Mount Agung have erupted anyway? These are untestable explanations; we cannot go back in time and see whether Mount Agung erupted if the priests had shown more backbone against Sukarno's pressure to perform the ritual at the wrong time.

Nevertheless, we can ask why religions exist or, less charitably, why people believe in all that stuff. Several explanations have been brought forth. First, we might ask what functions they serve.

Are religions indeed the opiate of the people, as Karl Marx would have it? Do they serve to promote social solidarity, as the sociologist Emile Durkheim would argue? Several such explanations have surfaced in recent years. Second, one might ask an epistemological question: do religions fill in the conceptual gaps left behind by science, however defined and however sophisticated or not? Do they explain the universe in areas that science cannot, whether the scientist is a thoughtful Azande tribesman or a philosopher of science at Harvard or Oxford? Third, and as a theme and variation of Marx's opiate theory, do supernatural cosmologies offer comfort to those uncertain as to what death is like and what the afterlife holds for them, if any?

Revitalization Movements

Over the past five centuries, Western countries and their powers elite—Western Europe, the United States, and for a time imperial Japan—have expanded their economic and political influence over the rest of the world. Changes have generated widespread insecurity among non-Western peoples over widespread regions, generating among other things **revitalization movements.** Such movements occur during times of extreme change in which religious leaders emerge to bring forth change, positive or negative. One may consider the definition offered by Anthony F. C. Wallace, who defined the term as "deliberate and organized attempts by some members of a society to construct a more satisfying culture through rapid acceptance of a pattern of multiple innovations.

According to Wallace, most revitalization movements follow a more or less regular pattern of five phases. (1) A society is in a state of equilibrium. (2) A society is pushed out of equilibrium by various forces, such as a climatic or biotic (biological environmental) change, epidemic disease, war and conquest, economic restructuring, and other factors. (3) The society undergoes disorganization and its member's disillusionment that accepted norms that no longer function. (4) Social deterioration sets the stage for a revitalization movement to bring about a society more satisfying to its constituents. (5) An individual or group constructs a new, idealistic model of culture that forms the basis of social action. If the movement is successful, the society reaches a new steady state. Examples abound: the Ghost Dance initiated by the Paiute of the Nevada Basin, the cargo cults of Papua New Guinea and Melanesia, even the transfiguration of the Virgin Mary to the Virgen de Guadalupe after Spain's conquest of the Aztecs.

Conclusion

In this section, we have examined a dimension that many cultures do not recognize as separate from the everyday reality we see around us. Supernatural phenomena (sometimes known as **noumena,** or things and events said to occur beyond the five senses and their extensions) are as routine in daily living among some cultures as eating or sleeping is anywhere. In a sense, this may reflect a culture-bound bias of our own. We cannot empirically test for ghosts, mana, gods (one or many), spirits, sorcery, or witchcraft; these are outside the ken of science. Yet because we cannot test for these things and events, how do we know they are not there? We cannot test for emotions (love, hate, anger) except through behavior; these qualities are intangible. At one time, it was thought that the sun went around the earth or the earth was flat, showing in both instances that our ordinary perceptions of these phenomena are wrong.

As these considerations show, there is much about this world to be learned. That all cultures recognize the supernatural demonstrate how much there is to know—perhaps much more than we do know. Even what we know is uncertain. Who would guess from unaided observation in ancient Greece that a gold ring is made up of atoms?

Summing Up

Indeed, the case studies that follow provide some evidence that modern cultures have a good deal to learn by their cohorts of today or cultures of the past. An instructive case is India. Who would have guessed that during the Golden Age under Gupta that the concept of the zero would have been developed, that pi (π) would be calculated, or that we live in a system of planets and suns we call stars? Yet it all happened. Who would have guessed that Islamic societies preserved Western culture, added more insights on the medical sciences, the science of optics, or invent the astrolabe—and bring the concept of zero to the West—while the Europeans were busy killing each other over whether God came in three persons or one and other such minutiae? This was the Dark Ages. Which one? The Middle Ages or now?

We have a lot to learn. Consider this collection as a first step.

PART 1

North America

CHAPTER 3

The Inuit: Peoples of the Arctic

Introduction

One of the best publicized cultures in the popular media is the so-called Eskimo, more accurately known as the **Inuit.** In fact, there are several different cultures in Arctic North America. Although the Inuit are well-known in the popular media with their igloos, their dog sleds, and their signature parkas, they are not the only cultures in the Arctic region of North America. There are the coastal peoples represented by the Tareumiut, who live in permanent dwellings and are semi-nomadic at best. The Aleuts and the Yupik have similar lifeways as the **Tareumiut,** so that this culture represents the settled communities in coastal Alaska and the Aleutian Islands.

Eskimo is derived from a Chipewyan slur meaning "eaters of raw meat," not exactly a compliment. Nevertheless, the term Eskimo is widespread, from the mascot of a football team in Edmonton, Alberta, Canada, to the brand name of an ice cream bar. The Inuit are best known for another trait: the adaptation of their culture to an extremely frigid environment. This is one focus of this presentation.

Climate and Environment

The Inuit (or Eskimo, if you must) are one of several peoples who have adapted to polar environments in various ways. There are the Lapps of the Scandinavian north, the Chukchee of northern Siberia, the Reindeer Tungus of north central Siberia, and, as mentioned, the Aleut of the Bering Strait between Russia and North America. The Inuit themselves range from central and northern Alaska through Arctic Canada to Greenland. The focus of this presentation is on two Inuit population: the Nunamiut, who live in central Alaska, and the Netsilik, who live in Pelly Bay on the western shores of Hudson's Bay, Canada. The Tareumiut, a settled population on the west coast of Alaska, are also described.

The two groups of Alaska have different adaptive strategies: the coastal Tareumiut, who have developed a village economy focused on whaling, and the nomadic band-level Nunamiut of the inland regions. The Inuit inhabit the edges of North America from the land split that starts the Aleutian Islands in the Bering Strait, extends northward then eastward along the Arctic Ocean to Hudson's Bay. They occupy the habitable islands north in the Arctic Ocean and the northern edge

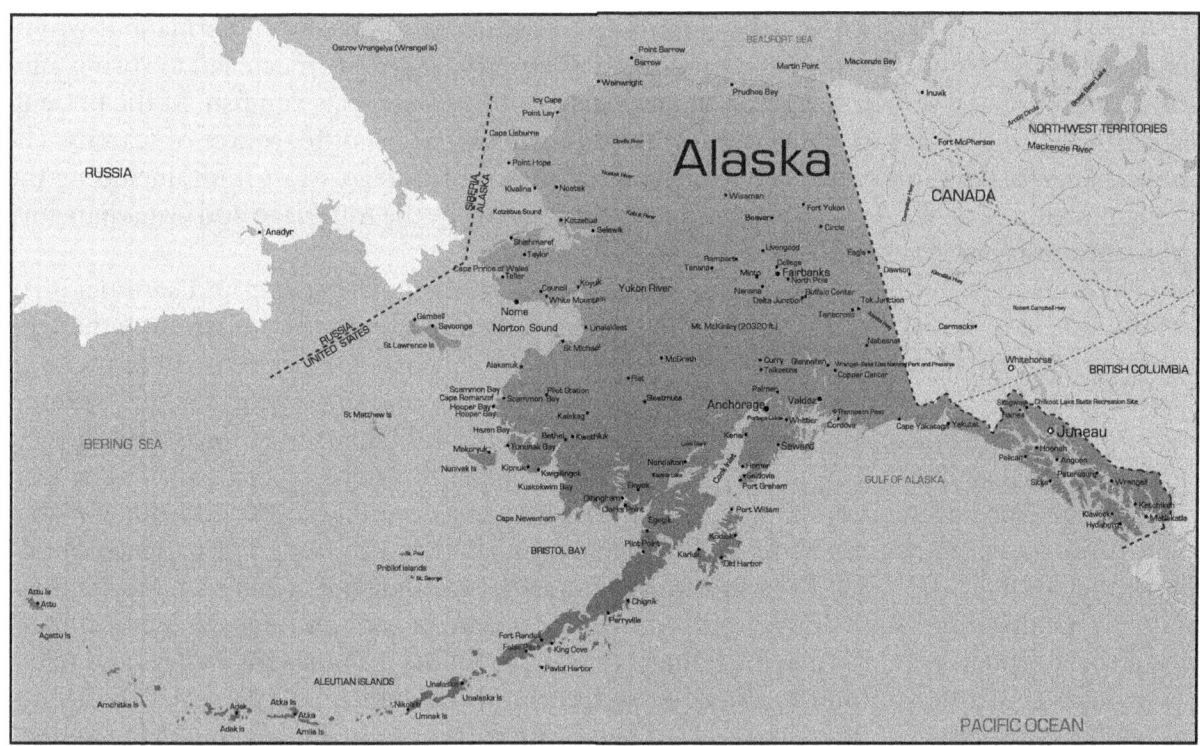

FIGURE 3.1

Alaska, Siberia, and Western Canada. The Inuit live in central and northern Alaska and across Arctic Canada to Greenland. The Tareumiut live along the central and northern coast; the Aleut live in the Aleutian chain and the Yupik live along the western coast and the adjacent coast of Siberia.

of Quebec and Labrador, and end in the habitable parts of western Greenland. The related Aleuts occupy their namesake, the Aleutian Islands of the Bering Strait. Other groups include the Yupik, located further south and share the same language family as the Siberian Yupik, who inhabit the eastern tip of Siberia and its offshore islands.

Foraging

The habitat of the Tareumiut comprised the North Shore of Alaska. Primary game included whales, walruses, seals, and polar bears. Whales, because of the large yield of meat and blubber, were the most prized game. Both the meat and blubber were preserved by storage in ice cellars dug into the permafrost. Up to 15 whales were taken during their spring migration southward. To hunt, the Tareumiut used large boats called umiaks, led by an *umealiq* ("boat owner"), tracking and harpooning whales, a dangerous undertaking inasmuch as the whale could capsize a boatload of hunters at any time. As among other northerners of any ethnicity, the Tareumiut now use snowmobiles and motorized umiaks. Other animal and fish, though hunted, were less prized because of their lower fat content; blubber was used for oil.

Unlike the stereotypical Inuit, the Tareumiut formed, and still do form, permanent winter villages. Like the Nunamiut, the Tareumiut faced a "hungry season" from late fall to spring after the caribou had ended their migration and the main sources were seals and fish. At the present, all northern peoples, including the Inuit and the Tareumiut, face another source of scarcity: climate change leading to a scarcity of game and the means of storage. Most Inuit, including the Nunamiut and Netsilik, now live in settlements constructed by the American and Canadian governments, respectively.

The Nunamiut live in the interior of Alaska's north shore. In late spring and summer, they enjoy a season of abundance. Grouping into large multifamily groups, the Nunamiut hunt caribou in their annual migration, and add smaller animals such as fox for pelts. In winter, the Nunamiut scatter into smaller family groups, and exploit the land during the "hungry season." Their primary game is seals, which are used for meat and for blubber used for the oil in their heating fire and lamps.

Like the Nunamiut, the Netsilik hunt a species known as ring-neck seal; little wonder that their name means "People of the Seal." Their technique requires a good deal of patience. Hunting is a multifamily effort. Seals may create as many as 30 breathing holes, and each hunter must wait at each hole. A piece of down is affixed to a small piece of caribou bone, so that it flutters when the seal breathes on it. Then the hunter waits . . . and waits . . . and waits. When, and if, the seal reaches one of the breathing holes, the down flutters and the hunter kills the seal with the harpoon, then pulls it to the surface. The seal is divided into parts and distributed among the hunters and their families. In both cultures, other animals are hunted or fished in various ways. Fish, principally arctic char, is trapped in a stone weir. Caribou herds are driven to a confined site or a body of water and shot there.

Social Organization

Both the Tareumiut and Nunamiut form nuclear families. Although conflict is rare, it does occur, and it is up to the family to control aggressive behavior lest it disrupt the household. Hunting partnerships are important, inasmuch as a successful seal hunt requires several hunters, as noted above, to watch the breathing holes in which the seals come up for air. There is an obligation to share if one household bags a seal, and in any case, a household must provide food if and when asked. Some families, feeling burdened by this obligation, may strike out on their own in the tundra, but the drawback is that they may find no game and so starve.

In this connection, Inuit social organization is simple as far as cultures go. Inuit bands are organized into bilateral families in which residence is patrilocal; that is, the bride moves in with the groom at his parents' residence. Feminists would clearly see this as a patriarchal society. On the other hand, Eskimo or Inuit cousin terminology is the same as that in Euro-American society in Canada and the United States. Sibling terms are different from cousin terms, but all the cousin terms are identical except, in some cases, those that differ by gender (Figure 3.2).

Although the preferred marriage rule is monogamy, two or more men may marry one woman, a polyandrous arrangement. Abduction of other men's wives are also reported, a common source of conflict. There are no larger kin groups, such as lineages or clans, although elderly parents live with their children. Several households did collaborate in seal hunts, weir construction, and caribou kills; once the meat was distributed, each hunter returned to his own family.

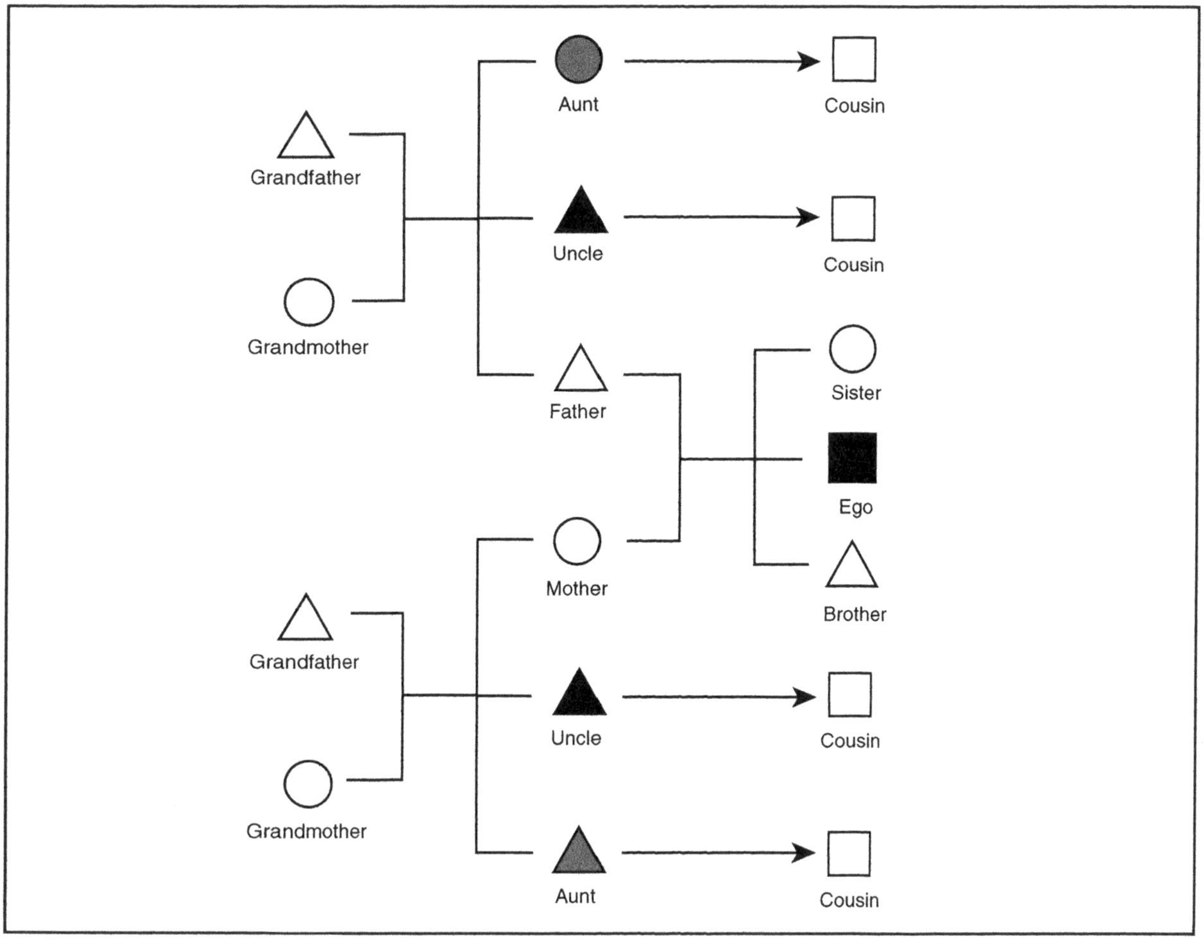

FIGURE 3.2
Eskimo or Inuit Cousin Terminology. Note that the brothers and sisters are distinguished from their cousins. In some kinship systems, the cousins are further distinguished by gender.

Inuit society is a case study of gender inequality. One factor of such inequality is the differential contributions that men and women make to the household economy. Women rear the children, chew the man's parka and leggings to render it soft and pliable, cook the meals, and attend to other domestic chores. But men's contribution to the household is vital: they hunt and so provide the food. Starvation is a constant fear if men do not supply the meat from seal, walrus, and fish. It is not surprising, therefore, that female infanticide is practiced whenever the dwelling is crowded or food is scarce. Gender inequality is also evident in the practice of wife-sharing, a tactic by men to strengthen their hunting partnerships.

As mentioned, warfare is rare. In a harsh climate, there is a strong incentive to keep aggression under control. Overaggressive men are ostracized from the group, and such ostracism amounts to death in a freezing environment. Interpersonal conflict is known to occur, often over women involved in extramarital sexual relations. Homicide of strangers who stray into another family's territory also occurs. The value of networks in trade and hunting tends to counterbalance these divisive acts.

Nor are there social class differences. Of the Netsilik, Asen Balicki reports their description of leadership as having no "bosses on top of each other." Leadership is implicit, and it becomes evident when hunting in groups. As in the seal hunt, leadership is advisory; no leader has the power to order people around. The sanctions of ostracism and the ridicule induced by the song duel, used with drums, keep would-be dominant males in check. Warfare is almost nonexistent, but conflict has been reported. Overall, the ideal man is, according to Johnson and Earle in their *Evolution of Human Societies,* "hard working, generous, who has no wish to place himself above the heads of others." They are a classic example of an egalitarian society, as discussed in Chapter 2.

Material Culture and Housing

Housing design is very different between the two groups. The Tareumiut live in larger settled communities and so their structures are permanent. Their housing is constructed from wood frames with sod walls, winter or summer. These houses are spread out along the coast, allowing each household to hunt walrus and seal, and allowing mobilization of hunters if a whale is spotted.

The Numamiut and the Netsilik, on the other hand, construct the well-known geodesic igloos, which can be constructed in a matter of minutes. (Figure 3.3) The dome shape reduces wind resistance, and a long entrance tunnel keeps out the cold winds. In some designs, the passage is curved to lessen the force of the winds. A clear ice panel allows sunlight to enter and this also helps to heat the inside when the sun is out.

The technology of the Inuit belies the stereotype of a "primitive" culture. Dog-driven sleds are a landmark of Inuit, and prodigious amounts of meat are consumed by both dog and man. Such clothing as the parka (Figure 3.4) and the muk-luks (boots) effectively resist the cold and have been imitated in industrial countries. Kayaks, or paddle-driven boats are enclosed at the top except for the paddler's perch; kayaks are easily righted if capsized. Long before Buckminster Fuller came up with his geodesic dome, the Inuit designed igloos of that design, which makes for low wind resistance. Most igloos have an ice window that lets in sunlight for illumination and heat.

The Netsilik (and other Inuit nomadic bands) illustrate the importance of sharing, an attribute also characterizing band-level societies of warmer climates. Yet there is a difference. As noted in Chapter 2, hunting fortunes vary in all bands. In warmer climates, most cultures lack a means of preserving meat. It has to be consumed shortly after the kill or it will rot. Because of the frigid climate, meat preservation is not a problem among the Inuit. Sharing is an imperative because of the cooperation needed for a successful seal hunt. Often, hunting partners name each other by the anatomy of the seal, so that they may call each other the rib, for example. If a man bags a seal, he gives the rib portion to his partner; when successful, the partner will reciprocate accordingly.

These examples show how Inuit and other cold-climate bands differ from nomadic bands in the deserts and in tropical rain forests. Colder climates required protective clothing and shelter which are unnecessary in warm regions. Unlike tropical bands, whose diet is mostly nuts, roots, and other plant foods, the diet of Inuit is almost all meat. There are similarities as well. Food is subject to seasonal variation, and there is a limit to which the environment can sustain a local population. Groups are small, and are generally family-based bands.

Image © Marteric, 2012. Used under license from Shutterstock, Inc.

FIGURE 3.3

Igloo. Note the geodesic dome, which render the structure resistant to high winds, and the entrance. In some designs, the entrance is a curved tunnel. Though not shown here, an ice window allows sunlight to enter and to heat the inside.

Image © Adisa, 2012. Used under license from Shutterstock, Inc.

FIGURE 3.4

Parka design. Notice how the hood is sewn to provide maximum protection against the cold.

Myths, Religion, and the Arts

Myths are commonplace among the Netsilik and other cultures, and shamans play an important role among the Inuit. One myth illustrates the process. Once day, a not very popular orphan girl named Nulisjuk (her name varies with Inuit band) is forced overboard from an overcrowded boat (umiak). When she tries to climb back on, her fingers are lopped off. Her severed fingers become the first seals and she gains supernatural power as a seal goddess. Now, not being especially fond of humankind she can—and does—prevent hunters from capturing seals. From this legend, hunters are expected to perform rituals of gratitude so that the seals' souls return to the sea and acquire new bodies. Nulisjuk furnishes the bodies and releases them—if her anger is placated and the hunters have observed appropriate taboos. Shamans also visit her abode with their offerings and respect.

In a harsh climate that is stingy with its game and that requires continuous work to survive, one might think that the Inuit have little leisure for the arts. This is far from the case. Inuit art dates back to hundreds of years. One of the most common forms of art is sculpture, depictions of animals or the Inuit themselves carved in soapstone, bone, ivory (from walrus' tusks), even wood. Masks made of skin and fur are common and used in ritual (Figure 3.5). Music comes in the form

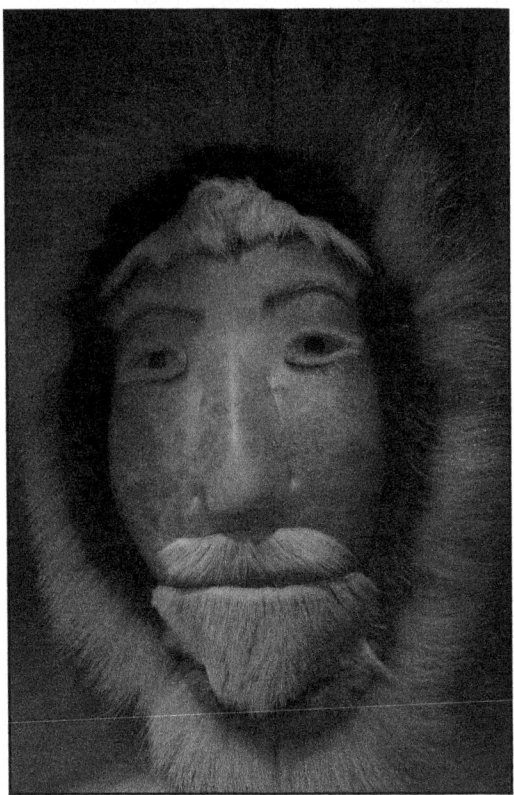

Image © George Burba, 2012. Used under license from Shutterstock, Inc.

FIGURE 3.5
Inuit mask of skin and fur, used in ritual. More typical of Inuit art was soapstone sculpture, dated several hundred years ago; ivory, bone, and wood were also common media.

of drums, which are used to accompany stories, often humorous accounts, and to decide disputes in the form of song duels, as mentioned previously.

Documentaries of the Inuit

Classical films of the Inuit are often re-enactments of life as remembered by the people whose hunting and gathering way of life were still fresh in their memories. Robert Flaherty's film *Nanook of the North,* produced in 1922, was based on such a re-enactment of an Inuit family who lived on Baffin Island. The accuracy of this film has been questioned but seems to be a faithful representation of the real thing. A popularized version called *The Savage Innocents* provides a reasonably accurate ethnography of the Inuit, despite the fact that the actors are non-Inuit. More recently, a Canadian-Bulgarian anthropologist, Asen Balikci, of the University of Montreal, filmed a comprehensive series titled *The Netsilik Eskimo,* with well over 25 hours of footage. It portrayed Zachary and his family and neighbors who recreated their technologies, such as their seal harpooning techniques, the construction of their igloos, caribou hunting, kayak construction, sled construction and use, and numerous others. The Netsilik lived in Pelly Bay, located on the western shores of Hudson's Bay. We discuss these reconstructions in turn.

Robert Flaherty, with *Nanook of the North,* was the first to produce what has become known as salvage ethnography. *Nanook* was a staged production. Nanook (actually named Allakariallak) was asked to use spears to hunt walrus, even though guns were commonplace by then. An actress played his "wife." Staging involved cutting away part of an igloo so that a camera, very bulky and hard to move at the time, could be used for domestic shots.

That the film was staged did not necessarily mean it was ethnographically inaccurate. Flaherty had been a mining prospector for many years in northern Canada, and so he was intimately familiar with the Inuit people there. He tried to portray Inuit life as it was—hence his insistence that Nanook use a spear instead of a gun for hunting scenes. The hunting itself involved actual animals, especially walruses and seals. The techniques of igloo construction were faithfully reproduced, although this igloo lacked a tunnel for its entrance. The ice window was installed, true to the original. Considering the technology of the time—oversized immovable cameras, lack of sound in motion pictures—this was an accomplishment indeed.

Another staged production was completed of an Inuit group located directly north of Hudson's Bay, using film technology available in the 1960s. This culture, known as the Netsilik, re-enacted the lifeways they had abandoned less than ten years before. The Netsilik ranged in a territory surrounding Pelly Bay, located due north from Churchill, Manitoba. Asen Balicki produced a series of 21 half-hour films on the Netsilik and authored an ethnography on this band. Although the Netsilik were settled in government houses in 1957, they recalled enough to recreate their lifeways six years later. The films were shot between 1963 and 1965.

It is clear that neither the Inuit of the Arctic, represented by the Nunamiut and the Netsilik, nor the coastal Tareumiut, were "primitive" cultures. The geodesic structure of the igloo enabled the Inuit to adapt to a climate of extreme cold and high winds because of its wind resistance. The well-insulated parka, the kayak which can readily be righted if capsized, and the dog-driven sled have all been emulated elsewhere. They are a case study showing how a species that evolved in the tropics could adapt to an environment of extreme cold.

The Arctic Peoples Today

One change that comes readily to mind is the effects of climate change or global warming. As the headlines inform us, the glaciers of northern regions from Alaska to Greenland and in the circumpolar region overall have been melting at a rapid rate. Even before climate change became a regional issue, however, the Inuit came under the influence of Canadian and American governments. First, settlements were founded in the 1920s as missionaries and the Royal Canadian Mounted Police (RCMP) sought to acculturate Inuit settlements into Western ways and national law. Introduction of health services and settlements combined to increase the Inuit population to levels beyond the carrying capacity of the regions. It reached its high point in the 1960s with the institutionalization of the High Arctic relocation policies, which was implemented to protect the sovereignty of Canada in its northern region, and to stem starvation of Inuit as their game resources became overhunted because of the population increase. Forced settlement policies were thereby implemented, accompanied by job opportunities and by the mid-1960s, most, if not all, Inuit were living in government-run communities. The establishment of the Distant Early Warning system initiated by the U.S. government at the outset of the Cold War in the late 1940s and 1950s also contributed to the relocation effort. As a result, the once free-ranging of a migratory people were transformed into a small, impoverished minority, lacking skills or resources to sell to the larger economy, yet dependent on it for its survival. Indeed, the anthropologist Diamond Jenness predicted their extinction (1964).

The Inuit themselves took the initiative to protect and maintain their culture. Activist movements emerged during the 1970s, arising from the Indian and Eskimo Association in the 1960s and leading to a few regional Inuit associations from 1971 to 1975. Land settlements were agreed to in James Bay and Northern Quebec in 1975. Others remain pending to the present day. One of the outcomes was the establishment in 1999 of a separate territory, Nunavut, which was run by the Inuit themselves. Other parts of northern Canada, including western parts of the Northwest Territories, plus a region called Nunavut since 2005, cover most of the traditional Inuit lands in Canada, and all were the products of these land settlements.

Another development is the emergence of international circumpolar organizations, the best known of which is the Inuit Circumpolar Council, a United Nations non-governmental organization (NGO) whose constituency comprises representatives from Canada, Greenland, Alaska, and Siberia, even though the Yup'ik of the latter two regions do not speak an Inuit dialect. Their primary concern is a fight against such ecological problems as climate change, which disproportionately affects the peoples in the Arctic.

Inuit culture, thought close to extinction in the 1960s, has undergone resurgence since then. Inuit art such as printmaking, soapstone carving, textiles, and throat singing are known nationally and worldwide. Inuit language such as Inukitut has become a widely adopted language and appears in several feature-length films and written novels. Cape Dorset is regarded as Canada's premier artistic center with 23% of the labor force participating in the arts.

Nevertheless, the assimilation of Inuit into modern society has had its negative effects. One of the major issues is diet, as fast food and imported products have led to an obesity problem among northern community residents. The integration of Inuit into a society alien to their own has led to a cultural dissonance, evident in the high suicide rate among teenagers. Myopia has increased among the youngest generation of Inuit, parallel with myopia reported in other accul-turated societies, such as those in Vanuatu. Social problems will no doubt increase in future years.

However, given their location in the High Arctic, the Inuit are some of the most direct wit-nesses of the impact of climate change. A recent example is evidence of global warming on Banks Island, the fifth largest and westernmost of the archipelago situated north of the Northwest Ter-ritories mainland. According to the film *Sila Alangotok: Inuit Observations on Climate Change,* made at Sachs Harbour, the only settlement, an air base, on Banks Island, the Inuit residents report major mudslides as permafrost melts in the hills, summers without ice where ice floes were common in July, lower seal populations throughout the year, and thundershowers usually non-existent in an arctic climate. Elsewhere in the North, residents report thinning ice, accidents in which hunters and their snowmobiles break through the ice, and new varieties of birds and flow-ers appear where none were there before. Such activists as the Inuit social worker Siila Watt-Cloutier have spoken at environmental conferences to warn of these developments and the worldwide consequences of climate change that Inuit see evidence of on a daily basis. Also a new development, the Northwest Passage that Frobisher sought in the 1500s is now opening up, cre-ating international competition for its control.

To conclude, the Inuit and related peoples had the Icelands of the High Arctic to themselves for unknown hundreds of years; the ethnographic present of the ethnographies represented here range from the early twentieth century to about the 1940s. As Euro-Americans and Euro-Cana-dians invaded the land from the 1940s onward—missionaries to save souls, military to secure the northern borders, the RCMP to control the population, corporate interests to tap oil and other resources in the north, and to control a previously nonexistent Northern Passage—the Inuit have been forced to abandon their igloos and hunting to live and work—or not work—in the new communities. Their future remains to be seen.

Selected Documentaries

Nanook of the North. 1922. Robert Flaherty. 60 minutes.

The Netsilik. 1965. Asen Balicki. 21 half-hour segments. Cambridge, MA: Documentary Educa-tional Resources and Montreal: Canadian Film Board.

Selected Literature

Balikci, Asen. 1970. *The Netsilik Eskimo.* Prospect Heights, IL: Waveland Press.

Chance, Norman. 1997. *The Inupiat and Arctic Alaska.* New York: Harcourt.

Reiss, Bob. 2012. *The Eskimo and the Oil Man: The Battle at the Top of the World for America's Future.* New York: Business Plus.

CHAPTER 4

Peoples of the Northwest Pacific Coast: Kwakiutl, Haida, and their Neighbors

Introduction

The peoples of the Pacific Northwest comprise a unique culture area. Few complex societies are supported by hunting and gathering alone; the cultures of this area rely on salmon as a staple and on a rich natural environment: thick stands of timber, abundant wildlife on land and in the sea, edible plants, nuts, and berries by the dozen. The population is dense enough to support chiefdoms. The carvings and paintings are distinct in style. Small wonder the Northwest Coast has attracted attention from anthropologists and tourists alike.

In precontact times, the Northwest Coast peoples ranged from Oregon through Washington State and British Columbia to southern Alaska. Among the best known cultures are the Kwakiutl (also known by the native term kwakwaka'wakw) of Vancouver Island and the adjacent coast of mainland British Columbia, the Haida of the Queen Charlotte Islands further north, and the Tlingit of southern Alaska. Others include the Salish of the lower mainland of British Columbia, the Nootka of western Vancouver Island, the Bella Coola of central coastal British Columbia, and the Tsimshian of northern coastal British Columbia.

The Northwest Peoples as Complex Foragers

As noted elsewhere and in the introduction, simple foragers are nomadic bands comprising 25 to 100 people. The native peoples of the Northwest Coast are different. What if you could yield large amounts of food and sustain a dense population without agriculture; that is what describes the cultures of the Pacific Northwest. They lived on salmon that could be netted and speared by the thousands and preserved by smoking for year-round use. They obtained oils for fuel from candlefish (or olachan). Other food sources included game ranging from rabbits to deer to bear, berries and pine nuts in season, and other species of fish. Peoples with a diverse resource base such as this are known as **complex foragers.** They formed settled communities and supported centralized forms of governance.

64

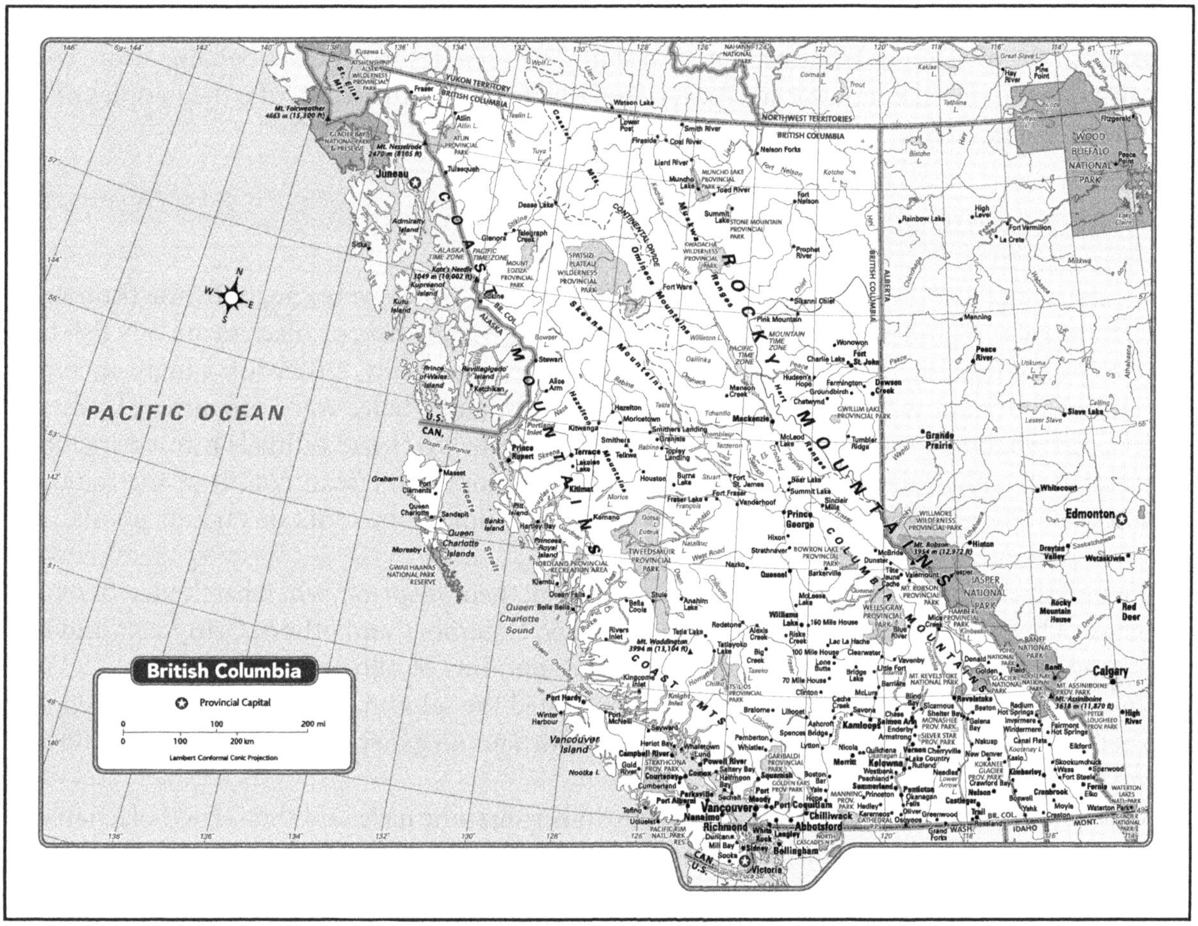

Image © Globe Turner, LLC, 2012. Used under license from Shutterstock, Inc.

FIGURE 4.1
Coastal British Columbia and Southern Alaska. These include Vancouver Island, home of the Nootka and the Kwakiutl, and the Queen Charlotte Islands, home of the Haida.

There are several characteristics of complex foragers. They are still food collectors; they do not cultivate. They don't need to. Their food sources are comparatively steady in the form of seasonal salmon runs—though they have been known to fail in some years. There are several types of food sources. Carrying capacity is relatively high; nomadism is unnecessary. Liebig's Law of the Minimum, which specifies carrying capacity in terms of the least abundant sources of subsistence, is much higher than of any known simple foraging culture. Even so, sources can fluctuate by year, season, and location. Some salmon runs are more abundant than others, and even the best runs can fail at times. The Northwest Coast Indians are the best known contemporary example. Several Middle and Upper Paleolithic sites are classic examples: the fishing villages of Nitano in Japan, Vedbaek of Denmark, Star Carr in England, and Mount Sandel of Ireland were all complex foragers, relying either on big game or a steady supply of fish and game throughout the year—not to mention the ever-abundant plant foods.

With a rich resource base, several other features are found. Communities become sedentary, and reliance on domestication of either crops or animal is not essential. The assemblage of tools and ornamental objects multiply in type and number. Populations increase. You can expect increases in the division of labor by craft and skill. The societies themselves become more complex and, more often than not, social classes arise. All of these features describe the peoples of the Northwest Pacific Coast.

Subsistence Base of the Northwest Coast

The primary staple of the Northwest Coast diet was salmon, which were caught by the thousands in their annual runs and preserved by drying or smoking. Candlefish, or olachan, an oily fish that is the source of heat, light, and cooking, also were netted seasonally. Other fish caught included cod and halibut, and sea mammals, such as otter, seals, and whales were consumed (only the Nootka did whaling; others peoples relied on beached whales). Land animals hunted included deer, elk, bear, and, in the northern regions, caribou, a North American cousin of the reindeer. Plant foods were not ignored: a wide variety of berries, pine nuts, roots of various plants, and greens in season.

Every fall, salmon run up the major rivers to spawn; their offspring, when hatched, will return to the sea. The major rivers include the Skeena, Fraser, Columbia, and others. Using nets and fish traps (known as weirs), the fishers catch prodigious amounts of salmon.

In recent years, dams and pollution have decimated the salmon. The salmon are gutted, cut into halves, and hung on racks to dry or to be smoked. Salmon generally keep in winter and early spring.

Olachan, also known as candlefish, is a highly oily fish; some have said that a fried olachan can burn like a candle if lit. Their runs begin in the early spring and are netted, again by the thousands. Their oil is rendered and stored in leakproof wooden bins. The oil provides heat and light, and is often used as a preservative. Oil is a valuable trade item, especially with the native Athabaskan peoples of interior British Columbia and the northwestern U.S. states.

The Nootka of the western side of Vancouver Island also took up whaling, using harpoons in large seagoing canoes. Other Northwest Coast peoples also consumed whale, but only those that were stranded on the beaches. Other fish was also netted, principally halibut and cod. Sea otter and seals were hunted. Most peoples did hunt land-based game, also for meat, but especially for hides, especially bear. Finally, there were ample berries, seeds, and nuts to be picked. Large stands of timber provided building materials for houses, seagoing canoes, and art objects from storage boxes to totem poles.

Spring, summer, and fall were devoted to outdoor activity, from hunting and fishing to longhouse construction and maintenance. Winter was more often rainy than snowy and most activities occurred inside. This was a period of feasting and holding ceremonies, principally potlatches held to observe important events, such as the passing of a chief or installation of his successor. Some hunting did take place in the winter, however.

Stability of resources was not absolute. Not all rivers or streams supported salmon or olachan runs, and many areas were short of other resources. Those rivers that did support salmon or olachan runs still could vary seasonally. Consequently, some groups would aid those in time of need, reminiscent of simple foragers such as the !Kung or Inuit. However, resource shortages also

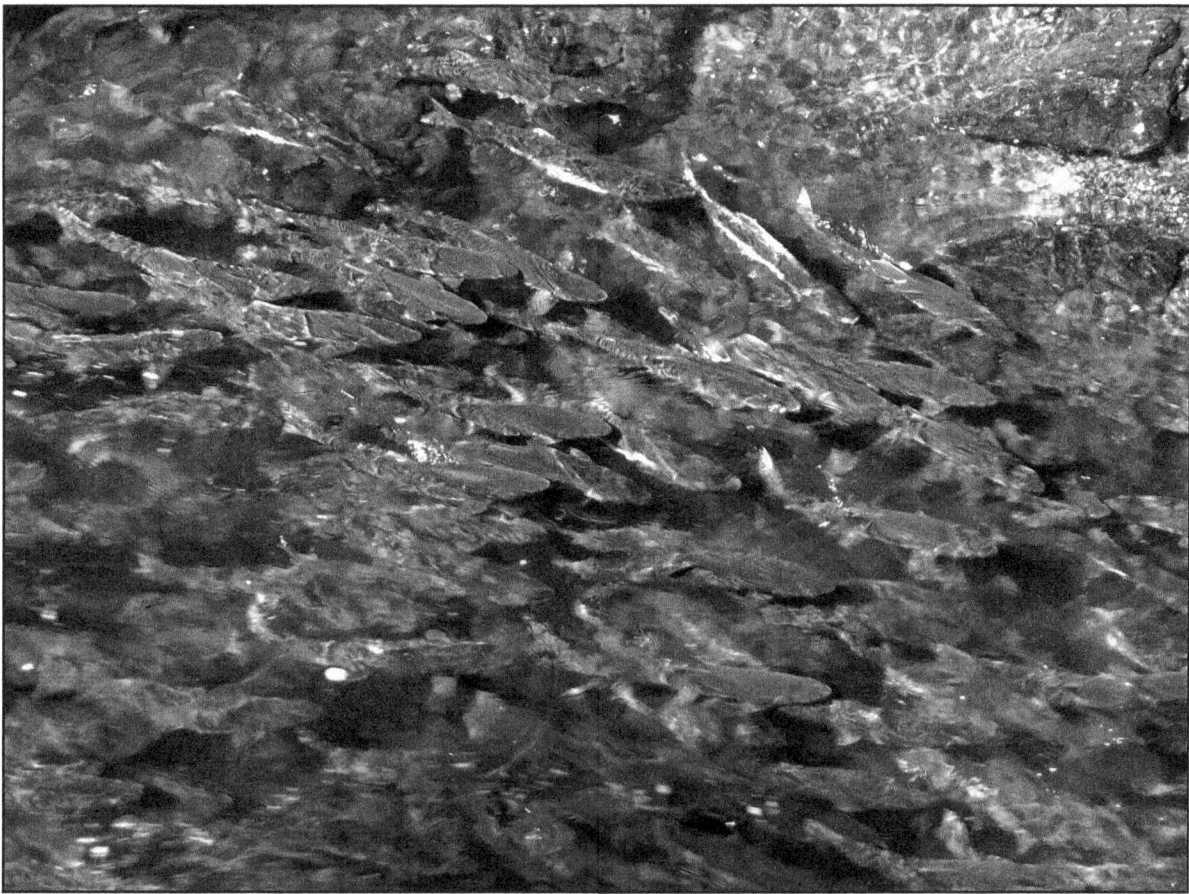

Image © Sarah Theophilus, 2012. Used under license from Shutterstock, Inc.

FIGURE 4.2
Salmon spawning in Kechikan, Alaska, a Tlingit culture area. Salmon were reported to be numerous prior to the construction of dams along Alaska and British Columbia river areas.

sparked competition for resource-rich areas and were causes of warfare, not unlike societies reliant on cultivation.

Given that the Northwest Coast is a temperate rain forest region, the extensive stands of forest sustained another set of skills: woodcrafters and builders. Not surprisingly, longhouses, seagoing canoes, so-called totem poles (which, bearing the likeness of the animal that symbolizes a lineage or clan, which signified the founder of the descent group), carved artwork, and decorated boxes were all built and/or crafted (see Figure 4.3 on page 69). Northwest Coast peoples were also expert in carving on stone, ivory (from the whales and walruses), and bone. Later, silver-smithing was added to the repertoire of crafts in post-contact time, and Bill Reid was famous for those art pieces. Totemic animals included ravens, killer whales, bears, and, among the Kwakiutl, the thunderbird. Totem poles vary from almost nonexistent among the Kwakiutl to the elaborately designed ones among the Haida and Tlingit. The founder of the clan (usually one of these totemic animals) is placed at the top of the pole, representing graphically the cultural obsession with ranking.

Sociopolitical Organization of the Northwest Coast

All Northwest peoples were organized into multifamily groups called lineages (those whose ancestors could be traced back to the ancestor) and clans (those whose ancestors could be only stipulated rather than demonstrated). The Kwakiutl, who live in east Vancouver Inland and the adjacent mainland of British Columbia, were organized into *numaym,* patrilineal groups with bilateral attributes. Women played a role in the possession and inheritance of valuables, which they often obtained through marriage. Thus, the precise nature of the *numaym* has never been clearly defined. We do know that they were residential units, and that each one was headed by a chief, probably succeeded by his eldest son who showed the desirable characteristics of an effective chief. Each chief had a speaker who held a talking stick while addressing the assembly.

Descent groups among northern chiefdoms were more clearly defined; they were all matrilineal. The best documented were the Haida of the Queen Charlotte Islands, the Tsimshian of the northern British Columbia mainland, and the Tlingit of southern Alaska. All functions of the household and larger groups were conducted through matrilineages of various levels, defined as descent through a line of females who women passed their affiliation through their daughters (see diagram in Chapter 2, Figure 2.3, for all members). Residence was matrilocal, whereby men joined their wives and their kin. The flexibility of affiliation found among the Kwakiutl was lacking in the northern groups. Among males, succession to the office of chief went from a man to his sister's son, as did male-owned property. We find a similar pattern among chiefs in the Trobriand Islands, covered elsewhere.

Levels of Social Organization: The Family. The social organization of all Northwest cultures occurred at five levels. The most basic unit was the nuclear family comprising father, mother, and children. The next level comprised the house group, consisting of several related nuclear families living in a common longhouse, and so could be regarded as an extended family. This comprised parents, their married children, and the children of these children, who might also be married and have children of their own. This is one defining feature of an extended family. Above the house groups were the lineages, which varied by tribe: patrilineal, matrilineal, or sometimes nonunilineal descent groups based on bilateral descent. Above those was the village, all basic political units headed by a chief. Finally, there were groups called supravillages, alliances of villages based on common concerns, ranging from resource control and exchange ceremonies to a common defense in warfare.

Despite the complexity of social organization among the cultures of the Pacific Northwest, the basic unit is the nuclear family, which comprises man, woman, and children. The family carries out the productive activities of the household: fishing, hunting, foraging for berries and pine nuts, and everything else. The harpoons, nets, and other tools are also done within the family. Each individual in the family has his or her assigned role in foraging during the summer. At the same time, families are not autonomous entities; they also work within the house group.

Individual families live in longhouses; the Haida in Skidegate (Figure 4.4) is an example. House groups manage the affairs of these wooden structures. Tasks needing interfamily cooperation are carried out by the house group: drying and smoking salmon; extracting and rendering oil from their olachan catch; and maintaining and using fishing equipment and the seagoing canoes used for that purpose. In a redistributive economy in which contributions of products

Image © trappy76, 2012. Used under license from Shutterstock, Inc.

FIGURE 4.3
Totem pole in Stanley Park, Vancouver, British Columbia. The thunderbird, perched on the top represented the founder of the Thunderbird clan among the Kwakiutl.

Image © Chris Howey, 2012. Used under license from Shutterstock, Inc.

FIGURE 4.4
Haida longhouse near Skidegate, British Columbia, with clan's totem pole indicating matrilineal affiliation, located on the Queen Charlotte Islands, also known as Gwaii in Haida. Lineages and clans made up multifamily residential units in many Northwest cultures.

had to be made to the chief, it was the house group that mobilized the labor and products of its members. Styles of housing varied from culture to culture, as these illustrations show.

There was a division of labor by gender and craftsmanship within the house group. Women formed the productive unit in that entity; it was they who cared for the children, made the clothing, smoked the salmon, rendered the oil, and managed the stores of blankets, clothing, and, in post-contact times, money. Nevertheless, men were not sitting around either. They made tools, carved wood posts of the longhouses and the totem poles that stood in front of the house, constructed the longhouses themselves, built the canoes, and handled all other tasks involving construction, carving, and ornaments.

One consequence of this division of labor is that women enjoyed a good deal of power, the consequence of being the ones who smoked and dried the salmon, which formed the basis of both subsistence and luxury wealth; salmon was the main course at potlatches and other cere-monial events. It is not surprising that the northern communities were both matrilineal and matrilocal; couples moved in with the bride's kin. Women also exercise considerable influence among the Kwakiutl and other southern cultures. Their influences may have played a part toward the bilateral bias of the normally patrilineal *numaym*. Upper status women often own the longhouse and sponsored potlatches in their own right, even though the chiefs and coun-cils were men.

Level of Social Organization: Lineages and Clans.
The next level of integration among the peoples of the Pacific Northwest was lineage and clans. In the literature, the Kwakiutl terms *numaym* or *numaymna* served as a gloss to refer to lineages and clans of all societies in that region. By definition, lineages are unilineal units of kin who can name the linking kin between the cur-rent generation and the founders of that entity. They are either patrilineal (the linking kin are males) or matrilineal (the linking kin are females). Using patrilineal descent as an example, this model of a segmentary lineage shows how larger lineages can form out of smaller ones.

Strictly speaking, clans are unilineal groups whose members are unclear as to how exactly they are descended from the ancestor. One ethnographer may call a group of kin a lineage; another may use the term clan. This is the product of a lack of standardized terminology over the years.

In this culture area, a single lineage might dominate a village, with all members regarded as co-owners of that village. Lineage membership is flexible: one individual might be a member of more than one lineage. Lineages could also extend across the boundaries of a village into another. The principal role of lineages was to facilitate trade and ceremonial relationships between vil-lages, saving the task of creating these networks. No less important, membership of two groups in a common lineage might reduce the incident of warfare.

Level of Social Organization: The Village and the Chief.
The village represented the next level of integration, over which the chief maintained authority. It was he who controlled the resources of the house group. The chief organized a complex economy, relying on his own spe-cialists and productive resources at a large scale, a minimal definition of capital. Construction of large-scale projects was also the role of the chief; it was he who organized the construction of dams, weirs (fish traps), and defensive structures such as walls. He also performed functions of conservation, regulating the use of salmon fisheries to prevent overuse and depletion of salmon.

The chief played other roles. He was the village treasurer in a cashless economy; he main-tained the community storehouse, paid debts to other chiefs, made loans, and performed other economic functions. He also was the community tax man. A successful fisher or hunter was required to provide the chief with one-fifth to one-half of his catch, game, or both. In return, the chief provided for the common defense, other common needs of the community—such as feasts—and to pay specialists for their services. Finally, at the supravillage level, he sponsored large, interregional ceremonies, such as the potlatch.

Was the chief an actual office or was he more like a big man similar to one in New Guinea vil-lages? In their book, *The Evolution of Human Societies,* Johnson and Earle (2000) contend that Northwest Coast leaders were more big men than they were chiefs. In their reasoning, the chief relies on a group of loyal followers whose loyalty is not guaranteed; some could join other lead-ers at any time, in the way that New Guinea tribesmen do. The problem with this analysis is that the chief and the position he holds has an established rule of succession. The successor may be a chief's eldest son among the Kwakiutl, or he may be the chief's eldest sister's son among the Haida or Tsimshian. The chieftainship itself is a permanent position; it must be filled when vacated by death or dismissal of the occupant. Furthermore, Northwest Coast cultures are ranked, divided into the power elite, the commoners, and the slaves. Individuals are ranked relative to each other and even villages are ranked. There is no such ranking among New Guinea big men; everyone has a chance to become a big man, and every village may have several big men, all vying for power. Thus, the term referring to Northwest cultures is usually chiefdom, and we retain this term here.

Ceremony: From Local Feasts to Potlatch

Several feasts were held for several occasions and for several functions. A village might hold a feast to formally claim a newly discovered salmon stream, for example; acceptance of the invitations implied recognition of the village's ownership of the stream. Potlatches commemorated important events, such as the installation of a new chief, announcement of a new heir, or a naming ceremony. Prior to the epidemics that swept the Northwest Coast in the nineteenth century, the ceremony was simply to celebrate an important event. This brought several tribes together. In the first phase of a potlatch, numerous ritual dances were performed, such as the Sea Monster Dance among the Bella Coola. The chief then would rise and give a speech. The visitors viewed the speech with a critical eye. Was he eloquent? Did he use the right metaphors? Did he stumble over words? The gifts were then distributed, the value matching the rank of the recipient. Again, the visitors watched carefully. Did he give a valuable gift to a commoner or a low-ranking noble? At the end, the guests rose and, in turn, acknowledged the performance of the host chief. How well did he deliver the speech and how appropriate were the gifts? Praise of the new chief was recognition of his legitimacy by the visitors.

These principles are exemplified by the **potlatch** of the several chiefdoms concentrated along the Northwest Coast of North America, which stretches from the extreme northwest tip of California through the coasts of Oregon, Washington, British Columbia, and southern Alaska. As stated in Chapter 11, the potlatch observed major events, such as births, deaths, or marriage of important persons, or the installment of a new chief. Families prepared for this event by collecting food and other valuables such as fish, berries, blankets, animal skins, carved boxes, and copper. At the potlatch, several ceremonies were held, dances performed by their "owners," and speeches delivered. The new chief was watched very carefully, the eloquence of his speech noted, the grace of his presence observed—including any mistakes, however egregious or trivial.

The distribution of gifts came next. Again the chief was observed in that process: Was he generous with his gifts? Were the value of his gifts appropriate to the rank of the recipient, or was he giving valuable presents to those of lower rank? Did his wealth allow him to offer valuable objects?

The next phase was critical to the chief's validation to his position. Visitor after visitor arose to give long speeches evaluating the worthiness of this successor to the chieftainship of his father. If he had performed to expectation, if his gifts were appropriate, the guests' speeches would praise him accordingly. They would be less than adulatory if the chief did not perform to expectation, and indeed the eligibility of the successor was not sufficient. He had to perform. If he did so, then the guests' praise not only legitimated the new chief in his role, but also it ensured some measure of peace between villages. Not only was the event festive, it also involved legitimation and diplomacy.

Much has been made of the **rivalry potlatches,** competitive gift giving by rival pretenders to the chieftainship. Philip Drucker in *Indians of the Northwest Coast* argues that the competitive potlatch was a product of sudden demographic changes among the Northwest Coast Indians. As smallpox and other diseases decimated thousands, potential successor as likely as not died out, leaving several potential successors who might be eligible for the chieftainship. Thus, competition became extreme, with blankets being repaid with ever larger piles, coppers being met with ever larger quantities, and valuables being destroyed in an effort to demonstrate one's wealth. So raucous did the events become that the Canadian government outlawed these displays in the early part of the twentieth century. Prior to this period, it was sufficient to present appropriate gifts by a successor who had been chosen beforehand.

However, much of the literature is based on ethnographies of the twentieth century, and the potlatch is described as a raucous affair. Helen Codere titles her book on the Kwakiutl *Fighting with Property*. Phillip Drucker, in his book *Indians of the Northwest Coast,* argues that rivalry potlatches developed after a series of epidemics decimated the native American population in the Northwest Coast, as they had elsewhere in the Americas. For the Kwakiutl, the population declined from an estimated 3,500 in 1853 to 1,335 in 1903. In any case, there were far more titles than for people to assume them. Some titles were more valued than others, and these became the object of competition.

As disease spread, the potential successors and heirs perished, leaving open the question as to who should become the next chief or inherit the most valued of all the titles. To prove his worth, each chief competed by giving his rival a large gift—stacks of blankets, copper plates, even slaves— to his rival. The rival could not refuse these gifts, lest he lose face. He had to return ever larger amounts of blankets or coppers as "interest." Thus, the cycle of gifts and countergifts continued to escalate until one rival was "crushed," conceding victory to his opponent. Often, rivals destroyed their valuables in a demonstration of their wealth. Coppers, such as the one from the Kwakiutl village of Cape Mudge, were often broken to "shame" the rival. Rivalry potlatches became so raucous that the Royal Canadian Mounted Police was often called in to quell the unrest. Eventually, potlatches were outlawed by the Canadian authorities, and the law remained in force for decades.

Thus, it is a myth, perpetuated by much ethnography, that the rivalry potlatch existed, long before British and American traders arrived at the locales. Drucker argues, in contrast, that the potlatch served as a means to cement intervillage relations, to enhance trade relations, and lessen the chance of warfare (1965). More important, in a broader context, the Northwest Coast chiefdoms were classic examples of how a chiefdom could develop on a subsistence system based, not on agriculture, but on fishing, hunting, and gathering.

Selected Films

Blunden Harbour. 1951. 22 minutes. Robert Gardner and William Heick. Cambridge, MA: Documentary Educational Resources. Settlement of impoverished Kwakiutl.

Box of Treasures. 1983. 28 minutes. Chuck Olin and the U'mista Cultural Centre. Cambridge, MA: Documentary Educational Resources. Recovery of confiscated potlatch objects owned by the Kwakiutl of Alert Bay, British Columbia. The objects were confiscated by the Royal Canadian Mounted Police in the nineteenth century.

Selected Literature

Drucker, Phillip. 1965. *Indians of the Northwest Coast.* San Francisco: Chandler.

Rohner, Ronald P. 1986. *The Kwakiutl of British Columbia. Prospect Heights, IL: Waveland Press.*

Sullivan, Robert. 2002. *A Whale Hunt: How a Native American Village Did What No One Thought It Could.* New York: Scribner. Revival among the Makah of a whale hunt.

PART II

Latin America

CHAPTER 5

Mexico:
From the Aztecs to the Present

Introduction

Although Mexico is the home of numerous indigenous cultures, the name itself is derived from the indigenous name of the Aztecs, the Mexica. Following an overview of Mexico, we examine the culture that gave the country its name, then at the cultures that followed the Conquest. The Mayan culture area of southeastern Mexico and Guatemala will be treated separately.

Mexico: A Geography

Mexico is, geographically, part of North America along with Canada and the United States. The new trade zone reflects this geographical by its very name, the North American Free Trade Agreement (NAFTA). Located south of the United States and northwest from the isthmus of Central America that begins with Guatemala and Belize, the country is bounded to the west by the Pacific Ocean and to the east by the Gulf of Mexico adjacent to the Atlantic Ocean.

Mexico is mostly a mountainous country. Baja California has a largely Mediterranean climate, much like California or Alta California with mild areas along the coast and hotter valleys and cooler mountains in the interior. The Sierra Madre dominates Mexico with stretches of desert to the north, and tropical rain forest to the western and eastern sides. The country is a land of contrasts, with an industrialized north region around the federal district known as Mexico City, and underdeveloped, peasant-dominated central, southern, and southeastern regions.

The Mexica or Aztecs of Central Mexico

All states are predatory, but some are more predatory than others. Along with the Mongols under Genghis Khan, and the Axis powers in World War II, the Aztecs or Mexica probably share the record as the most predatory state in the world.

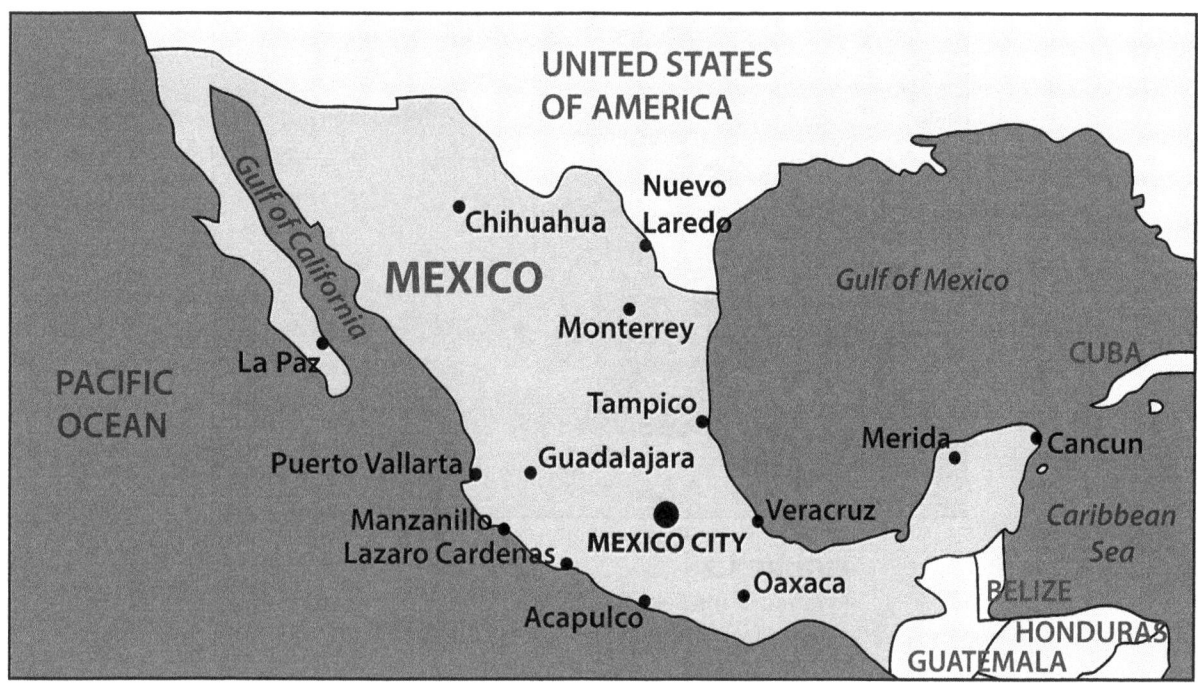

FIGURE 5.1

Mexico. Geographically, it forms part of North America but culturally is distant from the other two countries of Canada and the United States.

No one really knows where the Aztecs came from. Historical linguistic data and legend alike suggest they came from the north—but how far north or where is anyone's guess. More likely, they lived in Tula for a while, acting as mercenaries for the Toltecs. With the fall of Tula, they migrated to Lake Texcoco, a lake near Mexico City which has since dried up. The area was dominated by what Wolf calls in his *Sons of the Shaking Earth* (1959), "Epigonal Toltecs." They were called "Chichimecs" by the Toltecs, who regarded them as "barbarians."

The word *Aztec* derives from a place name of their supposed origin, probably mythical, of Aztlán, which means "Land of the Herons." The preferred designation is *Mexica,* whose full name is Colhua Mexica when they allied themselves to the Colhua of Colhuacán. *Tenochca,* another designation, was used in honor of a legendary hero of that name; this is how the capital, Tenochtitlan came to be called. After they left their homeland—wherever that was—the Aztecs migrated to the Valley of Mexico. For a time, they served as mercenaries (soldiers paid for fighting) for the Toltec of Tula. When the Toltec empire collapsed, the Aztec migrated to Lake Texcoco and adjacent lakes, home of the so-called Epigonal Toltecs.

There were five basic groups along the lakes: Atzcapotzalco, an Otomí-speaking people on the western shores of the lake, Xalltocan, located on the northern shore of the lake, the Acolhua on the eastern shore, Colhuacán, in the southwestern part of the Valley of Mexico (at the cusp between Lake Texcoco and Xochimilco), and a small state called Xicco. The Acolhua were later to be organized as a fighting force by the Aztec, still known by the contemptuous term "Chichimeca."

Image © f9photos, 2012. Used under license from Shutterstock, Inc.

FIGURE 5.2
Pyramid of the Sun, Teotihuacan. The identity of its builders is unknown, but may have been Toltec or their ancestors. The Aztec served the Toltecs as mercenaries for a time.

Initially, none of the Toltecs would take the Aztecs in and they were compelled to find a place to camp. According to myth, their god Huitzilopochtli (Hummingbird to the Left, also known as their Sun God) commanded them to settle where they would see an eagle perched on a nopal cactus, devouring a serpent. When they saw this event, they settled in a swampy area at Lake Texcoco. The eagle, cactus, and serpent became the center emblem of the Mexican flag (Figure 5.3).

When they arrived at this swamp, the Aztecs had to revert back to their hunting and gathering strategies, subsisting on green algae, snakes, indeed whatever they could find. Later, they invented *chinampas,* or platforms constructed out of the swamp using wood poles as support. By placing reed bundles at the bottom and alternating layers of mud with swamp plants, they built platforms that proved to be highly fertile soil. Later, they developed irrigated fields on drier lands and planted crops on hillsides. *Chinampas* were also built to extend dry land as the population grew.

Although Tenochtitlan, at the site of today's Mexico City, would become the capital of the Mexica (Aztec) empire, they did not settle there at first. They allied themselves with the western city of Atzcapotzalco as mercenaries against the Acolhua. Later, the Aztecs had a falling out with their allies and so switched sides and, now allied with the Acolhua, overthrew Atzcapotzalco. By 1427, they formed a Triple Alliance with Acolhua, and a breakaway group from Atzcapotzalco called Tlacopán. By 1500, they had established a hegemonic empire.

Data sources on the Aztec come in many forms. First, there is the codex (plural is codices), a book written on animal skin or bark, which are strung together like folding screens. Second, there are glyphs on stone surfaces—walls of monuments, stelae, pyramids—that can be deciphered; which has been done. Third are the chronicles of various observers, some Aztecs literate in Spanish, some Spanish witness accounts—such as Bernal Diaz or Bernardino Sahagún for the Aztecs and Diego Landa for the Maya.

Image © Daboost, 2012. Used under license from Shutterstock, Inc.

FIGURE 5.3

Flag of Mexico, displaying the omen of an eagle devouring a snake while perched on a nopal cactus. This signaled the Aztec, according to legend, to establish their empire on a swamp at this site.

From what we can tell from archaeological and written sources, the Aztec started as a mud village and rose to become an empire in fewer than 200 years later. Their success implied the need for flexibility of organization, and so they were flexible—but how? Just what kind of a society are we talking about when we refer to Aztec society? Frances Berdan, noted authority on Aztec ethnohistory, describes Aztec society as it was just before the Conquest. Even so, we do not know whether they were bilateral or patrilineal. Spaniards destroyed large numbers of codices, so there is much that is inferred.

One thing we do know is that they were organized in units known as *calpulli* (singular and plural). The term means "big house," and we know that there were 20 of them. We know that they were landholding groups, and that they were organized by territory. They had their own councils, and they had their own temples. Most likely, they were commoners. What we do not know is whether they were kin groups as well.

There is some likelihood that they were kinship based. For one thing, they were probably a tribal group 300 years before, when they still lived in the mythical place of Aztlán. Some writings indicate that there was a preference for "junior lines" when resources and political favors were allocated, but other information suggests that they might have been of bilateral descent. They did involve councils.

Berdan says that most evidence indicates that Aztecs reckoned their kin bilaterally. Kin on the mother's side and the father's side were equally recognized. Perhaps this reflected the extreme instability that rapid formation of a state implies. If you need allies to keep your family together, you are unlikely to much care how your allies are related to you. You might even take in strangers and define them as your kin.

Another suggestion is that *calpulli* might have developed into administrative subclasses. You could have *calpulli* that organized not only peasants, but also craftsmen of various kinds. For example, in Texcoco under the emperor Hungry Coyote (Netzahualcoyotl), *calpulli* were organized into crafts, namely feather workers for one and goldsmiths for another. There is some indication that the merchant class, called *pochteca*, formed a *calpulli*. We do know for certain that this was a hereditary trade. Sons of the merchants also became merchants.

As the Aztec conquered more and more states, Tenochtitlan became more ethnically diverse. That meant that the *calpulli* might comprise not only kin but allies as well. Kin terms might be extended to the "foreigners," making for fictive kin. The Spanish custom of giving every child two godparents, namely co-parenthood or *compadrazgo*, would be well accepted among the Aztec, and this is indeed the case in today's villages. What is at issue is what were the *calpulli* like before the Spanish Conquest, and even before the Aztecs' own conquests. That debate will go on.

We also know that *calpulli* were landholding units. The *calpulli* owned the land, but use rights were allocated to individual members. They "owned" their plot so long as they used it and paid their taxes. Land would go back to the *calpulli* if they discontinued use and payment. Land could be rented to others, but it could not be bought or sold.

There were also rules of marriage. Marriage was endogamous by class. Nobles (called *pipiltin*; singular was *pilli*) could marry only other nobles. Peasants (*macehualltin*, singular *macehual* or *macehualli*) would marry only other peasants. Husband and wife could not be from the same family; the incest tabu applied here as it does in almost every other society of the world. That did not mean, however, that one could not marry one's cousin. Cross-cousin marriage was frequent: the marriage of a couple linked by both a parent and the parent's sibling of the opposite sex. Polygyny (marriage of one man to two or more wives) was common among the nobles, but not among the peasants. Marriage linked not only the couple but their two families.

Marriage involves an economic dimension, and Aztecs were nothing if not traders. There were two kinds of markets. One dealt in ordinary goods, such as a food market in Tenochtitlán. The other kind of market dealt with luxury goods; this was the major focus of this market in Texcoco. City markets met daily. It was required by law to trade only within markets; one could be imprisoned and the goods confiscated for trading outside marketplaces. The reason was to enforce taxation for goods bought and sold.

Texcoco is of special interest to economic anthropologists because it had existed long before the Aztecs rose to power. Though a daily market, it held a much larger market every five days with as many as 50,000 buyers and sellers. One hereditary group comprised the *pochteca*, the long-distance traders already mentioned. They, too, probably traded long before the Aztecs, but they also provided information to the emperor about events in the provinces. Even so, they were in a precarious position. Their economic power was constantly perceived as a threat to the empire. Not surprisingly, they hid the wealth—as Mexican peasants do today.

If trade in markets was required by law because of taxation, then taxation means there is a state. What was the nature of the Aztec state? We turn to that topic next.

As mentioned earlier, Aztec society comprised two basic social and economic classes, the *Pilli* (*Pipiltin*) or nobles, and the *macehual* or *macehualli* (*macehuallin*) or peasants. Nevertheless, there were social subclasses in both broad categories. Furthermore, at least in the early years of the empire, a peasant could hope to become a noble through his performance in battle. First, we have to refine this conception of social classes by looking at their subdivisions.

Image © Fedor Selivanov, 2012.
Used under license from Shutterstock, Inc.

FIGURE 5.4
Aztec noble. The Aztec formed a stratified society but did allow social mobility for warriors with unusual skills.

To begin with, at the top were the emperors, or kings. They were the rulers, and they enjoyed privileges unmatched by any other group. Moctezuma, for example, was said to have 200 wives. The nobles also were privileged, allowed to wear insignia and fine clothing denied the peasant. They also had rights of polygyny. The occupations of nobles included high military officer, tax collector, and judge.

Next in the hierarchy were priests, warriors, and merchants of various statuses. As mentioned, *pochteca* were wealthy, long distance traders, but not all merchants were wealthy. The status of each depended on performance and birth.

At the lowest rung of the hierarchy were the artisans, who again varied in rank. There was more prestige, for example, of being a feather worker or a goldsmith than to be a weaver, sandal maker, or stone tool manufacturer. Peasants formed the bulk of the population. Of course, peasants could become a warrior (involuntarily sometimes), and many rose to become nobles through battle. Slaves were usually either criminals or war captives. Even they had rights (they could own property, for example) but they were always potential candidates for human sacrifice.

How did stratification emerge? In a highly populated area, some coordination is always necessary, and chinampas provided a rich source of food that supported a growing and dense population. The emperor and his noble retainers owned or controlled the most productive land and access to water, important in a semiarid environment like the valley of Mexico. For peasants, leaving was not an option. They were hemmed in by mountain ranges and other empires. Thus, they could not escape taxes, forced labor, possible human sacrifices, and other abuses associated with all states.

All states depend on legitimization, or public justifications for being. One is a probable myth about a war with the Tepenacs of Atzcapotzalco. In a council, the nobles opted for war, and the commoners chose peace. Then Obsidian Snake arose and said that if the Aztecs lost the war, the nobles would offer themselves to the commoners to be eaten. The commoners then replied that if they won the war, they would submit to the servitudes for the nobles. Though probably mythical, the story is one source of legitimation of imperial rule by the Aztec elite.

The political structure reflects the social structure of the Aztec, but in the early years at least, there were two kinds of nobility: the nobility of lineage, in which nobles inherited their position, and the nobility of service, which encompassed commoners who had risen in the ranks to become part of the elite themselves. The Aztec were expanding their empire, and they were always in need of warriors. And this was where the nobility of service came in.

Image © Antonio Abrignani, 2012. Used under license from Shutterstock, Inc.

FIGURE 5.5
Teoyaomicqui, Aztec god of dead lost souls. There were numerous gods in the Aztec pantheon besides Quetzalcoatl and his dark rival Tezcatlipoca. They included Tlaloc, the rain god, and Hummingbird to the Left, the patron god of the Aztecs. The afterlife was not hopeful for the departed.

FIGURE 5.6

Wall of stone skulls, on display at the Museum of Tenochtitlán in Mexico City. Skull racks were a common sight near the Templo Mayor, site of most human sacrifices.

The nobility of service comprised commoners who distinguished themselves in war or in trade. They were often called "knights" or "Sons of the Eagle." Apart from getting new blood into the ranks of the military and the elite, it also served to divide the commoners. Revolt might be forestalled by offering the hope of mobility. Nevertheless, as Aztec society matured, the nobility of lineage resisted the idea of sharing their position with the newly advanced commoners. In later years, the commoners were restricted in their nobility and stratification had become calcified at the eve of the Conquest.

A source of legitimation was ideological in terms of religion. The belief was prevalent that the world was always in danger of a chaotic, cataclysmic end. The only way to forestall it was to feed the gods with humankind's most precious substance—its blood. Thus, at the command of Huitzilopochtli, the only way to postpone the day of cataclysm was to sacrifice humans to the altar. This was nothing new; the idea was inherited from the Toltecs.

Most of the gods were of Toltec heritage. Quetzalcoatl, who was said to oppose blood sacrifice, was the plumed serpent who was a beneficent ruler. Tezcatlipoca (Smoking Mirror) was the exact opposite. He demanded blood sacrifices and is often identified with Huitzilopochtli as one manifestation of himself. According to myth, using trickery, he banished Quetzalcoatl to the east. There was a promise that Quetzalcoatl would return from the east to reclaim his kingdom. This myth was a small but significant factor in the Aztecs final downfall. Tlaloc was the god of rain and with Huitzilopochtli, had a shrine in his honor at the Templo Mayor. There were others, such as Xipe Totec, the flayed one.

With the dangers of a cataclysmic world, what was the self-concept of the Mexica? The ideal Mexica was expected to confront danger, whether the real one in battle or the imaginary one of a universal catastrophic end, with bravery and moderation in behavior. The ideal Mexica did not drink to excess, he spoke softly, he deferred to authority, and was sexually continent. One may wonder, with the wealth and women available to them, whether the emperor and nobility met these ideals.

The Conquest of Tenochitlán

The conquest was symbolized in an emperor's nightmare. The penultimate emperor Moctezuma, also known popularly if inaccurately as Montezuma, dreamed that Quetzalcoatl was about to return. The date in the Mayan calendar, which the Aztec had long adopted, was One Reed—the first day of a new 52-year cycle. The year was 1519. In 1519, Hernán Cortez and his troops landed in the site of Vera Cruz.

This interpretation of Moctezuma's dream was the first of many events that rendered the Mexica vulnerable to the Spanish Conquest. Moctezuma sent a party of emissaries to the imagined Quetzalcoatl to welcome him—and to invite him to leave. They met, and soon Cortez's demand for ever more gold and his capture of Moctezuma dispelled any remaining belief that he was the Feathered Serpent. The Aztec elite had done much to alienate their population through heavy taxes and demands for human sacrifice on a massive scale. The still unconquered states, especially Tlaxcala, saw in the Spaniards a way to be rid of the threat posed by their Aztec neighbors. Thus the Spaniards were able to exploit these weaknesses. Other factors were their superior military technology and the smallpox they brought into the New World that wiped out much of the population in 1520 and after. Tenochitlán was captured in 1521 and the remainder of central and southern Mexico was in Spanish hands by 1530. Although most of the Maya, too, were under Spanish domination by 1546, Maya uprisings were common throughout the sixteenth to even the nineteenth century, long after Mexican independence. The last Maya city-state fell at Flores, the Petén, in 1692.

The Colonial Era

After the conquest of the Aztecs and other peoples of Central Mexico, the towns were restructured on the Spanish model of indirect rule and of consolidated communities laid out in a grid. The trajectory of events in central Mexico went as follows. In the interim period, the Spaniards initiated the process of congregación, or combining smaller communities into larger ones. Each congregación was governed by a system of indirect rule. Local government were headed by Indian appointees who themselves were local chiefs or caciques. Theirs was the job to make assignment of labor and tribute quotas to individual residents. Aztecs also assumed the managerial functions of the church, whose priests were frequently absent because there were not enough of them to supervise the church in every community.

According to Wolf, the peasant communities replaced the traditional Aztec belief system with a syncretic religion that combined Christian with indigenous beliefs. The formation of what he calls closed corporate communities was the product of Spanish policy of restructuring Aztec communities for Spain's ends. The communities were designed to exploit indigenous labor and resources for the gain of the then-developing gold and silver mines or of large landed estates called *haciendas.*

The communities were the products of a mass conversion to Catholicism that led to syncretistic beliefs and practices. The converts became Christian Catholics in name, but Aztec in practice. The spirits lived behind the statues of the Saints, renamed variously as Santa Maria, San Juan, Santo Tomas, or any other saint in Spanish, but otherwise playing the roles of the indigenous spirits. The saints were the brothers and sisters of God, not their servants.

In the meantime, colonial administrator and priest left the management of civil and religious affairs to the indigenous residents themselves. The communities were reorganized into civil and religious administrations for this purpose: mayors, council members, and police-messengers in the civil wing, and sacristans, mayordomos, and altar boys in the religious wings. As time went on, the twin institutions evolved into theocratic civil-religious hierarchies in their own right.

They formed the core of what Wolf calls closed corporate communities. They were corporate in that, under the deeds issued by the Spanish authorities, the community at large owned an estate of communally held land. A body of rights and obligations was established around this estate.

The rights were usufruct land tenure for the whole community. This meant that the members of the community had rights to the use of the land, so long as they paid a small annual tax and used it to grow corn, beans, and other crops on a yearly basis. Such land could never become a commodity, that is, be neither bought nor sold. If the tenant stopped using the plot, it would revert back to the community and was subject to allocation to another tenant.

The primary obligations were service to the community, and this came in the form of the civil-religious hierarchy, which consisted of a stratified system of offices (known as *cargos* with the double meaning of offices and burden) that had been fused into a theocracy. The younger men might start off as messengers or minor police functionaries in the civil wing of the hierarchy or as altar attendants in the religious wing. Those passing these lower ranks might become mayordomos (the names varied by community and ranking), whose prestige varied by the obligations they incurred; the greater the obligations, the higher the rank. Senior participants became councilmen and the mayor in the civil wing, senior mayordomos in the religious wing. At the end of the service, the participants would retire as seniors, known variously as *pasados, principales,* or some other title. Their opinion carried weight in community decisions, and they were honored for a lifetime of service.

The obligations were demanding; hence the second meaning of *cargo*, namely "burden." Each official served without pay, and they had to support the functions out of their own pocket. For the mayordomos, each was expected to pay for the costs of the annual fiesta: the *mariachi* bands (the name probably was indigenous), the ceremonial drink and food, the saint's new clothing made annually, the trappings of ritual—the list was endless. The costs of official functions were borne by the civil functionaries as well. Furthermore, they could not tend their own fields during the year of service. Small wonder that there was a correlation between the costs of serving in office and the prestige attached thereto. Many anthropologists see this function as a wealth leveling device; cargoholders ended their service in considerable debt.

If the communities were corporate, they were also closed. They were endogamous; the partners had to be from the same community. One can see where there might be problems of land inheritance if the partners came from two different communities. The dress styles were distinct for each community. What men or women wore in Zinacantán was not what women or men wore in Chamula. Only in more recent years did men start to wear western-style clothing. Women continued to wear indigenous dress.

Other barriers separated indigenous communities. Each community spoke the local dialect of a language. The Nahuatl spoken in Tepoztlán, say, was not the Nahuatl spoken in any of the other villages in that language area. Furthermore, each village had a semimonopoly over a particular product, ensuring that it had a demand for its product at the next weekly market or in a central market in the town serving the region.

Wolf argues that the close corporate communities existed in what he calls a "hostile symbiosis" with landed estates in the region. Short of cash and reliant on few exports outside the region, let alone the colony, the haciendas regarded the communities as sources of labor without needing to pay wages year-round. The communities provided labor in return for products and protection against the authorities or other communities. When not needed, the communities provided for their own subsistence. This would change with the Mexican Liberal Reforms of 1857 under Benito Juárez, of indigenous descent yet with Liberal aspirations in economic policy and Mexican politics.

Post-Independence Mexico

Like other Latin American countries at the time, Mexico obtained independence formally on September 15, 1821, after a war that began in 1810. Both dates are commemorated today. As elsewhere, Mexico underwent competition between the Conservatives, who favored regional economies dominated by haciendas and a hierarchical form of government, and Liberals, who preferred external commerce, internal economic development dominated by industrial firms, and a federal form of government.

Power in Mexico seesawed between the Conservadores and the Liberales in the interim leading to the 1880s. A federal form of government was instituted in 1824. Then followed a period of conflict that involved the machinations of Antonio López de Santa Anna, whose centrist rule began in 1836. The Constitution of 1824 was suspended, leading to revolts that led to the formation of the Republic of Texas, the Republic of the Rio Grande, and Yucatan. As a product of his often unstable and discontinuous rule, Mexico lost Texas, other Southwestern territories, and Alta California, all to the United States during the Mexican American War of 1846–1848. Then, also during his dictatorship, the Yucatan erupted in a rare if temporary successful indigenous revolt called the War of the Castes in 1847; it remained in power in the Yucatan until the 1930s. Partly as the product of his fiscal mishandling, France, in an effort to collect its debts and establish a Roman Catholic enclave, invaded Mexico and installed the Habsburg Ferdinand Maximilian in 1861. In the series of wars that followed, Mexican forces deposed Maximilian in 1867 and he was executed on June 29, 1867. The annual *Cinco de Mayo* celebration commemorates one of the key battles that turned the war in favor of the Mexican rebels.

Over the decades, the Liberals ascended to power. Under the Plan de Ayutla drafted in 1857, Benito Juarez assumed the presidency of Mexico the same year, and with his Liberal allies, defeated the Conservadores in the Reform War in 1861. His forces, which were also led by future President Porfirio Díaz weathered the French occupation during the 1860s and reasserted dominance with the defeat of Maximilian in 1867. Even the Conservadores allied with the Liberals in his ouster, along with periodic attempts to rid the presidency of Santa Anna.

Though historically modern Mexico began with the 10-year instability initiated by the Mexican Revolution of 1910, the roots of modern Mexico actually begin with the ascension of Porfirio Díaz. He governed Mexico, with one early four-year interruption, from 1876 to his overthrow in the 1910 Revolution.

It was during this period, known as the *Porfiriato,* that Díaz implemented the policies of industrial development, construction of the railways that link all of Mexico to this day, and put the country's agriculture on a commercial footing. His were the policies to finance the arts, music, and dance for which Mexico has become famous worldwide. He did so by centralizing the government of Mexico down to the provinces, in ways that Justo Rufino Barrios would do in neighboring Guatemala. He promoted American investment in enterprises ranging from agriculture to steel to railways.

Development came at a price. The Plan of Ayutla had developed these and other policies under Juárez, but it was under Díaz that the policies were implemented in a comprehensive way. One was the privatization of Indian communal land. The lands were seized, divided into plots, and sold to individual entrepreneurs. The political wing of the civil-religious hierarchy fell under control of the national infrastructure that Díaz had implemented. With the outbreak of the revolution, peasants throughout central to southern to southeastern Mexico attacked the local elites who had been part of the Porfiriato and who had overseen the land grabs privatized under that regime.

From the Mexican Revolution to the Present

The revolution began with a pattern that has plagued Mexican presidential elections to the present, including the elections of 2006 and 2012 that have dominated the headlines: accusations of electoral fraud. In 1910, Díaz ran again, this time against Francisco Madero. Díaz's self-proclamation of victory was widely rejected, sparking widespread revolt. An interregnum followed of several leaders including the Liberal Francisco Madero, who assumed the presidency in 1911 only to be assassinated by Victorano Huerta, one of Diaz's generals in 1913.

Others entered the fray. José Doroteo Arango Arámbula, better known as Pancho Villa, led the revolution in northern Mexico, seeking to distribute ranch land to the peasants there, and relied on banditry to finance his adventures. Emiliano Zapata led a series of peasant revolutions in southern Mexico, and, after a failed set of negotiations with Madero, outlined a Plan de Ayala, which called for the direct return of the lands the peasants had lost under Díaz. Others, first Madero and then his successors, attempted to control the land reform process by constitutional means. Zapata's strategy incorporated the Anarchist philosophical writings of Flores Magón, one of the architects of the principles behind the Revolution. Zapata was assassinated in 1919 by a patrol sent out by one of his rivals, Venustiano Carranza.

The same Venustiano Carranza was one of the authors of the Constitution of 1917 which now is used to govern Mexico. Among the more important articles are Article 27, which sets up the guidelines for land redistribution and reform, and Article 127, which provides for labor reform. Plutarco Calles established, among others, the foundations of the Mexican state, which

FIGURE 5.7

Pancho Villa in a commemorative postage stamp marking the 100 years since his birth. Villa was one of two icons of the Mexican Revolution. The other was Emiliano Zapata.

included the implementation of land redistribution, a tripartite political party initially known as the National Mexican Party, later to be renamed the Institutional Revolutionary Party (Partido Revolucionario Institutional or PRI), which has governed Mexico (with a twelve-year hiatus from 2000 to 2012) to this day. PRI regained national power in the Election of 2012 and has retained most of the state and local power even in those years.

PRI is governed by three interest groups—white collar functionaries, labor unions, and agrarians—and is based on maintaining a balance of all such groups and, some have argued, has survived the years because of this comity of interests. It has gone through phases from the peasants' interest. Calles, who ran on a populist platform, made good his promise of land redistribution and labor laws. One of his successors, Lázaro Cárdenas, who governed the country from 1934 to 1940 in the midst of the Great Depression, established an *ejido* system of communal land that lasted until the Salinas administration. He also nationalized the petroleum industry under Pemex, introduced a thoroughgoing set of labor reform laws, and instituted other social services policies somewhat imitating Roosevelt's New Deal.

Since then, Mexico has undergone a series of dramatic developments that has changed society as a whole. The PRI, despite a 12-year hiatus, never left the states or the localities. Now Enrique Peña Nieto appears to restore the PRI to the executive branch. Under Salinas Gotari, the ejido reforms were reversed and public enterprises were sold to private organizations. Then, in recent years, the drug trade has reached unprecedented scope and violence.

Conclusion

Mexico represents one of the oldest civilizations in the New World. Founded on the Olmec tradition, the region included an unknown peoples who constructed the Pyramids of the Sun and the Moon in Teotihuacan, supported the Toltec, the Tarascans, and the Zapotec in periods before the Aztec emerged as a developing state around 1327 AD. Even after their conquest by the Spaniards in 1521, the influences of the Aztecs and other peoples have persisted to the present, ranging from cuisine (tortillas, maize, beans, squash, and chiles) to fiesta traditions to the arts and music.

Mexico also has traditions that, in a sense, are walking contradictions. The 1917 Constitution represented as a model for constitutions of other countries, such as that of Weimer Germany in the 1920s and even that of the Soviet Union (if the government practiced what it preached, there might not have been a Cold War). The problem is its implementation. Presidential elections have been held on schedule every six-year interval since Calles. Yet accusations of electoral fraud occur almost equally on schedule the day after the election. Mexico has enjoyed periods of economic prosperity—but economic collapse seems likewise routine. Nevertheless, the cuisine, the arts, the songs and dance, and the architecture render Mexico an interesting place for study.

Selected Films

Blossoms of Fire. 2000. 105 minutes. English and Spanish. San Francisco: Film Arts Foundation.

Central America: The Burden of Time. 1991. 57 minutes. Michael Wood. London: Carlton. Includes material of Teotihuacan, Tula, and Tenochtitlán (Mexico City).

Little Injustices. 1981. 59 minutes. Cambridge, MA. Documentary Educational Resources.

Mayas, Aztecs, and Incas. 2004. 25 minutes. New York: Educational Media Resources.

The Other Conquest. 2007. 105 minutes. Spanish and Nahuatl with English Subtitles. New York: Union Station Media.

Selected Literature

Blair, Kathryn. 2011. *Forging a Nation: The History of Mexico from the Aztecs to the Present.* New York: Creating Space: Independent Publishing Platform.

Coe, Michael, and Rex Koontz. 2008. *Mexico: From the Olmecs to the Aztecs.* 6th ed. London: Thames and Hudson.

Joseph, Gilbert M., ed. 2003. *The Mexico Reader: History, Culture, Politics.* Durham, NC: Duke University Press.

Lewis, Oscar. 1951. *Life in a Mexican Village: Tepoztlán Restudied.* Urbana: University of Illinois Press.

Martin, JoAnn. 2005. *Tepoztlán and the Transformation of the Mexican State: The Politics of Loose Connections.* Tucson: University of Arizona Press.

Wolf, Eric. 1959. *Sons of the Shaking Earth.* Chicago: University of Chicago Press.

CHAPTER 6

The Mayan Culture Area

The Mayan Culture Area consisted of several cultures belonging to a family of languages collectively referred to as Mayan and with several common cultural attributes, such as a distinctive pyramid style, a vigesimal (twenty-based) numerical system, and a complex intersecting system of calendars. Their range included southeastern Mexico (principally Chiapas, the Yucatan peninsula, and Quintana Roo), Guatemala, and parts of Honduras and El Salvador. This section begins with an ethnohistory of the pre-Conquest Maya then continues with a survey of cultures in southeastern Mexico and Guatemala, and concludes with their integration into a global corporate economy.

The Ethnohistory of the Mayan Culture Area

The Maya were one of the earliest civilizations in the Americas. In pre-Hispanic times, the Maya comprised city-states with shifting alliances. They had number systems that were vigesimal (based on twenty) and writing based on glyphs, or carved symbols that were pictorial but could also be phonetic or syllabic. They also included calendars for divining (predicting) the future or for recording history. We look at the Maya as reconstructed through archaeology and ethnohistory.

Central America connects the continents of North and South America. It is southeast of Mexico, which geographically forms a part of North America. In the southeastern part of Mexico and the northwestern part of Central America, principally Guatemala, several Mayan city-states developed. Among the best known were Chichén Itza, Mayapan, and Uxmal in northern Yucatan, Palenque and Tikal in eastern Mexico and the Petén, and Copan and Quirigua in the south.

As elsewhere in the Americas, hunters and gatherers populated Mesoamerica, including big game hunters. Along about 1800 BC, villages began to form and agriculture began. At first, the main plants were squash, which were valued not only for their flesh but also for their seed. Then production shifted to maize, which were bred from Teosinte. Teosinte evolved from a grass to a stalk. The ear evolved from a barely edible spike of teosinte to corn that is familiar to us today. The seeds were transformed from ears that easily shattered to those tightly packed in husks, so they cannot reproduce without human intervention.

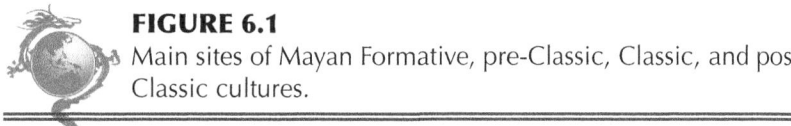

FIGURE 6.1
Main sites of Mayan Formative, pre-Classic, Classic, and post-Classic cultures.

Domesticated Plants in Mesoamerica

Gradually, as corn and other cultigens became important, settled communities became more commonplace, displacing nomadic bands. The size of corn ears increased. As perception of the value of maize became widespread, the Mayans perceived corn as "flesh of the gods." The god of maize came to be worshipped.

Other crops assumed importance. Beans are an important source of protein, but wild bean pods are brittle and the seeds are impermeable to water. Therefore, they were bred for the size and permeability of the beans and toughness of the pods. Furthermore, corn consumes vast amounts of nitrogen; beans generate nitrogen. Squash, in the meantime, provide shade to the earth and so minimize weeds. Not surprising, Mayan farmers planted all three in the same hole during sowing season.

The Formative Era

The Formative Era (1500–500 BC) of the Mayan Culture Area began with the Olmec, consisting of chiefdoms who left behind massive basalt heads with baby-face design and long-headed figurines, often with jaguar fangs. Locations included settlements along the southeastern coast of the

Image © Naaman Abreu, 2012. Used under license from Shutterstock, Inc.

FIGURE 6.2
Olmec Baby-Face sculpture, typical of art from that period.

Gulf of Mexico, such as La Venta, San Lorenzo, and Tres Zapotes. Settlements in the adjacent highlands included Llano del Jicara, site of a nearby basalt quarry. Stepped pyramids were constructed in or near the settlements. Reconstructed centers suggest populations of around 1,000.

The Olmec characteristics were defined by their art. One typical feature concerns a massive baby-faced sculpture with what appears to be a helmet. Basalt was the stone of choice. Another design is a figurine that has the fangs of a jaguar. These were found in the coastal areas, but basalt quarries were 40 miles inland, in the highland region. How they got to the coast remains a topic of debate. They did not last long as a tradition but were widespread, the defining characteristics of a horizon in archaeological terminology. The dates of this tradition are set from 1150 to 750 BCE (Before Common Era, a religious neutral expression that means the same thing as "Before Christ").

The Olmec were probably chiefdoms and not yet a state. One indication is a group of 16 male figurines who are standing in a circle and appear to be listening to a leader giving a speech. These figurines were discovered in the original circular arrangement, thereby suggesting a chiefdom. Another figurine, nicknamed "the wrestler," suggests that wrestling was one of the sports among the Olmec.

Writing may also have been a feature of the Olmec. A greenstone plaque recovered in San Andres, near La Venta, suggests the first evidence of writing. A bird carved into the plaque is associated with a glyph deciphered as "King 3 Ajaw" and his date of birth. Was the bird uttering the name of the king? Could it be the symbol of the king's clan? Perhaps the deciphering of more text will yield the answer.

The Olmec were probably the first chiefdoms that may be precursors of a state, which is a political entity that controls society through monopolizing the legitimate use of force. Generally, they govern a large area using an army with defined rights to use force and an administrative apparatus. Law is generally written in legal codes which define procedures for resolving civil disputes and punishing crimes, always defined as acts against the state. If they formed a state, it was probably by controlling resources, such as valued products like cacao (the cocoa bean that became currency among the Aztecs) and minerals.

Other pre-Classic cities included Nakbe, located in the Petén rain forest located 215 miles northeast of Guatemala City. The platforms, built over earlier structures, and the pyramids with three small temples suggest they might have been divine kingships. Until more texts are deciphered, these questions remain speculative.

El Mirador, when it was discovered, was unexpected; it was much larger than other pre-Classic cities. Population was estimated at 100,000 in 900 BCE. One can observe a few pyramids from the 200 structures that were found there. Writing was in evidence, suggested by glyphs inscribed on potsherds and the stucco covering of sculptures. There was a raised road from El Mirador to a second city, Calakmul, located 24 miles to the northeast. Evidence indicates two occupations; it was abandoned once and repopulated. The second abandonment left the city to tropical rain forest for 1,000 years.

Mayan Classic Period

The Mayan Classic period, which ranged from 250 to 925 CE (Common Era, identical to the Christian AD or Anno Domini or "Year of our Lord"), began with the prominent features of Mayan Society and ended with the Mayan Collapse. Divine kingdoms predominate, beliefs in the underworld become important, and writing, numerical, and calendrical systems are developed to the

Image © Mark Yarchoan, 2012. Used under license from Shutterstock, Inc.

FIGURE 6.3
Tikal, which was both ceremonial center and a market center.

maximum extent. Trading networks and market cities come into being with regional specialization: salt in Komchen in the northern Yucatan, food from the raised fields in Belize, and others.

One of the most noteworthy is the Temple of the Inscriptions, located in Chiapas, Mexico. Pacal's (also spelled Pakal) sarcophagus (stone coffin) has inscriptions that recount his life, his ancestry, and his royal progeny. Other inscriptions are written on stone panels or plaster of the temple. Palenque was one of the major political centers of the Maya. Much of the history of the Maya was deciphered here, and we know much more than we did in the 1950s. Similar structures dominated the lowland regions of the Maya.

Another noteworthy Maya center during the Classic was Tikal. Here (Figure 6.3 on page 93) you see the man temple of Tikal while, off to the right, one can see the extent to which it was covered in tropical rain forest for centuries after abandonment. The city was a market center of an estimated 40,000 persons. Therein hangs a tale.

Tikal was a ceremonial center with a temple honoring past kings, but it also was a commercial center, with estimated populations up to 40,000. Beginning in the 1960s, excavation showed the surrounding mounds to be residential. The rectangular mounds were possibly raised fields (chinampas). The location of Tikal near the trade route connecting the Caribbean Sea to Mexico suggested that it was a market town, rivaling nearby Caracol. Various times, both cities took turns in dominating the region. The shifting alliance, allies one year, enemies the next, characterized all Mayan city-states.

Apart from the main city-states of the Classic, there were developments in writing and numerical system. We turn to these topics next.

Maya Writing, Numbers, and the Calendar

One of the hallmarks of the Classic Period, not only of the Maya but of several Mesoamericans, was writing. The Mayan were the best-known of writing cultures, but the Aztec of Central Mexico and the Zapotec and Mixtec of southern Mexico also had their own form of writing. There are three kinds of writing: phonetic, or sound-related script like our alphabet; pictographic, like Egyptian hieroglyphic and much of the Mesoamerican; and ideographic, which are abstract symbols much like our numbers. These recur in most languages of the world: "one" in English reads "eins" in German and "uno" in Spanish, but the symbols are the same.

Writing media varied. The codices, or writing on skins or bark, provided a rich source of history but most codices were destroyed in the Spanish conquest. The Dresden Codex, discovered at a museum in Dresden, Germany, is one of the most complete codices in the world. Other media include mural and stone carvings on walls of temples and pyramids, and pottery design. One important source is the stela (plural, stelae). This stela at Tikal is a rich source of history in that city. Pacal's tomb, mentioned earlier, was also ringed with writing.

Maya writing is called logosyllabic. It is a set of glyphs that also reflect the syllables of a language. For example, one glyph contains, in its center, a hair knot in the back of the person's head. There is, in the prefix, two symbols, *ku* and *ajaw*. The two together mean "Supreme Lord." This shows that pictographic symbols can represent sounds. Egypt's hieroglyphic sounds are also expressed in pictures.

The Maya also had a unique numerical system. As you can see in Figure 6.4, there are three basic symbols: a shell for zero, a dot for one, and a bar for five. Four dots represent four, but a bar

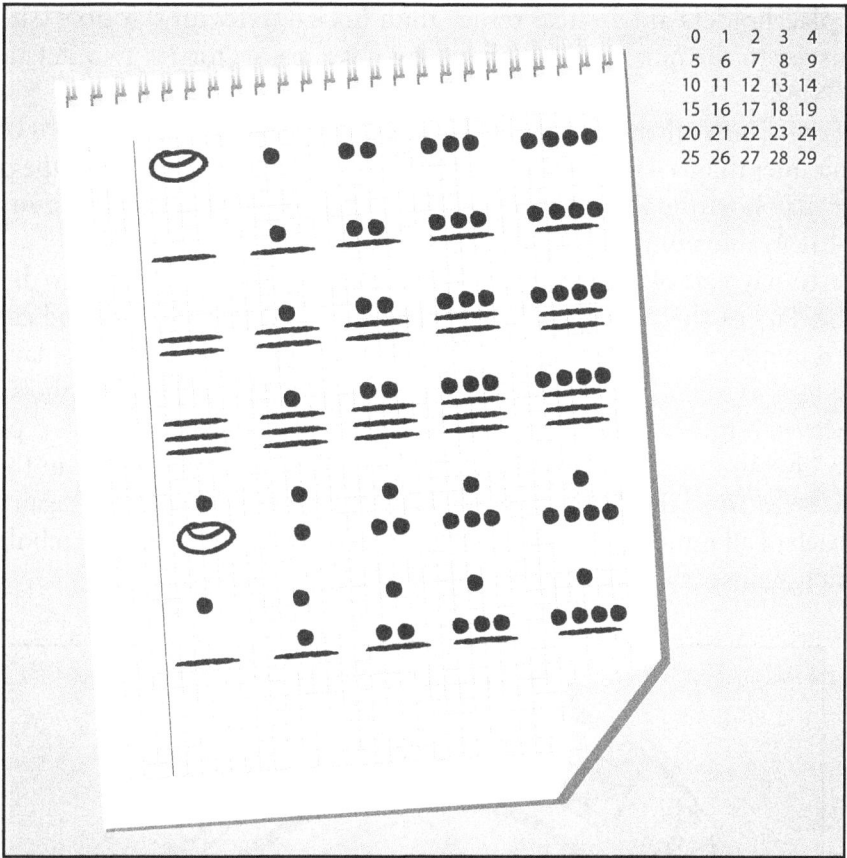

Image © dicogm, 2012. Used under license from Shutterstock, Inc.

FIGURE 6.4

The Maya numerical system. A vigesimal or base-20 system, the Mayan calendar has a shell representing zero, a dot representing one, and a bar representing five. Note that the position of the dot and bar determines its value. The higher the figure, the greater the value. See text for further description.

represents five dots. Stack two bars, and you get a ten. At nineteen you have three bars and four dots. But for twenty, a single dot is located above the shell. The dot suddenly represents twenty, not one, and the shell represents a digit of zero. In other words, you get twenty by multiplying the dot for one with twenty, the value represented by the place. The next number is twenty-one, formed by a dot in the place for one, below the placeholder dot for twenty. How do you get twenty-five in the lower left hand corner? What do you suppose thirty would be? How about forty? Answers appear below.

The Mayan numerical system is unique to this culture. As seen from the diagram, they use three symbols: a shell representing zero, a dot representing one, and a bar representing five. Their mathematical place is vertical. Ours are horizontal. If we place 1 at the right end, we get a one (1). If we place it next to the right end followed by a zero, we get a ten (10). If we place it to the third from the right followed by two zeros, we get one hundred (100). As you see from the preceding diagram, the placeholders are vertical rather than horizontal with symbols (shell, dot, or bar) below. The answer to the quiz: one dot above, two bars below for 30; two dots above, one shell below for 40. Why?

This chart represents other numerals in Mayan. Remember that the system is based on a vigesimal (20 base) rather than a decimal (10 base) principle. Remember, too, that the placeholders are vertical rather than horizontal, like ours. Can you figure out how the Mayan numerical system is equivalent to the Arabic numbers below each column of Mayan numerals?

This is the 20-day part of a lunar calendar or *tzokin,* used by the Mayan to divine, or predict, the future. The days of this calendar matches 13 numbered days of a second calendar, and the two are rotated to match each other to total 260 days, as represented by a 13-day cycle and a 20-day cycle for a total of 260 days. The permutations are of the two sets of symbols. The first set of symbols are Mayan numbers from 1 to 13; the second set consists of symbols representing natural objects. To give an example from this pair, if we take the number 1 from the left cycle and match it with Ahaw from the right cycle, the two symbols will not match again until 260 days have passed. Each of all numbers will match with each of all natural object symbols at some point. None will match again for 260 days.

Image © Alexander Ryabinstev, 2012. Used under license from Shutterstock, Inc.

FIGURE 6.5
The lunar or *tzokin* calendar is divided into two parts; this is the 20-day calendar which meshes with a numbered 13-day calendar whose permutations total 260 days. The figure in the center is known as a year bearer. See text for full description.

The two sets of symbols that make up the 260-day calendar round are known as the *tzokin.* They then match in combination with a 365-day calendar round called the *haab.* That gives us three sets of symbols, all permutating until the same three sets match again. That occurs every 52 years. For the Aztec, every 52 years meant a crisis—in one of these cycles, the world would come to an end.

The Maya also had a linear dating system called the Long Count. A *kin* was a day. Twenty *kins* made one *uinal.* Then the 20-count system was compromised with the *tun,* which equaled 18, not 20 *uinals,* making 360 days. Five intercalary days were added to make the 365-day year. Going further, 20 *tuns* made a *katun* (see chart for number of *uinals* and 7200 kins). Finally, the highest unit, the baktun, equaled 20 *katuns,* or 400 *tuns,* or 144,000 *kins.* (All terms are from the Yucatec dialect of Mayan.)

To review: the lunar calendar consists of 13 cogged (toothed) wheels. The first wheel comprises 13 numbered days; the second comprises 20 named days (animal, plant, or other natural object). This is the *tzokin* and is used for divination. A third calendar keeps track of a solar or "vague" year. That calendar is divided into 18 months of 20 days each, plus five intercalary days. The solar and lunar calendars begin with the same number, one and Reed, every 52 years. At the beginning of the new cycle, the world undergoes renewal—or possibly destruction. It was One Reed that Cortés's forces landed in Vera Cruz—in 1519.

Writing, numbers, and calendars were products of the Mayan Classic. The final period was the post-Classic. For reasons yet to be fathomed, one city after another was abandoned, the structures allowed to decay and collapse, the fields unattended. Mayanists offer three factors: The first was that the population outstripped the land resources, which could no longer sustain it. The second is that, as demands of the kings increased, the population rose in revolt. A variation of this theme was that wars broke out among the city-states, and both resources and populations were exhausted. The final variable was the onset of a long-term drought. Most likely, all three factors—resource exhaustion, wars, and drought—played a part.

One post-Classic development was the invasion by the Toltec of the Yucatan, and possibly other regions. The architecture of Chichén Itza reflects this development. Themes of war with Toltec warriors appear on the murals of temples. The puuc style of construction, with limestone masonry covering a rubble core, makes its appearance. Evidence of human sacrifice appear in the limestone wells called *cenotes;* human skeletons with gold and jade jewelry. *Chac mools,* reclining figures with bowls designed to receive the hearts of sacrificial victims also appear. Racks of skulls are carved on stone. And ball courts are constructed.

In recent years, some Mayanists have argued that there may not have been an actual Toltec invasion of the Maya, but rather the Toltec styles of architecture, themes of war, and even of human sacrifice may have been the product of diffusion. The debate on this issue continues.

Still, there is evidence of Maya influence on Chichén Itza as well. Textual sources indicate that Toltec warriors, if they were present, were speaking a Mayan language. Vault construction is distinctly Mayan. Corbeled, or stepped, walls support the ceiling, and there is an arched structure of masonry. Thus, the evidence of invasion versus diffusion remains ambiguous.

The Castillo of Chichén Itza marks the landscape of this site. As evidence of human sacrifice brought into the region by Toltecs, according to the invasion hypothesis, carvings of skulls planted on racks are depicted to the right. The Maya appeared to have retaken Chichén Itza in the twelfth

Image © aquatic creature, 2012. Used under license from Shutterstock, Inc.

FIGURE 6.6
Chichén Itza. Note Toltec influence and compare it with Tikal.

century, the advocates of the invasion hypothesis assert, inasmuch as Mayan themes are also represented in the murals and carvings. As said before, the debate continues.

In the meantime, the collapse did not mean the Mayans left the regions. They still populated, and populate today, the Yucatan, the tropical rain forests of the Petén, and highland areas of what are now Chiapas and Guatemala. At the time of the Conquest, they were organized into patrilineal clans that controlled agricultural land on a communal basis. They were still warring kingdoms. They retained the calendrical systems, the base 20 system of numbers, the logographic style of writing.

The Conquest of Central America

In 1523, Pedro de Alvarado, one of Cortez's lieutenants entered and conquered southeastern Mexico; in 1524, his forces defeated the forces of Tecun Uman at the plains of Xelajŭ and went on to occupy Utatlán. Most of central Guatemala was in Spanish control by 1530, but much territory would remain in Mayan hands for several years. Yucatan was not subdued until 1546 and Petén remained under Mayan control until 1692.

Unlike the Aztecs, in which the fall of Tenochtitlan meant the surrender of the entire empire, the Mayan had to be subdued one by one. The fall of the Quiche kingdom, for example, did not mean the fall of the Cakchiquel or the Mam or any of the other city-states. Furthermore, gold was scarce or nonexistent, so that Central America lacked what New Spain and Peru had—ample quantities of gold and silver. It was not a priority either of Conquest or of colonization.

Colonial Guatemala/Central America

After the conquest led by Pedro de Alvarado, Guatemala and Central America was restructured on the Spanish model of indirect rule and of consolidated communities laid out in a grid. Guatemala was captaincy-general of Central America (including Chiapas). As time went on, Spain lost interest in Central America. The new colony lacked the gold and silver deposits that the Spaniards discovered in New Spain (colonial Mexico) and Peru. Thus, most of the colonial administrative resources and staff were directed to these two colonies.

The trajectory of events in Central America, especially Guatemala, went as follows: Initially, the Spaniards mined for gold and platinum, which were never in great supply. Most of these metals were taken from deposits in the rivers and streams of Guatemala. As the metals became exhausted, the Spaniards grew cacao for foreign exchange. Inasmuch as other parts of the colonies were better suited for the product, the cacao industry collapsed in Central America. Interest diminished from the sixteenth century onward: only one ship landed in a decade on average in the regions of Central America as a whole.

In the interim period, the Spaniards initiated the process of congregación, or combining smaller communities into larger ones. For Santiago Atitlan, congregación involved the consolidation of hamlets called *chinamit* into larger communities (*amak* were pre-Columbian versions of these hamlets); a system designed to attach Indian laborers to the haciendas under a system called *encomiendas*. The aim of the *congregaciones* was to facilitate access to labor under the *repartimiento* (labor quota) system after the *encomienda* system failed and to gather tribute and taxes.

Each congregación was governed by a system of indirect rule. Local government was headed by Indian appointees who themselves were local chiefs or *caciques*. Theirs was the job to make assignment of labor and tribute quotas to individual residents. Mayan also assumed the managerial functions of the church, whose priests were frequently absent because there were not enough of them to supervise the church in every community.

In a sense, the system backfired. By 1600, Central America came to be neglected. In due course, the Mayan and other indigenous peoples gained autonomy from the colonial administration and the Church by default. The formation of the local communities has been attributed to two ethnohistorical interpretations by Mayan specialists: Maya discontinuity or continuity. According to the discontinuity interpretation, the communities replaced the traditional Mayan belief system with a syncretic religion that combined Christian with Mayan beliefs. Advocates of the continuity model argue that the usual syncretic explanation is too simplistic. It underplays the force of the Mayan belief system that was as strong after the Conquest at it was prior to the Conquest. We review the longer-held discontinuity interpretation first, and then look at the continuity model.

Discontinuity Model. According to the discontinuity model posited by Eric Wolf in *Sons of the Shaking Earth* (1959), the formation of what he calls closed corporate communities was the product of Spanish policy of restructuring Mayan communities for Spain's ends. The communities were designed to exploit indigenous labor and resources for the gain of the then-developing *haciendas* or large landed estates.

The communities were the products of a mass conversion to Catholicism that led to syncretistic beliefs and practices. The converts became Christian Catholics in name, but Mayan in practice. The spirits lived behind the statues of the Saints, renamed variously as Santa Maria, San

Juan, Santo Tomas, or any other saint in Spanish, but otherwise playing the roles of the indigenous spirits. The saints were the brothers and sisters of God, not their inferiors.

In the meantime, colonial administrators and priests left the management of civil and religious affairs to the Maya themselves. The communities were reorganized into civil and religious administrations for this purpose: mayors, council members and police-messengers in the civil wing, and sacristans, *mayordomos,* and altar boys in the religious wings. As time went on, the twin institutions evolved into theocratic civil-religious hierarchies in their own right.

They formed the core of what Wolf calls closed corporate communities. They were corporate in that, under the deeds issued by the Spanish authorities, the community at large owned an estate of communally held land. A body of rights and obligations was established around this estate.

The rights were usufruct land tenure for the whole community. This meant that the members of the community had rights to the use of the land, so long as they paid a small annual tax and used it to grow corn, beans, and other crops on a yearly basis. Such land could never become a commodity, that is, it could be neither bought nor sold. If the tenant stopped using the plot, it would revert back to the community and was subject to allocation to another tenant.

The primary obligations were service to the community, and this came in the form of the civil-religious hierarchy, which consisted of a stratified system of offices (known as *cargos* with the double meaning of offices and burden) that had been fused into a theocracy. The younger men might start off as messengers or minor police functionaries in the civil wing of the hierarchy or as altar attendants in the religious wing. Those passing these lower ranks might become *mayordomos* (the names varied by community and ranking), whose prestige varied by the obligations they incurred; the greater the obligations, the higher the rank. Senior participants became councilmen and the mayor in the civil wing, senior *mayordomos* in the religious wing. At the end of the service, the participants would retire as seniors, known variously as *pasados, principales,* or some other title. Their opinion carried weight in community decisions, and they were honored for a lifetime of service.

The obligations were demanding; hence the second meaning of *cargo,* namely burden. Each official served without pay, and they had to support the functions out of their own pocket. For the *mayordomos,* each was expected to pay for the costs of the annual fiesta: the marimba band, the ceremonial drink and food, the saint's new clothing made annually, the trappings of ritual—the list was endless. The costs of official functions were borne by the civil functionaries as well. Furthermore, they could not attend their own fields during the year of service. Small wonder that there was a correlation between the costs of serving in office and the prestige attached thereto. Many anthropologists see this function as a wealth leveling device; cargoholders ended their service in considerable debt. In Guatemala, the mayordomos served as members of a *cofradía,* or confraternity, responsible for their functions.

If the communities were corporate, they were also closed. They were endogamous; the partners had to be from the same community. One can see where there might be problems of land inheritance if the partners came from two different communities—to whom would the land belong, husband or wife? The dress styles were distinct for each community. One could identify a woman from Almolonga by her zigzag *huipil* (blouse) design, and a woman from Zunil by her purple striped *huipil.* In Guatemala, men of some communities retained the distinctive style of their dress. Men from Nahualá wore checkered brown and black kilts and black *chaquetes* (jackets); men from Todos Santos Cuchamatanes wore striped, pajama style pants and inner shirts.

Many men in Guatemala communities dispensed with their distinct clothing for western style menswear.

Other barriers separated indigenous communities. Each community spoke the local dialect of a language. The Quiché spoken in Chichicastenango was not the same style as that spoken in Cantel, or Santa Cruz del Quiché or Momostenango. Furthermore, each village had a semimonopoly over a particular product. Zunil and Almolonga specialized in garden vegetables. Momostenango produced woolen goods, such as *chaquetes* or blankets. Salcajá produced a bootleg liquor called *caldo de fruta* and were subject to periodical raids from the authorities. The semimonopoly for each community assured it would have a market for its products at the next weekly market demand.

Wolf argues that the close corporate communities existed in what he calls a "hostile symbiosis" with landed estates in the region. Short of cash and reliant on few exports outside the region, let alone the colony, the *haciendas* regarded the communities as sources of labor without needing to pay wages year-round. The communities provided labor in return for products and protection against the authorities or other communities. When not needed, the communities provided for their own subsistence. This would change with the Liberal *reforma* of 1871.

Continuity Model. Other interpretations see the Mayan communities as a continuation of pre-Conquest Mayan society. Advocates of this model find Wolf's and others' interpretation is simplistic, failing to assign proper weight to the pre-Conquest beliefs of post-Conquest Mayan communities. Citing Santiago Atitlán, Guatemala, to make this case, Robert Carlsen in *The War for the Heart and Soul of a Highland Maya Town,* argues that communities maintained sociocultural structures and practices that are pre-Columbian in origin. The symbol of Flowering of the Dead is described to demonstrate this continuity.

These practices were well hidden from the authorities, explaining in part the underemphasis of pre-conquest belief; they were hidden for good reason. For example, Diego de Landa, the friar who governed the church's conversion efforts in Mérida, the Yucatan, ordered the destruction of the codices as products of the Devil. As a result, there are only four known codices that document the written language of the Maya. The autos-da-fé of the Inquisition were legendary both in the Iberian Peninsula and Spanish America. There was ample reason for the Mayan to keep their beliefs under wraps, similar to the efforts of the Jews and the Muslims to keep their beliefs hidden in the Iberian Peninsula after the Christian reconquest of Spain in 1492.

Furthermore, even after consolidation, transplanted *chinamit* or *amak* residents kept their affiliation. There was enough documentation to warrant the bringing by members of two *amaks* of their cases to the courts in the twentieth century. This brings the assumption that Mayan lack the memory of their original beliefs into serious question.

The central theme among the Mayan of Santiago Atitlán is the identification of an organizing principle called *Jaloj-K'exoj.* According to the Romanian religious historian and philosopher Mircea Eliade, every religion has a center, an *axis mundi* about which it rotates. To the Mayan, *Jaloj-K'exoj* is that axis. In its agriculture, for example, *Jaloj-K'exoj* is the source of continuity to the earth and the products that it yields. In its etymology, *Jal* means "husk": the change in a thing as it goes through its life cycle: life begins in death. *Kex* means "seed" and entails generational change: from one (seed) springs the many.

From this concept, the symbol to Atitecos (residents of Santiago Atitlán), *Jaloj-K'exoj* generates the symbol of the Flowering Mountain-Earth, which links vegetation with all aspects of the

FIGURE 6.7

Woman from Santiago Atitlán. This halo headband is characteristic for women of that village; every Mayan community has its own distinctive style of dress.

human life cycle—kinship, production modes, religion, the community's political structure and, more broadly, to time and the celestial movements. The primary manifestation of the Flowering Mountain-Earth is a maize plant, a sacred entity to the *Atitecos*. The Flowering Mountain-Earth is the Original Tree of Life, for which the cross is not Christian but Mayan. The deity became pregnant with endless possibilities.

Thus, to the *Atitecos*, the original tree represented all that there was in the beginning. The branches of the Tree yielded all things, the "fruit," from rocks to fruit to deer to lightning—all things of the earth. The branches become so heavily laden that the fruit dropped; striking the ground, the fruit broke, scattering its seeds. Soon, all its fruit sprouted and trees grew under the Shade of the Original Tree, which was also called Father/Mother. From death springs life.

Larsen links this myth of death transformed into life to the Hero Twins of the *Popul Vuh*, one of the original books of the Mayan. The Twins die when they enter the Mayan version of Hell, called Xibalba, but they are reborn after tricking the gods in a series of adventures. The alter carving at the church in Santiago Atitlán reflects this cosmology of *Jaloj-K'exoj*. Every year, the members of one of the cofradías ascend the side of a mountain. At the top of the mountain is a maize stalk, representing the Tree of Life. So long as this tree is "fed," it will continue to generate the "seeds." Such "feeding" may be literal, as farmers feed their seed through a hole of the land that symbolically represents the umbilicus. It may be metaphorical, as they conduct their ritual through the rising smoke of the copal they burn. Through this construct, the metaphorical and the real become as one.

The Flowering Mountain Tree is reified every spring when farmers plant the seed. These are dead (corn) seed, or "little skulls," that will be transformed into life. Seeds sprout into seedlings, the "little ones," or children. Seedlings then mature, yielding flowers, then maize. Then the maize dies, yielding ever more "little skulls." The life cycle is completed, yet begins again. This represents a metaphor of the human life cycle. This recurrence represents to the Maya metaphorical generations, ancestries, lineages of the living. The ceiba tree represents the tree of life, its roots being the home of bats and the underworld, the trunk the refuge and feeding place of insects, and the leaves a protected canopy.

Based on this series of convoluted metaphors and symbols, Larsen, along with Tedlock, Thompson, and Schele, argues that Mayan belief is much more than a syncretic combination of Christian and Mayan beliefs. The cross is a Mayan symbol, and so the Christian cross was not alien to them. Blood sacrifices are thematic to both Christian and Mayan beliefs. So, argues Larsen, the religious themes of death transformed into life were integral to the Mayan throughout the Conquest and its aftermath, and remain so today. To see the changes as discontinuous ignored the theme conceptualized in *Jaloj-K'exoj*.

The Liberal Transformation: 1871 to the Present

Among the Spaniards and their nationalist successors after Central America's independence in 1821, there has been a contentious relationship between Conservatives and Liberals. The Conservatives, representing the *hacendados* (owners of *haciendas*), see the road to wealth and prosperity through self-sufficiency. Conservatives limit international trade and preserve their wealth in the form of land and subsistence crops. The indigenous population exists to provide labor as needed, then go back to their communities. Communal land serves the interests, not only to the Indians, but to the owners of landed estates as sustaining reserves of labor until when needed.

The Liberal road to wealth is very different. To them, wealth can only be obtained through development of the national economy, which can be made only through external trade. After independence, Central America was initially dominated by Liberals but soon split up into five republics: Guatemala, El Salvador, Honduras, Nicaragua, and Costa Rica. The province of Soconusco initially was a part of Guatemala but was later annexed by Mexico as a part of the state of Chiapas.

Guatemala fell under the Conservative government of Rafael Carrera, who held sway over the country until 1865, then under a change of presidents until 1871. With exceptions, the economic policy was consistent with the Conservative strategy, but cracks emerged even during this period. Coffee, which was introduced in Costa Rica in the 1840s, found a lucrative market in the United States and parts of Europe. This crop was introduced into Guatemala in the 1860s.

The Liberals seized control of Guatemala in 1871 under Justo Rufino Barrios, who soon implemented a series of reforms in the country. He thought that Guatemala, to survive and prosper, needed to industrialize, and the key to industrialization was to develop external trade, both to find exports in Guatemala of high demand abroad and to foster entrepreneurs into the country or to attract them from abroad.

After trying various exports—quinine, among others—Barrios found that the most successful export was coffee. Thus, by 1877, he pursued policies that fostered the expansion of the coffee industry. The first concerned land. Much of the land was tied into communal holdings controlled by Indian communities. To this end, he withdrew legal recognition of communal land, declared them as vacant lands (*terrenos baldios*), and extended provisions for the private registration of land thus declared as vacant. The second concerned labor. Coffee is a labor intensive crop, first requiring care for the seedlings to mature, then needing a large labor force to pick the berries, separate the coffee seeds from the flesh, and to dry the beans in the sun before marketing. To that end, he reestablished a forced labor policy requiring communities to furnish quotas of labor to the new coffee plantations. Debt peonage was also legalized.

The results were dramatic. Hundreds of entrepreneurs, most of them Ladino (of mixed Indian-Spanish descent) flocked to the communities to register the now officially vacant lands; some lands and houses were sold from under individuals who had lived and farmed at those sites for years, decades, even centuries. Entire communities were taken over by plantations, as was the case of El Palmar. Agents bought land, suitable for coffee or not, in order to entrap peasants and create *fincas de mozos* (farms to produce workers). To get access to land, peasants now had to work for the plantations. Those peasants who somehow escaped takeovers were still obliged to work outside the community. Land agents who recruited, by fair means or foul, created an army of indebted peasants.

Coffee was not the only motor force of land and labor capture. Barrios also sought to attract that industry. To that end, he approved in 1884 an application to establish a textile factory in Cantel, near the second city of Quezaltenango, and privatized a communal plot for that purpose. The six council members of the town joined a conspiracy to overthrow Barrios in retaliation. When the conspiracy was discovered, Barrios ordered the six Canteleños executed. A stela was erected in their memory at a cemetery. As if to mock the villagers, a bust of Barrios stands at the entrance to the village (Anonymous in Grandin and others' *The Guatemalan Reader*, 2011, p. 165).

After Barrios was killed in battle in 1885, his successors continued his policies and added to them. Military dictatorships became the norm well into the twentieth century. Jorge Ubico added vagrancy laws requiring individuals owning less than a stipulated amount of land to engage in 100 or 150 days of wage labor. The distribution of land became skewed, and by the 1960s, it was not uncommon for a small percentage of a community to own 85% to 90% of the land.

A revolution in 1944 reversed these trends over a 10-year period. Juan Jose Arevalo, elected on a platform he called "spiritual socialism," initiated legislation that included a minimum wage, a 40-hour work week, and a land redistribution program. His successor, Jacob Arbenz Guzman, adopted more radical policies that included, in 1952, the redistribution of unused land owned by the banana-growing United Fruit Company; *sikatoka,* or Panama disease, had rendered this land useless for growing bananas but still usable for other crops. These and other policies induced calls from the company and from the U.S. State Department to Arbenz's ouster as a communist allied with the Soviet Union in the midst of the Cold War.

In a coup led by Carlos Castillo Armas and sponsored by the Central Intelligence Agency, a counterrevolutionary army entered Guatemala and overthrew the Arbenz regime. Castillo Armas was assassinated a year later, and successive regimes eliminated the reforms initiated by the Arevalo and Arbenz presidencies. In 1960, a group of younger military offers began an insurgent movement in eastern Guatemala that developed into a thirty-year civil war. Up to four guerrilla armies were formed during the period between 1960 and the mid-1970s. Initially a Ladino-based movement confined to the east, the movement expanded to involve the rural indigenous population in the 1970s that involved the assassination of a plantation owner in northern Quiche province.

In response to the guerilla warfare that had spread, the American military, through the offices of the School of the Americas (SOA), which provided training for military dictatorships throughout Latin America, including Argentina, Chile, Paraguay, Nicaragua, and El Salvador, fostered an efficient counterinsurgency force in Guatemala, comprising the army, the National Police, and death squads such as the White Hand (Mano Blanco) and the Anti-Communist Secret Army. There followed a scorched-earth policy in which entire villages were massacred. Although the genocide occurred during the 1970s, the worst of the massacres occurred under the evangelical president Efrain Rios-Montt from 1982 until his overthrow in 1983. In partial response to these developments, the four existing guerrilla groups merged into an umbrella force, the Guatemalan National Revolutionary Unity (URNG) in 1982.

Over the years of the civil war, more than 450 Mayan villages were destroyed, and around a million Mayan people were displaced inside Guatemala or to the border regions in southern Mexico. More than 200,000 lost their lives during the civil war. After years of conflict, the national Guatemalan government and the URNG met and signed a peace accord in 1996. URNG became a political party, whose success has been modest at best. A variety of centrist and center-left parties have since been elected to the presidency and the national congress (The Chamber of Deputies). In the meantime, the families of more than 45,000 activists have taken part to document these years of genocidal war. Although much work has been done in this effort and one police chief has been convicted, the election in 2011 of former General Otto Pérez Molina to the presidency threatens to halt the investigation. He was the head of intelligence in Guatemala during the civil war, and according to witnesses, was present during a massacre in 1982 of villagers in Quiché province.

Guatemala has since moved toward a neoliberal society. *Maquiladoras* (branch-plant factories) have sprung up in Guatemala City, Chimaltenango, and elsewhere. A collection of essays by O'Neill and Thomas titled *Securing the City: Neoliberalism, Space, and Insecurity in Postwar Guatemala* (2011) looks at the changes in the cities and countryside, such as the progress of foreign apparel industries in Guatemala since the war's end and the displacement of street vendors by a "Maya" retail chain in Guatemala City. Another book, this one by J. T. Way titled *The Mayan in the Mall,* traces the roads of modernity in Guatemala from the 1920s to the present, symbolized by a Mayan-themed shopping mall named Gran Tikal Futura ringed by neighborhoods of gated communities whose iron fences replaced the walls topped with broken glass (2012). In the meantime, Otto Pèrez Molina was elected president on the promise to suppress a burgeoning drug trade now developing in Guatemala.

Conclusion

One may legitimately ask what the future holds for Guatemala and its Mayan population. Elsewhere in Latin America, there are hopeful signs. Argentina has since rejected the neoliberal model, arising from its economic collapse in 2001, and a factory recovery movement is in progress. Venezuela and Bolivia have nationalized their recourses: oil in Venezuela and natural gas, tin, and lithium in Bolivia. On the other hand, Honduras underwent a coup overthrowing a liberal president, the former Sandinista leader Daniel Ortega as newly elected president of Nicaragua has been less than enthusiastic in pursuing a nationalist agenda, and Chile has elected a conservative president despite its years under the Pinochet regime. So far, Guatemala seems to be in a neoliberal camp, continuing the past begun under Justo Rufino Barrios a century and a quarter ago. Time will tell.

Selected Films

Central America: Burden of Time. 1991. 57 minutes. Michael Wood. London: Carlton. Includes material of Teotihuacan, Tula, and Tenochtitlán (Mexico City).

Mayas, Aztecs, and Incas. 2004. 25 minutes. New York: Educational Media Resources.

The Maya: Lords of the Jungle. 1981. 91 minutes. Odyssey Series. Cambridge, MA. Documentary Educational Resources.

When the Mountains Tremble. 1984 [2004]. 90 minutes. Pamela Yates. Skylight Pictures.

Selected Literature

Bunzel, Ruth. 1952. *Chichicastenango: A Guatemalan Village.* Seattle: University of Washington Press.

Grandin, Greg, et al. 2011. *The Guatemala Reader.* Durham, NC: Duke University Press.

Tedlock, Dennis. 1996. *Popol Vuh: The Definitive Edition of The Mayan Book of The Dawn of Life and The Glories of Gods and Kings.* New York: Touchstone.

Watanabe, John M. 1992. *Maya Saints and Souls in a Changing World.* Arlington: University of Texas Press.

Way, J. T. 2012. *The Mayan in the Mall: Globalization, Development, and the Making of Modern Guatemala.* Durham, NC: Duke University Press.

Wolf, Eric. 1959. *Sons of the Shaking Earth.* Chicago: University of Chicago Press.

CHAPTER 7

Andean America

Introduction

Along the western side of South America arises the Andes cordillera. This has been the site of several relatively small state-level cultures, such as Moche, Chan Chan, Nazca, and others. The main language spoken here is Quechua, followed by Aymara. Later, these states would be conquered by a Quechua population centered in Cuzco and became known as the Inca. We review the formation and florescence of the Inca then look briefly at the Spanish conquest under Pizarro and the outcome at present.

Andean South America: A Geography

The Andes form a narrow but highly elevated mountain chain over the length of the southern Pacific Rim from Colombia through Ecuador, Peru, Bolivia, and on to Chile near the Argentina border. Most of the region is bounded to the east by the Amazon rain forest, occupied mostly by Brazil, but also by eastern Colombia, Ecuador, and Peru. The region rises from a coastal desert band to an extremely wet and cold climate in the higher elevations.

As you can see from the map in Figure 7.1, South America is located in the Southern Hemisphere. It does not include Central America, nor does it include Mexico—that country is geographically part of North America. The empire itself was long: it stretched from present-day Colombia through western Ecuador, Peru, and Bolivia into northern Chile. Yet it was narrow as far as empires go, from the Pacific coast through the Andes mountain range and stopping at the Amazon region.

Indigenous Andean Cultures

The Inca Empire was unique in several ways, as we shall see. The Inca were one of the world's largest empires. It had no writing, unheard of among other empires. All accounting was done with knotted ropes. It had a highway system that was made up of little more than pathways, yet it kept the empire together. Other than the llama, which could carry no more than 100 pounds, there were no draft (or work) animals. They had no pulleys, metal tools, or cranes, yet they built huge stone buildings. And they had what was probably the first socialist economy.

Image © gregs, 2012. Used under license from Shutterstock, Inc.

FIGURE 7.1

South America. The Inca Empire and its predecessor empires of Moche, Chan Chan, Nazca, and others were located in present-day Colombia, Ecuador, Peru, Bolivia, and northern Chile with boundaries extending to northwestern Argentina.

The photograph in Figure 7.2 shows the Inca capital city of Cuzco, translated as "the navel of the earth." It was located in the central part of the empire, in present-day Peru. The sacred site of Machu Picchu was located northwest of the capital city. Tiahuanaco, an Aymara city and empire, was one of the few market centers in pre-Inca years; it is located at the banks of Lake Titicaca. Other early empires included Nazca in the southern coastal region, Huari and Chancay slightly north of Nazca, and the city-states of Moche, Chimu, and Chan Chan located much farther north on and near the coast. Cajamarca was a northern city-state well into the Andes, and Quito, capital of modern Ecuador, was the northernmost city of the empire.

One of the most analyzed infrastructures in the Inca Empire was the road system that covered the entire empire. Tampus, combined garrisons and granaries, were spaced a day apart. The roads themselves would not be recognizable as such by today's standards. They were more paths than roads, many stretches were unpaved, and they went straight up and down the mountainside rather than curve upward to fit the contours. Messengers ran in relays so that messages could reach from one end of the empire to the other in a week. Often one runner would shout out the message as he approached the tampus, so that the next runner would be on his way before the first one arrived.

FIGURE 7.2
Cuzco, former Inca capital, now a regional city in central Peru.

Ecology of the Andean Region

Though narrow, the empire comprised numerous ecological zones (see Figure 7.3 on the following page). The Pacific area was extremely dry, yet teeming with fish and shellfish. Foothills were forested leading to the Andes highlands. To the east was the montaña, much moister, followed by the impenetrable rain forests of Amazonia. With so many ecological zones so closely together, it was possible to provide fish and seafood from the coastal area, bananas and plantains from the montaña, potatoes and duck from various elevations, and different varieties of corn, also differing in type by the elevations.

The climate of the Pacific coast was, and is, the driest of all coastal areas around the world. Although cloudy days are common, an inversion prevents rain from falling there. Yet an upwelling of the southward current produces an abundance of sea life. Most of the water utilized comes from rivers originating in the Andes, providing ample irrigation. It is not surprising, then, that the first settlements began at the coast.

The Andes comprise a series of peaks and valleys, including grassy plateaus called punas. Most of the rainfall captured by the Andes flows eastward toward the Amazon and its tributaries rather than toward the west and the Pacific plains.

Andean Domesticates

The staple plant of the Inca was the potato, a tuber that does well in cold climates such as the Andes. Another indigenous grain is quinoa, which was used for making a kind of bread. Also an

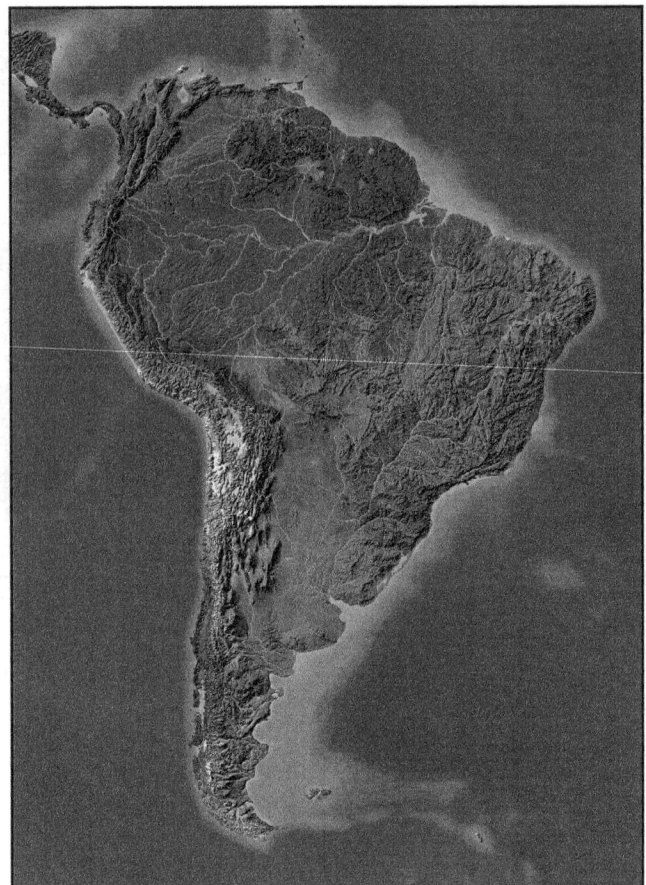

Image © AridOcean, 2012. Used under license from Shutterstock, Inc.

FIGURE 7.3
Relief map of South America. The Inca and their predecessors lived in the Andes mountain range throughout the western edge of the continent.

important but non-indigenous plant is maize, or corn, which originated in Mesoamerica and diffused into the Andes about 4000 BC. It is the primary ingredient for making chicha, a kind of beer. As for animals, the most important were the camelids, South American animals related to the camel. The llama is the only beast of burden in the Andes, and for that matter, anywhere in the Americas. The llama, together with the alpaca and the vicuna, are valuable sources of wool and meat. Duck and guinea pigs round out most of the domesticated animals.

Ethnohistory of the Inca and their Predecessors

There were several regional empires prior to Inca expansion. As stated before, Moche, Chan Chan, and Cajamarca dominated the north. Sipan was also a coastal empire, while Nazca dominated the southern coastal area and Tiahuanaco was an Aymara empire located at the banks of Lake Titicaca. Chanca, or Chancay, was the principal rival of the developing Incas, and that is where the expansion of the Incas got its start.

Image © J Duggan, 2012. Used under license from Shutterstock, Inc.

FIGURE 7.4

Inca road passing through the Sacred Valley. Though often no more than an unpaved trail in many parts, the road was key to integrating the empire over its 2600-mile length.

The Inca actually began as a small village founded in AD 1000. Around 1440, Pachakuti led his troops to defeat the rival Chanca State and began its expansion. The typical pattern of development was to expand northward across Peru and western Ecuador and southward into present-day Bolivia, northern Chile, and northwestern Argentina. The final expansion went deeper into Ecuador and southern Colombia. A typical pattern of Conquest was for the Inca to provide gifts to the conquered and allow them to retain their social organization and culture. Nevertheless, labor taxation integrated the colonies thoroughly into the empire.

The road system (Figure 7.4) was the key to maintaining the 2600-mile-long empire. The roads were limited access; only officials, the military, and transporters of essential goods were allowed on the roads. As mentioned above, *tampus* were constructed a day's travel apart. Llamas (Figure 7.4) and humans were the transporters of cargo, and runners maintained the communication network of the empire.

The Inca probably represents the first known prototype of a socialist economy. The peasants worked off *mita*, or labor tax—constructing roads, raising public buildings, and farming on the lands controlled by the emperor. Peasant land was owned by clans called *allyu*, and was free to provide for their own needs of subsistence and households. They were then recruited as *mita*. Rewards for such labor were said to be generous; *chicha* (beer), entertainment, and the highly prized textiles.

The beasts of burden were not used for agriculture; there were no plows to pull. Instead, the native people turned the soil using foot plows. The principal crops, as stated, were potatoes, quinoa, and corn. Duck, guinea pigs, and camelids were the animals. The Inca invented a unique system of preserving food. Potatoes and duck were freeze-dried. During the day, they were dried

Image © andreanord, 2012. Used under license from Shutterstock, Inc.

FIGURE 7.5
Typical llama, one of three major types of camelids. The others are
the much smaller alpaca and vicuña.

in the sun, and then frozen at night in storage bins. Temperatures varied from hot in the daytime to freezing at night. Food would keep for more than a year.

Products, ranging from potatoes to corn brew to meat, were warehoused and accounts kept on the supply. Lacking writing, the Inca used knotted rope, called *quipus,* to keep accounts. Thin, knotted cords were suspended from a main rope; the cords represented numerals, probably based on a decimal system. Each cord or set of cords kept track of human populations, live animals, and the contents of the warehouses.

In most civilizations, writing originates as accounting systems; both Egyptian hieroglyphics and Mesopotamian cuneiform writing began as accounting devices. However, there is no evidence that the Inca had any writing at all. Scholars have inferred pre-Conquest history by murals, sculptures, clay pottery images, and stone engravings, by oral tradition, and acculturated Incas who described their culture. Therefore, *quipus* took up the accounting function that writing assumed elsewhere.

This is how the *quipu* system works. Knots are spaced at intervals, the knot furthest from the main cord, representing the lowest values, namely ones. The next knot indicates tens, then hundreds, then thousands. The value of each part is indicated by the number of knots in a specific place on the cord. To take an example, visualize on a cord three knots in the place of one, making a three. At the place of ten, there are four knots, indicating forty. Six knots in the 100 place indicates 600. On that basis, how do you get the numeral 3643? Hint: there is a fourth knot closest to the main cord, which represents thousand. How many knots are there in that position?

The censuses were color-coded by category. Population would be represented by one color, labor tribute by another, tribute of other kinds by yet another. If you needed to count the amount of laborers allocated to a particular region, you had a color for quick reference.

Image © vdLee, 2012. Used under license from Shutterstock, Inc.

FIGURE 7.6
Machu Picchu, ceremonial center of the Inca.

The sociopolitical structure of the Inca was based on the myth that the emperor was descended from the Sun God. Since the sun, in their view, was the giver of all life, it was essential that the lineage derived from the Sun God be kept pure. Thus, royal incest was practiced; the emperor married his sister, who bore children of pure royal stock thereby. Needless to say, upward social mobility was limited, if it existed at all.

Administratively speaking, the Inca state was divided into four quarters. The Inca name for their land, Tawanitimsuyu, meant "Land of Four Quarters." Each quarter was further subdivided into units called *waranqa,* comprising 1000 laborer/taxpayers each. Because of their policies of allowing conquered peoples to retain their customs, the ethnic diversity of the Inca was considerable. Therefore, they used a system called *mitmaq* both to utilize any new resources such as copper, gold, or stone for tools and to keep tight control to prevent revolts. Huanaco Pampa and other administrative towns strengthened centralized control.

Like many other complex cultures, the Inca were governed by a theocracy. Although the administrative center was Cuzco, the ceremonial center was Machu Picchu (see Figure 7.6). Some have regarded the site as a summer residence of the emperor, but others, such as the archaeologist Johan Reinhard, attribute religious significance to the site because of the presence of ritual remains under platforms at the site and because of its location amid the mountains, itself of religious significance according to the Inca themselves. Others argue for the role of Machu Picchu as a center for controlling the economy, a prison site, and a center for grading potatoes and other food crops.

Finally, the Inca were master builders. At first glance, one might think that the trapezoidal blocks reflected poor workmanship. Yet, not only did they manage to lift heavy blocks into place without pulleys or horses, they were able to place the blocks together so precisely that one could

Image © Kobby Dagan, 2012. Used under license from Shutterstock, Inc.

FIGURE 7.7
Inca wall, built from uneven but precisely measured stone blocks. One could not insert a quarter in the spaces between the blocks.

not insert a coin between them. Gold was used in profuse quantities. The surface of the Temple of the Sun, for example, was covered with a gold frieze (a decorative plate). Of course, that did not escape the notice of the Spaniards, and there is no gold covering any of the public structures today.

The Conquest and Its Aftermath

Francisco Pizarro was nothing if he wasn't a ruthless and cunning conquistador, and like Cortes in Mexico, he relied on Indian allies to overthrow the Inca. In fact, in *The Great Inca Rebellion,* it is another native culture that finally does the Inca in—and they even have their own Malinche, the woman in Mexico thought to have betrayed her own people by serving as Cortes's translator and mistress. But the greatest ally of the Spaniards was disease, smallpox, which decimated the Inca population even before Pizarro set foot into the region. Indeed, Atahualpa and Huascar were at war for the crown because their father had died from smallpox. That some 188 soldiers could subdue a population in the hundreds of thousands is telling.

Like other Spanish colonies, Peru, the main successor to the Inca empire, was along with Mexico one of the principal sources of gold and silver for the Spaniards. When these metals began to run out, the Bourbon reforms, under the leadership of the Crown that fell under the French-origin Bourbon king, attempted to diversify the economy while maintaining Peru and other colonies as sources of raw material. Peru was the last of the South American colonies to declare independence, under the principal leaderships of Símón Bolívar and José de San Martín.

After independence, Peru went through long periods of political and economic instability. Though sustained for a period of time with a high demand for guano, rich deposits of bird droppings along the coastal regions, depletion of the source ended that period. Years of internal and sometimes external conflict (The War of the Pacific with Chile for example in 1879 to 1883) have kept Peru, among other Andean countries in decades of political and economic instability.

Throughout the period, Incan peasants have largely retained their culture from Incan times. The Spaniards used the *mita* system to recruit workers for the mines and the plantations. Their stone houses with distinct kitchen design have been maintained through the centuries and their indigenous cuisine of potatoes, the corn *chicha,* and quinoa grains have remained, albeit with Spanish and Japanese variations. Coca remains the primary means of suppressing hunger in a resource-poor environment. Only in the mid-nineteenth century did the communal land tenure of the Inca shift to the Liberal privatization policies similar to Mexico in 1857 under Juárez and in Guatemala in 1871 under Justo Rufino Barrios.

The twentieth century saw the rise of British and later American imperialism that transformed Peru into a resource outlet for developed countries. Like other countries, Peru saw a period of military dictatorships punctuated by liberation movements during the early decades of the century. Peru also saw an attempt by the Maoist Shining Path to overthrow the then-President Alberto Fujimori. Fujimori won, only to be ousted and later imprisoned for corruption. Finally, the anti-neoliberal movement of the twenty-first century that has swept their neighbors Ecuador (under Rafael Correa) and Bolivia (under the indigenous leader Evo Morales) has not taken hold in Peru. *La lucha continua.*

Selected Films

Apu Condor (The Condor God). 1992. 28 minutes. Cambridge, MA: Documentary Educational Resources.

Aymara Leadership. 1984. 28 minutes. Hubert Smith. Cambridge, MA: Documentary Educational Resources.

The Incas. 1980. 59 minutes. Michael Ambrosino. Cambridge, MA: Documentary Educational Resources.

Weaving the Future. 1997. 24 minutes. Mark Freeman. Cambridge, MA: Documentary Educational Resources.

Selected Literature

Buechler, Hans J. and Judith Maria Buechler. 1970. *The Bolivian Aymara.* New York: Rinehart and Winston.

Davies, Nigel. 2008. *The Incas.* Boulder: University Press of Colorado.

Kolata, Alan. 1993. *The Tiwanaku; Portrait of an Andes Civilization.* New York: Wiley Blackwell.

Kolata, Alan. 1996. *Valley of the Spirits: A Journey into the Lost Realm of the Aymara.* New York: Wiley.

CHAPTER 8

Amazonia and the Orinoco Region

The Amazon and Orinoco river basins in South America were the home of hundreds of tribal societies, and remain so today. Most of the tribes live in Brazil, but many others live in the tropical rain forest areas of southern Venezuela, Colombia, Ecuador, Peru, and Bolivia. This chapter looks at a sample of South American cultures. Primary emphasis will be placed on the Yanomamö tribal societies in Venezuela, but with comparative material drawn from the Kayapó of the Xingu River in central Brazil and the Waodani of Amazonian Ecuador.

All of these cultures are located in South America, which is one of seven continents around the world. It is often confused with Central America and often lumped with Mexico, which is actually part of North America. This map shows the location of South America with portrayals of Venezuela (the Yanomamö), Brazil (Kayapó), and Ecuador (the Waodani).

Yanomamö: An Overview

The Yanomamö have been the subject of Napoleon Chagnon's *Yanomamö* (originally titled *Yanomamö: The Fierce People*) that has gone through five editions since it was first published in 1966. Most students who took cultural anthropology probably read this text, and even nonspecialists in South American ethnography know something about the Yanomamö.

Chagnon's study of the Yanomamö became the center of controversy in the 2000s when Patrick Tierney in his book *Darkness in El Dorado* accused Chagnon and his colleagues (principally James Neel) of using some Yanomamö individuals as subjects of an epidemiological experiment that led to their deaths from measles and of staging one of the filmed episodes, *The Ax Fight,* to portray the Yanomamö as an inherently violent culture. These and other accusations led the American Anthropological Association to launch an investigation in 2002. Although most of these allegations were refuted in 2005, the debate has continued to this day. A video titled *Secrets of the Tribe* reviews some of these allegations against Chagnon and other colleagues, including Jacques Lizot, against whom it was alleged he induced Yanomamö boys to engage in homosexual behavior in return for favors.

Image © Serban Bogdan, 2012. Used under license from Shutterstock, Inc.

FIGURE 8.1

Map of South America. The Yanomamö are located in southern Venezuela and northern Brazil, the Kayapó are in central Brazil at the Xingŭ River, and the Waodani are in eastern Ecuador.

This section will focus on the basic elements of Yanomamö culture and society, noting the debated topics as they occur. The questions lie principally in the issue of violent behavior and persistent warfare; such areas as tropical horticulture, cross-cousin marriage, and the *hekura* (forest spirit) beliefs have been relatively free from controversy.

Setting of the Yanomamö

The Yanomamö are located in southern Venezuela and northern Brazil along the banks of the Orinoco River, which flows through Venezuela to the Atlantic Ocean in the north (see map). The region is tropical rain forest, and like cultures everywhere, the Yanomamö rely on slash and burn cultivation, in addition to hunting and gathering.

They start the horticultural cycle first by cutting down the trees and brush at the beginning of the dry season. After allowing the slash to dry over this season, they burn it just before the rainy season begins and plant their crops, mostly cuttings for their staple manioc, along with other varieties. After two or three years, the Yanomamö abandon the site piecemeal as they clear a new site for their next harvest. Valued peach palms and plantains continue to be exploited at the old site until the forest reclaims it. Meggers cites the horticultural practices of five other tropical rain forest peoples in the Amazon basin and describes the natural forest cycles to which such cultures adapt (1996).

Yanomamö live in a village complex called *shabonos,* or palisades comprising thatch housing surrounding an open plaza. Oval in shape, the *shabonos* are structures that are sectioned off into living spaces for each family household. Housing is thatch and has to be replaced every two years because of the heavy rainfall (Figure 8.3).

Image © AridOcean, 2012. Used under license from Shutterstock, Inc.

FIGURE 8.2
Southern Venezuela and northern Brazil, the home of the Yanomamö.

Image © Alexander Bark, 2012. Used under license from Shutterstock, Inc.

FIGURE 8.3
Interior of a *shabono*. Note thatch and poles used as roofing and walls.

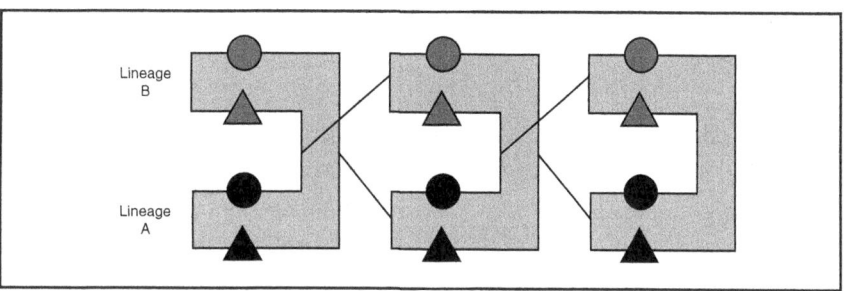

FIGURE 8.4
Bilateral Cross-Cousin Marriage. Notice how the married cousins come from outside their own lineage.

Households are patrilocal in basic organization. When a young man marries, he performs labor for his bride's family to prove his worth as a provider of game and other wild and cultivated foods. After a year or so, he is then free to bring his wife to his own dwelling. Polygyny, or marriage of a man to two or more women, is the ideal norm which varies in actual practice. Female infanticide is practiced, leading to a female underpopulation. For that reason, one common cause of war is the abduction of women from neighboring villages.

Yanomamö reckon their kin affiliation, or through the male line (see Chapter 2 under kinship). As you can see from Figure 8.4, a man often marries his cross-cousin related to him through either his mother's brother or his father's sister or, preferably, both.

As you can see, the cousins who marry belong to separate lineages, so in effect, the marriage is not incestuous by definition of the Yanomamö themselves. (Biologically, of course, inbreeding takes place, showing how culture often trumps biology). This explains why Yanomamö, like other tribal peoples of Amazonia and the Orinoco basin, are organized into two lineages called moieties. The Kayapó, for example, are similarly organized into dual lineages, separated by the lower and upper plaza of their villages.

The Yanomamö and other tribal societies in Amazonia and the Orinoco basin also organize themselves into patrilineages. Groups are organized by the principle of patrilineal descent as described in Chapter 2. Because they practice bilateral cross-cousin marriage, every village will ideally be organized into two lineages: one's own and one from which one will obtain his/her wife or husband. That is why they are organized into moieties. They are two intermarrying lineages. That means that when a village splits into two, each of the new villages will always have two inter-marrying lineages. If you think all this is complicated, it's perfectly natural to the Yanomamö. Does that make them geniuses? No. It only means they've grown up with their arrangement all their lives.

That marriage arrangement explains their cousin terminology. To us, we have only one term for all Ego's cousins on this chart. You guessed it: cousin. The Yanomamö use the same term as brother and sister to apply to their parallel cousins: mother's sister's daughter (or son) and father's brother's daughter (or son). But a different term is applied to the cross-cousins: suaböya for mother's brother's or father's sister's daughter, and shoriwä for mother's brother's and father's sister's son. As in-laws, female cross-cousins can marry Ego, and in fact suaböya also means "wife."

Politics and Warfare

Historical buffs may remember von Clausewitz's definition of war: politics by other means. The Yanomamö are a tribal society; in this instance they have two segments in a village and this segment has a cross-cutting institution—marriage. Every village is autonomous and linked together by weak alliances, if they are linked at all. If we take Chagnon at his word (and many anthropologists would not; see Good, Lizot, Tierney 2000), the village is led by a headman who has limited control over that village. As one headman known as Kaobawä notes, he gives orders only if followers will obey him, such as occurs in the midst of a raid or battle (Chagnon 1992). Unlike heads of states, the headman has no policing power, no army, and no way to control his followers through the use of institutionalized violence.

According to Chagnon, the Yanomamö value the quality of fierceness in their society. They have a name for it: *waiteri*. Warfare is frequent, and the issue, according to Chagnon, is abduction of women from other villages. Yet even they see the value of preventing war, and to do so, they first trade with each other, as a way of extending peace feelers. They then hold feasts. This is risky, because the hosts could massacre the guests at any time, and the guests could massacre the hosts. So when things get out of hand, they have a device to defuse tensions.

They start with chest pounding duels. One man lands a fist on the chest of the other; that man then hits his opponent with his fist. If things don't calm down, they continue by slapping the sides of their opponent with the shafts of their spears. The next level of violent escalation is the club fights. Only then do the arrows start to fly. At every stage, they try to defuse the tension. Still, tension is always present.

They do form alliances, however, and trade is the first step, then the feasts, and finally marriage alliances with another village. This is very risky because the woman does not have the protection of her brothers who live on the opposite side of the plaza. Marcel Mauss came up with a book, *The Gift*, which argued that gift exchange was what kept stateless societies from each other's throats. The obligation to give, to receive, and to repay involves not just the items given, but the relations they establish.

Animism and Shamanism

The Yanomamö also co-exist with a world populated by spirits they call *hekura*. They reach the world through the use of a hallucinogen called *ebene*. One man blows the substance into the nostrils of his partner. In the video *How Cultures are Studied*, Dedeheiwa trains Chagnon in the arts of attracting *hekura*. Often, *hekura* spirits are sent to bring sickness or death to one's rival.

The Yanomamö have their own conception of the cosmos, existing at four levels. Earth is the second plane from the highest. The highest plane is devoid of life. The third plane is where the dead go and the lowest plane is their Hell. That is where the stingy go for their tightfistedness.

A Synoptic Comparison

This presentation has set the stage for comparison. This section provides the leading videos on Yanomamö, Kayapó, and Waodani as representative rain forest tribes. Many of these videos can be accessed on YouTube. Classics on the Yanomamö include *The Ax Fight* and *The Kayapó*. In The *Kayapó*, two tribes called the Gorotire and the Kapot deal with another gold mining invasion in different ways, and in a later film they face the prospect of displacement through flooding by a five-dam project. The feature length film *The End of the Spear* depicts a Waodani killing of four missionaries and the reconciliation that follows.

All three cultures have faced pressures for acculturation. The Yanomamö have been subjected to a series of invasions from Brazilian gold prospectors, known as *garimpeiros*, beginning in 1987. Though many operations were based in northern Brazil, some entered into Venezuela as well. More than 40,000 miners were in Yanomamö region by the end of the year. Clashes between miners and Yanomamö soon followed, with four killed in one village. Almost overnight 100 airstrips in Yanomamö territory in Brazil and Venezuela were laid out to set up mining operations. *The garampeiros* not only destroyed Yanomamö territory on both sides of the border, but spread measles and other diseases, wiping out much of the indigenous population that lacked immunity to these epidemics. Although Venezuela cleared airstrips on their own to establish security in its part of Yanomamö territory and newly elected Brazilian President Ferdinand Collor de Mello moved to scale back the mining operations in Brazil, operations resumed later that year. Most of the 14 airstrips that had been dismantled by order of Collor were back in operation because his military officers and other officials countermanded the closure. By 1991, illegal miners were again flocking to the operations. Other developments included the continued spread of the epidemics and expansion of control of the Salesian missions over Yanomamö villages in Venezuela. Adverse publicity of these and other developments forced both the Brazilian and Venezuela governments to adopt policies ameliorating the conditions of Yanomamö in both countries. Chagnon describes these issues in his most recent monograph titled *Yanomamö* (2012).

Similar developments beset the Kayapó populations in the Xingu River region of northeastern Brazil. First, two subtribes, Gorotire and the Kapot adopted different strategies to handle the incursion of a gold mining company. The Gorotire opted to negotiate terms of the mining operations with the company; the Kapot refused to have anything to do with the company or its propositions. Results have been mixed for both strategies. Second, the Kayapó as a whole have been threatened by the construction of a five-dam project by the Belo Monte Corporations, which would flood out most of the population of the Xingu region. So far, the suits and countersuits over the past 30 years have led to projects start-ups subsequently halted. In the most recent development, unidentified natives blasted open a channel to one of the nearly completed dams, allowing the water to flow again into the lower Xingu. The efforts continue (Rabban 2005).

A third culture has been far more resistant than either the Yanomamö or the Kayapó. The Waodani were fiercely independent warriors, resisting not only Americans and Spanish Ecuadorans but also other tribes. The film *End of the Spear* describes the murder of four American missionaries and the reconciliation between the Waodani murderer and the family of Nick Saint, one of the four victims. Though the film and the book on which it is based, *Jungle Pilot,* take a Christian perspective of the incident, the changes are described in terms of an ideological perspective other than Marxist or academic liberal. One may reasonably argue that an intersubjective approach is the most likely way toward an accurate ethnography.

Finally, there is a film that reinforces the cannibalistic stereotype of Amazonian peoples: *How Tasty Was My Little Frenchman.* Set in the seventeenth century, a Tupinamba tribe captures a French explorer and, after keeping him prisoner for a few years, and even allowing intimacy and marriage with one of the Tupinamba women, cooks and eats him. Just before he is slaughtered and butchered for the feast, the Frenchman issues a prophecy—that others will conquer and colonize the tribe. The twenty-first century has verified this prophecy for all of Amazonia.

Conclusion

One theme that dominates the literature on the Amazonian peoples is the ecological adaptation of horticulturalists and hunters and gatherers in a tropical rain forest that, despite their diversity, has lasted for unknown generations of their existence. The search for gold, the damming of a major region, the wanton massacre of the Yanomamö or anyone who stands in the way of "progress" have damaged, if not destroyed, this balance between humankind and nature.

Selected Films

The Ax Fight. 1975. 30 minutes. Cambridge: Documentary Educational Resources.

The End of the Spear. 2008. 102 minutes Jungle Films.

Feast. 1970. Chagnon, Napoleon. 28 minutes. Cambridge, MA: Documentary Educational Resources.

How Tasty Was My Little Frenchman (*Como Era Gostoso o Meu Frances.*) 1971. 84 minutes. Condor Filmes (Portuguese with English subtitles).

The Kayapó. 1987. 51 minutes. Cambridge, MA. Documentary Educational Resources.

Secrets of the Tribe. 2010. 98 minutes. Cambridge, MA: Documentary Educational Resources.

Selected Literature

Borofsky, Robert. 2005. *Yanomami: The Fierce Controversy and What We Can Learn From It.* Berkeley: University of California Press.

Chagnon, Napoleon. 2011. *Yanomamö.* 6th ed. Belmont, CA: Wadsworth.

Fabben, Linda. 2004. *Brazil's Indians and the Onslaught of Civilization: The Yanomami and the Kayapó.* Seattle: University of Washington Press.

Hitt, Russell. 1997. *Jungle Pilot.* Grand Rapids, MI. Discovery House.

Meggers, Betty. 1996. *Amazonia: Man and Culture in a Counterfeit Paradise.* Washington, DC: Smithsonian.

Tierney, Patrick. 2000. *Darkness in El Dorado.* New York: Norton.

PART III

Middle East

CHAPTER 9

Egypt: Kingdom to Nation-State Along the Nile

Introduction

Egypt is the longest lasting empire in history with continuity to a nation-state. This module looks into the reasons why.

Whatever opinion historians and archaeologists may hold about Egypt, they agree on one thing: it lasted a very long time. After Narmer (or Menes) led his armies to unify two parts of Egypt—Lower and Upper—the empire lasted at least 2500 years. This was interrupted by a

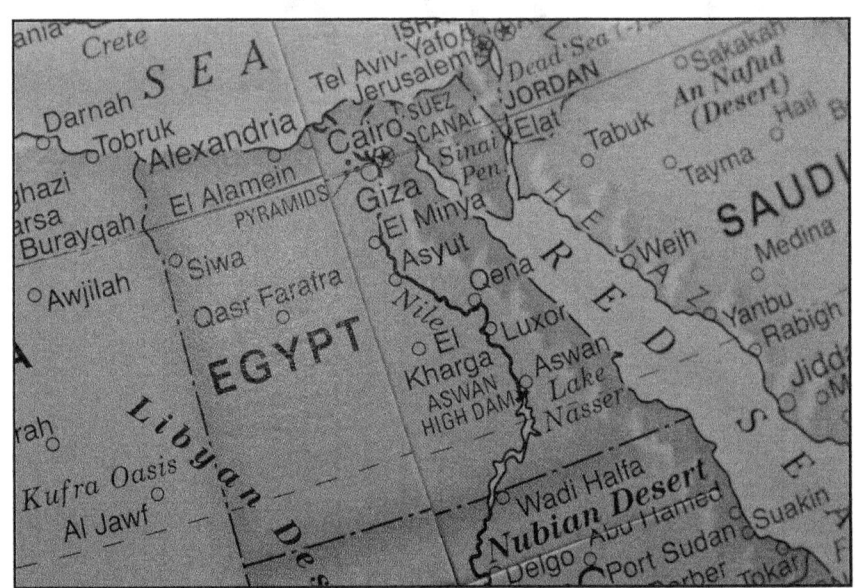

Image © Condor 36, 2012. Used under license from Shutterstock, Inc.

FIGURE 9.1
Egypt, showing the Nile and some of the ancient sites.

200-year period of regionalism, from 2200 BCE to 2000 BCE. BCE means Before Common Era. Though it means the same thing as BC, or Before Christ, BCE takes a neutral perspective in terms of religion. CE means Common Era, and is the same as AD, or Anno Domini, or "The Year of Our Lord."

Egypt: A Geography

Egypt is 800 miles long and averages about six miles wide along the banks of the Nile River. Lower Egypt means "Lower End of the Nile River" and refers to the delta, when the Nile breaks into several rivers toward the Mediterranean Sea. Upper Egypt comprises the upper part of the Nile River, which goes on to the Sudan. The river floods—very predictably—the banks every spring as the result of the rains further south in Africa. The desert on either side of the river contributed to its isolation from the rest of the world—and thereby its political and social stability, simply because it was hard for outsiders to invade Egypt.

The flooding and the isolation of the Nile rendered Egypt a self-sufficient entity. The regular flooding added silt to the land every year, ensuring the fields would always be fertile; the agriculture was of the flood plain type from the beginning. Not only that, but Egypt was rich in natural resources. It had ample limestone for construction, more than enough flint and other crystalline rock to make stone tools from, and large deposits of gold and precious stones for ornamentation. Because there were no invasions in Egypt's early years, almost the entire population was ethnically the same.

Egyptian Neolithic

The Neolithic, or "New Stone Age," is defined as the invention of agriculture, in which both plants and animals are domesticated. The early plants were special kinds of grass, namely wheat and barley. Flax was used for fiber in weaving. The earliest animals to be domesticated, or tamed, were typical Near Eastern animals: sheep, goats, cattle, and pigs. Merimbe, formed in 4900 BCE near the Nile delta, consisted of subterranean oval houses with roofs made of sticks and mud. Grains were stored in ceramic jars, pits, and baskets. There was a threshing floor lined with clay. Badari was the site of burial customs that would characterize burial customs of later times. Bodies were buried with grave goods, such as ivory spoons and vases. Apparently the message that you can't take it with you was not taken seriously.

Egypt has always been a society marked by two features: social stratification and death, or more accurately, the afterlife. Nagada (also spelled Naqada) was a case in point. Not only did sumptuous burials indicate high social status of the dearly departed, but large stretches of land appear to have been controlled by this city by 3500 BCE (5500 BP or Before Present in archaeological jargon). Nehken (which the Greeks called Hicrakonopolis) developed a distinct pottery design that was found throughout Egypt. More important was the colony of tombs, earning it the reputation of a necropolis, or city of the dead. Both cities were precursors of the Egyptian society that would emerge.

Egypt Under the Pharaohs

The gods that eventually emerged were associated with nature, particularly the sun, and with specialties of culture and society. The principal god was Amon, also known as Re, Ra, and Aten. He is portrayed as the sun's rays or a solar disk. Sometimes the scarab, a type of beetle, represents him because, like the sun, the scarab emerges in the morning. Aten is often portrayed separately, as the sun's disk, and in later years, he was the only god worshipped; this was the first hints of monotheism, or worship of one god only. There was Anubis, the jackal-headed god of embalmers and cemeteries, reflecting the importance of death and mortuary preparation for the afterlife. Hathor was the mother, wife, and daughter of Ra, the sun god.

Other principal gods included Osiris, the god of the underworld and his wife, Isis, who is the goddess of fertility. According to myth, Set or Seth, the god of storms and violence, murders Osiris; Isis brings him back to life but he must rule the underworld for all eternity. Horus is the son of Isis and Osiris. He is the source of royal power of the pharaohs, the monarch of Egypt.

There were other gods. The falcon-headed Thoth was the god of the scribes, lord of language, and inventor of writing. Because the hieroglyphic style of writing is difficult to learn, it took specialists to learn the script, and so they were ranked third in the hierarchy, after the pharaoh himself and the nobles. Ma'at (below), pronounced with a glottal stop between the two vowels of {a}, was the goddess of truth and universal order. She was the wife of Thoth. Hearts of the dead were weighed with an ostrich feather that you see on top of her head (lower right). Phat was the creator of humankind and the patron of craftspersons. Bes was the helper of women in childbirth and the protector against snakes. Venomous snakes such as the cobra and the asp were commonplace in Egypt.

Image © Kharidehal Abhirama Ashwin, 2012. Used under license from Shutterstock, Inc.

FIGURE 9.2

Ma'at, the winged goddess of justice, with Isis, Osiris, and Queen Nefertiti. Note the ostrich feather atop Ma'at's head. Ostrich feathers often were affixed to legal documents.

Given the role of gods in the intervention into human affairs and Egyptians' obsession with the afterlife, it is unsurprising that Egypt became a theocracy from early on. The monarchs, known as pharaohs, were the representatives of the Sun God. The term *pharaoh* originally meant a place, a "Great House," but eventually came to mean the monarch. In many conceptions, the pharaoh was a god himself; at least, the will of the Sun God flowed through him. The symbol of power is the Sphinx, which guards the entrance to the pyramids of Gizeh (Giza). The Sphinx is represented by the head of Khafre, Khufu's son and successor, and the body of a lion. Power is well represented by the symbol; political power of the pharaoh and of the king of beasts.

The cult of the dead occupied much of the Egyptians' time, especially when a pharaoh died. His body was carefully prepared for entombment in the pyramid. In most pictures, one sees the jackal-headed mortuary god Anubis preparing the body of a pharaoh. He will later be placed in the center of the pyramid, the queen placed in her chamber below him. Pyramids were built during flooding season, when farmers were idled and could not work the fields.

The *Egyptian Book of the Dead* prepares the soul for judgment as a condition for entering the afterlife. In one scene, a man and his wife enter the room of judgment. The jackal-headed god Anubis weighs the heart (considered to be the seat of a person's emotions, intellect, and character) against the feather of Ma'at, the goddess of universal order. If the heart is heavier than the feather, the defendant is condemned to nonexistence and is consumed by the animal usually depicted to the right of a typical picture, which is part crocodile, part lion, and part hippopotamus.

Discussion now shifts to the development of the empire from two countries prior to 3100 BCE (5100 BP) into one. The two countries were Lower Egypt, named for the lower reaches of the Nile River at the delta, and Upper Egypt, the part of Egypt south of the delta. Memphis was the border city between the two Egypts. Upper Egypt stretched from Memphis to Nubia, a separate kingdom in present-day Sudan and Ethiopia.

Forces from Upper Egypt led by Narmer (also known as Menes) conquered Lower Egypt and unified the countries under one crown. In recognition of the importance of Lower Egypt, Narmer combined the conical white crown of Upper Egypt with the boxy red crown of Lower Egypt to fashion a double crown.

The symbol of unification is reflected in a double engraved palette discovered at Hierako-nopolis, which for legal reasons has to be described without the illustration. On the obverse side, Narmer (wearing his white crown) subdues the captive, who is held by Horus, the falcon, by a feather. To the right, papyrus blossoms symbolize Lower Egypt. Defeated warriors are seen at the bottom. On the reverse side of the palette, two long-necked lions symbolize the integration of the two powers. Defeated decapitated warriors are stacked in the panel above the lions, along with Narmer himself. A bull at the bottom symbolizes royal power.

Once united, Egypt went through a series of phases, which we now discuss. Including Narmer/Menes, there were 33 dynasties of the pharaohs. The Archaic period (3100 BCE) begins with the consolidation of Upper and Lower Egypt into a single state. The Old Kingdom then emerges in 2920 BCE and lasts until 2134 BCE, when regional feudalities emerge. The era is marked by the construction of the largest pyramids in Egyptian history under highly despotic pharaohs. The Sphinx is depicted in Figure 9.4 with the Pyramid of Khafre in the background. This is the era that the governmental and economic institutions of the pharaohs are established, writing is invented and developed, and the artistic traditions are established.

The Archaic Period might be defined as the formative after Narmer's rule. Horus Aha, the first known pharaoh after Narmer, continues consolidating the empire. The myth of pharaohs as divine kings spreads, to the point that the purity of the lineage must be preserved through royal incest, that is, brother-sister marriage. He establishes centralized authority over labor, granaries, and taxation. Under his rule and that of his successors, large-scale temples, palaces, and pyramids are constructed. One key development is the introduction and development of hieroglyphic writing.

Hieroglyphic writing was invented, in part, to exercise control over the population. This is a writing system in which pictorial symbols serve to convey particular sounds, objects, and/or meaning. The writing system was so complex that only trained scribes could create and interpret them. Thus, they held enormous power, ranked third after the pharaoh himself and the nobility.

Image © Nicole Gordine, 2012. Used under license from Shutterstock, Inc.

FIGURE 9.3
Egyptian alphabet, which can be both pictographic and phonetic.

Initially, they were used as accounting devices, indicated by small bones and ivory tags attached to containers of linen and oil. Discovered by Gunter Dryer, the tags were found in Abydos, 250 miles south of Cairo, and dated 5200 BP (7200 BCE).

Notice from this chart that each hieroglyph stands for a sound. One symbol, however, could represent two sounds. For example, a basket could represent a "c" but also a "k". Even though it could represent speech sounds, glyphs could also represent objects, such as the symbols for man and woman (not depicted here). Thus, it was not a purely phonetic alphabet, but it was not entirely one in which pictures represent whole words.

The Old Kingdom continued with the consolidation of central power. One good way to establish centrality was to build pyramids. Zoser (Djoser) began the tradition with a stepped pyramid, the only one built in stages. The others for Khufu (Cheops), Khafre (Chephren), and Menkaure (Mycernius) were built in a single stage and were smooth-sided rather than stepped—they were never meant for climbing. In Khufu's pyramid, one can still see the relatively smooth top part.

The primary function of the pyramid was to inspire awe among all the subject population. Because it was constructed during the flood season, the peasants were recruited to construct the pyramid. By feeding the workers during this season, the pharaoh and his retainers reinforced his power even further. It involved careful planning and massive labor. The design added an aura of mystery to the pyramids. They were solely the house of the deceased pharaoh and his wife in their journey to eternity. That explains the centralized position of the pharaoh's chamber accessible only by complex passageways and with fake ones to deceive any intruder.

The pyramids played but one art in establishing the institutional power of the pharaohs. They played on the beliefs that they were divine and had such power that they could control the flow

Image © michelepautasso, 2012. Used under license from Shutterstock, Inc.

FIGURE 9.4
The Pyramid of Khafre, the second pyramid built at Gizeh, guarded by the Sphinx thought to be a likeness of Khafre, the successor to Khufu or Cheops.

of the Nile, the rise and setting of the sun, and other natural forces. They were the top of a complex bureaucracy and were the lawgivers themselves. Codified law, systematized in Mesopotamia, would come later. Even in death, the pharaoh was said to be dwelling in the pyramid; his double had moved on to the other worlds.

By 2134, the Old Kingdom was in disarray. The economy simply could no longer sustain the costs of building the pyramids, and even the second and third pyramids at Gizeh were progressively smaller than that of Khufu's, the first pyramid. Then a drought occurred, which belied the Pharaoh's ability to control natural forces such as the rising and receding of the Nile. Provincial nobles arose in power and had pyramids built in their own right. As the central power waned further, warfare broke out in competition for political supremacy.

As the disunity itself became problematical, pharaohs began to be more modest in their ambitions. No longer could they claim absolute divinity, and focus shifted to lesser degrees of despotism and a greater efficiency of public services. Irrigation canals were expanded, granaries were increased in size (now that drought was an easily remembered reality), and external trade was fostered. Seafaring technology improved, emphasizing the need for secure borders. Nevertheless, leadership still relied on personal attributes. Amun was a typical pharaoh in the Middle Kingdom (2040–1640 BCE), and the capital was moved to Thebes.

By 1640 BCE, Egypt was no longer so isolated as it once was, and the invasion of Asians (known as the Hyksos) invaded Lower Egypt, forcing a division between the Hyksos-dominated Lower Egypt and an Upper Egypt under the domination of the traditional Pharaohs. Ironically, it was the very same foreigners that introduced the technology that the Egyptians would be forced to adopt: bronze, whose tin strengthened copper tools, horse-driven chariots, and new weaponry. It would also set the stage for a new type of pharaoh—the military hero.

King Ahmose arose to power and expelled the Hyksos from Memphis and then from the eastern part of the delta, driving them back to Palestine and destroying their stronghold. After putting down an uprising in Upper Egypt, he invaded Nubia and eventually consolidated the borders north and south. Ahhotep, his queen mother, maintained the peace in Thebes and later, the whole of Lower Egypt.

After Ahmose, the New Kingdom was established. Amun (Ra) again was worshipped as the Sun God. A new area arose on the west bank of the Nile, and a temple was built at Karnak. The dynasty included Akhenaten called the "heretic," who worshipped Aten, the god of the solar disk, as the sole god. Though it did not survive his death, the cult set a precedent for monotheism that would dominate Western religion. Tutankhamun, the "boy king" was not as famous as the ruler of Egypt as his face mask. He died after 10 years. The shaduf was invented, a lever and bucket that transferred the Nile water to higher ground, thus minimizing peasant dependence on flood-plain agriculture.

The terminal period saw the decline of the Pharaohs, despite the adventurist policies of Ramses II. Persians invaded Egypt in 525 BCE, were expelled once in 404 BCE, and returned in 343 BCE. Alexander the Great expelled the Persians in 322 and become an occupier himself. Then, in 30 BCE, the Romans came to stay.

Formation of Egypt after the Pharaohs

By the Late Period (1070–30 BCE) Egypt went into steep decline. Ramses II attempted to expand Egypt's territory, but was turned back at Syria, beginning a series of military disasters. The Nubians invaded the south in the eighth century BCE; Assyrians and Persians also invaded. Finally Alexander the Great annexed Egypt to the Hellenistic empire in 332 BCE, and established the Ptolemaic dynasties from its new capital at Alexandria. The Romans conquered Egypt in 30 BCE. Later, in 639, Egypt fell under Islamic rule with a succession of dynasties that included the Ottomans and the Arabs. Islam has remained, and the ascension of the Muslim Brotherhood to power in the person of Muhammad Mursi may create a new principle of democracy free from dictatorial rule whose precedents date back five thousand years.

Egypt has a long heritage that began with the pharaohs. Much of their art, their architecture, and even their personal habits reflect this heritage. The Coptic Church, though Christian, is distinctly Egyptian. The Holy See of the church is in Alexandria and is said to have been founded by St. Mark the Apostle.

Conclusion

Egypt has a long history, and the pharaohs occupy the longest part of that history. The government was personalistic rather than institutional, and it was supported by the supposed divine power from the founder Narmer, or Menes to the Middle Kingdom, after a drought brought to question the pharaoh's ability to control natural events, namely the pattern of flooding and receding of the Nile. Along with Mesopotamia, Egypt was one of the earliest monarchies in the civilized world.

With the overthrow of a contemporary leader, a military dictator named Hosni Mubarak, Egypt may be setting a new precedent, a state that may well prove democratic in the true sense of the word. His expulsion of the military council may indicate a new trend in the form of governance, not only in Egypt but in other countries, such as Tunisia (which set the tone) and Libya. Will the Arab Spring set this pattern? Events in the next several years will tell.

Selected Films

Egypt: The Habit of Civilization. 1991. 60 minutes. Michael Wood. New York: Ambrose Video Publishing.

El Moulid: Egyptian Religious Festival. 1990. 38 minutes. Fadwa El Guindi. Cambridge, MA. Documentary Educational Resources.

Houses of Eternity. 1980. 30 minutes. Washington, DC: National Geographic.

Young Arabs. 2008. 25 minutes. Michael Grazian and E. Joong-eun Park. Cambridge, MA. Documentary Educational Resources. Muslim and Christian boys grow up in a Jesuit school in Cairo.

Selected Literature

Cook, Steven. 2011. *The Struggle for Egypt: From Nasser to Tahrir Square.* New York: Council on Foreign Relations.

Osman, Tarek. 2010. *Egypt on the Brink: From Nasser to Mubarak.* New Haven, CT: Yale University Press.

Shaw, Ian. 2004. *The Oxford History of Ancient Egypt.* Oxford, UK: Oxford University Press.

CHAPTER 10

Mesopotamia to Iraq: Cradle to Grave of Western Culture?

Introduction

Iraq makes every day's headlines—but did you know that the country was where Western civilization got its start? Read on.

Mesopotamia/Iraq

Mesopotamia comes from the Greek meaning "Between Two Rivers." The two rivers are the Tigris and the Euphrates; the Tigris passes through Baghdad. States came and went: first Sumeria, then the Semites with their Babylon, then Assur (Assyria) with its Nineveh.

Iraq, formerly Mesopotamia, is bounded to the southeast by Saudi Arabia and Jordan, to the northeast by Syria and Turkey, and to the east by Iran. To the southeast lies Kuwait, which was invaded by Iraq in 1990 over a dispute of an oil deposit that lay near the borders of the two countries.

Mesopotamia in the Neolithic

Mesopotamia is part of the Fertile Crescent, the earliest known region where agriculture got its start. The crescent begins at the Levant (today's Israel and Lebanon), then curves upward into the Taurus Mountains of southern Turkey and Syria, then southward into Iraq and the Zagros mountains of Iran. The Neolithic, or New Stone Age, which defines the domestication of plants and animals, begins at roughly 10,000 BP (Before the Present in archaeological parlance) or 8,000 BCE (Before Common Era, a religious neutral expression that is identical to BC, or Before Christ).

The most common grass that eventually became grain was wheat, which was of two initial varieties, the einkorn and the more productive emmer wheat. The spike (ear) of wheat includes a rachis (part attaching the grain to the stalk) and protective glume (part covering the wheat grain). In the wild, the rachis was brittle, ideal for propagation with the wind, and the glume was

Image © pavalena, 2012. Used under license from Shutterstock, Inc.

FIGURE 10.1
Iraq and its neighbors. Note the two rivers, the Tigris and Euphrates, which gave the earlier Mesopotamia its name.

tough, to protect the seed until it germinates. But humans don't want the seed to fly all over the place with high winds, and they do want easy access to the grains; therefore, they bred wheat with a tough rachis and a brittle glume. Bigger grains didn't hurt either.

Although wheat was the mainstay of the Near East, other plants were important. They included barley rye, and legumes, such as peas, beans, and lentils. All of these, too, were cultivated and bred for size. Flax, used for fiber, was also domesticated in the Near East. As you can surmise, the long leaves were stripped and teased for fibers, which were then made into thread.

Animals were also bred for desirable features from the human standpoint: more meat, more milk, and more wool. Sometimes they were bred for temperament. The wild boar was not an animal you would want to tangle with; domesticated pigs are more amiable. Another example is a wild black sheep of Inner Mongolia; not only is it noted for a relative lack of wool compared with the white domesticated ones, its meat is stringier and lower in yield.

A classic site among many Neolithic sites is Abu Hureya, located in the Euphrates Valley in Syria. In a study of animal bones, the count of gazelles was high relative to sheep prior to 6500 BCE. Starting in 6500 BCE, the count of sheep bones relative to wild gazelles increased dramatically, and by 6000 BCE, the percentage of sheep bones was around 80% compared to gazelles. Similar patterns were shown for cattle and pig bones, and the amount of plant material remains for grain and legumes likewise increased.

Abu Hureya also showed other signs of settlement. Clay containers were recovered, although none of it was fired pottery. Trade was also evident: cowrie shells from the Mediterranean, turquoise artifacts from Sinai, obsidian and other crystalline stone from Turkey. The site was abandoned in 6000 BCE; drought was the most likely factor. It is possible that some of the inhabitants took up herding animals and migrated to the Zagros Mountains in Iran; the farmers possibly migrated to the upper part of the Tigris and Euphrates rivers.

Mesopotamia: The First Civilizations

The first villages of Mesopotamia were found in the upper regions of the Tigris and Euphrates River around 6000 BCE, but the villagers were soon attracted to the greater rainfall of the southern reaches of the two rivers. Even so, rain varied from year to year, with barely a trickle one year and a season of flooding the next. Flood plain agriculture was practiced in the north, but problematical because of the unpredictable rain patterns. The structures consisted of several houses in the village, with roof entrances.

The first period was the Ubaid era, which saw the spread of irrigation canals, construction of temples, and a distinct monochromatic pottery design with triangles, grids, and zigzag lines. They were made on a potter's wheel, which later gave rise to the wheel as a mode of transport. Mesopotamia lacked crystalline stone such as flint or obsidian, and so the earliest tools, namely sickles, hammers, axes, and mullers were made of fired clay. They were not very sturdy.

Eridu was one of the earliest villages that developed into a shrine. Almost all structures were residential at the beginning. Shrines and ritual centers were erected, and they were built piece-by-piece. They started with the smallest shrine, constructed in 5000 BCE. Eventually the shrines evolved into a full-sized structure called a ziggurat, a combined ritual and administrative center that was constructed in 3000 BCE.

Eridu showed little sign of the extreme social stratification that was to come. We find no elaborate tombs, no sumptuous grave goods, and no slaves or retainers interred with the deceased. If anything, southern Mesopotamia lacked any central city. Only later would centers emerge, and even then, they were city-states competing for dominance. None ever achieved that dominance for long.

Uruk was the first city of any size, reaching a population of 10,000. The city itself was overshadowed by the Anu temple (named after Anu, the principal god of the Sumerian pantheon). As Eridu's ziggurat had been, the temple was constructed over earlier shrines. Indeed, the White Temple was constructed over the Anu temple. Both temples were constructed by massive labor: 7500 man-years each. Elitism was all too evident; the structures separated the priests from the commoners.

Changes in style marked the Uruk period. On the one hand, pottery design shifted from the decorative to the merely utilitarian. On the other hand, the agricultural base diversified. Plows with wooden shares with metal tips came into widespread use. They were more efficient than digging sticks, even though the metal for tips had to be imported. Wheat, barley, flax, and dates were among the products grown, and cattle and fishing also contributed to the rural economy.

Because Sumeria was resource poor, it relied on trade to obtain necessities and luxury goods. The main trade routes connected Uruk to southern Turkey and Persia (Iran). Precious metals such as gold, silver, and semiprecious stones came from the Persian Gulf. Textiles, skins, ivory, and timber also came from Persia. On the other hand, timber came from the northern regions of southern Anatolia (Turkey). Seals, distinctive of the Indus River Valley, were also found, indicating that products were exported from regions as far as Southern Asia.

Cuneiform Writing

Because of the extensive trade networks, accounting systems arose out of necessity to keep track of the goods exchanged. Thus, cuneiform writing—writing on clay tablets with wedge-shaped implements—first arose from forms used to indicate products. Denise Schmandt-Besserat, in her book *Before Writing: From Counting to Cuneiform* describes a five-step process in the evolution of cuneiform writing. First, accounting systems began with 16 basic shapes, such as geometric or animal. By 6000 BP, there were 300 forms with varied markings (one pair of markings distinguished raw from finished materials).

By 5500 BP, tokens indicating the accompanying products were encased in bullae, or clay envelopes, presumably for security reasons—you could not deceive your customer or tax collector by changing the tokens. The bullae and tokens of one type indicated oil. By 5200 BP, however, flattened tokens replaced the bullae, which were eliminated altogether. By 5100 BP, this information was now entered onto clay tablets with cuneiform writing. This tablet (lower left hand corner) indicated the number of sheep and goats owned by the party in question.

From that point on, cuneiform writing underwent refinements. From the early texts that contained 1500 symbols, the number went down to 750. A system that had a one-to-one representation of a commodity could now categorize products into classes of goods. Nevertheless, the system

Image © Fedor Selivanov, 2012. Used under license from Shutterstock, Inc.

FIGURE 10.2
Cuneiform Script. Note the wedged-shape of the markings. Clay, which was plentiful along the two rivers, was commonly used. About 1500 symbols were initially used, later pared down to 750.

was still cumbersome. It lacked the advantages of an alphabet that can represent anything the writer or accountant wants.

Mesopotamian Sociopolitical Organization

From that point on, the trends begun in Eridu and Uruk intensified in the Early Dynastic Period (3100–2370 BCE). The populations of Uruk itself increased to 50,000 inhabitants and, reflecting the increased militarism of Sumerian society, defensive walls were constructed. City-states rose and fell. The city of Ur, only 75 miles away, became Uruk's main economic and military rival, and power shifted back and forth between these two cities. Other cities also competed for power. As trade increased and products became more valuable, highwaymen raided the caravans. (For a contrasting case study in which walls apparently were not defensive, see the section on the Indus River Valley or Harappan Civilization in the chapter on India.)

The extreme stratification was reflected in the burials. Sir Leonard Woolley, specialist of Near Eastern city-states, unearthed 250 burials. One extreme case concerns Queen Shub-ad. She was laid on a bed accompanied by female attendants. Two wagons bearing the bed and grave goods were backed down into the entry ramp. They were drawn by oxen driven by male servants. The retainers of the queen were bedecked in finery and finely crafted ornaments. The oxen were killed, all the retainers consumed poison, and the tomb sealed. By contrast, the remaining grave had few grave goods or, in most instances, none at all.

Mesopotamia also developed a legal system, given trade and extreme social stratification. Hammurabi, the first king of Babylon, a Semitic city-state, created the first legal code. As a priest-king, he held all of Mesopotamia for a time, but his successors were unable to maintain it. The code sets forth standards for resolving commercial disputes and guidelines for personal conduct. It also sets forth crimes and their punishment. For example, a woman of god could be burned at the stake for entering a wine shop. A man who stole a draft animal would be forced to compensate his victim 10-fold if the victim was a commoner, and 100-fold if he was a noble. If he could not pay, he would be put to death.

Cosmology of Mesopotamia

The cosmology of Mesopotamia is a system dominated by gods with human personalities and with various specialties. Sometimes, the deities can have contradictory functions. Ishtar (or Inanna) is the goddess of erotic love but also the goddess of war. The commonalities are that they are larger than life, to the point of abstraction. Priest-kings were not infused with divinity like the Egyptian pharaohs, but were their agents. Gradually, the kings became secularized.

The chief God was Anu but not without predecessors of gods who were also the head gods. The large hypnotic eyes in one depiction gave him, along with the rest of the pantheon, an eerie quality. Adad was the rain god and of storms; he reminds one of the Egyptian god Seth, also of rain and storms, as well as discord. Dumuzi was the god of vegetation and the underworld; he was also the husband of Ishtar. Ishtar, or Inanna, was the goddess of erotic love and patron of the temple whores. She was also the goddess of fertility, so giving her an affinity to her husband. But she was also the goddess of war, the nemesis of the epic hero Gilgamesh.

Image © Morphart Creations inc., 2012. Used under license from Shutterstock, Inc.

FIGURE 10.3

Inanna or Ishtar, also known as Astarte. Here, standing on a lion, she exudes divine power. Another representation has her connecting the heavens with the nether world. She holds a ring of power.

Represented here is Astarte, also known as Inanna and Ishtar. Perched atop a lion, she is characterized as a goddess of considerable power. Another common representation of Inanna often has her standing nude, perched on two lions representing power and flanked by two owls, representing wisdom. She wears a crown and holds two rods and rings, all representing power derived from heaven. Yet her feet are the talons of a predatory bird, perhaps an owl, representing the nether world, suggesting that she connects the two worlds. According to one interpretation, her body represents the earthly link between the heavens and the netherworld. Not surprisingly, in Babylon, she is the patroness of prostitutes in the Temple of Ishtar.

Other gods people the pantheon. Apsua is the god of primeval sweet waters. Ea is the god of wisdom and patron of the arts. Enlil is the god of the elements namely earth, wind, and air. Ninhursag is the mother goddess and creation of vegetation. She is also the wife of Enlil. Nisaba is the goddess of grain. Skanash is the god of the sun, but he is also the judge and law giver. He is also the god of wisdom. In a way, he reminds us of the Egyptian goddess Ma'at the goddess of universal justice. Sin (Nanna) is the goddess of the moon.

In Mesopotamian mythology, Gilgamesh is the personification of Mesopotamia itself, from Sumeria to today's Iraq. He is two-thirds god and one-third human blessed with beauty and courage. However, he is also an extremely harsh monarch of the city state of Ur. He meets up with Enkidu, with whom he at first fights, but later becomes his best of partners. Then, when he refuses the love of Ishtar, she seeks revenge (she is also the goddess of war, after all). He compounds his trouble by killing the Bull of Heaven, thereby earning him the wrath of the other gods. The first punishment is the death of his dearest male companion Enkidu.

He then goes on for a quest for everlasting life. When he finds a root that has this life-preserving quality, he bathes in a river, leaving the root on the shore. A serpent seizes the root and spirits it away. He is left with a vision of death, a "house of death," and a space of inescapable sadness. The theme of the serpent, you may recognize, recurs with the serpent that tempts Eve to eat the fruit of the Tree of Knowledge and so leads to the Fall of Man.

Modern Iraq: A Thematic Interpretation

Are the troubles one sees in Iraq, over its decades-long conflict with the United States and its allies, a recasting of the cosmology of the gods and of the cultural legend Gilgamesh himself? Mesopotamia was one place of western culture.

Michael Wood, in his film *Iraq: Cradle of Civilization,* contends that the entire history of Iraq and the city-states going back to Sumeria is thematic in the Epic of Gilgamesh. Like Gilgamesh, Iraq leads a life enviable by all. Prior to the war, Iraq was one of the most developed and cultured of Middle Eastern society. But like Gilgamesh, it comes to a disastrous end, first in the Persian War in 1991 then with the American invasion of 2003. Likewise, Ur is today a desert, destroyed by the salinization of its water. Baghdad, the political and cultural center in the thirteenth century, was sacked by the Mongols in 1236. Is this the theme dominating Iraq today? In fact, is it a theme that dominates us all?

Selected Films

Iraq: Cradle of Civilization. 1991. 52 minutes. Michael Wood. New York: PBS.

Iraq for Sale. 2006. 75 minutes. Brave New Films.

The Iraq War. 2008. 357 minutes. New York: A & E Home Video.

Selected Literature

Leick, Gwendolyn. 2003. *Mesopotamia.* London: Penguin Books.

Roux, Georges. 1993. *Ancient Iraq.* 3rd ed. London: Penguin.

Tripp, Charles. 2007. *A History of Iraq.* Cambridge, UK: Cambridge University Press.

PART IV

East Asia

CHAPTER 11

China: World Power:
Past, Present, and Future

China: Its Geographical and Archaeological Context

China was unprecedented in the world's cultures in many respects. It developed complex bureaucracies relatively early and sustained it over the centuries. Numerous inventions began with China: a standardized coinage, an elaborate road and canal system, gunpowder, and, last but hardly least, the Great Wall of China, which was better at keeping its citizenry inside than the northern barbarians outside.

China has always had the dubious honor of being the most populous country in the world. The mandarin bureaucracy was appropriately named. The legalistic movement was the prototype of China's totalitarian regimes up to and including the People's Republic of China. Even the republican, then the socialist, regimes that succeeded the Manchu Qing Dynasty retained these characteristics. Minorities have always formed part of China, dominated by the Han. They include Uighurs (pronounced Weegers) and Kazakhs to the west, Tibetans in the southwest, and Mansuo toward the south.

China: A Geography

China, at 1.3 billion population is the most populous nation in the world. It is also among the largest. As the map shows in Figure 11.1, it is bounded by several countries: the Islamic states of Kazakhstan and Kyrgyzstan to the northwest; Russia and Mongolia to the north; the Koreas, Japan, Taiwan, and the Pacific Ocean to the east; the southeastern Asian nations of Indo-China, Burma, and Thailand to the south; and India and smaller Himalayan countries to the southwest.

The country includes disputed territory; Tibet, which was invaded by Chinese troops in 1951 and annexed thereafter, is still seeking independence even after being populated by Han Chinese over the years since. China also lays claim to Taiwan, which was taken over by the Nationalist Chinese government after the Chinese Communist Party completed its revolution in 1949. The People's Republic of China asserts its claim over the island to this day.

Image © pavalena, 2012. Used under license from Shutterstock, Inc.

FIGURE 11.1
China. Note location and its leading cities.

Neolithic China

The terrain of Northern China consists of grasslands and desert in a cold region, one too cold to grow rice under natural conditions. At the beginning of the Neolithic, the staple crop was millet and other grains such as wheat. Southern China, being warmer and mountainous, was conductive to rice cultivation. It was not surprising that the Neolithic of the two regions was very different. They were unified only with the rise of the Qin dynasty under Shih Huang Ti.

The Neolithic begins roughly about 6000 BCE; pigs and millet were the primary domesticates in Northern China. In Southern China, rice became the dominant crop. Domesticated animals were pigs and possibly water buffalo. Canal irrigation was found in both regions, but because of its mountainous terrain, terracing was found in the south.

As noted above, the staple crop was millet; crops also included sorghum and hemp. Mulberry plants, which support silkworms and their cocoons, were also essential to northern China. Loess, a soft silt, was the dominant soil type in northern China, thus facilitating cultivation with digging sticks. Again, pigs were the primary domesticated animals.

One of the most notable Neolithic cultures was the Yang Shao, whose river valleys supported irrigation by terraces and flood plains sustained irrigated crops. Houses were either circular huts or tentlike pyramids whose roofs reached the ground. Although Chinese Han are strongly patrilineal and patrilocal, evidence indicates that the Yang Shao units were matrilineal and matrilocal. There was some evidence of a ranked society, as some houses were larger and more centrally located.

In the south, ranging from southern China to South and Southeast Asia, rice was the standard crop. Rice requires flooding, and this is seen on both the plains and the terraces. Water was stored most likely by damming rivers and streams and channeling the runoff in a region marked by heavy rains. Richard McNeish, better known for his sequence of cultures work in the Tehuacan Valley in central Mexico, developed, with Yan Wenming, a sequence of four cultures from foraging to settled communities in the Xianrendong and Wangdong caves in Central China.

The late Neolithic of southern China shows evidence of ranked or stratified societies. The Daxi site contained cemeteries with jade, bone, ivory, and ceramic objects used as grave goods. Stratification is evidenced by the differential size of dwellings, the opulence of grave goods, and the presence of defensive walls, indicating possible warfare.

Imperial China

Early States in Imperial China

China shows early stratification in a sequence of warring states, the Shang dynasty, the feudal era exemplified by An Yang; the unification, initially by warfare and later by forced labor and shrewd organization, under Shih Huang Ti; and finally consolidation of a unitary administrative structure of the Han dynasty.

In northern China at or near the banks of the Huang Ho, three known dynasties—the Xia, Shang, and Zhou dynasties occurred in rapid succession; the history is as much shrouded in legend as in fact. Chances are that all dynasties began as chiefdoms and became stratified as the leaders acquired more productive land and the peasants who tilled it. As they expanded, the growing principalities controlled both the Huang Ho and the Yangtze regions. Since most available archaeological evidence come from the Shang dynasty, this takes up most of the discussion.

Rule under the Shang was harsh. Warfare was frequent and gravesites yield beheaded skeletons by the hundreds. The Yueh axe was one of the executioners' tools. The Shang was a confederacy of competing kingdoms that eventually occupied seven capitals along the Huang Ho. This is one of the earliest indications of a strong patrilineal organization, which clearly indicated patriarchal families. In 1557, Shang kings moved to Ao, whose dwellings were surrounded by an earthen wall 33 feet high that enclosed five square miles. The elite lived within the walls; workers and peasants lived in sites surrounding the walled fortress. Workshops were in evidence outside the walls, including two bronze factories.

In 1400 BCE, the capital moved from Ao to An Yang, located on the northern bank of the Huang Ho. There it remained until the Shang dynasty fell in 1150 BCE. Warfare continued and stratification increased. These were indicated by the large number of sacrificial sites. There were hundreds of sacrificial sites containing decapitated victims and grave goods such as bronze vessels. One of the large tombs at the site is that of a General Cao Cao.

The Shang Dynasty was the birthplace of many technological innovations. Bronze work, mostly of burial artifacts, was prolific. Molten copper and tin were melted, alloyed, and cast into molds. Unlike the bronze technology of Southeast Asia, there was no lost wax casting or annealing; for this reason, the artifacts are considered indigenous to the region. Other artifacts were mostly vessels, chariot and horse fittings, weapons, and musical instruments. Decorative pottery was a common feature, and there were also bone implements—fishhooks, awls, hairpins. Bone for these artifacts was both human and animal. All these crafts were a royal monopoly.

Writing was another innovation in the Shang Dynasty, which developed from scapulmancy. This was developed from heating the scapula, or shoulder blade, of water buffalo or cattle, or from the carapaces (shell) of turtles. Divination consisted of written questions that could be answered with a yes or no. Writing was developed, carried out, and controlled by professional scribes. Writing itself comprised 3000 symbols that were pictographic, ideographic, and phonetic in combination. Beside scapula and turtle shells, inscriptions have also been found on pottery, bronze, and stone. Perishable media, such as silk, bamboo, and wooden tablets, may also have been used.

Many of the precedents of Chinese stratification are seen in the Shang dynasty. The society was divided fourfold: royalty and nobility, craftsmen, peasants, and slaves. Residential differences were substantial, as were tombs that might contain opulent artifacts, chariots and sacrificial horses, and sacrificial victims who might have been the retainers of the royal or noble deceased. Peasants, on the other hand, relied on the same stone hoes, digging sticks, harvest knives, and the small-scale irrigation their ancestors had used. Their food was simple fare: millet, supplemented by rice and wheat. Bowing and the kowtow were expected from inferiors during the Shang.

Qin Dynasty under Shih Huang Ti

If his predecessors had been ruthless, tyrannical—and innovative—before, Shih Huang Ti was all these things to an exponential degree. He conducted a war that spared no prisoners to conquer the six other feudalities. He tolerated no betrayal, including his mother. He forced the monarchs he conquered to move to Xianyang, the capital of his own feudality. With the principles and ideology of legalism, he institutionalized totalitarianism that survived into the twenty-first century. And he laid the base of the institutions that persist today, despite dynastic changes and revolutions throughout the history of China.

Having conquered his six rival kingdoms, Shih Huang Ti moved to consolidate his power. To prevent invasion from the north, he extended the fortresses of earlier kingdoms into a structure that would be known as the Great Wall of China. It was the longest cemetery as well; thousands died there of overwork and they were entombed in the Wall. He saw Confucian principles as a challenge to his power. Scholars who preached a benevolent state founded on Confucian principles were rounded up and buried alive. Confucian texts were burned, a pattern that has been repeated throughout history from Alexandria by a Muslim monarch to book burning in Nazi Germany. Finally, Shih Huang Ti organized the largest standing army of that time: namely one million soldiers.

If he was one of the most ruthless of monarchs, he also fostered many innovations. Under his rule, Chinese script was standardized so that its writings could be read throughout the country. If his scholars developed a systematic totalitarian apparatus, they also added consistency to the law by specifying crimes and their punishment. His drive for standardization extended to weights and measures, including the size of chariot wheels. He built roads and canals that would link the entire country; some canals are still in use today. Paper was invented during his reign. And he created a standard coinage that would facilitate commerce.

Image © Hung Chung Chih, 2012. Used under license from Shutterstock, Inc.

FIGURE 11.2
The Great Wall of China, often known as the Great Cemetery of workers who died during its construction.

One of Shih Huang Ti's best known projects was a three-acre gallery containing terra cotta soldiers, horses, and charioteers, who "guarded" the eastern side of the tomb (Figure 11.3). The soldiers were said to be faithful reproductions of individuals; they were slightly larger than life size. Horses and the chariots were also faithful reproductions of real animals and vehicles. Dressed in battle regalia with varied colors that have since worn away, they stood in battle formation. The designers of the security system to protect this gallery were entombed as soon as they had completed their task.

The Qin dynasty ended in ruins. The Great Wall, the tomb, the soldiers, and other projects exhausted both the subjects and the resources of their realm. Shih, ever in quest of immortality by drinking small amounts of mercury that he had been persuaded was the elixir of everlasting life, died deranged of the poison, according to one account. His eldest son and successor was forced to commit suicide, making way for the second son whom the royal court thought was more easily controllable.

Han Dynasty and After

The Han dynasty, which succeeded Qin rule under Shih Huang Ti, extended the innovations begun in the Qin period and before. Iron tools were adopted; wet rice cultivation techniques were perfected. Ox-drawn plows were invented and improved upon, while new technologies were designed to improve the roads. The crossbow was invented to improve military effectiveness. Even a seismometer to measure earthquake was invented.

No less important was the administrative apparatus that was improved during the Han dynasty. One aim had been to endure stability, and this would be reflected in the years that fol-

FIGURE 11.3
Terra cotta soldiers at Shih Huang Ti's tomb.

lowed. Improvements were made in weights and measures and in standardized coinage. The world's first census was conducted in AD 1 and 2; according to the results, the population stood at 57 million; one Han city had an estimated one million. The most complex administrative for an agricultural state up to that time, the Han dynasty cast the die for a durable and stable administrative system that not only ensured long periods of stability between dynasties, but also would survive the dynastic changes that inevitably followed, including the last of these, the Manchu dynasty founded by a Mongol elite.

The Philosophies of Lao Tzu and Confucius (Kong Zi)

It was also during the imperial period that philosophical belief systems were founded. The Tao, often translated as "the Way," was attributed to Lao Tzu, whose existence has been a matter of debate. A naturalistic philosophy, the first sentence of the *Tao Te Ching* reads "The way that can be named is not the constant way." The unity of opposites, represented by the yin/yang dichotomy, is a part of the belief. Overall, one is admonished to follow the principle of nonaction—or action that is natural, not contrived.

Another philosophical system that is distinctly Chinese are the principles set forth by Confucius (Kong Zi in Pinyin script) set forth the principles of right conduct at all levels: individual, the family, and the state. The way of the superior man, he declares, is to inculcate harmony through virtue. Virtues involve not only benevolent love, but also duty, truth, wisdom, and propriety in the five relationships: toward ruler, father, wife, elder brother, and friend. The most oft-cited source of his works is the *Analects*.

Also integral is a religious belief system originating in India but spread throughout China and Japan: Buddhism. Like Hinduism, Buddhism posits the idea of *samsara*, or illusion, in which we all live, and whose forces is driven by *karma*. Nirvana, or liberation from illusion, is the underlying theme of both systems of belief. Distinct to Buddhism are the Four Noble Truths: the universality of suffering, desire as the root of all suffering, the end of desire as the way to end suffering, and the path of nirvana thereby being the Eightfold Path: right belief, thought, speech, action, livelihood, effort, mindfulness, and meditation.

Later Pre-Republic Dynasties

The Ming dynasty showed the first sign of modernization with the promotion of trade at home between city and rural district in the fifteenth century and the largest fleet in history under the Muslim admiral and eunuch Zheng He. Although the fleet went on seven voyages, reaching as far west as Persia and Arabia, the voyages were immediately halted under the reign of the Hongxi emperor and his successors for reasons still not understood. The last voyage was made in 1433; thereafter, the remaining Ming emperors followed a policy of autarky, or self-sufficiency. Thus what could have become an imperialist power in its own right was aborted.

The Manchu dynasty overthrew the Ming in 1644 and underwent a period of expansion to Xinjiang to the west and Tibet to the southwest. The dress style, which was forced upon the male population along with queues, became standard throughout China. In the nineteenth century, as western powers expanded eastward and as Meiji Japan underwent industrialization of its own, the Qing dynasty began to lose control over its economy. The 1842 opium war with Britain forced the sale of opium from India into the country, and the Open Door policy forced China to trade with five countries, including Japan. The Boxer rebellion, instigated by Chinese anti-imperialist forces, was suppressed by 1901 and the Qing dynasty, among other punishments, was forced to pay an indemnity of 67 million pounds to the eight embassies that the Boxers had taken over in Beijing. The chain of events that followed led to the Dowager Empress to abdicate her throne and the revolution of October 10, 1911, at the Wuchang fort.

Modern China and Its Precursors

Republican China

Imperial China would last, under several dynasties, until 1911, when a revolt at a military base spread throughout China and installed Sun Yat-sen as the first president of republican China. Despite the years of unrest that ended with the Chinese Communist Revolution of 1949, many of the attributes of Imperial China would persist into the early twenty-first century. They included extreme social stratification, centralized political power, technical innovations that served Chinese society, infrastructural projects from canals to dams to highways, standards of weights and measures, and, despite an atheistic interlude under Mao Zedong, the influence of the Tao, of Confucian philosophy, and of Buddhism. We will see how these have played out in China since 1911.

This is an overview of modern China, which went through several metamorphoses. The Republican era saw the overthrow of the Qing dynasty, which had dominated China since 1644. Sun Yat-sen was the first president of the Republic of China, but did not last long. China went through a warlord era until the Kuomintang under Chiang Kai-shek established a relatively stable period during the 1920s; the communists, massacred in 1927, went through the Long March, which finally established a socialist base at Yenan in northern China under Mao Zedong. Japan entered the picture with a takeover of Manchuria in 1931 and the invasion of eastern China in 1937 that saw the so-called Rape of Nanking that year. Throughout World War II, the Communists and the Nationalists retained an uneasy alliance at the front with Japan, continuing their conflict behind the lines. Four years after the end of World War II, the Chinese Communist Party assumed control of Beijing (Peking) on October 1, 1949; the Nationalist forces were forced to retreat to the island of Formosa, later renamed Taiwan, under Chiang Kai-shek, which has persisted since then as the Republic of China. Mainland China, now named the People's Republic of China (PRC), underwent a series of failed socialist experiments. Since 1972, the PRC gradually transitioned from a socialist to a corporate capitalist state. This next discussion traces the history from China's Ming and Qing roots to the present.

The Republican Revolution and Its Aftermath

China underwent a revolution on October 10, 1911, a day still celebrated in Taiwan, officially known as the Republic of China. The Wuchang uprising of October 10, 1911, led to the secession of 16 provinces from China. Although Sun Yat-sen, as the first president installed on March 12, 1912, is considered to be the father of modern China, he was forced out by Yuan Shikai, who declared himself emperor and so sparked another revolt. Yuan's death in 1916 initiated a power vacuum filled by competitive warlords. This set the stage for civil war between the Nationalists under Chiang Kai-shek and the Communists that would soon be led by Mao Zedong.

During the warlord period (1911–1927), famine swept the rural areas across China. Eventually, after the death of Sun Yat-sen in 1925 and the assumption of power by Chiang in Nanking in 1927, stability returned to China's economy. New factories opened in the urban areas, benefiting from the demand induced by World War I and its aftermath in Europe and from a boycott of foreign goods. Rural areas prospered from a high demand for export cash crops that supplanted the traditional rice-based subsistence economy. The prosperity was shortlived. The world depression of the 1930s, combined with the Japanese invasion of Manchuria of 1931 and eastern China later in the decade, disrupted China's industrialization.

Rivalry between the Nationalists and the Communists developed in the 1920s. Sun Yat-sen, who had formed an alliance with the Chinese Communist Party (CCP) in south China in the early 1920s, died of cancer in 1925. Thereupon, Chiang Kai-shek seized power over the Kuomintang (KMT) and initiated the Northern Expedition to suppress the warlords. In 1927, he ordered the massacre of every known Communist in Shanghai, forcing the CCP to abandon the cities and form a power base in the rural areas of the country. The Long March under Mao Zedong, began in the western provinces and ended at the CCP stronghold in Yenan. The civil war would continue through the Sino-Japanese war until 1949, when the CCP officially declared the formation of the People's Republic of China on October 1 of that year.

Japan had been one of several imperialist powers that harassed China at the turn of the century. In 1931, part of an effort to add land and resources to its burgeoning population, Japan occupied Manchuria in 1931, renaming it Manchukuo. It then expanded into northern and much of eastern China in 1937, occupying and destroying much of Nanking that same year. Chiang was kidnapped by a faction led by Zhang Xueliang and held hostage until he agreed to ally the KMT with the CCP against the impending Japanese invasion. Nevertheless, the alliance held only at the front: the CCP and the KMT continued the conflict away from battle lines between China and Japan. The alliance collapsed entirely after Japan's surrender in 1945.

The CCP exploited its advantage in rural areas. By implementing land reforms under its control and by hit-and-run tactics, the CCP gained one victory after another. By 1949, the CCP controlled most of the mainland and the KMT forces under Chiang retreated to the island of Formosa (now Taiwan). On October 1, 1949, Mao declared the formation of the People's Republic of China. For nearly a decade, China was to model its economy after that of the Soviet Union, which provided material aid and expertise to the fledgling country.

Peoples Republic of China

After the war years, the government of the People's Republic of China (PRC) sought to recover from the conflict. The CCP took over the state-owned enterprises that the KMT had founded during the 1920s and early 1930s, but allowed private firms alone initially. The hyperinflation that had ruined postwar China was brought under control. Land was redistributed to peasants, and they were encouraged to join mutual aid teams that eventually formed the basis of the communes later to come. By 1952, the economy had recovered entirely.

In 1951, following the Soviet model, the PRC initiated its first Five-Year plan. Heavy industry—steel, coal, cement—was given priority over light industry and agriculture. These objectives were realized by 1956: 67.5% of the plants were state owned, and 32.5% were joint public-private enterprises. Agriculture also underwent consolidation; by 1957, 97.5% of farm households had joined collectives through mutual-aid teams. Despite the priority given heavy industry, agricultural productivity had also increased, but problems arose to bringing rural products to the cities.

Several developments led to Mao's decision to launch the Great Leap Forward in 1958. Fears developed that tensions developing between China and the Soviet Union would soon lead to a cutoff of aid and technical assistance, partly because of Khrushchev's secret speech that denounced Stalinist policies and practices. With this in mind, agricultural enterprises were consolidated into giant communes, which would incorporate industrial, educational, and other functions into these entities. The well-publicized backyard pig-iron furnaces formed part of this strategy. Attempts were made to abolish families and move the peasants and workers into dormitories. This was quickly abandoned. The belief was that surplus manpower would be released for the vital tasks of developing agriculture in parallel with industries.

The Great Leap Forward proved a disaster. Even before it started, collectivization of agriculture had produced a famine in 1956. Although poor weather was partly to blame for the famine, food production dipped even lower; there were shortages of raw material for industry as well. Communes produced poor quality goods, and the iron produced in backyard furnaces was useless. Poor management also led to deterioration of the plants. Both worker and cadre officials were exhausted from trying to make the systems work. By 1959, it was evident to all that the Great Leap Forward would end in failure. Assuming responsibility for the failure, Mao resigned from the chairmanship of the PRC, though he retained the chairmanship of the CCP. Liu Shaoqi succeeded Mao to the PRC post.

After Liu Shaoqi replaced Mao, the Politburo began to moderate its agricultural and industrial policies. The still-extant commune system was modified to allow production teams more control over its administrative policies. Realizing how bureaucratic arrogance had fostered the disaster, the Politburo gave production managers more power to attend to the technical needs of

Image © John Lock, 2012. Used under license from Shutterstock, Inc.

FIGURE 11.4
Propaganda poster during the Great Cultural Revolution depicting an image of Mao and of the Red Guards holding up the Little Red Book for all to see.

the enterprises rather than structure their decisions in accordance with the party line. Agriculture was also given greater priority as compared with industry. By 1966, productivity increased in both agriculture and industry, surpassing the beginning of the Great Leap Forward—and has improved ever since.

Until 1962, Mao had stayed in the sidelines, but he became alarmed at what he interpreted as creeping capitalism in China, and so he launched efforts to restore socialist purity. In 1962, he launched a Socialist Education Movement to reintegrate socialism into the bureaucracies, the schools, and especially the People's Liberation Army (PLA). Then in 1966, Mao launched the militant phase, the Great Cultural Revolution (GRC). The Red Guards, a cadre of youth, were formed under his influence and, armed with the *Quotations of Chairman Mao* (the Little Red Book), they harassed other Chinese and enforced Mao's directives of drafting intellectuals, from bureaucrat to professor, into manual labor. One major consequence was that the country's economic development was stalled not only during the period of 1966 to 1968, but for several years after.

Market Socialism or Corporatism?

As the consequences of the GCR became evident, the leadership began to reconsider a pragmatic approach to economic development. Though the PLA gained influence during the GCR, it was divided between the radical and the pragmatic factions. Eventually, the PLA saw the need to modernize military technology and to support development policies. Lin Biao, initially supported by

Mao, attempted a coup on the government that failed. Then in 1971 Liu was killed in a plane crash in Mongolia as he tried to flee the country; circumstances of the crash are unknown. By 1972, the "rehabilitated" pragmatists, such as Deng Xiaoping and Zhou Enlai, increased their influence. In that year, an American president, Richard Nixon, made an official visit to China for the first time. Deng and his allies initiated reforms in 1978.

The decade of the 1970s saw a checkered transition. As the Great Cultural Revolution was perceived by many as a disaster, some tried to preserve the ideological purity of Chinese society; in this, the so-called Gang of Four tried to do so through a media campaign. This ended when, after Mao's death in 1976, preceded by Zhou Enlai's demise in January of that year, Hua Guofeng ousted the Gang and restored Deng to power. The Gang of Four were tried in 1981; two, including Jiang Qing, Mao's fourth wife, were sentenced to death, but the sentence was later commuted to life imprisonment.

The transition led to an incipient transition toward a market-based economy. A responsibility system was initiated in the agricultural sector, in which individual farmers were allowed to sell products for a profit; industry would be added later and the entire arrangement systematized. Enterprise managers were allowed greater autonomy, and production of goods outside the Five Year Plan was allowed. Small scale entrepreneurs were now allowed to operate and so proliferated. Foreign firms were allowed to trade with individual domestic firms outside the scope of the Ministry of Foreign Trade.

Technological dominance gradually supplanted ideological purity. Although the Four Modernizations—in agriculture, industry, national defense, and science and technology—were promulgated as early as 1963, this strategy became the centerpiece of Deng's economic strategy. The responsibility system drove agricultural development, whereas technological expertise and development were to be improved with the help of foreign investment and assistance. After the PLA underwent its struggle, those advocating improved military technology and strategy won out. Finally, improvements in science and technology suffused all three of these sectors.

Deng Xiaoping had a checkered career, first gaining influence in the early 1970s, then being purged in the mid-1970s, and then gaining permanent influence by December 1978 as the new policy began in earnest. The household responsibility, initiated in agriculture in 1984, was expanded to industry. After meeting a certain quota, the producers were free to reinvest or consume the product. If there was a loss, they had to absorb it; there were no longer provisions for the state to absorb the loss.

China's economic policy has increased the role of the market system in the allocation of the country's resources. Socialist-run policy has been displaced by capitalistic attributes: market-driven decisions, managerial autonomy, and flexibility of output accordingly. These have led to greater efficiency of industrial and agricultural enterprises, increases in enterprise growth, and improved entrepreneurial opportunities. Although bureaucratic clearance was still required, managers had the power to hire and fire. Foreign trade expanded from 15% in 1980 to 35% in 1986. In the meantime, the environmental costs have also increased. In the steel-making city of Wuhan, for example, the sky was so dark with air pollution that cars' headlights were on during the day. Only recently has the Chinese government addressed this issue, and cleanup policies adopted.

The Maoist period included job security, metaphorically called the Iron Rice Bowl, for every Chinese worker and peasant, though security gravitated toward the Communist bureaucracy.

Image © testing, 2012. Used under license from Shutterstock, Inc.

FIGURE 11.5

Model in Beijing showing off a Buggatti Venron sports car at the 2010 Beijing International Automotive Exhibition. To be rich is glorious, said Deng Xiaoping. . . .

With Deng's rise to power, the Iron Rice Bowl was the first social program to go, with widespread protests and strikes breaking out (China Airlines workers' strike was one example). Migratory labor increased as peasants migrated to cities or the better developed areas. One condition for China's entry into the World Trade Organization was to abolish this policy.

If, as Deng Xiaoping once declared, to be rich is glorious, the glory did not extend to all, or even to most. Extremes in wealth and poverty increased. Land became overpopulated, forcing many landless peasants to move to the cities. Slums sprung up in areas surrounding the cities. As in Nationalist China in the late 1920s, crime and corruption returned to China, increasing over the years since 1982. Factory conditions remain poor at best, and slave-like conditions dominate many enterprises.

Social and Economic Conditions in the New China

China, at 1.3 billion, is the most populous nation on earth. Acknowledging this crisis, China initiated a one-child policy in 1976 and added enforcement provisions in the years following. Failing to adequately acknowledging the patrilineal descent norms of its culture, female infanticide and abortion became widespread, leading to an imbalance in the male-female ratio of China's population over the long term. Hence, there is an oversupply of male suitors, female children are often adopted abroad, and overprotected boys often have an obesity problem. Exemptions allowed include rural families whose first child is female, ethnic (non-Han) minorities, and wealthy couples, who recently have used fertility drugs to increase the number of births. Who said money doesn't talk?

International Trade

One consequence of overpopulation is a glut in market supply, so it is not surprising that China has the lowest wages in the world. Thus, China has drawn *maquiladoras* into China by the hundreds; tags on clothes increasingly state "Made in China." This has drawn accusations that China employs slave labor, although the country's government denies the charge. There have also been widespread reports of child slave labor at brick kiln plants in southwestern China, although authorities claim the police have halted these practices. The issue has become international. China has invested in mining and other sectors in Africa, sending its surplus labor there and recruiting African workers as well.

China has become incorporated into the corporate-dominated global system of production and trade. Statistics indicate that China is the second largest recipient of foreign direct investment (FDI); FDI accounts for 40% of all China's exports. Other constraints on foreign trade persist, such as the rule that 51% of joint ventures must remain in China's hands. Chinese investors are now seeking to enter in both developed and underdeveloped countries, as symbolized by a Chinese container vessel, docked at Mumbai, India. China holds most of the U.S. national debt.

The news of July 2, 2010 (second day after opening Xinhua News Service in English) also included U.S. news (Obama's proposal of a $2B investment in solar power and vows to create more such power sources), science news (isolating "longevity DNA"), other foreign politics (Poland's presidential elections), accidents (the Congo's tanker disaster), Islamic news in China (script of a mosque in Xinjiang), and Paris Hilton's and Lindsay Lohan's latest escapades. One may ask whether this news agency actually produces news or imitates western-style propaganda of the National Enquirer/New York Times genre. You be the judge: log onto http://www.xinhuanet.com/english2010/ or put English.News.cn on your browser.

China is a land of contradictions. On the one hand, there has always been a centralized government, based on a redistributive economy—first feudalism, then a command economy in various guises. Yet it also has a system of market towns as we shall see, and the Chinese are among the most entrepreneurial peoples of the world. The Chinese made many innovations, from a relatively effective bureaucracy to coin and paper money to gunpowder. They created a fleet that might have been the envy of the known world. Yet their power elite destroyed the fleet and pursued a policy of isolation that persisted from the Imperial lords to the Chinese Communist Party under Mao. Now they appear to becoming a model of a globalized economy. There is much that remains to be learned about China. What is its influence on the localities within its sphere? A case study will serve to illustrate, namely the case of Taitou in Shandong Province.

Taitou: A Chinese Peasant Village

Introduction

Perhaps one of the best indicators of national history is local history, inasmuch as by definition, peasantry is part of a larger nation, its state, and its society. Alfred E. Kroeber, one of the preeminent anthropologists during the 1940s, referred to peasants as "part societies with part cultures," in societies that contain urban areas. To Robert Redfield, peasant societies are little traditions whose belief systems, styles of clothing, oral traditions, and other features reflect the norms

Image © Janelle Lugge, 2012. Used under license from Shutterstock, Inc.

FIGURE 11.6
Panorama of a typical Chinese peasant village. Not everyone shares in the glory of wealth.

of the great traditions of nations and empires. To Eric Wolf, "primitive cultivators" reliant on local technology and cultures but linked to the state through tribute, taxes, and forced labor separate peasants from independent agrarians. In these respects, the people of Taitou in Shantung Province, China, are indeed part of a larger society with linkages ranging from cultural attributes to the domain of a state.

The Economy of Taitou

Taitou is located in Shantung (now Shandong in the pinyin Chinese system of translation) province in northeastern China. The principal city of the province is Qingdao. The village was densely populated, but peasants in the village were autonomous.

All land was privately owned. Each family had land in different ecological zones. Lighter, terraced, sandy plots on hillsides supported peanuts and sweet potatoes. Moist bottom soils supported rice cultivation. Flatlands yielded millet and wheat. At one time, most families enjoyed diversified and secure crop yields.

Although their plots were small, they were productive. Every plot of land involved multiple cropping with several crops at any one site. Fertilizer was a must, and came from several sources: human and animal waste, ashes, and other organic material, all composted. All families owned a few animals—including horses and oxen—all used for plowing and harrowing their fields.

Although wealth distinctions were evident, they were deemphasized. A few families owned twenty acres of land at any one time, a larger number owned around ten, and the majority owned around two. Dietary patterns were the same, based on rice as a staple, but the better off might enjoy fish and bread. Although the wealthier individuals might display their wealth in the form of multi-roomed housing, fine clothing, and fat oxen, stratification was deemphasized and there was no conscious effort for the elite to separate themselves from the others. Envy for the wealthy might exist, but it was not institutionalized, as one might find in Mexican villages.

Family and Household Relations

Taitou, unlike many other villages in China, was organized by nuclear families. One married son might stay with his parents, forming a stem family, but the other sons would have to leave to form their own families. Division of labor by gender was more or less distinct: women attended to domestic chores and to the children; men performed agricultural tasks from plowing to much of the harvesting and engaged in trade and politics. Everyone contributed to the household economies by handling different jobs.

At the village level, every household produced for the market: pigs, peanuts, soy beans. Women bought cotton and spun it for the households, but they might employ specialists—dyers and weavers. There were several specialists in the crafts. Some made and repaired tools; others were oil pressers, carpenters, or masons. Professionals in the village were teachers and public officials.

Market Towns

Every region was dominated by a market town. Taitou was one of 20 villages within the sphere of one market town, Hsinanchen. Each town had amenities the villages lacked, including shops ranging from bakeries to bookstores. Each town had its own market days, which were coordinated with market days of other towns so that itinerant traders could do their business in all of them. Large markets were open to serve the surrounding communities.

Traders were all men. Not only did they buy and sell products, but also met in tea or wine shops to exchange information about the economic conditions and opportunities in regions. Credit was essential to trading and to maintain production. Even if they had nothing to sell, they went to town with empty baskets to exchange information and to make payments to maintain their credit.

Market towns were termini of wider networks; the elite formed part of this network. Although these were administrative centers, the primary function of the elite was economic, involving more distant trade. There was a hierarchy of ever wider centers.

Patrilineal Descent and Marriage

Like other Chinese villages, the people of Taitou traced their ancestry patrilineally. All marriages were arranged by families, and the couple might not meet each other until the wedding. Each family was more concerned with forming strategic alliances than compatibility between couples. Nevertheless, the husband-to-be worked for the future wife's family, turning all his earnings over to her father, a practice known as bride labor. After the marriage, the couple moved in with the groom's father; the son now passed his earnings over to his father. Though patrilineal, women held tight control over the household assets, and the daughter-in-law was subjected to the demands of her mother-in-law.

Unless the son was to become the next household head, he would seek to find independence, first seeking land to develop his own farm; the daughter-in-law encouraged the split, equally motivated to escape the dictatorial hold of her mother-in-law. It also helped that both daughters and daughters-in-law performed odd jobs whose earnings were theirs to keep, thereby loosening the father's domination over the couple.

Extended families did have their advantages. For one thing, having so many people under one roof enforced frugality of its member to increase their savings and assets. For another, the members could divide their labor into specialized economic activities, thereby widening the scope of the family's activities. For example, one son would work the land, other sons took up commerce and trade, and still others would hire themselves out for farm work or engage in crafts and the arts. Extended families were also in a better position to obtain more land.

Though comprising nuclear families, reckoning included nonresidential kin. Families formed extended families, though their constituent families. In turn, several extended families would form lineages, and several lineages formed into clans. Their functions were to provide mutual aid and to support family members who were less well off—widows, orphans, the elderly, and the sick.

Village Governance

At the village level, there were several functions the family or even clans could not provide for themselves. As of 1945, when China was still governed by the Kuomintang (KMT), the village was organized to defend against bandits by setting up barricades to village entrances and organizing night patrols. This was necessary because the national government was weakened by the civil war between the KMT and the Chinese Communist Party (CCP). Taitou entered into alliances with other villages and hired full-time crop watchers to defend the fields against both pests and thieves.

Village governance was maintained not so much by public officials as by informal means. Gossips, "loss of face" or public shame, and ostracism were the primary means of keeping villagers in line. Disputes were resolved by village elders who had acquired both wealth and personal honor in their lifetimes. In addition, formal patron-client ties between the wealthy and the poor involved exchanges between services in return for material favors—whether bound by kinship or not. Legal disputes and appeals to public officials were rare, and government officials were ranked lowest in the village hierarchy.

Taitou under the PRC

China passed into control of the Chinese Communist Party in 1949. For the first years after the transition, the village was left alone to run its own affairs. Then, as the central government formed mutual aid teams and later communes, village control passed to the leadership of centrally appointed cadres. Under the Five Year Plan, each village was assigned a specialized crop. Taitou provided wheat, barley, and sweet potatoes. No longer was the village allowed to produce crops that it had produced before: peanuts, millet, soybeans, and fruit. Households no longer could own small plots of land or raise pigs or other animals.

Over the years that included the Great Leap Forward and, later, the Great Cultural Revolution, many central decisions influenced the economy of Taitou. For example, the soy oil pressers, who had performed their trade for decades, were forced to close because of the prohibition of soybean production. In 1966, as the result of the Cultural Revolution, the carpentry shops were closed when their owners were condemned as "capitalist roaders." After the demise of the Gang of Four and the reforms beginning in the late 1970s, the village began to enjoy prosperity to some degree. Now the village could produce grain, and a nearby factory opened that provided employment (but no investment technology). Its fate was still determined from outside. Taitou was passed over for the status of a "model village" in favor of a nearby impoverished village.

Taitou under PRC Reform. In 1980 and after, Taitou was allowed greater autonomy. Private plots were allowed, and "sideline" production increased in livestock, poultry, and crops. Small shops appeared, and some men were hired for construction projects outside the village. Liberalization enhanced village income as a whole.

As the reforms of the central government progressed, the Taitou householders enjoyed greater control of their economy. The "Iron Rice Bowl" of official policy was displaced by what they called "a rice bowl of their own." Villagers now could make decisions regarding what they produced, how much, and the amount of profits they could retain. Women now have greater economic independence than they had even before the CCP's assumption of power. The redistributive economy of the CCP now was replaced by systems of market exchange and reciprocity. Even the changing media underwent change as radios and television provide households with alternative sources of information and entertainment.

Despite a Communist hiatus, the household remains the basic economic unit of Taitou. Wealth distinctions remain predominant, and lower classes may be envious of the upper class, but there are not the wealth leveling systems that are found elsewhere, such as in peasant Mesoamerica or during the height of socialism under Mao. Entrepreneurship remains an important motor in Taitou's economy.

Conclusion

From the foregoing accounts of the country of China as a whole and one of its constituent villages, it is clear that what goes on at the national level impinges on the events at the local. Change is evident at both levels. As one of the rapidly developing countries, called BRIC by Goldman Sachs (Brazil, Russia, India, and China), we are looking at a power shift from a unipolar political economy dominated by the United States to dominance by four or perhaps even more economic powerhouses (South Africa has recently been added to this acronym in the more recent BRICS). CNN recently predicted that China will overtake the United States in gross domestic product (GDP) during the 2020s. Yet this is never a sure thing. *The Guardian* of August 13–17, 2012, reported a slowdown in the economies of China and other countries. Marx's model of business cycles is as true in Communist—or Corporatist—China as it is in the United States, or in any country for that matter. The role of anthropologists is to keep up on these rapid changes at all levels of society, from the globe to the locality.

Selected Films

China: The Mandate of Heaven. 1991. 60 minutes. Michael Wood. New York: Ambrose Video Publishing.

Herdsman. 2001. 88 minutes. Wei Bin. Cambridge, MA. Documentary Educational Resources.

Sprouts of Capitalism in China. 1997. 20 minutes. Wen-jin Qin. Cambridge, MA. Documentary Educational Resources.

Trading Women. 2003. 77 minutes. Cambridge, MA. Documentary Educational Resources. Sex trade in China and other Asian countries.

Without Fathers or Husbands. 1995. 26 minutes. Hua Cai. London: The Royal Anthropology Institute.

Wuxing People's Commune. 1978. 59 minutes. Richardson, Boyce, and Tony Ianzelo. Cambridge, MA. Documentary Educational Resources.

Selected Literature

Chang, Leslie. 2009. *From Village to City in a Changing China.* New York: Spiegel and Grau.

Hessler, Peter. 2007. *Oracle Bones.* New York: Harper. Everyday life in the new China.

Jacques, Martin. 2012. *When China Rules the World: The End of the Western World and the Birth of a New Global Order,* 2nd ed. London: Penguin.

Keay, John. 2009. *China: A History.* New York: Basic Books.

McGregor, Richard. 2010. *The Party: The Secret World of China's Communist Rulers.* New York: Harper.

Midler, Paul. 2011. *Poorly Made in China: An Insider's Account of the China Production Game.* New York: Wiley.

Neville, Peter. 2007. *China: People, Place, Culture.* New York: DK Publishing.

Potter, Sulamith Heins, and Jack Potter. 1990. *China's Peasant: The Anthropology of a Revolution.* Cambridge UK: Cambridge University Press.

Safran, William, ed. 1999. *Nationalism and Ethnoregional Identities in China.* London: Routledge.

Walter, Carl. 2012. *Red Capitalism: The Fragile Financial Foundation of China's Extraordinary Rise.* New York: Wiley.

CHAPTER 12

Tibet: A Buddhist Theocracy

Introduction

One of the most thoroughly theocratic kingdoms of the world is Tibet. We take an overview of this kingdom and introduce the current literature and videos that accompany this presentation.

Ever since the Chinese invasion of Tibet has received public attention, Tibetan Buddhism has been romanticized considerably. The Dalai Lama has become a godlike public figure and China has acquired a demonic image that matches Satan himself. But like all demonogies, the truth is likely somewhere in-between. There is more to the real Tibet than meets the eye, and also much less. The model of the universe in Tibetan Buddhism is interesting, namely *samsara,* the world of illusion, the hope to see the bright white light that promises *nirvana* or *moksha,* the end of all illusion. Yet in the daily life of the herder, the peasant, life is more mundane. We look at both these aspects in Tibetan Buddhism.

Tibet, a Geography

Tibet lies to the southwest of China and northeast of India and is adjacent to Nepal and Bhutan. It consists of highland plateaus broken by peaks and mountain ranges.

The country is not called "the Roof of the World" for nothing. This topography (Figure 12.1) shows the plateaus that average 16,000 feet in elevation, making it the highest region in the world. It abuts Nepal, which contains Mount Everest, the highest peak in the world.

Everyday Life of Tibetans

At such a high region, it is not surprising that arable land is scarce. Those Tibetans who are not peasants are herdsmen, and some communities combine both enterprises. The best known animal is the yak, an ox whose matted undercoat and shaggy outer hair protect them. They serve both as beasts of burden and providers of meat, milk, cloth, and hides. Other animals herded are horses, sheep, the ubiquitous goat, and even camels. Crops grown in the harsh landscape include wheat, barley, rye, and buckwheat. Salt is also an important product in some regions.

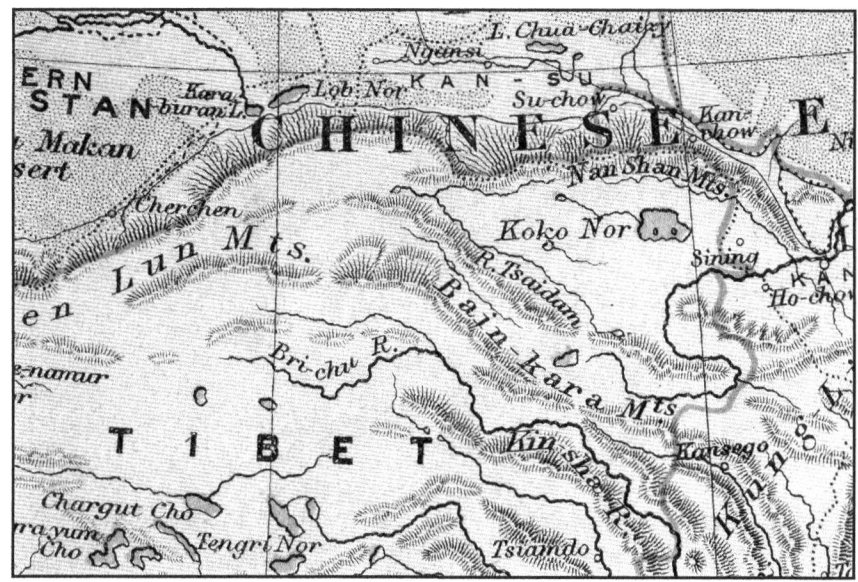

Image © Chad McDermott, 2012. Used under license from Shutterstock, Inc.

FIGURE 12.1
The Tibetan plateau, which justifies the name "roof of the world."

Sociocultural Characteristics of Tibet

Socioculturally speaking, the Tibetans are famous in the anthropological literature for a rare but consistent marital practice: polyandry. This is the marriage of one woman to two or more men. In Tibet, the preferred form is fraternal polyandry, whereby a woman marries two or more brothers (of each other, not of the woman). Since a woman can bear only one child every nine months (at most), the population is likely to increase only slowly, very adaptive to land scarcity. Not only that, but it militates against division of property. No one knows who the father of the child is, nor does anyone much care. Property is inherited as one piece from one generation to the next.

Tibet is traditionally a feudal society. It is a matter of debate as to how oppressive the system was to the peasants. According to Michael Parenti, the vast majority of 1.2 million Tibetans (namely 700,000) were serfs allowed a parcel of land and worked either for the monasteries or secular lords. Attempts to escape were frequent and those captured were severely beaten. Some peasants, he argues, actually welcomed the Chinese invasion. His argument can be accessed by typing in the internet "Friendly Feudalism: The Tibet Myth."

Joshua Frei, in "A Lie Repeated: The Far Left's Flawed History of Tibet," (also accessible on the internet) argues that Parenti relies on secondary sources that were themselves supportive of Chinese propaganda and tended to romanticize Maoist society. Neither he nor those whose argument he supports have interviewed the Tibetan refugees themselves. I suggest you do your own research and draw your own conclusions. For both arguments, again search the respective titles on Google or other internet sources.

Image © zhang kan, 2012. Used under license from Shutterstock, Inc.

FIGURE 12.2
Potala Palace, the (former) residence of the Dalai Lama.

The capital of Tibet, the home of Tibetan Buddhism, is Lhasa. The Dalai Lama, the supreme lama of the Tibetan Buddhists, lived in the Potala palace, perched high above the city on a hilltop. Since the Chinese takeover, the palace has been a tourist attraction.

The Theology of Tibetan Buddhism

Like other major religions, such as the varieties of Hinduism and Buddhism, the Tibetan Buddhists subscribe to a concept of *samsara:* we all live in a world of birth, death, and rebirth that are all built on illusion. *Karma* drives our fate; our rebirth depends on our past deeds. Nirvana amounts to recognition of samsara as illusion and so the illusion dissolves with this recognition.

To the Buddha, the source of all suffering is desire. The life cycle we call *samsara* brings suffering, including old age and death. The road to nirvana (called Moksha by some), is the ending of desire. But, according to Alan Watts, the late Zen expert, can the end of desire itself reflect desire? That is to say, isn't wanting to end desire a desire in and of itself?

Several schools dominate Buddhism. One is the Mahayana, or great vehicle, school, and it is the Mahayana school that Tibetan Buddhism follows. The principle behind it lies in reaching a state of Buddhahood or enlightenment. In so doing, the lama, or monk, helps all other sentient beings attain that state. Sometimes defined as a state of omniscience (the knowledge or awareness of all), the Buddhist principle states that all things derive from mind. By so doing, all limitations to help others achieve enlightenment are thereby removed. Still, the karma of sentient beings limits the Buddhists' ability to help them.

To the Tibetans, what matters is the internal state of Buddhism, not the outward formalism. A favorite tale of theirs is the story of Aryadeya, a Buddhist saint, who began scrubbing the out-

FIGURE 12.3
Prayer wheels in a Buddhist temple.

side of a cesspot, a pot used for defecating. After a while, one of the disciples asked why he was not cleaning the inside. He replied that like his action, ritualism also ignores the essence of Buddhism. To the Tibetan, there are two essential steps to achieve Buddhahood: one, to take refuge from the external, the surface, the superficial; and two, to observe the Four Seals of Dharma.

The four seals of dharma, or duty, are these: First, that all things that are complex in nature are impermanent. The complicated ritual build up over the years of Buddhist practice can never last. Second, that all emotions are painful, and they must be extinguished. Third, that all phenomena are empty and lack coherent existence. Finally, that nirvana is beyond extremes. In the absence of these Four Seals, Buddhism would be nothing of a theistic, religious dogma, a body of rigid rules and beliefs without substance or life. The external of Buddhist practice would displace the internal, the vital force that drives the ultimate aim of religion, of reaching nirvana. The external is the ultimate illusion that is *samsara*.

Buddhist practice among the Tibetans begins with three elements of preliminary practice. Such practice entails renunciation of the world, then a wish to attain enlightenment called *bodhicitta* and a recognition of emptiness that we call wisdom. After the preliminaries come what the Buddhists call *Vajrayana,* or "skillful means." This is the fastest way to reach Buddhism, but also the most dangerous. Misapplied, the practice increases the problem of the ego that is to be overcome and thereby increases greatest suffering. Therefore, preliminary practice must be pursued under the direction of an adept lama, one who knows the practice firsthand.

There are four schools of Tibetan Buddhism, each with their variations. The first school is the oldest: the *Nyingmapa,* or "Ancient Ones." This school was founded by the Indian sage Padmasambhaya. The second is the *Kagyupa,* or "oral lineage," from which several sub-sects have sprung. The third is the most scholarly of the traditions called *Sakyapa,* or "gray earth." The last tradition is the *Gelugpa,* or "Way of Virtue." This is the tradition that dominates Tibetan Buddhism today and one which the present Dalai Lama belongs. The Dalai Lamas of that school began their rule in the seventeenth century and continued into the twentieth until the Chinese takeover in the 1950s.

Cutting across these schools are two translations of Tibetan scripture: the Old Translation on which the *Nyingampa,* the oldest traditions, depend. This is the oldest translation of the Buddhist scriptures that guide Tibetan thought. The New Translation is the one on which the other three traditions rely, including the now-dominant *Gelugpa.* Another tradition is the color of the hats the lamas wear: the Red Hat worn by the lamas of the first three traditions, and the Yellow Hat that lamas of the *Gelugpa* tradition wear. You may have seen pictures of this hat.

The major document among Tibetan Buddhists is the Tibetan Book of the Dead. This is a guide between death and rebirth that a lama recites to the person during and after death. The recitation continues even after the corpse has been cremated. The interval between death and rebirth is known as the *bardo.* It is not so much a place as a level of awareness. Some would say that we are living in a *bardo* right now.

There are three *bardos.* The first is the *Chikhai Bardo,* the bardo at the moment of death. This is the moment of meditation and prayer. The second *bardo* is the *Chonyid Bardo,* in which the spirit of the dead experiences various Buddhist forms. The great white light is the one the spirit first perceives; it symbolizes the recognition that all life is an illusion. The spirit reaches *nirvana* if it recognizes the light; most spirits do not. The spirit faces the wrathful and peaceful deities, but they are but projections of the being itself. *The Sidpa Bardo* is the *bardo* of judgment and rebirth.

These are mandalas—there are hundreds—of a wrathful deity and a peaceful deity. The figure of the peaceful deity is the Buddha with a consort in an erotic pose. Both are but projections of the being's own perceptions, and they come during the *Chonyid Bardo.*

The Chinese Invasion of Tibet

The Chinese People's Liberation Army invaded Tibet in 1951 against a weak resistance force. It was a destructive process, with hundreds of monasteries destroyed. Atheism became the official state ideology. Many Tibetans, including the Dalai Lama, were forced to relocate to India, many in Darmsala, or to Ladakh, and Tibet itself has been repopulated with Han, or ethnic Chinese. Since then, a worldwide movement has been launched to recover the country from Chinese rule.

Conclusion

So we have seen that Tibet is a classical theocracy. Whether the system was a benevolent system or an oppressive one has been open to debate. In either case, the economy is sustained by herders, peasants, or a combination of both and they are part of a feudal system dominated by monasteries or secular lords. The Tibetan tradition of Buddhism is oriented to the Mahayana, or Great Vehicle schools, and of the four traditions in Tibetan, the Gelugpa is the current dominant one, to which the Dalai Lama belongs. The model of the universe includes the transition from death to rebirth in the *Tibetan Book of the Dead.*

Selected Films

Mystic Vision, Sacred Art. 1996. 28 minutes. Raju Gurung. Cambridge, MA: Documentary Educational Resources. Technique of Thanga art, a Tibetan art form.

Summer Pasture. 2010. 86 minutes. Lynn True et al. Cambridge, MA: Documentary Educational Resources. Tibetan herders move to summer pastures.

The Tibetan Book of the Dead, 2 parts. 1999. Leonard Cohen. Wellspring Media.

Tsundu: Becoming a Lama. 1997. 17 minutes. Raju Gurung. Cambridge, MA: Documentary Educational Resources.

Selected Literature

Kapsten, Matthew T. 2006. *The Tibetans.* New York: Wiley.

Laird, Thomas. 2007. *The Story of Tibet: Conversations with the Dalai Lama.* New York: Grove Press.

Ricard, Mathieu. 2012. *Tibet: An Inner Journey.* London: Thames and Hudson.

Sogyal Rinpoche. 1994. *The Tibetan Book of Living and Dying.* San Francisco: Harper.

Van Schaik, Sam. 2011. *Tibet: A History.* New Haven, CT: Yale University Press.

CHAPTER 13

Japan: From Feudal to Corporate State

Introduction

Japan is one of the most noteworthy countries in the world. First, it contains one of the largest ethnic groups in the world that make up an entire nation; the term for ethnic Japanese include *Yamato, wajin,* or simply Japanese-Japanese (*Nihonjin, Nipponjim*). It has the third largest GDP in the world, after the United States and the People's Republic of China. It is a leading country in technological innovations, including semiconductors and other computer-related technology. After Singapore, Japan has the lowest homicide rate in the world, and other crime rates are similarly low. It is the home country of Zen Buddhism.

Officially, Japan is known as Nippon, with an informal variant, Nihon. Both terms mean "The Land of the Rising Sun," an allusion to its location east of China (see Figure 13.1). The flag is white centered with a large red solid circle alluding to the sun, and former flags include the sun's rays emanating from the circle. The term Japan is an exonym (foreign-derived name) that probably came from Malay, *jepeng,* which in turn may have come from an old Chinese name. Early Portuguese traders probably borrowed this term from the Malay to refer to Japan/Nippon. The Portuguese likely brought the term to Europe where Japan or variants thereof became part of the Western vocabulary.

Japan consists of nearly 7,000 islands; four islands are home to 97% of the Japanese population: Honshu, the largest and most populous, Sikoku, Kyushu, and the northernmost, Hokkaido. A fifth island, Okinawa, is part of the Ryukyu chain located midway between Japan proper and Taiwan. Principal cities include Tokyo, largest city in the world at 30 million; nearby Yokohama, the principal seaport; the sacred city of Kyoto; the northernmost city of Sapporo; and Nagoya, Los Angeles's sister city, among others. One of the features that structure Japan's culture and society is its high population density; 127 million people are crammed into the 33% of the usable land of Japan; most of the country is volcanic mountainous area. Japan is in the so-called ring of fire, and the Tohoku 9.0 temblor and tsunami of March 11, 2011, was a grim reminder that Japan is nothing if not earthquake country.

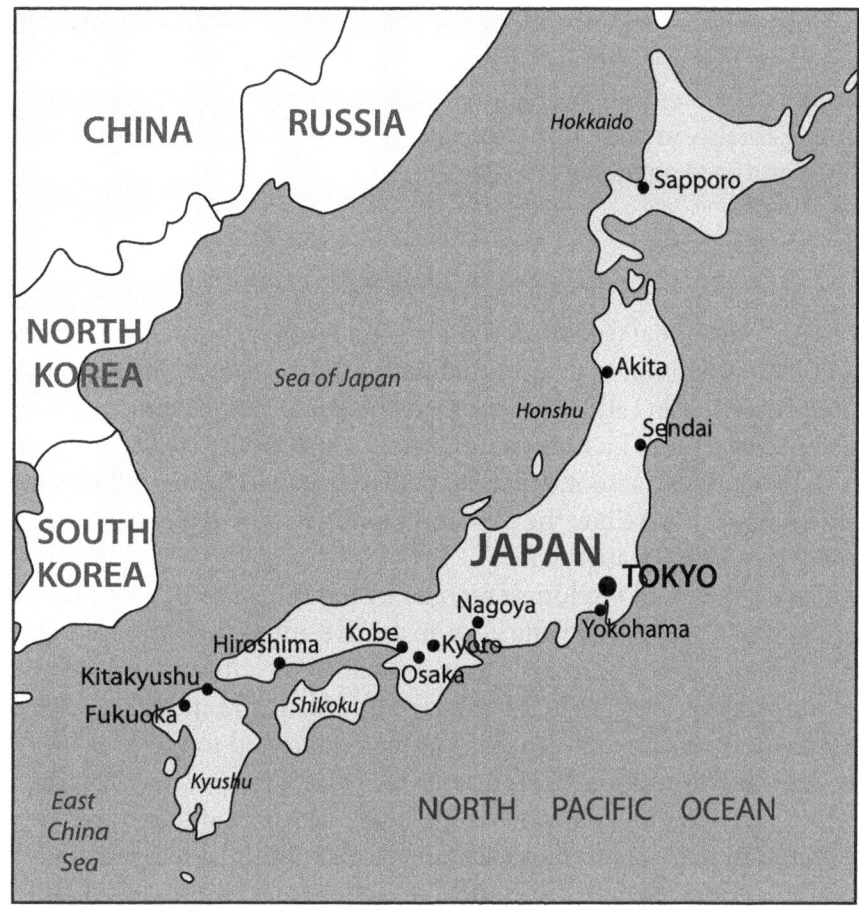

Image © pavalena, 2012. Used under license from Shutterstock, Inc.

FIGURE 13.1
Japan. The site of the nuclear disaster is near Sendai.

Pre-Feudal Japan

Archaeological evidence indicates that Japan had settled communities long before agriculture. Although the Jomon communities were still peopled by foragers, they were capable of elaborate artwork such as pottery and permanent housing. The Jomon period lasted more than 10,000 years, from 10,500 BCE to 300 BCE. The communities were laid out in a horseshoe pattern centered around a ritual shrine or community hall.

One Jomon site is Sannai Maruyama (near Nittano, which was the original name), located on the northern shore of Honshu Island, as the map above shows. That the settlements were permanent was indicated by the complex assemblages of tools, including knives, scrapers, and stone drills; milling stones, mortar, pestles, which are too heavy to move easily; and pottery, with elaborate designs. A reconstructed site indicates the horseshoe style of settlement design.

The remains indicate heavy dependence on sea resources, and most of the fish and seafood was taken except during the winter. Fishhooks, harpoons, and seagoing canoes all indicate the importance of fishing. Land resources were not ignored, and the bones indicate that hunting was a year-round occupation. Remains include bones of deer and boar, and 180 plant sources have been identified by pollen and seed analysis.

Feudal Japan

Japan went through a long feudal period, and the period is often compared with the patrimonial systems of Europe, including France. Commonalities for both areas include a contract providing the lord's military protection in return for the serf's personal services and provision of agricultural products. The contract also includes bonds of personal loyalty (fealty in France; *bushido* in Japan). In Japan, the system displaced independent villages such as Sannai Maruyama and rice cultivation displaced foraging. For a time, the maximum polities were regional lords, but they would soon be replaced by an administrative state.

In recorded history, the first kingdoms emerged by the third century CE; the strongest kingdom was the Yamataikoku realm. A strong administrative apparatus emerged by the eight century CE at Nara. Though strong, this state was unable to contain the warring feudalities dominated by samurai. Nevertheless, the Mandarin administrative model of China was adopted at Nara and became the structure that would dominate Japan up to the present. Written literature emerged by 720; Lady Murasaki's *Tale of the Genji* was written after 794, during the Heian period, as were the lyrics of Japan's national anthem, *Kimigayo*. Buddhism was introduced from China by 538. Though initially resisted by the Yamato clan, Buddhism eventually amalgamated with Taoism, also introduced from China, and the indigenous Shinto belief to form a distinct religious culture.

Shoguns became the principal monarchs of Japan, leading the still-warring kingdoms. They were often subject to overthrow by the feudal lords known as *daimyo*—even shoguns who successfully dominated the entire country could be kicked out of office at any time. Below the daimyo were the *samurai,* elite warriors bound to their lords by an intense vow of loyalty known as *bushido*. At the time Commodore Matthew Perry landed at Edo in 1853, Tokugawa Leyasu was the shogun for the entire nation of Japan. He would be overthrown in the Meiji Restoration of 1868.

The foundation of Japanese society from the end of the Mesolithic to the modern era were peasants. Though occupying the lowest rung of Japanese society, peasants were stratified among themselves. Farmers who owned their own lands independent of the feudal lords were the highest of the peasant strata. Artisans, or craftsmen, formed the next rung; the most important were woodworkers, metal workers, and the most prominent of these, sword makers, upon whom the Samurai depended. Merchants formed the next stratum; they were often despised as being parasites for the rest of society, but later would become the strongest force in Japan, especially after the Meiji restoration. At the bottom were the serfs, farm workers of the lords' (daimyo) lands.

As time went on, Japan's Middle Ages arrived with the dominance of regional feudalities. Their period is usually set from 1334 to 1568 CE. Each daimyo was jealous of his powers, and resisted integration into larger polities. By then, foraging had been displaced (except for the Ainu of northern Japan, the Kurile Islands, and Sakhalin), by two varieties of rice cultivation, wet and dry. The population increased dramatically and ways were found to intensify land use to areas pre-

FIGURE 13.2
The samurai were the principal warriors in Japanese feudal society.

viously thought to be unusable. A military aristocracy integrated previously independent extended family households into their realms.

In a later phase of the First Middle Ages, households became clustered around the lord's manor, and they became autonomous communities, with their own water supply, land, and agricultural systems. Craftsmen made their appearance and incipient trading systems arose; however, towns and cities were yet to emerge. Over the long term, land holdings increased in size, as did populations.

The second Middle Ages began in 1568 and survived into the Tokugawa period, which ended in 1868. As more powerful lords arose, backed by their increased wealth, their samurai, and their improved military technology, lesser lords could no longer resist the trend toward centralization. New waterways were constructed, which connected villages and added to the water supply of the fields. Markets emerged, reflecting the new interdependence; feudalities could no longer supply their needs on their own. Populations increased and individual plots of land diminished in size.

The later phases of the Second Middle Ages saw the consolidation of Japan itself. Iron tools were now introduced, increasing the efficiency of both agriculture and nonfarm industry. New rice varieties were introduced, increasing both productivity and the population that relied on rice. Fertilizers were introduced as well, in the form of fish cakes, fish oil, and human manure; production costs increased as well. Agriculture underwent an involutionary process. As field sizes declined, their per-unit productivity increased. Draft animals were now adopted to plow and harrow the fields. That also meant the marginal areas previously unsuitable for agriculture could now be exploited. There was a drawback, however: sources of firewood and fodder for the animals were correspondingly reduced.

These developments meant that interdependence among all productive units of society expanded at an unprecedented scale. Markets burgeoned as single crops were grown for sale on the market, displacing multiple crops intended for subsistence. Manufactured products now had to be bought; no longer could peasants produce crafted goods for their own use. To obtain them, peasants and their lords now had to produce something for sale. As commerce expanded, so did the police force, courts and their laws, and regional daimyos (now "great lords") in order to regulate the trade and enforce security. As time went on, fewer and fewer daimyos went on to dominate ever greater regions of Japan.

As land became scarcer and scarcer, contracts enforcing loyalty between servant and master became even more necessary. In fact, peasants might no longer be peasants as they lost their land in droves and became proletarians, i.e., workers without land. Peasant revolts became commonplace, such as the Shimabara revolt (a rebellion of peasants and unemployed Samurai) in 1637–1638. Partly sparked by Christian converts, the rebellion was suppressed in 1638 and Christianity outlawed. This consolidated the rule of the emperor as supreme shogun.

Institutional Roots of Modern Japan: Meiji Restoration to World War II

Modernity of Japan had several roots. First, the institution of legal contracts converted land from a fiefdom into a commodity that could be bought, sold, and deeded. The once-powerful daimyo lost their wealth to the industrialists, merchants, and bureaucrats who now came to control and administer the means of production. Power passed to a unitary monarch, now the emperor, and an administrative apparatus emerged under his sway. Thus, one can say that the apparatus of a modern nation-state had developed even before Commodore Matthew Perry arrived at the shores of Japan in 1853, the first of two visits.

Japan before 1854 pursued a policy of isolation ever since the Portuguese traders and missionaries created problems, including a rebellion, for the nation-state and its emperor. Nevertheless, trade elsewhere in Asia, principally China, could no longer be ignored, and Japan now had to come to terms with the now expanding international economy. The flashpoint came when Commodore Matthew Perry and his fleet entered Edo harbor and refused to leave when ordered to do so. He presented an ultimatum to Japan: open the country to U.S. trade or be invaded. The Japanese then relented and in the following year, on his second visit, the two countries signed a treaty allowing for U.S.-Japan trade and for American whaling ships to dock and load up supplies in Japanese harbors.

As the external political and economic environment changed, factional tensions built up within Japan itself. By 1868, a civil war erupted between the Tokugawa and Meiji factions. This led to the victory of the Meiji faction, and the new regime established rule in what became known as the Meiji Restoration. The Meiji emperor moved from the old capital to the modern capital of Tokyo. Under the new regime, the daimyo and samurai were stripped of their power and remaining assets, and the 75 prefectures (reduced from 300), passed into imperial control. From 1868 on, the Meiji regime adopted a conscious policy of industrialization by sending teams to study the var-

Image © tristan tan, 2012. Used under license from Shutterstock, Inc.

FIGURE 13.3
Postage stamp depicting a fateful encounter when Commodore Matthew Perry forced Japan to open its ports to American trade—and to whaling ships.

ious systems in Europe and the United States—steelmaking, automotive, postal services—and to select the ones that seemed to work the best.

The conditions were ideal for rapid industrialization. Some of the technology perceived to be the best were adopted—the postal service from the United States, steelmaking from the Germans, railway systems from the British and Americans—and the newly unemployed workforce were put to work to build the new infrastructure. Apartments were constructed for the workers needed for the task. Typically, a conscious effort was to recruit peasant girls into the new factories, inasmuch as they were perceived to be docile workers and less likely to join in labor unions than their male counterparts. Programs were initiated to ensure their "purity."

Japan soon acquired the reputation of being the world's model imitators. As mentioned, the U.S. postal service was emulated in Japan. Britain's navy was the model for Japan's navy. Heavy industry from Germany was likewise emulated in Japan. Family-based corporations, called *Zaibatsu,* became the motor force for development. Eventually, four zaibatsu became the principal entities in Japan: Mitsui, Mitsubishi, Sumitomo, and Yasuda.

Along with industrialization, Japan underwent militarization. From their view, they had a country to defend against the Western imperialist powers. The Imperial Japanese Army was formed and incorporated the latest military strategies of the Western armed forces; among the advisors was a team from France. Conscription was imposed in 1873 on all males reaching the age of 21. Although the samurai was now dismantled, they now found posts in the bureaucracy and the imperial army. They were also a good source for Japanese propaganda, analogous to the now cattle-less cowboys of the western United States.

Japanese Militarism

The Japanese were not reluctant to exercise their newfound military power. As the overpopulation of Japan became a problem—and with Western powers a continuing threat—the Japanese went on a number of military adventures. The Russo-Japanese war and the first Sino-Japanese war led to Japanese annexation of the Sakhalin peninsula of Russia and the takeover of the Korean Peninsula in 1905. The second Sino-Japanese war, beginning in 1931, led to the annexation of Manchuria; a renewed conflict in 1937 led to the annexation of northeastern China in 1937, which included the defeat, massacre, and rape in Nanjing (Nanking). Coverage has ranged from denial to allegations and documentations of beheadings, massacres, and rapes in the hundreds of thousands. Iris Chang's *The Rape of Nanking* has been the definitive work on the topic—including the interesting assertion that even Japanese who bring up the issues of that incident, or Hirohito's role in the war, have been threatened with death or actually assassinated—as was the case of Hitoshi Motoshima, who was shot in connection with his claim that Emperor Hirohito bore some responsibility for World War II.

War with the United States began with an attack on Pearl Harbor on December 7, 1941, and a prolonged Pacific War that ended only in 1945 in an unconditional surrender to the United States and its allies. For six months American forces remained at a disadvantage as Japan captured Singapore, expelled the British from Southeast Asia, forced the Americans out of the Philippines, took over most of the Pacific islands, and created a Japanese sphere of influence in the so-called Greater Asian Co-Prosperity Sphere. The tide of the war changed in June 1942 with a decisive defeat of the Japanese navy at the Battle of Midway, which saw the destruction of four of six Japanese aircraft carriers and a heavy cruiser. U.S. code breakers (mostly Navajo Native peoples) revealed Japan's strategy on Midway and proved also a factor in the reversal of fortunes. From then on, Japan proved unable to keep up with the needed pilot training and ship construction while the Americans succeeded in both.

After the Pearl Harbor attack, under Executive Order 9066 issued by Franklin D. Roosevelt on February 19, 1942, authorizing an exclusion zone that forbade Japanese to live on the West Coast, most, if not all, Japanese residents were relocated to race tracks in selected cities, and then interned into camps when the barracks were completed. The barracks were devoid of kitchens, bathroom facilities, and even running water—hardly fit for families. Allowed only what they could carry, Japanese families lost farms, businesses, and homes. Eventually, some Japanese-Americans were recruited into the U.S. Army as an all-Japanese 442 Infantry Brigade, which fought in Italy, southern France, and Germany, becoming the most decorated unit in the U.S. Army and also suffering the most casualties. Their motto was "go for broke," derived from pidgin English meaning "risk everything." The Japanese were released beginning in February 1945. Not one Japanese person was convicted of espionage, and during the 1980s and 1990s, the surviving internees and their estate received a formal apology and nominal reparations.

After the decisive battle of Midway, the allies entered an offensive involving heavy military hardware and a strategy called island hopping, whereby the U.S. forces bypassed the less strategic valued island and captured those valuable for air landing strips. But Japanese determined resistance slowed American progress in the war. Guadalcanal was taken in February 1943 after only six months of battle; Japanese allowed Americans to take over parts of the island and pinned them

Image © Nikonaft, 2012. Used under license from Shutterstock, Inc.

FIGURE 13.4

Atomic bomb, nicknamed Little Boy, used to devastate Hiroshima. Whether nuclear weapons were necessary to end World War II remains a matter of debate to this day.

down with heavy fire. Tarawa was won in six days but of 2,600 Japanese soldiers, only 17 survived. Iwo Jima and Okinawa both involved heavy casualties on both sides.

The dropping of nuclear bombs in two major Japanese cities, Hiroshima and Nagasaki, effectively ended the war, but debate remains whether the Japanese would have surrendered by August 1945 without these weapons. On the other hand, postmortem analysis of Japanese prison camps indicated that the Japanese starved and overworked the allied POWs, violating the Geneva accords providing for humane treatment. Both events have raised questions about war crimes committed by both sides of the war.

Japanese War Crimes

Japan has been responsible for some of the most heinous war crimes in World War II: the Rape of Nanking and of other parts of China, the brutal treatment of Allied prisoners of war, and a bacteriological research program known as Unit 731. One of the most debated issues is the conduct of the International Far East Military Trials Tribunal (also known as the Tokyo War Crimes Tribunal). Although some of the perpetrators of the Pacific War, such as Hideki Tojo, Japanese prime minister who planned and promoted the war offensive, and Iwani Matsui, the general who oversaw the Chinese theatre that included the Rape of Nanking, were hanged for their crimes, others escaped without so much as a trial. They included Emperor Hirohito (also known as Showa) and others of the royal family who participated.

Especially worthy of note was the release of Shiro Ichii in a deal with General MacArthur. Ichii was the director of Project 731, which oversaw the vivisection-based research on bacteriological weapons based in Harbin, Manchuria, China, from 1936 to the conclusion of World War II. The victims ("subjects" or "logs") were dissected while alive to test the effect of bubonic plague among others. Neither Ichii nor the others participants—at all levels—were tried, and indeed many, including Ichii himself, were appointed to high responsible positions of the medical professions and corporations after the Pacific War/World War II. MacArthur, the Supreme Commander of the Asian Pacific (SCAP), had his own motives for allowing these exonerations—to use Hirohito as a figurehead in the postwar reconstruction of Japan, and to use the research findings of Unit 731 with the cooperation of its staff. The incentives for both were tied in the newly developing Cold War with the Soviet Union, and, later, the People's Republic of China. A growing literature suggests that Japan was not the only country to use atrocities for political ends, nor was Hitler's Germany; others such as the United States and the United Kingdom have been no less guilty. The My Lai massacre and the Abu Graib prisoner tortures, both in recent history, come to mind.

Modern Japan

Under the guidance of General Douglas MacArthur, who accepted the surrender on September 2, 1945, Japan made significant recovery from the war. Institutional changes in Japan's society included universal suffrage by secret ballot, restoration of the Japanese Diet (legislature), retooling of Japan's industries from cars to telecommunication, labor rights (under a Republican!), and relative freedom of the press. The recovery strategy in Japan paralleled the recovery of postwar Europe (including former Nazi Germany) under the Marshall plan. It is also of interest that zaibatsu of the same families, such as Matsui and Mitsubishi, have led the redevelopment of corporations with an alliance with MITI under an administrative state, nicknamed Japan Inc.

Japan signed a formal peace treaty with the Allies, representing 48 nations, on September 8, 1951, in San Francisco. By then, Japan renounced imperial military policy, settling only for a Self-Defense Force. This released investment for a thoroughgoing industrialization policy, ranging from automobiles to telecommunications to—eventually—computers. A corporate society was re-established built from the original *zaibatsu*. A model of Japanese management came into being, guaranteeing lifetime employment for former students who passed what they called "examination hell." This was a reaction to the labor unrest during the 1950s when massive layoffs of coal miners were threatened by Matsui. Japan has become one of the strongest industrial powers in the world. Nevertheless, Japan has not escaped the deleterious effects of globalization. The lifetime employment policy has since gone by the board, and much of Japan's workforce has been "hollowed out" as Japanese companies, not unlike those of other countries, have sent their manufacturing overseas in pursuit of cheaper labor. The "Japanese Miracle" has proven less than miraculous over the late twentieth and early twenty-first centuries.

Ethnic and Social Minorities

One of the ethnic features of Japan is that there are few ethnic minorities. The Nipponese, or Nikons, are the most unitary in the world's nations. The main indigenous minority comprises the Ainu, a peoples in northern Japan (Hokkaido, the Kurile Islands, and Sakhalin peninsula—the last two are Russian possessions). Traditionally foragers, this minority still seeks to preserve its ethnic traditions. The Ryukyu form the main ethnic group in Okinawa and the nearby Ryukyu Islands. The remainder are immigrant Koreans, Chinese, Peruvians, Filipinos, and possibly Portuguese and Dutch descendants. Then there is a castelike minority called the Burukamin, Japanese in appearance but clearly as discriminated against as the untouchable *Dalit* in India.

The Ainu are perhaps the most publicized minority in Japan, located as they are in Hokkaido and points north—the Russian-dominated Kurile Island and the peninsula of Sakhalin. Though thought to be Caucasians, DNA tests suggest they are unrelated to the peoples of the Caucasus regions. They are traditional hunters and gatherers, hunting bear, horse, badger, and other game. Men traditionally wear long beards; the women sport tattoos around their mouths and faces. Both genders traditionally wear robes of a distinctive design. Their dwellings are traditionally one-room reed huts with the hearth at the center of the room and a hole in the roof to allow the smoke to escape. Among their arts is a distinctive weaving design, such as the ceremonial robe commonly worn on formal occasions.

In many respects similar to the caste system of India, the Japanese had a system of class—the shoguns, or emperors; the daimyo, or feudal lords; the samurai, or warriors; artisans; merchants (regarded as parasites); and peasants. They also had a castelike group similar to the *Dalit* or *Harijan* "untouchables," called *burakumin*. Like the untouchables of India, the burakumin were defined as a kin-linked occupation that involved death—executioners, undertakers, butchers, leatherworkers. They are descendants of outcasts in feudal Japan. Although the Meiji regime abolished this category, their descendants, identifiable from the neighborhood place names as registered in official records registrations, have remained outcasts to this day. In recent years, the Burkumin Liberation League was formed to oppose discrimination, which has limited this form of apartheid to some extent.

Japan: Its Cultural Features

One of the hallmarks of Japanese culture is miniaturization. In a nation comprising a population of 127 million people, it is scarcely surprising that this population has had to make do with less. A thematic example is the cultivation of *bonsai* plants, which are grown and bred to fit in small places. One such is the *bonsai* tree that is bred small enough to fit in a window sill. Housing design itself makes effective use of small spaces. In a typical Japanese room, the same room might serve as a dining area, den, and bedroom. One finds this process in industry. The Japanese made the first transistors, which effectively replaced the bulky tubes of North American radios. They brought the personal computer to new heights, with Apple and Microsoft being effective imitators and tossing the block-length computers of the 1940s and 1960s into the dustbin of history. To the Japanese, small is indeed beautiful.

Much of the theme in Japanese art and architecture is the theme of *shibui,* whose underlying theme is the balance between simplicity and complexity. A sake cup reflects the tension between perfection and irregularity. The cup is characterized by irregular form and muted colors, yet such a design is often preferred over the finely crafted porcelain cup that also characterizes Japanese pottery. Indeed, the main artifact of tea ceremonies are irregularly designed teapots and teacups. Another example of shibui is the interior design of a typical room, which balances the primary colors with gray to create a coordinated silvery scheme.

One of the most prominent attributes of Japanese culture is the geisha tradition. Geishas are women trained to create a fantasy world for all-male parties. They do so with elaborately designed hairdos and kimonos and with their skills in the dance, in song, in the playing of stringed instruments, and in serving food and drink. Contrary to popular stereotypes, they are not courtesans or prostitutes—in fact, male performers originally played the geisha role. They may have started as courtesans, but had developed a profession of their own by the eighteenth century. Their clients were, and are, high-status men, today senior government officials and business executives. Often compared with Hollywood stars, their costumes do not reveal their figures, but the nape of the neck is often uncovered and considered erotic.

Religion and Philosophy

Japan has two major religious traditions, Shinto and Buddhism. Shinto developed in Japan proper whose origin myths are centered in the country itself. The term is derived from *shin*, which means *kami*, or essences or spirit, and *to*, meaning a philosophical path, akin to the Chinese word *Tao*. It is believed that *kami* are inseparable from humans; they may be deities or animistic spirits, or essences of nature. Shinto was the state religion in prewar and World War II Japan. Buddhism, which came from China, is focused more on the intellectual. One can be both Shinto and Buddhist, and the two beliefs are often compartmentalized. One refers to his/her Shinto beliefs in conducting one's life according to *kami;* Buddhists rites are often associated with one's funeral at death.

To the West, the best known school of Buddhism in Japan is Zen Buddhism. Daisetz T. Suzuki introduced Zen to the West through such books as *The Essentials of Zen Buddhism,* published in 1960. In Buddhist theology, Zen is perceived as the ability of the meditator to reach satori (enlightenment) through direct experience rather than intellectual discipline. We all have a chatterbox mind, a mind that harbors one thought after another, the Zen masters say, and by *koans* that direct the mind to firsthand experience, one perceived reality directly. For example, to a query about the Buddha-nature, the master might reply with a seeming non sequitur—"It is windy this morning." The master substitutes the everyday experience for a painful elaboration about the Buddha-nature. "If you meet the Buddha on the road," reads another "kill him on the spot."

Culture and Behavior

In a crowded environment, polite behavior is essential. Thus the practice of *enryo,* or restraint in expression and action toward other people. Often, Japanese society is often seen as a passive society reflecting the effort to avoid conflict. For example, Japanese avoid the direct answer "no" to avoid offending others. They might say "your request is very difficult" as an indirect way to say no. The expression "Thank you for not smoking" is more indirect—but perhaps more effective—than the direct command "no smoking." This raises the question: if *enryo* smoothes over human relations in a mass society like Japan's, can it create new problems, such as releasing unpleasant information, for example, the effects of a record-breaking earthquake, its tsunami, and the damage of a nuclear facility?

Culture and Catastrophe: The Tsunami and Fukashima-Daichi of 2011

On September, 11, 2011, at 2:46 PM Japanese Standard Time (JST) an earthquake measuring 9.0 on the Moment Magnitude Scale (Mw) struck 43 miles off Tohoku at the eastern coast of northern Honshu Island, the main island of Japan. The nearest city of Sendai was severely damaged, first by the quake, then the tsunami that the earthquake generated. The tsunami inundated 420 miles of coastline with waves ranging from 11 feet to as high as 39 feet (this at the Sendai Airport). So far, more than 15,000 are known dead and some 7,500 are missing.

The tsunami, cutting a swath of 420 miles of coastline along eastern Japan, carried cars, trucks, and even ships miles inland. It also destroyed extensive acres of agricultural land. The official death toll stands at 15,431 and 7,937 are listed as missing. Many people were caught in areas thought to be high enough to avoid the tsunami.

Particularly destructive was the destruction of the Fukushima-Daiichi nuclear facility, consisting of six nuclear reactors, located between Sendai and Tokyo. A seawall had been constructed, but it could withstand only a 19-foot high tsunami; this tsunami was measured as being 46 feet high.

The Fukushima-Daiichi facility is a major nuclear site. It consists of six boiling water reactors, which are maintained by the Tokyo Electric Company (TEPCO). So far, three nuclear reactors have melted down and the fourth reactor is uncertain. The fifth and sixth reactors had been shut down for maintenance, but even they are at risk of overheating. The electronic grid was destroyed, exposing all reactors to the risk of overheating and eventual meltdown. As of March 20, 2012, the facility has been decommissioned and will not resume operations after the crisis has passed. The

Image © Maxx-Studio, 2012. Used under license from Shutterstock, Inc.

FIGURE 13.5
The Fukushima nuclear facility before the tsunami. Note its location near the sea where the tsunami struck on September 11, 2011.

government itself has set the level of the International Nuclear Event Scale (INES) at 4, despite calls to declare the level higher. It was later raised to the maximum INES of 7. Throughout, the Japanese government and TEPCO have been criticized for failing to fully disclose the impact of the disaster.

Conclusion

Japan is dominated by an administered state with a corporate economy, a long-standing pattern at least since the Tokugawa period and reinforced by the Meiji Restoration of 1868. Japan begins with the Jomon period, with settled, well-designed communities even while still dependent on fishing, hunting, and foraging, even before agriculture was introduced. The country went through periods of warlordism and feudalism of classical design. It went through the Russo-Japanese war and two Sino-Japanese wars, the second leading to World War II. Nevertheless, the corporate administrative state has remained intact to this day. Whether the country will survive the Tohoku earthquake and the nuclear disaster it caused remains to be seen.

Selected Films

Japan: Memoirs of a Secret Culture. 2004. 170 minutes. New York: PBA.

The Last Kamikaze: Testimonials from WWII Suicide Pilots. 2007. 55 minutes. Masami Takahashi. Cambridge, MA: Documentary Educational Resources.

Makiko's New World. 1999. 57 minutes. Media Production Group. Cambridge, MA: Documentary Educational Resources. Transitioning of farm women to factory workers in 1910 Japan.

Neighborhood Tokyo. 1992. 30 minutes. Theodore C. Bestor. Cambridge, MA: Documentary Educational Resources.

Shugendô Now. 2010. 88 minutes. Abela, Jean-Marc and Mark Patrick McGuire. Cambridge, MA: Documentary Educational Resources.

Tamiya: Japan's Hidden Christians. 1997. 34 minutes. Christal Whelan. Cambridge, MA: Documentary Educational Resources.

Selected Literature

Dower, John. 2000. *Embracing Defeat: Japan in the Wake of World War II.* New York: Norton.

Gordon, Andrew. 2008. *Modern History of Japan: From Tokugawa Times to the Present.* Oxford, UK: Oxford University Press.

Kaplan, David E. 2003. *Yakuza: Japan's Criminal Underworld.* 2nd ed. Berkeley: University of California Press.

Lu, David. 1996. *Japan: A Documentary History: The Late Tokugawa Period to the Present.* New York: M.E. Sharpe.

McClain, James. 2002. *Japan: A Modern History.* New York: Norton.

Varley, M. Paul. 2000. *Japanese Culture.* 4th ed. Honolulu: University of Hawaii Press.

PART V

Central, South, and Southeast Asia

CHAPTER 14

Central Asia: Land of the Equestrian Nomadic Herdsmen

Introduction

Central Asia has always been the subject of stereotypes. This is Siberia, where Russians out of favor with the czar or Josef Stalin or the commissar of the week were sent. Or if it was thought of at all, it was the middle of nowhere. Central Asia, however, was also the land of the Mongol hordes under Genghis Khan, who is still celebrated today in the Republic of Mongolia. More recently, it has attracted U.S. interest for a pipeline, and in June 2010, there was a massacre in Kyrgyzstan of the Uzbek minority. The region is likely to remain in the news for some time to come.

Central Asia, that land in the middle of nowhere where the Mongol hordes arose, is the region of the former Soviet Republics. Kazakhstan was the site of nuclear testing during the Soviet era. Since then, oil and gas have been discovered in Central Asia, resource regions of interest to both Russia and the United States.

Geography of Central Asia

Central Asia comprises five former Soviet Republics when the Soviet Union dissolved in 1991: Turkmenistan, Kazakhstan, Kyrgyzstan, Uzbekistan, and Tajikistan, all Islamic republics. Across the Caspian Sea are three more republics: the Islamic republic Azerbaijan and the two Christian republics Armenia and Georgia.

As has been the case elsewhere—Africa, the Middle East—tribal cultures overlap across nations. The best known feature is the Silk Road, which started in Xian, the former capital of Imperial China, and extended westward through western China and Central Asia, continued through present-day Iran, Iraq, and Syria, ran through the countries north of the Mediterranean Sea, and ended at the Italian city-state of Venice. Nomadic peoples were threats to traders along the road, including Mongols, Kirghiz, and Kazaks until Genghis Khan united the region with his conquests and so provided relative security to the traders along the Silk Road and others.

This map (Figure 14.1) shows the political geography of the region. Beginning in 1991, five former Soviet republics became known as the Islamic states of the region: Kazakhstan, formerly a nuclear testing region, Turkmenistan, Uzbekistan, Kyrgyzstan, and Tajikistan. Afghanistan is

Image © Olinchuk, 2012. Used under license from Shutterstock, Inc.

FIGURE 14.1

Central Asia, including the five former Soviet republics, all Islamic states. Some would extend the borders westward to include Armenia, Georgia, and Azerbaijan west of the Caspian and Black Seas.

sometimes regarded as part of Central Asia and Pakistan is sometimes thought as a candidate. Central Asia is bounded to the north by Russia, to the east by China (which includes Xianjiang, whose Uighurs share the cultural attribute of other Central Asian tribes), to the west by the Caspian Sea, and to the south by Iran, Afghanistan, and Pakistan.

In terms of physical geography, Central Asia consists of a wide variety of landscape: mountains, such as the Caucasus mountains to the western part of the region, the Tian Shan mountains to the south and southwest, a wide expanse of deserts (Taklamakan, Kara Kum, and Kyzyl Kum) to the north of the Tian Shan, and several bands of grassland—the steppes—between the deserts and the arctic.

Like other grasslands of the world, the steppes were unsuitable for nonmechanized agriculture, not only because of the cold, but also because of the sod, which no hoe or other hand implement could penetrate or break. Draft animals, especially horses, were the most effective in exploiting the steppes for human use. Not surprisingly, the cultures of this region included some of the best horsemen in the world. Other cultures exploited grassland for other animals—cattle in East Africa, goats, sheep, and camels in the Middle East, and horse and bison among Plains Indians of North America.

Genghis (Chinghis) Khan and the Mongols

The steppes long had a reputation for so-called barbarians of the north from the Chinese perspective and, later, that of the Europeans. In the beginning, the several warring tribes seemed

Image © rook76, 2012. Used under license from Shutterstock, Inc.

FIGURE 14.2

Genghis Khan or Temujin commemorated on a Mongolian postage stamp. He is still regarded as the national hero.

unlikely to form an empire. How they did so has become a highly relevant topic. The expanding empire began as five tribes as of 1206: Naimans, Tatars, Uighurs (pronounced "Weegers"), Merkits, and Mongols. By 1237, they developed into the largest empire in the world, past and present. Their sway extended from the Caspian Sea to modern-day Manchuria and coastal Siberia. Much of the following information comes from *The Secret History of the Mongols* whose author is unknown.

The Mongol empire expanded under Temujin, later to be crowned as Genghis Khan (also written as Chinghis Khan). There is no doubt that as a warrior, he was nothing if not ruthless. As a boy, he murdered his half-brother Bekhter over the spoils from a hunt. Indeed, he was said to be born with a blood clot in his fist, an omen that he would become a great warrior. Despite his ruthlessness, he was said to regard war as a last resort if negotiations failed. He started small; in turn, he defeated the four rival tribes: the Tatar, who had poisoned his father; the Merkit, who had kidnapped his bride Borte; the Naimans, and the Uighurs. As he conquered his rivals, he integrated the survivors into his own tribe and shared his spoils of war with them. Yet disloyalty and betrayal brought swift retribution. In one incident, he sent emissaries to Samarkand in a bid to establish trade relations with the shah of the Khwarezmid Empire. The emissaries were murdered, provoking a war that led to the slaughter of the entire empire.

His strategies combined speed, the siege, and technology in ways that, it is said, is still emulated by today's armed forces, including West Point. His soldiers, expert horsemen, traveled light and relied less on supply lines. Their rapid mobility, combined with their skills as archers and lancers, compensated for their lack of armor. They might seem to retreat, then make a surprise attack on the pursuing forces. When subduing walled cities, they laid out a siege and used catapults and rockets, finally wearing down the defenders.

Less known is his administrative effectiveness. He devised a code called yassa. The key canon of this philosophy is that nobility, including the khan himself, share the same hardships with his soldiers. Rather than kinship loyalty, promotion was based strictly on merit. Honesty was enforced with death for theft and robbery, and this law was enforced on the trade routes long after the empire was established; it was safe to travel in the empire, a point that even Europeans commented on. Religious tolerance was practiced, and Muslims, Buddhists, and Christians were free to maintain their beliefs.

After the death of Genghis Khan in 1227, the empire continued to expand from the borders with Europe to China to the Pacific east coast. The Silk Road, which had been established in 1168, continued to carry trade from Xian to Venice, and European traders were frequent travelers. Marco Polo was the best known of these traders. The *yam,* a postal system, became known worldwide, and the American Pony Express was said to be modeled after this system. Many elements of modern society were implemented under Genghis Khan: religious co-existence within the region regardless of faith; merit-based appointments to administrative office, not one that were kin-based; a rule of law that ensured that even the Khan himself had to obey. He established all these principles of effective administration in his lifetime and passed them down to his descendants.

Successors of Genghis Khan

The years following Genghis Khan's death involved further expansion to the west into Eastern Europe and into China under his son and successor, Ogedei Khan. Ogedei founded the capital, located centrally in the Mongol empire, in 1235; it was completed in 1238. His armies conquered Russia, Poland, and Hungary in the west and the Jin Empire in China toward the south. Only with Ogedei's death in 1241 did the expansion halt—but not for long. Under Mongke Khan, the empire expanded to the southwest into Iran, Iraq, and Syria, only to halt in Egypt. Mongke set up an infrastructure of the empire, introducing into the new regions a postal system, a policy of equitable taxation, and a census, completed in 1258. He assigned his brothers Helegu to administer Persia and Kublai to rule China. Kublai founded the Yuan Dynasty in China with himself as emperor. Mongke died in 1259, and the empire began to disintegrate soon after.

The Silk Road is one of the principal landmarks of Central Asia. Originating in Chan-An (now Xian), the Road wended its way into western China and bifurcated into two routes at the eastern edge of the Taklamakan Desert, one of the harshest deserts in the world; local peoples called it the "Land of Death." The northern route crossed the Gobi Desert then skirted the edge of the Tian Shan Mountains ending at Kashgar, at the foot of the Pamirs. The southern route skirted south of the Taklamakan Mountains and passed the city of Loulan before rejoining the northern route at Kashgar. The route then proceeded through the Pamirs. They then divided again, one going over the Pamirs to Samarkand and the other through India, both ending at the Caspian Sea. Other routes ran through Iran, Iraq, Syria, and eventually to the Mediterranean. More routes went to Egypt or to Venice, Italy. The routes were dangerous, mostly because of sandstorms from the Taklamakan and other deserts, and because of bandits. Although the western part of the road was developed first, originally because of Alexander the Great's conquests and later because of Rome's interest in silk, the eastern part of the route was developed later. The road reached its fluorescence during the Ming Dynasty of China and, later, the pacification by the Mongols under Genghis Khan and his successors. Over the years, precious goods in addition to silk—gold, precious stones, ivory, glass—were trafficked, as was religion (Buddhism first, then later Christianity and Islam). The Road declined as sea traffic proved safer and less expensive in East-West trade initiated by the Portuguese, the French, and the English.

Much of the Silk Road is found in China, whose principal ethnic minorities are Uighurs, who were driven from Mongolia into today's western Chinese province of Xinjiang in the eighth century AD. Initially Buddhists, they were soon influenced by Islam; half of the population in Xinjiang province today. All Turkic in descent, other ethnicities include the Kirghiz, Kazaks, Uzbeks, Tajiks, Turkmen, and Tatars.

Imperial and Soviet Russia

As time wore on, the regions of Central Asia became subdivided into units of an expanding Russian Empire, which passed into Soviet hands by the early 1920s following a civil war between the Imperial (White) and the Communist (Red) Russians. Both were to colonize the tribal groups that dot Central Asia, and eventually Central Asia was annexed to the Union of Soviet Socialist Republics, or the Soviet Union.

In the years that followed, the individual tribes and chiefdoms took on the features of the Russian political infrastructure: a charismatic leader, a decision-making politburo, a rubber-stamp congress, and an appointive administrative superstructure. Although granted independence in 1991 and invited to join the Confederation of Independent States, the newly formed states retained the attributes of the former regime; only later were there moves to establish democratic forms of government among some of them.

Post-Soviet Central Asia

Central Asian states went through a Soviet state, either as a satellite (Mongolia) or as Soviet republics. With the disintegration of the Soviet Union in December 1991, they all became independent republics, democratic in form, but military dictatorships in reality under presidents for life. They have all faced economic instability, though some had proven reserves of oil and gas. Environmentally, the drying up of the Aral Sea has proven a threat for states at its shores. Ethnic conflict is a constant threat, realized in April 2010 when Kyrgyz massacred Uzbeks in Osh located in southwestern Kyrgyzstan. A constitutional crisis that led to the ouster of the strongman Kurmanbek Bakiyev led to the creation of a caretaker government under Roza Otunbayeva. In turn, she called a constitutional referendum that was held on June 30, 2010. As of this writing, the constitution was adopted by a 90% vote of approval.

Kirghiz: An Ethnographic Case Study

As mentioned before, there are numerous tribal groups. The best known are the Turkic tribes; the Kazakhs, Turkmen, Uzbeks, Tajiks, and Kirghiz are the primary examples. This ethnographic section focuses on the Kirghiz of Afghanistan, who, because of border closures with Russia and China, were isolated from other segments of the Kirghiz. Their homeland is centered around the Pamir Mountains, and they are traditional pastoralists. The primary source of these Kirghiz is

Image © Makushin Alexey, 2012. Used under license from Shutterstock, Inc.

FIGURE 14.3
Kirghiz yurt, a typical dwelling in much of Central Asia.

The Kirghiz and Wakhi of Afghanistan: Adaptation to Closed Frontiers and War by M. N. Shahrani (2002). The ethnographic present is from 1940 to 1979.

Like other pastoral peoples, the Kirghiz migrate seasonally to higher pastures during the summer and to lower elevations in winter; this cyclical migration is called transhumance. They herd a variety of animals: sheep, goats, Bactrian (double-humped) camels, yak (oxen adapted to the cold), and, of course, horses. Like other pastoralists in Central Asia the Kirghiz live in felt yurts, or circular tents occupied by a nuclear, extended, or polygynous family. One of the changes in recent years has been the higher demand for animal products; as populations increased, land became scarce. Those two variables have led to increased stratification in recent years.

Sheep and goats are herded together as "companion animals," inasmuch as their grazing patterns differ. Sheep graze low-lying plants, typically grass, whereas the goats browse from higher growing plants, such as brush; thus, they do not compete with each other for food. Other matters of adaptation are the yaks, or cold-country oxen. They grow two layers of matted hair, which act as insulation against the cold. These are two examples of how a culture like the Kirghiz proves adaptive to a high elevation, cold climate that yields only grass and brush.

The basic unit of Kirghiz social organization is a household that average 3.5 persons. Of family types, 80% are nuclear, comprising the two parents and their children. The remaining families are extended (comprising three generations of married couples) or polygynous (with a man married to two or more women together with their children). Most households live in a circular felt tent that can be collapsed and loaded onto a horse or camel in a matter of hours. Recently, however, as tribes have been encouraged to settle, many families have constructed and moved into stone houses.

With the passage of time, the Kirghiz have formed chiefdoms in which one man controls much of the tribe through an *amanat* system. In this arrangement, a wealthy sheep owner lends

Image © Tracing Tea, 2012. Used under license from Shutterstock, Inc.

FIGURE 14.4
Nomadic Kirghiz woman in festive dress in Kyrgyzstan. Note the Bactrian camels in the background, distinctive for Central Asia.

part of his herds to individuals for their personal use: milk, wool, and dung use for heating. In return, the borrower repays the owner with lambs that the sheep have borne; this increases the owner's herds. Sheep is then sold in Kabul, Afghanistan's capital. Two-thirds of the households studied by Shahrani have few herding animals or none at all. Thus, the *amanat* system, coupled with land and animal scarcity and border closure have been factors in the formation of chiefdoms among the Afghan Kirghiz and the process of stratification.

Kirghiz after the Soviet Invasion

The ethnographic present of Shahrani's study ranged from the 1940s to the 1970s. In 1979, the Soviet Union invaded Afghanistan and occupied the capital city of Kabul. The Kirghiz lost the market for their sheep and other animals. Feeling themselves threatened by the Soviets, who had shut them out of the Soviet sector of their tribal lands, the Kirghiz decided to move. Some, under the khan or chieftain Haji Rahman Gul, migrated into Pakistan. Others migrated to Turkey and elsewhere. The move to Pakistan proved maladaptive: the only places to move to were tropical regions of the country, where the group lost their animals and more than 100 died. Later, the group found refuge in Turkey, whose cold climate and grassland topography enabled them to redevelop their herds. The source of study of this phase is Shahrani's "Afghanistan's Kirghiz in Turkey" in *Cultural Survival*, Vol. 8, pp. 31–34.

Conclusion

As this ethnohistorical sketch shows, Central Asia hardly represents a collection of obscure tribal cultures that live in the middle of nowhere. Nor was it simply a horde of bloodthirsty thuggish tribesmen. To be sure, they were ruthless tribesmen, but theirs was a study of military tactics that even today are studied by military theorists, even at West Point. Their principles of administration by merit rather than kinship anticipate the U.S. civil service reforms under the Pendleton Act by centuries. Finally, geopolitically speaking, Central Asia is a vital source of oil and gas and the pipelines that transport these resources.

Selected Films

The Feast-Day of Tamar and Lashari. 1998. 73 minutes. Hugo Zemp. Cambridge, MA: Documentary Educational Resources. Documentary of syncretic religious feast bonding Greek Orthodox with pre-Christian themes.

Genghis Khan. 2008. 40 minutes. Mandarin with English Subtitles. Beijing: GZ Beauty.

Genghis Khan: To the Ends of the Earth and Sea. 2008. 136 minutes. Shinichiro Sawai. Tokyo: Funimation Productions.

Herdsmen. 2001. 88 minutes. Wei Bin. Cambridge, MA: Documentary Educational Resources.

The Song of Harmonics. 1990. 38 minutes. Hugo Zemp. Cambridge, MA: Documentary Educational Resources.

Selected Literature

Hiro, Dilip. 2009. *Inside Central Asia: A Political and Cultural History of Uzbekistan, Turkmenistan, Kazakhstan, Kyrgyzstan, Tajikistan, Turkey, and Iran.* New York and London: Overlook Press.

Hopdick, Peter. 1992. *The Great Game: The Struggle for Empire in Central Asia.* New York: Kodansha International.

Sahadeo, Jeff, and Russell Zanca, eds. 2007. *Everyday Life in Central Asia: Past and Present.* Bloomington: University of Indiana Press.

Shahrani, M. Nazwef Mohib. 2002. *The Kirghiz and Wakhi of Afghanistan: Adaptation to Closed Frontiers and War.* Seattle: University of Washington Press.

Weatherford, Jack. 2005. *Genghis Khan and the Making of the Modern World.* New York: Broadway.

Zanca, Russell. 2010. *Life in a Muslim Uzbek Village: Cotton Farming After Communism.* Belmont, CA: Wadsworth.

CHAPTER 15

Afghanistan: Graveyards of Empires

Once upon a time, most Americans saw Afghanistan as one of those places in the middle of nowhere. If you needed to escape the authorities, this was the place to hide. In 2010, this is no longer the case. Ask any American soldier who has served there. This module will show why.

It is not for nothing that Afghanistan is often called the graveyard of empires. Often empires have invaded and occupied Afghanistan only to be caught in a tribal morass. Hit-and-run warfare, rugged country, and an arid climate were all factors in the failure of Alexander the Great, the Mongols under Genghis Khan, the Russians, and the British to retain their hold on Afghanistan for very long. Now the American troops seem about to have the same experience—30,000 troops or not.

Afghanistan: A Geography

Afghanistan is a landlocked country. Throughout its history, its boundaries and ethnic composition have changed. Predominantly, it is a tribal society in which empires have come—and often gone. Today's Afghanistan is bounded to the south by India, to the east by Pakistan, to the west by Iran, and to the north by the former Soviet Union—now Turkmenistan, Uzbekistan, and Tajikistan.

Besides being landlocked, Afghanistan is mostly mountainous country. This is one reason no one empire could hold its grip for very long. Eastern and Central Afghanistan is all mountain, whereas the plains to the west and the south are hot, dry desert. But it is also centrally located, with India to the south, Russia to the north, and Iran to the west. It has always been a crossroads for traders and military forces on their way to another region.

Ethnicity of Afghanistan

Practically all the tribes are strongly independent, yet they are capable of banding together to defeat a common enemy, as they did against the British in the nineteenth century, the Soviet Union in the 1980s, and—so far—the American and NATO forces in the 2000s. In the absence of a common adversary, they have been known to engage in longstanding feuds among themselves.

Image © pavalena, 2012. Used under license from Shutterstock, Inc.

FIGURE 15.1
Afghanistan. This is a landlocked country, yet no empire held it for long.

The Afghans are competitive even in their sports. Buzkashi is a form of polo in which the object of the game is the beheaded carcass of a goat or sheep, which two teams of horsemen compete for; one side wins a point when the carcass is deposited at an inner circle after the horsemen have rode to the outer edge of the field. Dog fighting is another sport. Even kite flying is competitive; the object is to use a glass-studded string to cut the opponent's kite away from its string.

The tribal Afghans have various degrees of loyalty. The first degree is to one's family, lineage, or clan. The second degree of loyalty is to one's chief who unifies the lineages and clans. The third degree is to one's tribe—Pashtun or Uzbek, or Waziri or any of 50 or so other tribes (more accurately, chiefdoms). The last degree of loyalty, if at all, is to one's nation-state. The Pashtun, for example, range from Iran to the west through Afghanistan to Pakistan to the east. The Uzbeks range into Uzbekistan and other former Soviet republics. The Baluchis of the southwest of Afghanistan also occupy southeast Iran.

The principal ethnic group in Afghanistan is the Pashtuns, variously known as Pathans, Pashtoons, and other spellings. They are also the second largest ethnic group in neighboring Pakistan.

Image © Dana Ward, 2012. Used under license from Shutterstock, Inc.

FIGURE 15.2
Buzkashi, an Afghan version of polo, but competing for a beheaded calf rather than a ball with long mallets.

(Note that the suffix –*stan* means "place of"). Their primary form of social organization is the patrilineage, or a group of kinsmen centered around a continuous line of males from their ancestors. They involve a segmentary lineage, which consists of a maximal patrilineage that encompasses all members. This patrilineage is divided (segmented) into smaller lineages (major segments), which, in turn, are segmented into even smaller lineages (minor segments) and eventually into minimal lineages (one step above from extended families). What makes them lineages is that every member knows how they are related to all the lineage founders up to the top. They may also recognize clans whose founders, by definition, they cannot identify nor can they trace their connection.

Afghanistan: An Ethnohistorical Review

Prior to 1747, when an empire was founded that incorporated them, the Pashtun and the other tribes were autonomous. In 1747, Ahmad Shah was elected by a *loya jinga* (grand assembly) of tribal leaders to become the king of the original Afghanistan. He was bestowed the title *Durani*, Persian for "Pearl." They faced challenges from outside forces: the Pashtuns had to jockey around the machinations of the British and the Russians, who were vying for access to India. (See "The Great Game" below). The Pashtun were major players in resisting the Soviet invasion, in bringing in the Taliban, and in kicking them out in 2001.

Before the Islamic conquest that started in 642 in western Afghanistan, most Afghans were Buddhist, Hindus, and to an unknown extent Zoroastrians. The recently destroyed Buddha sculptures at Bamiyan come from this era. Today, about 99% of Afghans are Muslim with a rough 85%/15% split between Sunni and Shia. Sufis are also found within both groups. Other religions still represented are Buddhist, Hindu, Sikhs, Jews, and Christians.

There were once several Buddhist sculptures in Bamiyan, a site southwest of the Afghan capital of Kabul. As noted before, Buddhism was one of the major religions that preceded Islam. The Taliban, a radical Islamic movement that ruled Afghanistan at the turn of the twenty-first century, ordered many of the Buddhas at the site defaced or destroyed. Islam prohibits any graven image of sacred beings, including the Prophet Muhammad himself. When Muhammad's forces entered Mecca, their first order of business was to destroy all the idols at the Kabala stone. The Taliban no doubt compared this act to Muhammad's destruction of these artifacts.

A consideration of the early history of Afghanistan will quickly explain why the country acquired its reputation and name of empires' graveyard. Waves of foreign armies invaded the country in historical times. Alexander the Great's army invaded the region and occupied part of the Bactrian empire before being driven out. Genghis Khan and his forces invaded western Afghanistan and depopulated much of the western region now known as Herat, but never subdued the entire country. In fact, much of his forces were absorbed into the country as peasant farmers.

The formation of the Islamic faith was a slow process. The Arabic Muslims occupied cities, including Herat, in western Afghanistan, but it was another 400 years before the entire country came under Islamic rule. For one thing, there were rival ethnic groups affiliated with Islam. The Turkic Muslims displaced the Arabs and extended the empire eastward and southward. By the eleventh century Mahmud of Ghazni consolidated the southern region and ensured the dominance of the Sunni division. This was the same Mahmud of Ghazni that desecrated the Hindu temples of southeastern India in one of the first Muslim invasions of that country.

The Great Game: Imperialistic Rivalry

During the nineteenth century, Afghanistan became the political football between Russia and Britain. Britain had wanted to protect India, by then its colony, from Russia and other foreign invaders. Both wanted to control Afghanistan for its strategic location between Iran to the west and India to the south and (at that time) southeast. This rivalry came to be known as the Great Game. The Afghans resisted foreign control and in 1842, in the First Anglo-Afghan War, defeated and killed the entire British army, sparing only William Brydon and his servant to report the disaster. The second Anglo-Afghan War in 1881 was equally disastrous. Nevertheless, the so-called Great Game between Britain and Russia continued until 1907, when rising concerns of Germany's power forced them to conclude a peace treaty.

Afghanistan after Independence

Afghanistan, after independence in 1919, continued to live under monarchial rule until 1973 when Zafir Shah, while away on official business, was overthrown by his brother-in-law Daoud Khan. Major reform came after another coup, by the People's Democratic Party of Afghanistan, led by Nur Mohammed Taraki, took place in 1978. Land reforms were implemented, farmers' debts were forgiven, and women's rights were granted, including running for political office. The conservatives, not enamored by these reforms, sought alliances to displace the PDPA.

By then, the U.S. Government, deep in its Cold War politics, sought ways to destabilize the Soviet state. The unrest in Afghanistan presented an opportunity; the Carter administration, with the support of Zbigniew Bzrezinsiki, provided covert military support to the conservatives.

FIGURE 15.3
Women wearing burkas while shopping.

Responding to the unrest in a neighboring state, the Soviets invaded Afghanistan on December 24, 1978. Ten years of war was to follow in which the U.S. government, first under Carter then under Reagan, supplied the Mujahedeen with arms and military advisors. The Soviet forces withdrew in 1989.

After Soviet withdrawal, the United States lost interest in Afghanistan. War among the several factions followed; out of the fray, the Taliban gained strength, winning a major battle in 1994, taking over Kabul in 1996, and occupying 95% of the country by 2000. Under Taliban rule, most of the civil rights were abolished. Women could no longer work or attend school, they were forced to wear burkas or robes covering head to toe, and freedom of expression was eliminated. Many academics and professionals left the country. Although the opium trade was curtailed, Sharia law was put into place; thieves were amputated and all forms of entertainment, including the traditional sport of Buzkashi, were outlawed. Long prison terms and death sentences were liberally applied.

The attack on the World Trade Center on September 11, 2001, induced U.S. military attacks on Afghanistan two months later. The issue: Afghan harboring al-Qaeda forces in the country; none of the 19 men involved in the attack were Afghans. The issue was that the Taliban had refused to surrender Osama bin Laden and other leaders of al-Qaeda. The Taliban were driven out of the country in a matter of weeks. Since then, the American forces (and other NATO) forces have been involved in yet another war of attrition, along with Iraq. The wars in Afghanistan (and Iraq) have continued to the present.

Since the 2001 invasion, U.S. forces have been bogged down in Afghanistan. The Taliban has undergone resurgence in both Afghanistan and Pakistan. Osama bin Laden remained at large until his assassination by U.S. Navy Seals in 2012 in Pakistan. U.S. forces have killed innumerable

Afghans and destroyed their infrastructure with little to show for it. In the meantime, the ban on opium has proven unenforceable and business in the drug is booming. American and other NATO troops have, so far, proven unsuccessful in either suppressing the Taliban or drawing many allied from the Afghan ranks. Using unmanned missiles ("drones") have drawn more enmity because the targets have as often proven to be civilians than military.

Conclusion

Although the excesses of the Taliban, particularly suppression of women's rights, have been curbed, the country has so far limited the effectiveness of the most recent empire, the United States and its NATO allies. Although the burka has been curbed for now, women still lack the rights in their own country. Women who have won seats in various offices and in parliament have been harassed, with one or two exceptions. Corruption predominates at various levels of government, including the Karzai regime at the national level. In short, the future of Afghanistan remains uncertain.

Selected Films

A Tale of Two Women. Experiences of the woman governor of Bamiyan province and a woman member of the Representative Assembly in Kabul. YouTube, http://www.youtube.com/watch?v=BRr21bkOdxs&feature=fvw

Afghan Nomads (*The Maldar*). 1974. 21minutes. David Hancock and Herbert DiGioia. Cambridge, MA. Documentary Educational Resources.

An Afghan Village. 1974. 44 minutes. Herbert DeGioria et al. Cambridge, MA. Documentary Educational Resources.

Child Brides in Afghanistan. Child betrothal, marriage, and outcome for the brides. YouTube. http://www.youtube.com/watch?v=dbkEahO161U&NR=1

The Coldest Winter in Afghanistan. (American patrol) http://www.youtube.com/watch?v=KsBQ_KU7pyY&feature=relate

Drug Baron in Afghanistan. YouTube. A very uncensored case study of an opium baron and his smuggling techniques. http://www.youtube.com/watch?v=Mxd5ugxNoAA&feature=channel

Taliban: Afghanistan. Taliban takeover and rule in Kandahar. http://www.youtube.com/watch?v=XyAerxHEWQo&feature=channel

Selected Literature

Barfield, Thomas. 2012. *Afghanistan: A Cultural and Political History.* Princeton, NJ. Princeton University Press.

Evans, Martin. 2002. *Afghanistan: A Short History of Its People and Politics.* New York: Harper.

Isby, David. 2011. *Graveyard of Empires: A New History of the Borderlands.* New York: Pegasus.

CHAPTER 16

India: A Culture of Futures Past

India is a complex country, geographically, socioeconomically, sociopolitically, culturally. We start with the *Bhagavad-Gita,* a narrative from Indian literature which encapsulates all these complexities.

The *Bhagavad-Gita* summarizes all that underpins Indian thought and action. The story is set just before the battle between Arjuna and his opponents, many of whom are his kinsmen and former gurus, and he is overwhelmed by the enormity of what he and his army are about to do. Krishna, the god in the guise of his charioteer, exhorts Arjuna to press on with the battle. The entire set of verses, about 700, uses the war as allegory of the life—and lives—every human faces in the illusory world of *samsara* and its liberation therefrom, *moksha.*

The *Bhagavad-Gita,* one of several scriptures of the **Upanishads** and the *Mahabarata* epics that undergird Hindu belief, summarizes the duties, the consequences of action, and the liberation of the human soul in the format of an allegory of a battle and sets the stage for Indian culture, not only of the past and the present, but of the future. This review starts with a schematic design of Indian culture, its caste system, its concept of *samsara,* and then continues with the periods of Indus River civilization, the sequence of cultures that bring Indian cultures to the present, and ends with an ethnographic case study: Village India as represented by S.C. Dube set in the 1950s. We also take a short look at a region near Chennai, formerly known as Madras, as discussed by Akash Kapur and set in 2003, a place that could just as well have been transplanted from Southern California. India lives in the days of futures past, as the soft rock band the Moody Blues might represent it.

India: A Geography

India itself is a subcontinent often known as Southern Asia. In terms of physical geography, the Himalayas form the north and northeastern parts of Indian, and it has cultures that look more like its neighbors Nepal and Tibet than the rest of India. Most of India consists of the Indo-Gangetic Plain, known for its hot, humid climate. Thar Desert to the west is cut off by the Aravati range. Besides the mainland, India also controls the Andaman Islands and the Nicobar Archipelago, located in the more distant Thailand and Indonesia. The large numbers of rivers that drain India include the sacred Ganga, or Ganges, whose site at Aligarh is the location of numerous pilgrimages throughout the year.

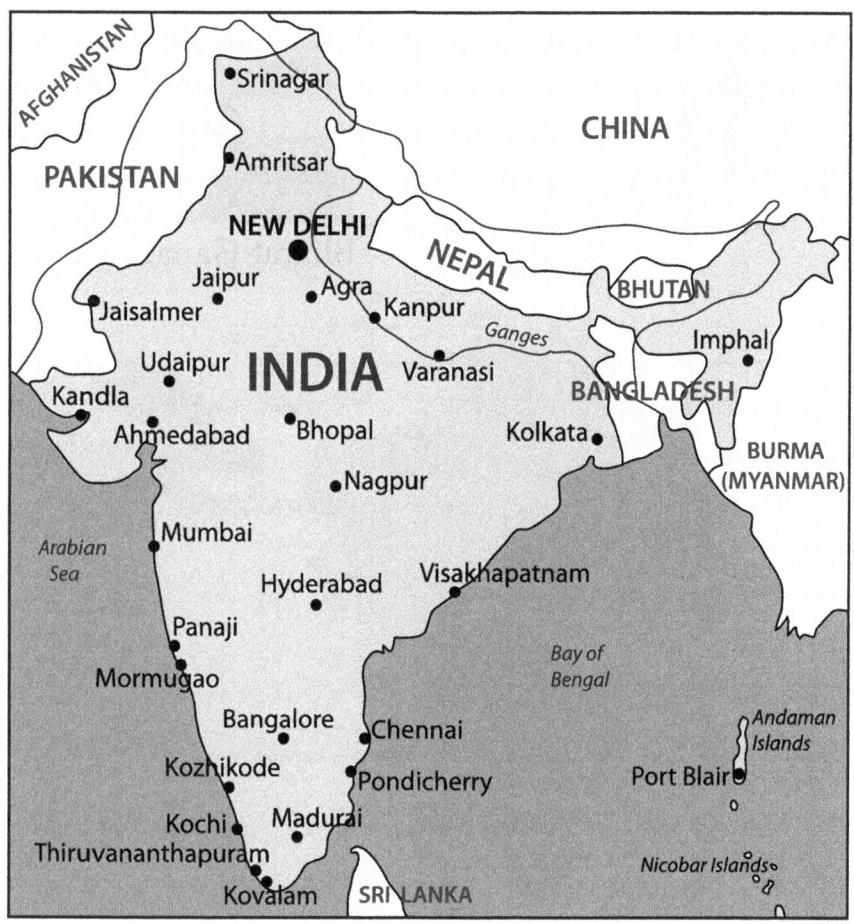

Image © pavalena, 2012. Used under license from Shutterstock, Inc.

FIGURE 16.1

Map of India showing location of major cities. Note neighboring countries and adjacent oceans.

India (see map, Figure 16.1) is bounded to the east by Burma and Bangladesh (formerly East Pakistan), to the northeast by China, and to the northwest from Pakistan, which received its independence along with India from Great Britain in 1947. The Arabian Sea is located to the southwest, the Indian Ocean is located to the south, and the Bay of Bengal is located in the southeast. At a population of 1.2 billion people, India ranks second after China as the most populous nation in the world. There are numerous cities over a million or more in the country; they include New Delhi, located in the northern interior; Mumbai, once known as Bombay, in southwestern India; Kolkata, formerly Calcutta, in eastern India; Chennai, formerly Madras; and many others, including Bangalore, the Silicon Valley of India. Bhophal is the site of the Union Carbide disaster, for which neither the company nor its successor Dow Chemical have taken full responsibility.

India, officially named in Sanskrit as Bharat Ganarajya, comprises 28 states in India plus New Delhi, the capital region for all of India. The flag includes the Chakra of Ashoka, a major warrior-king who renounced war and became a Buddhist convert after the Battle of Kalinga (now Orissa). Almost all states are represented at some point in the lecture.

Image © Richard Laschon, 2012. Used under license from Shutterstock, Inc.

FIGURE 16.2
The 28 states of India. Note the national emblem of three lions to the left and the flag of India to the right. The wheel is known as the chakra of the warrior king Ashoka, who pursued a peaceful unity after he converted to Buddhism and renounced war after his victory at Kalinga (now Orissa). Bharat Ganarajya is the Sanskrit name for India.

The name India itself is derived from the Indus River, the site of the earliest Indian civilization and whose name is Old Persian for Hindu. Although Hindus comprise about 80.5% of the population's religions, three other religions originated there: Buddhism, Sikhism, and Jainism. It also contains the most adherents of Zoroastrianism and the Baha'I faith. Finally, large numbers of the world's Christians and Muslims live in India; Islam forms an integral part of Indian history and it represents the third largest number of believers in the world, after Indonesia and Pakistan. It is also a very multilingual society. The main language families are Indo-Aryan (74%) and Dravidian (24%). Because there are 21 so-called scheduled languages in the country, with Hindi the most used, English has become the *lingua franca* of the country. The country is also multiethnic; there are 212 scheduled tribal groups in India. Nevertheless, the caste system is the most salient feature, together with Hindu religion and philosophy that sustain it. Other social features include patrilineal descent groups, patriarchal joint family structure, arranged marriage, and the high frequency of child marriage involving those 18 years or younger.

India: A Sociocultural Design

Hindu religion and its underlying philosophy is complex, to say the least, but there are a number of broad concepts involved with them. First is the belief that humankind at large live in a world of illusion called *samsara,* sometimes called *maya.* As Krishna reiterates to Arjuna time and again in the *Bhagavad-Gita,* we live in a continuous, repetitive cycle of birth, maturation, aging, death, and rebirth. We are born with *dharma,* a lifelong set of duties that govern ourselves through life. Our destiny is dominated by *karma,* or the consequences of our behavior from our past lives, not just the one preceding this one but many before that. Good and evil involve a balance between the forces of growth and creation versus those of decay and destruction. Yet there is liberation. Through many efforts involving the varieties of yoga, among other forms of meditation, we may at last recognize the reality beyond illusion, and so obtain liberation, or moksha or nirvana. This is not the state of grace in the sense of arriving in heaven, as represented in vernacular Christianity. This state, to the practiced Hindu, is but another state within the cyclical illusion of *samsara.*

The caste system represents, theologically, one of the states one has attained as the result of past lives. Castes are endogamous descent groups whose boundaries are rigidly fixed. One can never move from one caste to another within a lifetime; change in caste, if any, occurs between one life and another. As implied by the term *endogamous,* the member of one caste cannot marry that of another. Finally, when it comes to access to resources, members of one caste are better off than members of another.

In India, there is a multiplicity of castes, but they are generally broken down to five broad categories. Four of them are called *Varna,* or "pure" castes; the fifth is called "impure." The four Varna caste are the Brahmins, or the priests; the Kshatryas, or warriors (which include the police); the Vaishyas, or the merchants and/or craftspersons or artisans; and the Sudras, or peasants or menial workers in nonpolluting pursuits. The first three are called "Twice Born Castes" for the sacred thread ceremony (*Upanayana*), in which male members are initiated into the second stage of life (*ashrama*) of a Vedic follower. Sudras are not eligible to participate in that ceremony.

The fifth caste is a residual category for those who are regarded "impure" for the polluting tasks they are born to perform. Indian society includes occupations that are necessary but are polluting in their scheme of reality. Those who are born into the caste that handles such polluting tasks as removal of dead animals, leatherworking, or handling human remains from removal to cremation are called "untouchables" and have been given various names. Today, they are collectively known as Dalits, and have been called Harijans in the past.

India's caste system is associated with notions of purity. At one level, the four Varna (pure) castes are self-defining; to be such is to be free of pollution. The untouchable (Dalit) castes are by

Image © paul prescott, 2012. Used under license from Shutterstock, Inc.

FIGURE 16.3

An elderly Brahmin in New Delhi. The Brahmins are the highest of four *Varna* or "pure" castes in India.

definition polluted. For one caste to have any relations with a higher caste is also polluting to the higher caste, even if the lower caste is Varna. Bodily functions also pollute, from sexual activity to menstruation to defecation.

Any action that pollutes a person requires that the individual must undergo ritual purification. So extreme is the interpretation that a Brahman who is touched by the shadow of a Dalit must immediately take a bath for purification.

One of the recurring themes of Indian culture is the concept of *ahimsa,* or nonviolence. From the Vedas, the sacred books of Hindu belief, the practice of ahimsa is extended to animals, a tenet that underlies the Hindu proscription to eat meat or to kill animals for their hides, which must come from naturally dead animals. Ashoka the Great, who used extremely violent strategies to expand his empire, later eschewed violence in any way, shape, or form for the rest of his reign. The most widely known practitioner of nonviolent resistance is, of course, Mohandas Gandhi, whose strategies and tactics proved effective in gaining India's independence from Great Britain in 1947.

Hinduism is usually thought to be polytheistic, but a deeper interpretation would depict a deity with many manifestations. There is, according to Hindu theology a Supreme Being known as the gloss Para-Brahman. All the other deities are an expansion of Para-Brahman, as suggested in a diagram of Vishnu. Adi Shakti is the concept, or personification of divine feminine creative

Image © Sarawut, 2012. Used under license from Shutterstock, Inc.

FIGURE 16.4
Brahma, the Creator and leading god of three gods; the other two are Shiva, the Destroyer and Recreator and Vishnu, the Preserver. The three faces represent the belief that God is one, but with many manifestations or forms.

power. Adi Parashakti is Divine Energy beyond the universe. The constituent affixes are Adi (Never Ending), Para (Beyond), and Shakti (Energy).

The following conversation is from a student questioning a sage about the multiplicity of gods as taken from the Upanishads line of questioning:

Student: "How many Gods are there?"
Sage: "Three and three hundred, and three and three thousand."
Student: "Yes, of course. But really, how many gods are there?"
Sage: "Thirty-three."
Student: "But really, how many gods are there?"
Sage: "Six."
Student: "Yes, of course. But how many gods are there?"
Sage: "Three." This line of questioning continues until the Sage finally replies that there is one god.

After the Sage's final answer, the Upanishads as represented here goes on to state that the many different "gods" are in fact just the One God. This one God is also known as the Absolute or Brahman. Each seemingly separate god is, therefore, a different manifestation or quality of the One God.

Are Christians so different? How about the patron saints in Roman Catholicism, or the Virgin Mary? Or how about the Holy Trinity? Do we not worship the Father, the Son, and the Holy Ghost, or, as a hippie once put it, Daddy-o, Laddie-o, and the Spook?

In an interesting parallel, Hinduism involves three recurring deities that are known collectively as the Trimurti, namely Brahma, or Supreme God and Creator, which represents order; Shiva, the Destroyer and Recreator of all things (disorder followed by the recombining of the elements); and Vishnu, the Preserver of Life. The three combined represent *samsara,* or the cycle of life, death, and rebirth.

Each of the Trimurti has their female consorts, collectively called the Tridevi. Brahma is creator, so he needs knowledge or the goddess Saraswati (Vaak) to create. Shiva is destroyer and re-creator, so he needs the goddess Parvati, Durga, or Kali or power. Finally, Vishnu is observer, so he needs the goddess of wealth and prosperity, the goddess Lakshmi or Shri. Neither the Trimurti nor the Tridevi are complete without the other.

The pantheon in Śrauta consists of deities numbering in the thousands. Gods are called *devas* (or *devatās*) and goddesses are called *devis.* The most ancient Vedic *devas* include Indra (the original Deva). Others include Soma (the medium of heightened consciousness), Rudra (the chief demon), and others that number into the thousands.

They include the ten or more *Avatars,* including Krishna (who figures in the *Mahabarata*) and Rama (involved in the Ramayana), both of whom come to earth to the aid of humankind.

The Harappan or Indus River Civilization

The first highly documented precursors of India are the cities and villages that made up the Indus River Valley Civilization (IVC), which existed from 3300 BCE to 1300 BCE, and stretched throughout today's Pakistan and western India to southeastern Iran and northern Pakistan. Though a full-fledged Bronze Age civilization that was highly stratified, there is little indication that it relied on military power to expand or maintain itself, no remains indicating weapon-caused deaths, and few monumental structures celebrating military heroes or kings. They had writing, but it still is yet to be deciphered and whether there is a sufficient corpus to indicate the linguistic state of these markings is unclear. Finally, the cities' layout reflected very careful urban planning; even the measurements of the bricks were precise.

The Indus River Civilization was at its height from 2600 BCE to 1900 BCE. The Indus River itself rises in the snow-capped mountains of the Himalayas, descends through present-day Kashmir and runs through the Pakistani plains. Every spring, the runoff floods the plains, leaving silt and, therefore, a soil that is soft enough to turn without the use of plows. The major cities of the civilization include Harappa, the city that gives the generic name Harappan civilization, and Mohenjo-Daro, which the historian Michael Wood dubs the "Manhattan of the Bronze Age."

The period of the Indus River or Harappan civilization was preceded by the Neolithic, of which Mehrgarh is the best documented example. The villages formed along the Indus around 6000 BCE. Among the primary domesticated plants was western Asiatic wheat, and domesticated animals that were native to the region were zebu cattle (with their characteristic humps at the shoulders), goats, and water buffalo. Even then, trade routes were forming, linking the Indus region with Mesopotamia to the west and, later, with northern and eastern regions as well.

The Neolithic continued with the formation of several small villages with limited land. Archaeological remains suggest that the Harappans were egalitarian, with no dwellings significantly larger than the others. Metal ores were absent locally. As suggested above, the soils were soft, fertile, well-watered, still without plows. Trade developed apace. From the Baluchi highlands to the west came metals, semiprecious stones, and timber, leading to symbiosis between the Indus region and Baluchistan both in trade and in transhumance of their cattle. This trade pattern may have led to the development of complex societies that were to emerge along the Indus River.

Trade with Sumeria may have contributed to further Harappan growth. Sumeria expanded trade with Meluhha, probably the Sumerian name for the Indus civilization. The port of trade was Dilmun, on the island of Bahrain at the Persian Gulf. Items obtained from Meluhha included ivory, wool, cloth, leather, oils, cedar, and cereals. Other experts claim that Harappan civilization developed independently without this trade.

The Harappan civilization was nothing if not for its cities, of which there were dozens. The best known are Harappa and Mohenjo-Daro, both in Pakistan; Gandwereiwala was also in Pakistan. Five other noteworthy sites were located in an adjacent region in western Indian, namely Dholavira, Kalibangan, Rakhigarhi, Rupar, and Lothal. Lothal especially became one of the leading port cities in the Harappan region.

The cities—and Mohenjo-Daro was archaeologically the earliest and one of the best documented sites in the region—were exemplary cases of urban planning. There was evident concern with public hygiene, with public baths, individual bathrooms, and a complex sewage system. The streets were organized into broad thoroughfares in a grid pattern, separated by secondary streets which, in turn, were separated by narrow pathways leading to residences and courtyards. The estimated population of each city starts at 35,000.

One of the primary sources describing the cities' urban design is Jane McIntosh's *A Peaceful Realm*, which emphasizes the absence of walls used for defensive purposes. All cities, including the layouts of Mohenjo-Daro and Harappa, reflect a uniform design. Each city was dominated by a citadel raised on a mud brick platform located on the western edge. The citadel was surrounded by large granaries, bathhouses, and other public buildings. It was encompassed by a monumental wall, which McIntosh argues was used for commemoration rather than for defense.

Typically, the residential areas were spread out on the eastern side of the city. Anticipation of population growth seems to have been an important policy in planning; all areas, even those located on the margins of the built environment, were orderly and rarely haphazard, if ever. Bricks for housing came in standard proportional dimensions 1:2:4; for example, the dimensions of a brick might be $7 \times 14 \times 28$ cubic centimeters.

Each city was surrounded by farming communities; the hinterlands might cover up to 300,000 square miles (775,000 km square) for each city. Other cities sprung up beyond the region of Harappa. Lothal, the principal port city of the region of Harappa civilization, was planned in the same way as Mohenjo-Daro and Harappa. Shortugai, a mining settlement located 621 miles east of the Indus River Valley, was the principal source of the country's lapis lazuli.

City planning extended to the economy of the city. A system of weights and measures was established throughout the realm, and each city was sectioned off for the various crafts: pottery, flint manufacture, shell work, and the well-known manufacture of decorative seals. Bead manufacturers and bakers each were marked off as well.

Imports of the realm were predominantly raw materials such as gold, agate, lead, carnelian, and others. Many were reworked and exported as finely finished products. So well-known were the seals that examples were excavated in Sumeria. The western markets of the products were transshipped in Dilmun, Bahrain.

The sociopolitical organization of the Harappan Civilization is one of the more paradoxical cases in archaeological history. Evidence suggests that the Indus River society was tightly regulated and centralized, at least in the cities. Stratification was evident: dwellings varied from multi-roomed mansions with courtyards with single-room apartments. Yet the class differences seem to have been underplayed. For example, a sculptured bearded figure looks like a priest or monarch but is unidentified. There are no lavish displays of wealth, nor any monument or sculptures of bombastic rulers boasting of their deeds in their lifetimes.

Indeed, there is little evidence of a militaristic state at any site. Again, according to McIntosh, the walls appear to be monumental in function; there is no evidence of major defensive works around the cities or villages throughout the Indus region. Artifact assemblages include no weaponry, such as spears, shields, or helmets. Uncremated skeletons lack war-related wounds such as a projectile point lodged in the ribs. Given the warlike features of civilizations at the scale of the Harappan region, it would be a mistake to call it an empire. Any evidence of an imperialistic state is lacking.

Nevertheless, writing appears to have been an attribute of the Harappan peoples, but scholars differ on that issue. Most writing is short, generally found on the iconic seals, and is yet to be deciphered. Some 400 different symbols have been identified so far, but a corpus of text is lacking, so their linguistic significance, if any, is yet to be established. Some scholars speculate that they may have been used to identify merchandise. The symbols may be a mixture of sounds and concepts. Some seals and their writing suggest the early presence of yogic postures.

That the Harappans were artistic, there is little doubt, and decorative seals are iconic. One seal portrays a zebu bull, and many scholars have interpreted it as a symbol for Shiva, Lord of Beasts. Other seals depict indigenous fauna, such as tigers and water buffalo, and mythical creatures such as unicorns. Ceremonial life is often depicted, such as the statuette of a dancing girl.

According to Sir Mortimer Wheeler, the Aryans destroyed the cities along the Indus and Saraswati Rivers, but the skeletons he cites as evidence are dated well after the decline of the cities. The general consensus is that the Indus River Civilization (IVC) declined because of climate change, discussed further later. The entire population moved to the Ganges over time. Rice replaced wheat and barley as staple crops. Iron technology emerged in the region. Sixteen kingdoms later developed along the Ganges and so the Classic Period of South Asia began. The religion of the Brahmins emerged, followed later by Buddhism. Invasion of outside powers, namely the Vedic branch of the Aryan expansion, occurred. Darius of Persia incorporated the Indus region to the Persian Empire in 516 BC.

Alexander the Great came along later but failed to conquer India. The Mauryan Empire developed from a virtual vacuum and dominated India from around 300 BCE to 185 BCE; its sway extended from Nepal to the Daccan region. The remaining developments are discussed later.

Similarities between the Indus River Civilization with other civilizations include a high-yield subsistence base, supported by irrigation, a centralized authority with stratification, and the presence of writing, still undeciphered. However, there were also important differences from other civilizations: no evidence of extreme stratification, no evidence of warfare, substantial evidence that the IVC was a highly planned urban society, and that it had an economy with standard weights and measures.

There have been several explanations advanced for the decline of the IVC. An oft-cited factor is the Vedic invasion originating near Turkey in which Aryans displaced indigenous Dravidians in one fell swoop. The hypothesis by Sir Mortimer Wheeler has already been cited and rejected for inconsistency of the skeletal finds. More likely, the second major river, the Chaggar-Hakra or Saraswati River, dried up, forcing the population to move elsewhere. Other probable factors include a shift in major trade routes, the deforestation and soil erosion of the IVC region, and the permanent flooding of the Indus River, which did seem to rely on flood plain agriculture. The book *Decline and Fall of the Indus Civilization* by Nayanjot Lahiri reviews and evaluates these explanations.

A leading hypothesis is that there was a climate change that decreased rainfall during the monsoon season. As the Saraswati River dried up and the Indus River changed levels, the population was forced to abandon the Indus River Valley and vicinity and migrate to the Gangetic Plain of northeast India. Archaeological evidence indicates that the first signs of urban civilization in the Gangetic plain occur in 1200 BCE; some Harappan sites were dated 1000 to 900 BCE, suggesting that there was a continuous population flow during this period. If this is true, then there might be greater continuity between the Indus River civilizations than previously thought.

Vedic Expansion

In the meantime, the Aryan invasions of northern India were not a single event but came in the form of several migrations. Over the period, Sanskrit gradually replaced the Dravidian languages in the Indo-Gangetic Plain. Horses and four-wheeled carts were introduced from Central Asia. The four Vedas, especially the Rig-Veda, became the basic literature in early India. The Vedas are part history, but they are mostly hymnals about the sacred themes of Hindu religious ideology.

The Vedic expansion was only one part of a general expansion of the Aryan peoples. Based in eastern Turkey or west Central Asia, the migrations took a westward route through the Ukraine and southern Russia and then to central Europe. A smaller migration entered into southern Europe. The eastern route extended into Persia, Central Asia, and northern China and a southern route entered south Persia, Turkmenistan, then through Afghanistan, Pakistan, and finally the Indo-Gangetic plain of India itself. This was the Vedic expansion and eventually forced the Dravidians southward before they were eventually colonized themselves.

Further evidence of the Aryan expansion is linguistic in nature. The Indo-European language is geographically the most extensive of all language families throughout the world. The Germanic languages (including English) and the Romance languages (Spanish, French, Italian) cover western Europe, Slavic language covers Eastern Europe including Russia, and the Middle East includes Armenian and Iranian or Persian; Arabic and Hebrew belong to other languages. India includes the Indic (which includes Sanskrit) and Namali, both on the Indian subcontinent. Dravidian was displaced by Sanskrit, an Indo-European language. The number of cognates is an indication of the Indo-European. For example, the words for father are similar in many languages: *pitar* in Sanskrit, *pater* in Greek, *pater* in Latin, *pudre* in Spanish, *Vater* in German, and *father* in English. Other examples abound.

The mainstay of Vedic literature is the *Rig-Veda,* which reconstructs the probable features of Aryan society. Horses, chariots, ox-drawn carts, and metal (bronze) weaponry are all described in the *Rig-Veda,* and all of these features are of Central Asian origin while none were present in pre-contact India. The geography described in the *Rig-Veda*—mountains and rivers flowing from north to south, describe the Greater Punjab, one of the routes that the Aryans probably took. Soma, a hallucinogenic substance, is not indigenous to India but is found only in mountainous regions and in Turkmenistan; this, too, is described in the *Rig-Veda.* Finally, the main concepts of Hindu cosmology—*dharma,* or duty, *karma,* or action and its consequences, and *samsara,* or illusion—are described. Even the concept of *ahimsa,* or nonviolence, is alluded to in the phrase "Do not harm anything." Like the literature of other lands, the Mahabarata describes the human condition that transcends all cultures, including India's.

The *Mahabarata* is perhaps the defining epic narrative of India itself. Written in Sanskrit, the epic recounts in several embedded stories the Kurukshetra War between the houses of Kaurava and Pandava. The story and its subplots were authored over the years between 800 BCE and 800 CE. The epic, a story-within-a-story structure, is about ten times the length of Homer's *Iliad* and *Odyssey* combined. The *Bhagavad-Gita,* an 18-chapter segment of the *Mahabarata,* tells of Arjuna's reluctance, at the beginning of the first battle, to kill soldiers of the opposing army, many of whom are his kinsmen and former gurus. Krishna, a god disguised as his charioteer, points out that all life is an illusion, and even though it involves killing, he—Arjuna—must perform his duty, his dharma. Death is but a part of the birth-death-and-rebirth cycle that for the aware is the road to *moksha,* the liberation from the illusions of *samsara.*

The title of the *Mahabarata* is broken down to two segments: *maha,* which means great, and *barata,* which, among other things, is the Sanskrit name of India itself and, by extension, humankind. The epic poem has been variously interpreted as history, as myth, and as religious or philosophical allegory, or a story framing a concept or belief system. All concepts, related not only to Hinduism but also to other beliefs in India, such as Jainism and even elements of Zoroastrianism, not to mention other beliefs that were to come, such as Buddhism and Sikhism, are represented here. Specific historical sites are referenced, especially the principal city of Hastinapur. The archaeologist B. B. Lal shows that the Flood and even painted grayware pottery, have been archaeologically reconstructed.

The second epic is the *Ramayana,* composed in Sanskrit somewhere between 500 and 400 BCE; its title is translated as "Rama's Journey" in reference to Rama, another god in the Hindu pantheon. The plot centers around the kidnapping of Sita, Rama's wife, by the demon king Ravana, monarch of Lanka, and the story continues with the wars that follow to bring Sita back to Rama. The story serves as allegory to portray ideal relationships among father, mother, son, daughter, servants, and other characters in an ideal kingdom. The theme of absolute duty— dharma—underlies this story. Versions of this story recur among the Jains, the Sikhs, and the Buddhists in such countries as Cambodia, Indonesia, the Philippines, and Thailand.

Jainism was the belief that guided Chandragupta, the founder of the Maurya Empire, and also the belief of Mohandas Gandhi's mother. According to this belief, themes included asceticism; compassion for all forms of life; the importance of vows for self-discipline; vegetarianism; fasting for self-purification; mutual tolerance among people of different creeds; and "*syadvad,*" the idea that all views of truth are partial, a doctrine that lay at the root of Satyagraha, or nonviolent

Image © Andrey Pils, 2012. Used under license from Shutterstock, Inc.

FIGURE 16.5
Arjuna and Krishna at the outset of battle in the *Mahabarata,* of which the *Bhagavad-Gita* is an integral part.

resistance (in Gandhiian terms). Authorities differ whether Jainism originated in the Indus River Valley or was one of the tenets of the Vedic tradition.

Maurya, Gupta, and Chola Empires

India has a complex history of kingdoms in various locales throughout the southern Asian sub-continent. The regions are ethnically diverse and boast of 22 different languages, mostly of San-skrit or Dravidian derivation. This series emphasizes the best-known kingdoms and their influences on cultures throughout India. One of the first known kings was Chandragupta, who, through a series of campaigns, unified northern and central India from Bengal to the east to Baluchistan and eastern Persia to the west, under the sway of the Maurya Empire. His was the first empire in India's history and he himself the first emperor; he ruled from 340 to 298 BCE. He later converted to Jainism and, according to legend, so committed was he to reaching moksha that he died of starvation while meditating. His son Bindusar succeeded him in 298 BCE and his grand-son Ashoka rose to power in 273 BCE.

Ashoka was heavily influenced by Buddhism, as we shall see. Buddhism, as is well known, is widespread throughout Asia but it started in India. Gautama Buddha (born about 563), also known as Siddhartha, grew up protected from seeing the suffering of the world outside his palace. Having been married with a son, Siddhartha first saw an old man and learned from his mentor that aging is the condition of all life. Stricken by the reality of suffering—aging, deformities, disease—he chose to leave his palace to wander as a mendicant throughout India. After living a life of meditation and deliberate self-deprivation, he came to realize that extreme asceticism leads nowhere. He then adopted the Middle Way between self-indulgence and self-denial and later,

Image © piyagoon, 2012. Used under
license from Shutterstock, Inc.

FIGURE 16.6
Buddha and enlightenment.

while meditating under a Bodhi tree, he reached enlightenment (known among Buddhists as *nirvana* and to Hindus as *moksha*).

He went on to teach by example the path to enlightenment. His teachings are summed up by his Four Noble Truths: The First Truth is that we all experience dukkha, that is, suffering, anxiety, stress. The Second Truth is that dukkha is rooted in desire or craving. The Third Truth is the cessation of dukkha. The Fourth Truth is that there is an Eightfold Path to enlightenment: Right Understanding, Right Thought, Right Speech, Right Action, Right Livelihood, Right Effort, Right Mindfulness, and Right Concentration. This practice and belief system would spread throughout Eastern Asia, though it declined in India. But the belief played an important role in Ashoka's reign.

As noted above Ashoka rose to power in 273 BPE and sought to expand the Maurya Empire established by this father and grandfather. The pivotal event in his life came in the conquest of Kalinga (now Orissa), which had resisted the Maurya dynasty for centuries. In the Battle of Kalinga, 100,000 soldiers were killed, including 10,000 of his own men. As he surveyed the devastation his successful venture had inflicted, he felt an overwhelming remorse over what he had done and changed his ways. He converted to Buddhism, sought counsel from a Buddhist monk and organized his kingdom based on the principles of ahimsa, or nonviolence. He renounced war and violence although he maintained a large army. He forbade hunting and cruelty to animals of any form. He launched public works program at home and friendly relations abroad to Greece and

FIGURE 16.7
The Indian flag adopted the Chakra of Ashoka as its emblem; it represents ahimsa, or non-violence.

other European principalities. The national flag of India bears the 24-spoked wheel called the Chakra of Ashoka.

The Gupta Empire was known as the Golden Age of India, and lasted from 320 to 550 CE. The empire's military expansions were extraordinary enough, stretching from the Himalayas to Central India at its height, and from Thailand to Afghanistan. Its legacy is best known for developments in astronomy and mathematics. For example, Aryabhata came up with the concept of *pi*, the theory of place and of zero in mathematics, and he also hypothesized that planets revolve around the sun and formed a system in outer space. The Indian scholar Vatsyayana composed the *Kama Sutra,* the original work on human sexual behavior and technique. War games were not ignored. The game of chess, called *caturaṅga,* was invented with pieces representing infantry, cavalry, war elephants, and charioteers, which later became pawns, knights, bishops, and rooks, respectively. Other innovations included epic poetry, architecture, coinage, and much else.

Another empire sprung up in south India, in the region of Tamil Nadu. Known as the Cholas, its founder was Raja Raja, or King of Kings. His empire expanded beyond the shores of India to as far as Indonesia and expanded northward to Kalinga. His best known accomplishments were an administrative system with an efficient revenue generation system. Also known was the Shiva Temple in Thanjavur, called Raajarajeswaram, reflecting his lifelong devotion to the god Shiva. Myth holds that, originally unwilling to serve as king, he was compelled to do so when a birthmark identifying Vishnu was found on his body. He was elected by consensus of the council, the first democratic process reported for India. And Raja Raja was a fastidious record keeper, preceding the British bureaucracy of India by centuries. The Cholas have left a detailed history of the kings and their peoples. Even the home addresses of the dancing girls were kept.

FIGURE 16.8

Detail from Raajarajeswaram Temple in Thanjavur, showing erotic theme and also showing Indian ambivalence toward sexuality.

Mughal Period

Islam expanded into India around the tenth century CE, expanding eastward from its origins in Arabia and entering Northwest Indian through Afghanistan and present-day Pakistan. Intent on destroying idolatry—Islam forbids graphic representations of any kind—the first Hindu temples were destroyed, creating tensions between the two belief systems from the start. In the city of Multan in Pakistan, Sultan Mahmoud of Ghazni ordered the destruction of a Hindu temple in Somnath, South India. Though destroyed as a pretext to destroy the infidels, the more likely explanation was looting the place. He also sacked seven other cities and their temples.

However, other invasions were to follow. One that involved the takeover of Delhi and its hinterland was to have more lasting effects on Indo-Islamic relations. In 1206, the first of five Sultanates was established in India and played substantial roles in forming a presence in the country. The Sultanates established control over northern and central India. In so doing, they kept the Mongols from entering and controlling India. It was they who fostered a syncretic Indo-Islamic cultural fusion in a wide area of crafts: architecture, the arts, literature, and language. For example, Urdu was, and is, a mix of dialects of Sanskrit with those of Persian, Arabic, and Turkish. This pattern was referred to as "the meeting of two oceans" metaphorically the Arabian Sea and the Indian Ocean.

Eventually the Mongols, descendants of Genghis Khan and Tamerlane, did enter India. The conquistador was Zohar us-din Muhammad Babur, whose forces displaced the Sultanate of Delhi. The forces were successful owing to a new piece of European military technology—the cannon. Unlike many of the Muslim invaders preceding him, Babur prevented the looting of Delhi and Agra and he was the first to enact into public policy the Sufi belief in the commonalities of all faiths. Like Tamerlane and other Mongols before him, he allowed the citizens to continue practicing their religions.

With Akbar the Great, successor to Babur of Delhi, came a second Golden Age of India. Crowned at age 13, Akbar began by mobilizing his troops against impossible odds to reestablish the Mughal kingdom and expand it to an unprecedented degree. Under the Sultanate, an unpopular tax had been imposed on non-Muslims. He abolished the tax and ensured their allegiance in other ways. It was Akbar who constructed the Golden Temple for the Sikh population. Although he rationalized the administrative structure, legal arrangements, and fiscal reforms, he did much more—sought common ground for all religions. To that end, he organized a conference inviting leading members of all religions in the country: Hindu, Buddhist, Muslim, Christian, Jews, Jain, and Sikh, even Parsi (Zoroastrians) to seek and find what theological points they could agree upon.

After Akbar died in 1605, his son Jahagir succeeded him, followed by Jahan Shah. The Taj Mahal, which integrates Hindu and Islamic themes, was the main achievement under Jahan Shah's reign. Like his other projects, the Taj Mahal incorporated Judgment Day into his themes and maintained the traditions of integrating the two religions in his policies. His son, Aurangzeb, was

Image © Matej Hudovernik, 2012. Used under license from Shutterstock, Inc.

FIGURE 16.9

Taj Mahal. Conceived by Jahan Shah, the architecture incorporates Hindu and Islamic themes. The right hand side represents paradise, with the bridge representing the Day of Judgment.

a strict Islamist and eventually arrested Jahan Shah and put him to death. For the next 25 years, he fought off the rising Hindu Maratha Empire, restarting the rift between Hindus and Muslims, which eventually created the split between India and Pakistan in 1947.

With the internal division created by Aurangzeb, the Mughal Empire weakened, though still maintaining regional hegemony. The Hindu Marathas under Shivaji and his successor Shahu never displaced the Mughals, but they did control coastal regions during the eighteenth century. The last significant port city fell to the British in the mid-nineteenth century. The Rajputs came under Maratha dominance after the Mughal decline and succumbed to British dominance along with the Maratha Empire. The Sikh Empire broke away from the Mughals around 1799, later to be defeated by the British in 1849.

The Sikh religion is often confused with Hinduism or Islam but is neither. Founded by Guru Nanak Ji, the first of 10 Gurus, the religion sees God as unknowable and the source of all beings and things. All humankind is seen as one, rejecting all castes, class, and other social, economic, and religious divisions. All assets are to be shared by the community. All initiated males have uncut hair, a turban, a sword, a comb, and long undershorts, all of which begin with the letter K in their language. All men are surnamed Singh (lion). All women are surnamed Kaur (Princess). Most Sikhs live in the Punjab region of northwestern India, but there is a worldwide diaspora.

Although Sikhism began in the fifteenth century, the Sikh empire did not form until 1799. Individual confederacies called *Misls* formed as early as 1707, as the Mughal Empire weakened and an alliance of Sikhs defeated the Mughals and the Afghans to the west. Ranjit Singh rose to power in a very short period, from a leader of a single Sikh Misl to finally becoming the Maharaja of Punjab. He began to modernize his army, using the latest training as well as weapons and artillery. After the death of Ranjit Singh, the empire was weakened by internal divisions and political mismanagement. Finally, by 1849 the state was dissolved after their defeat in the Anglo-Sikh wars.

British Colonialism

India was now no longer exporting manufactured goods as it long had, but was instead supplying the British empire with raw materials, and many historians consider this to be the onset of India's colonial period. By this time, with its economic power severely curtailed by the British parliament, India itself became an appendage of the British empire. After the Battle of Plassey in 1757, in which the East India Company (the Company) took over the commerce and taxation in Bengal, India effectively became the colony of the Company until 1858. Later wars ensured the Company control over Calcutta, the Company began to more consciously enter non-economic arenas such as education, social reform, and culture. An appreciation of Indian culture was promoted by Thomas Stewart, major general for the Company. He worshipped the Hindu gods daily, bathed in the Ganges, and even thought English women should abandon their hoop skirts in favor of the sari.

Historians consider India's modern age to have begun sometime between 1848 and 1885. The appointment in 1848 of Lord Dalhousie as Governor General of the East India Company rule in India set the stage for changes essential to a modern state. These included the consolidation and demarcation of sovereignty, the surveillance through a census of the Indian population, and the education of its citizens. Technological changes—among them, railways, canals, and the telegraph—were introduced not long after their introduction in Europe. However, disaffection set in after years of colonial policy that included invasive British-style social reforms, harsh land taxes, and summary treatment of some rich landowners and princes. This set the stage for the Sepoy Mutiny in 1857.

The Indian Rebellion, also known as the Indian or Sepoy Mutiny, erupted in 1857. The mutiny was named after the Sepoys, who were Indian soldiers in service of the Company. The rebellion rocked many regions of northern and central India and shook the foundations of Company rule. The tensions leading to the revolt came with the increasing intolerance of evangelical Christians toward both Hindu and Muslim beliefs. Using cow and pig fat for greasing musket cartridges, which was offensive to both Hindu and Muslim soldiers, was the immediate cause of the rebellion. The revolt and the repression that followed decimated the population of New Delhi and leveled other cities such as Lucknow. Karl Marx, writing for the *New York Tribune* at the time, railed against the failure of the British press to report on British atrocities against the Indian rebels.

Although the rebellion was suppressed by 1858, it led to the dissolution of the East India Company and to the direct administration of India by the British government itself. Proclaiming a unitary state and a gradual but limited British-style parliamentary system, the new rulers also protected princes and landed gentry as a feudal safeguard against future unrest. In the decades following, public life gradually emerged all over India, leading eventually to the founding of the Indian National Congress in 1885.

The rush of technology and the commercialization of agriculture in the second half of the nineteenth century were marked by economic setbacks—many small farmers became dependent on the whims of far-away markets. There was an increase in the number of large-scale famines, and, despite the risks of infrastructure development borne by Indian taxpayers, little industrial employment was generated for Indians. There were also salutary effects: commercial cropping, especially in the newly canalled Punjab, led to increased food production for internal consumption. The railway network provided critical famine relief, notably reduced the cost of moving goods, and helped nascent Indian-owned industry. Nevertheless, the policies on the whole proved inimical to the Indian commercial and political elites and in the long run of the Indian population at large.

The movement begins in the aftermath of the Indian Rebellion. The Indian National Congress was formed in 1885 under the tutelage of Allan O. Hume, a British civil servant who supported the move for Indian independence. One of the strands affecting independence was the division by religions, fostered by the census which listed religion as the first criterion. Everyone for the most part was listed either as Hindu or Muslim, and that reinforced the division between the believers of the two major religions. The religious categories are retained from 1881, the first decade on the census, up to 1991 through ten-year segments. After World War I, in which some one million Indians served, a new period began. It was marked by British reforms but also by repressive legislation, including the Rowlatt Act, passed in 1919, which limited rights of peaceful protest and the limit of public assemblies to a maximum of four participants.

On April 13, 1919, a group of 20,000 peaceful protestors were assembled in the holy Sikh city of Amritsar in Punjab to protest the loss of civil rights under the Rowlatt Act. The assembly was perceived by the authorities as an insurrection and a violation of the four-person limit to assemblies. Without warning, the troops under General Reginald Dyer opened fired on the crowd, killing 400 to 1,500 (depending on estimate) and wounding many more. Dyer was forcibly retired but received a hero's welcome back home in London. This massacre provided the motor force for an independence movement.

The massacre, coupled with further repressive legislation, led to more strident Indian calls for self-rule, and to the beginnings of a non-violent movement of non-cooperation, of which Mohandas Karamchand Gandhi would become the leader and enduring symbol. During the 1930s, slow legislative reforms were enacted by the British; these delays contributed to electoral victories by the Indian National Congress. The next decade was beset with crises: Indian participation in World War II, coupled with the formation of the Muslim League, and the Congress's final push for separation contributed to the ultimate independence of the subcontinent.

Among the key players of the independence movement were Mohandas Gandhi, Mohammad Ali Jinnah, and Jawaharlal Nehru. Mohandas Gandhi had developed his principles of nonviolent and noncooperative tactics while a lawyer in South Africa. Initially, the Independence movement was confined to commercial interests, but by 1920, the Indian National Congress adopted Gandhi's principles of nonviolence and noncooperation to serve the population overall. In violation of the Salt Tax, Gandhi led the Salt March in April 1930 to the sea and made salt, along with thousands of other supporters; the British imprisoned 60,000 over that incident. Gandhi attempted several objectives: abolition of the untouchable caste, institution of local economic autonomy, elimination of religious separatism, and support of participatory principles over politics in decision making. Many of these aims went by the board as the council drafted the terms for independence.

All these moves led to independence in 1947, but tempered by the bloody partition of the subcontinent into two states: India and Pakistan. With the speedy passage through the British Parliament of the Indian Independence Act 1947, at 11:57 on 14 August 1947 Pakistan was declared a separate nation, and at 12:02, just after midnight, on 15 August 1947, India also became an independent state. The formalities of state formation came later. After independence, millions of Indians migrated to India, and Pakistanis to India, eliciting considerable bloodshed in the few years that followed.

There were fault lines between the two religions that were evident in early modern India, such as the first census in 1881, which listed religious affiliation as the main criterion. Much earlier, the Mughal raja Aurangzeb, a strict Islamist, cast the die for Islamic separatism from Hindus. Despite historical precedent under such Mughal rajas as Akbar and Jahan Shah and later movements as the Lucknow Renaissance, division between Hindu and Muslim persisted to independence. Mohammad Ali Jinnah led the separatist faction, even though he hoped for later reunification. That reunification was never to happen. The Muslim League pressed on for separation throughout the 1930s and early 1940s, leading to a partition at the very moment of independence in 1947.

Post-Independence India

Vital to India's self-image as an independent nation was its constitution, completed in 1950, which put in place a sovereign, secular, and democratic republic. In the more than 60 years since independence, India has been a mixed bag of successes and failures. The country has remained a democracy provided for in the constitution, with civil liberties, an activist Supreme Court, and a largely independent press. Economic liberalization, which was begun in the 1990s, has created a large urban middle class, transformed India into one of the world's fastest-growing economies, and increased its geopolitical influence. Indian movies, music, and spiritual teachings play an increasing role in global culture. Yet, India has also been weighed down by seemingly unyielding poverty, both rural and urban; by religious and caste-related violence; by Maoist-inspired Naxalite insurgencies; and by separatism in Jammu and Kashmir. It has unresolved territorial disputes with China, which escalated into the Sino-Indian War of 1962; and with Pakistan, which flared into wars fought in 1947, 1965, 1971, and 1999. The India–Pakistan nuclear rivalry continues. India's sustained democratic freedoms are unique among the world's new nations; however, in spite of its recent economic successes, freedom from want for its disadvantaged population remains a goal yet to be achieved. Evidence is mixed, although the official poverty rate of 22% may indicate progress—or it might involve some manipulation of the figures.

A rising generation of well-educated and skilled professionals in scientific sectors of industry began propelling the Indian economy, as the information technology industry took hold across India with the proliferation of computers. The new technologies increased the efficiency of activity in almost every type of industry, which also benefitted from the availability of skilled labor. Foreign investment and outsourcing of jobs to India's labor markets further enhanced India's economic growth. A large middle-class has arisen across India, which has increased the demand, and thus production of a wide array of consumer goods. Unemployment is steadily declining—to what extent is anyone's guess. Gross Domestic Product growth increased to beyond 7%. While serious challenges remain, India is enjoying a period of economic expansion that has propelled it to the forefront of the world economy, and has correspondingly increased its influence in political and diplomatic terms. Equally important is the breakdown of the caste system and the ethnic barriers that has hindered India's unity and development in the past. This is reflected in the fact that the current prime minister of India is Manmohan Singh, a Sikh.

Shamirpet: A Case Study

As a holistic discipline, anthropologists need to connect local studies in a larger context. We have done in this review of India so far, but what about rural villages? In this light, we now look at an ethnographic case. A representative study concerns a village called Shamirpet, near Hyderabad, capital city of Andhra Pradesh, central India, as of the 1950s. This is a straight ethnography of Village India, as represented by S. C. Dube's *Indian Village*. We then close with a broad sketch of changes in a region near Chennai, formerly Madras, in Tamil Nadu.

Shamirpet is a village located 30 miles north of Hyderabad. The population of 2,494, as of the 1951 census, comprises 2,124 Hindus and 340 Muslims. The Hindu population comprises 1,434 "clean" castes and 680 "untouchable" or "scheduled" castes. The Muslims are Sunni. The dominant language of the Hindus is Telugu and that of the Muslims is Urdu. Most are bilingual in the two languages. Most villagers are agriculturalists, but some pursue specialized crafts.

Although the Indian constitution abolished the category of untouchables, the caste system is strong in Shamirpet. The Brahmins comprise only one family in the village and they are the counselor for almost all Hindus. The next highest caste is the *Komitis,* who are the traders, namely shopkeepers and money lenders. The next castes are the agriculturalists, potters, and shepherds, who are mutually separate and endogamous. The agriculturalists form more subcastes, including, besides the farmers, barbers, launderers, and even minstrels. There are two untouchable subcastes, namely the *Mala,* ranked above the *Madiga.*

The concept of pollution permeates all intercaste relations, including the belief that contact between different-caste persons pollute the upper-caste individual, who must undertake purification ritual. The Brahmins are the highest rank and may not accept food from any caste members but their own. With rare exceptions, castes may not accept food from any other, whether or not equal in rank. Again with a few exceptions, different castes may not eat with each other. All castes are endogamous, though families and lineages are exogamous.

Yet again with exceptions, most of the trades are the monopoly of one subcaste or another. For example, only Brahmins may officiate at public rituals; only *Mangalis* may cut hair, and only the *Panch* can do carpentry and metalwork. The monopolies extend to the Dalits: only the untouchable *Madiga* can remove dead cattle or do leatherwork. There are exceptions: even those of a specific occupational case may cultivate their own fields or hire themselves out as field hands.

The restrictions apply to the relationship between service providers and their clients. Except for casual work, a long-term arrangement requires that the provider and receiver of service maintain the relationship across the generations. A weaver wanting to cut ties with a barber because of poor service cannot do so without taking the matter up to the local council.

In the area of political organization, there are two categories: the officials of the state and national administrations and the local leaders. The local leadership consists of the following: *Deshmukh,* who is the head of the village, and also the richest man of the village; his is a hereditary position of influence within and outside the village (e.g., with state and national government officials). The next locus of leadership is the *panchayat,* or a council of village elders representing subdivisions of the community.

Next are the *ganadi,* who are organizers of village ritual. *Kulam-pedda* is the headmen of different castes. Finally, the *Peddamansh* are the heads of each family. Overall, caste, relative wealth, and connections, both external and internal, determine local influence and power even among the castes and families.

The individual goes through four stages in the life cycle. The first is the formative and celibate stage. This involves acquiring the skills and values prerequisite to adult life. Sex outside of marriage is condemned and indeed the sex act itself is polluting. The second stage is to marry, beget children, and to rear and educate them. The third stage is cultivating an attitude of detachment of all worldly things and events. The last stage is to renounce all things and relations prior to death.

Ideally, family residence is patrilocal, comprising full brothers, unmarried sisters, and sons and unmarried daughters. Descent is patrilineal. However patrilocal extended family households normally thought to be the ideal is not observed in practice. In recent years, according to the author's survey, sons have separated from their parents within two years in 34% of the cases in the period under study. In only 22% of the cases were the ideals met in practice. Extended families were found mostly in higher caste and wealthier families.

Contrary to common stereotype, child marriage is rare in Shamirpet. Although cross-cousin marriage is stated as preferred, analysis of data indicated that only 18% were cross-cousins. Marriages are arranged; elopement is frowned upon. Ideally, marriages involve a dowry from the girl's parents to the boy's parents, who then pay for the wedding. If the boy's parents are too poor to arrange a marriage, the boy provides bride service to the in-laws. Divorce is tolerated but relatively infrequent; of 380 marriages in the author's survey, only 79 ended in divorce.

Almost all Muslim families in Shamirpet are former Hindus in their heritage; Hindus of both high and low castes have converted to Islam. They share with the Hindus beliefs in spirits, both malevolent and benevolent. They participate in all community-wide festivals and ceremonies. The practice of renunciation of the world is similar between Hindus and Muslims. In the past, Shamirpet was a Muslim feudality, and the village name itself is of Muslim derivation, named after a benefactor named Shamir who donated a water tank to the village. When power shifted to India as a nation in 1947, the Hindus attacked and insulted the Muslim minority, who were said to have endured the harassment. These conflicts have since subsided and inter-religious relations are relatively peaceful. The tensions have not ceased in the region, as shown in a recent Muslim riot in Hyderabad.

The overall pattern for both Hindus and Muslims is to retain current beliefs and practices, yet Western-based changes have been incremental. Basic individual ideology involves adjustment to the universe through the principles of *dharma*. These comprise ritual, sacrifices, caste relations, and other attributes of the "correct way of life." In terms of social relations, hierarchical arrangements persist, given caste relations and the recent history of feudalism. New ideas are usually greeted with dismay and skepticism, although they have not been totally disregarded. Western medicine and other material culture is accepted if affordable or publicly provided.

In 2012, one cannot find Shamirpet online—or if one can indeed find it, it is no longer a peasant village. The place called Shamirpet is now a housing development with all the features of a modern dwellings—town houses, apartment complexes, detached houses. According to one advertisement online, the area is developing "thanks to a flourishing real estate industry." Shamirpet also encompasses an artificial lake and a deer park. The town reflects what other outlying districts of Hyderabad have become: comprising a booming city of industrial parts surrounded by a new Suburbia.

Modernity in Local India

Over the past decade or more, India's cities have undergone a technological transformation. Akash Kapur makes this clear in his *India Becoming*. In the 1980s, when Kapur last lived in a village, the East Coast Road that runs from Chennai southward in a rural setting was a country road cutting past rice fields, coconut plantations, and rural villages. When he returned to India from the United States in 2003, East Coast Road had transformed into a 160 km highway. The highway was paved with toll booths and bordered by guard rails. Many rice fields and plantations were gone; many ancient trees were felled despite environmentalist protests. The highway was now lined with beach resorts, movie theatres, open air restaurants; Southern California seemed to have invaded the East Coast Road.

Beginning in 1991, India started to change. National growth in the GDP mushroomed from 3.5% yearly to 8% or 9%. Trade barriers tumbled and cities like Chennai, Bangalore, Mumbai, and others sprouted industrial parks, software centers, shopping malls, not to mention the lifestyles defined by cell phones, DVDs, and bars in which young men and women freely mingled. Even in the villages, one could detect a few ATMs amid the thatched huts which would soon be displaced by bungalows and apartment complexes. Farmers and fishermen were now setting up guest houses; in Kaddapakkam, a formerly poor son of a landless laborer now owned a tea house and a motorcycle, and he sent his children to a private school.

Conclusion

As we have seen, India has a history that matches China's and other ancient civilizations, and exceeds other, such as Mexico's. Yet it is one of the leading developing countries in the early twenty-first century. What have been the changes at the local level? Results are coming in, some dated as they are compiled and published. A promising item of longitudinal research is *Behind Mud Walls,* which has been studied from the 1930s to the 2000s, first by William and Charlotte Wiser and then by Susan Wadley. The growth of BRIC (Brazil, Russia, India, and China) countries (all developing nations) has recently stalled, according to *The Guardian* of August 17–23, 2012, and booms followed by bust effects is a pattern first observed by Marx more than a century ago.

Selected Films

Dadi's Family. 1981. 58 minutes. Camerini, Michael, and James MacDonald. Cambridge, MA: Documentary Educational Resources.

India. Empire of the Spirit. 1991. 81 minutes. Michael Wood. New York: Ambrose Video Publishing.

The Lover and the Beloved: A Journey into Tantra. 2011. 70 minutes. Andy Lawrence. Cambridge, MA: Documentary Educational Resources.

Running Out of Time. 1996. 55 or 104 minutes (two versions varying in show time). Abhijay Karlikar. Cambridge, MA: Documentary Educational Resources.

The Story of India. 6 Parts. 2008. New York: Public Broadcasting System and Maya Vision International.

Selected Literature

Beals, Alan. 1980. *Gopalpur: A South Indian Village.* New York: Holt, Rinehart and Winston.

Dube, S. C. 1956. *Indian Village.* London: Routledge and Kegan Paul.

Dull, Ramesh. 2010. *Maha-bharata: The Epic of India Condensed into English Verse.* New York: Fili-Quarian Classics.

Dumont, Rene. 1981. *Homo Hierarchicus: The Caste System and Its Implications, 2nd ed.* Chicago: University of Chicago Press.

Guha, Ramachandra. 2008. *India after Gandhi: The History of the World's Largest Democracy.* New York: Harper.

Kapur, Akash. 2012. *India Becoming: A Portrait of Life in Modern India.* New York: Riverhead Press.

Keay, John. 2000. *India: A History.* New York: Grove Press.

Luce, Edward. 2008. *In Spite of the Gods: The Rise of Modern India.* New York: Anchor.

Oberoi, Harjot. 1994. *The Construction of Religious Boundaries, Culture, Identity, and Diversity in the Sikh Tradition.* Chicago: University of Chicago Press.

Wiser, William, Charlotte Wiser, and Susan Wadley. 2000. *Behind Mud Walls: Seventy-Five Years in a North Indian Village: Updated and Expanded Edition.* Berkeley: University of California Press.

Wood, Michael. *India.* 2007. New York: Basic Books.

CHAPTER 17

Bali: A Study in Cultural Integration

Introduction

Bali, long immortalized in American stereotypes produced by the song "Bali Hai" in the musical *South Pacific* and in *The Road to Bali* starring Bing Crosby and Bob Hope in the 1950s (with Dorothy Lamour playing Princess Lala), the Indonesian Province of Bali is much more interesting than the stereotypes. Bali is a culture in its own right. If a culture is holistic and integrated, Bali is a classic illustration. Whether it will remain so after a massive population increase and bombings that harmed tourism remains to be seen.

Geography

Bali (Figure 17.1) is a small island located east of Java in the nation-state of Indonesia. The province is a Hindu enclave in a country that has the largest number of Muslims in the world. Bali is known as a tourist resort area with excellent surfing and sport fishing. The temples, the temple dancers, and religious plays also attract large numbers of tourists from Indonesia, Australia, and around the world. Ethnographers, such as Stephen Lansing, regard Bali as a classic example of a well-integrated society.

Bali is located about 5 miles east of Java, the principal province of Indonesia—Jakarta, Indonesia's capital, is located in western Java. Bali is a very small place, 5633 kilometers, or 0.003% of the total land area of Indonesia. One could drive around the island in two hours were it not for the heavy traffic. Even with the traffic, you can circumnavigate the island in a day.

Bali's center is a mountainous area dominated by Mt. Agung and Mt. Bator (below). The land slopes down toward the south to a tropical rain forest plain which has long since been cleared for irrigated rice paddies run by a series of water management entities known as subaks. The flow of water is regulated through a system of temples, which determine the allocation of an uneven supply of water.

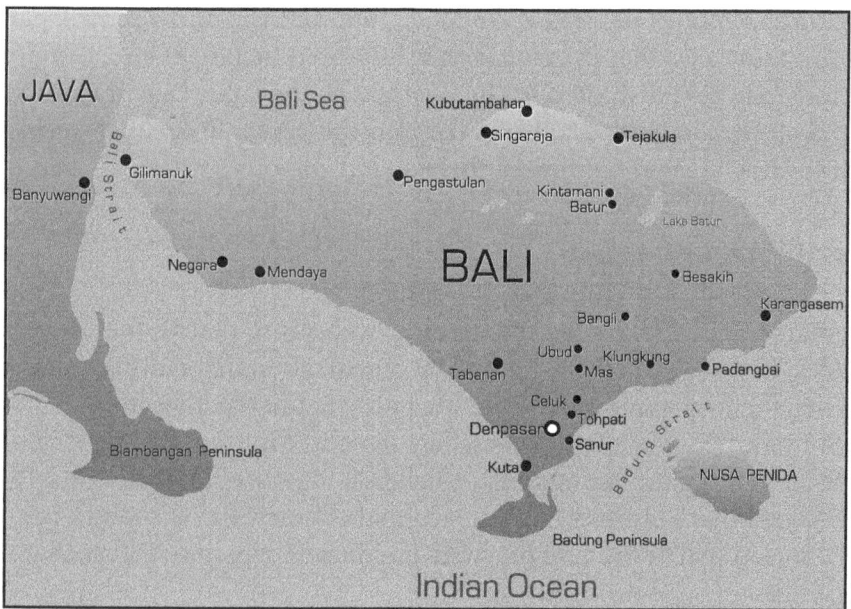

Image © Olinchuk, 2012. Used under license from Shutterstock, Inc.

FIGURE 17.1
Bali, located due east of Java, home of Jakarta, capital of
Indonesia.

Image © joyfull, 2012. Used under license from Shutterstock, Inc.

FIGURE 17.2
Mount Batur overseeing Lake Batur, which supplies most of the
irrigation water in Bali.

Mount Agung and Mount Batur (Figure 17.2) dominate the north central part of the island. Though there are four lakes that provide irrigation water, by far the most important source is Lake Batur, whose temple is dedicated to the Goddess of the Lake, Dewi Danu. Most of the irrigation is located on the slopes and a broad plain to the south. Shorelines surround the island, and most of the tourist areas are in the southern peninsula.

Culture of Bali: An Overview

One of the fundamental concepts in anthropology is holism, that is, the idea that cultures are integrated wholes. In this perspective, the family organization of a culture, their members' ways of making a living, their religion, and the like are parts that fit together into an integrated system. Often, that is not reflected in some societies. Tasmanians, for example, are islanders and yet did not consume fish in an ocean that was full of fish, among other dysfunctions. Robert Edgerton in *Sick Societies* gives other examples of dysfunctional cultures. Bali, however, is a classic example of an integrated society, partly because of a well-organized irrigation system that has lasted more than a thousand years.

Bali is a holistic society. The Balinese cosmos consists of three worlds: the upper world inhabited by gods, who represent the forces of growth and creation; the lower world inhabited by demons, who represent the forces of decay and destruction; and the human world, whose task is to balance the forces of the gods with those of the demons. As shown below, Bali is a local adaptation of Hinduism, which came to Bali centuries ago. Their lives are ordered by a complex system of calendars. As mentioned, *subaks* and temples regulate their system of irrigation, which is a study in ecologically sustainable agriculture.

The Balinese Cosmos

The basic cosmic model in Hinduism, both Balinese and Indian, involves endless cycles of birth, death, and rebirth in a complex world of illusion known as *samsara*. How one is reborn is determined by the forces generated by one's behavior in their lives; these forces are collectively known as *karma*. The Balinese model of balance between creative and destructive forces originates in East Indian Hindu beliefs. *Nirvana*, or *moksha*, is not so much heaven in the popular sense as it is a recognition that *samara* is an illusion, thereby freeing oneself from it. *Moksha* is liberation from this illusion; hence the doctrine of detachment forms all things on earth.

Karma itself is a cosmic force that is influenced by not only the acts one committed in this life, but also in all previous lives. Reward is rebirth in a higher state. If one has performed good deeds while in poverty, one will be reborn in a wealthier state. Punishment for evil deeds leads to rebirth in a lower state. The force involves all beings, from stone to plant and animal life to humans, and even to gods.

Based on the three worlds, Balinese recognize two polar opposite directions, *kaja* and *kelod*. Vertically, *kaja* is upward; *kelod* is downward. In the human body, *kaja* is of the head, and so is sacred; *kelod* is of the feet that touch the dirty earth. Geographically, Mount Agung, the most sacred landmark and home of the gods, is *kaja*; the sea, the home of the demons, is *kelod*. Ironically, a people who belong to the Malayo-Polynesian stock, which occupies the Pacific islands, do not swim out of fear of the demons. Even the homes are divided between *kaja*—the shrine—and *kelod,* the entrance with a demon wall that prevents demons from entering.

In addition, the Three Worlds of Bali each have their own names: *Swah* refers to the Upper World of the Gods; *Bhur* refers to the lower world beneath the earth, and the world of the demons; and *Bwah* refers to the middle world of the humans. These terms are applied to other contexts. For Bali itself, the mountains (including Mt. Agung) are called *Swah;* the middle plains of Bali are called *Bwah;* and the ocean is called *Bhur.* Villages are similarly divided: upstream of the village is called *Swah,* the village itself is called *Bwah,* and the cemetery (usually located to the south) is called *Bhur.* Even the human body is not immune: head and neck are *Swah;* the torso, *Bwah;* and the body below the knee is *Bhur.*

The housing structures correspond to the kaja-kelod orientations. Houses comprise rooms with an open courtyard surrounded by a wall. Temples are of a similar design. *Kaja* refers to the side entrance to the compound. The entrance is protected by a demon wall. Demons are said to travel only in straight lines, so when they enter the compound, they run into the demon wall and are frustrated. The polar *kaja-kelod* opposites apply to all aspects of the house. Sleeping rooms are oriented with the head oriented toward the mountains, which are *kaja.* Even boards are aligned based on how the tree grew; the part of the boards from the tree tops is always *kaja.*

Balinese Arts and Drama

Art—paintings, carvings, sculpture—are so commonplace that the Balinese have no word for art; art is an integral part of Balinese material culture. Even pig fat, prepared for every ritual, is made into a thing of beauty, such as the shape of a flower. The sacred texts also come from nature. The palms of the lontar tree are used to write scripture. One example is the *Mahabharata,* an epic heroic poem from India.

A distinctive Balinese art form is *wayang,* or shadow puppetry. The puppets are decorated leather representations of Hindu and Indian gods and demons, not to mention the heroes of Indian lore. Ordinary people cannot, the belief holds, perceive beings of the other worlds directly. *Wayang* interprets these worlds and the tradition for the audience. Particular extended family practice the art of *wayang.* One quality of the performers is *taksu,* which both refers to the family shrine and to the trancelike state into which a puppeteer enters when performing.

There is a metaphorical quality of *wayang* (Figure 17.3). The puppets are brightly painted representations of the characters depicted—the gods, the demons, the heroic figure of the epics. And yet the audience cannot see them directly; they only see the shadows cast on the screen by the gas lamps used for that purpose. Symbolically, these images represent *maya* or illusion, whose screen filters out the real—the puppets themselves. This replicates the cosmic representation of the gods, the demons, and the worlds they inhabit.

A keystone of Balinese society is the system of temples. In contrast with Indian Hindu temples, which are closed structures, Balinese temples are open courtyards that lead to the shrine, which is always built at the *kaja* end of the courtyard. Festivals are numerous; they consist of the distinctive gamelan music, dancing, and dramatization of the epics. Temples number into the thousands; there are 53 in the village of Sukawati alone. Although the Balinese are not rich, the support of the temples and their activities come from taxation of the local villagers; larger temples own the rice terraces whose products generate their revenue.

Image © A.S. Zain, 2012. Used under license from Shutterstock, Inc.

FIGURE 17.3
Wayang, or shadow puppetry. To the Balinese, *wayang* is a window to the real world, which humans cannot perceive directly.

The Balinese Calendar

As stated above, the temple ceremonies, the irrigation, and even marriage and cremation, are timed by the calendars. There are two systems: the *pawukon* (also known as *uku* or *wuku*), a system of ten calendars whose components mesh with each other, and the *saka,* a lunar calendar. The oft-used *tika* version of the *pawukon* is used for the more important events. We first start with an overview of the Gregorian calendar—the one used in the Western world including North America; then we look at the more complicated Balinese system of the two types.

The Gregorian calendar, used in the Americas and Europe and indeed around the world wherever business is conducted, was introduced by Pope Gregory XIII in 1592. The year starts on the assumed conception of Christ as AD 1 (there is no AD 0, so that the prior year is 1 BC, or Before Christ). Every fourth year (leap year) contains an extra day to make up for the .24 day in the 365.24-day astronomical year. To eliminate the Christian bias, CE (Common Era or Christian Era) and BCE (Before Common Era) are often used as a religious-neutral system.

The first system, the *pawukon* (*wuku* or *uku*) system is a repetitive cycle of 210 days. This system comprises 10 "weeks" ranging from a 1-day week to a 2-day week, a 3-day week, and so on up to a 10-day week. They all run concurrently. Each week has a Sanskrit-derived name, and each day is individually named. They total 55 days. Because of their importance for determining a good day for even mundane tasks such as chopping wood, every Balinese can recall both week and day names.

Nevertheless, the weeks are not equal. The most important weeks are those of three, five, and seven days. The three- and five-day weeks are the market days; three days in Bali, five days in Java. Both these numbers are ritually important. Three represents the triad of the most important Hindu gods: Brahma, the creator; Shiva, the destroyer and renovator; and Vishnu, the preserver. Five represents the cardinal directions: the directions north, south, east, and west, plus the vertical center. The seven-day calendars represent the sun, moon, and the five planets that can be seen with the naked eye.

The *tika* calendar keeps track of the important weeks and days of the *Pawukon* (*uku* or *wuku*) 210-day cycle. Balinese consult the calendar and the experts who read them for everything, from the most mundane tasks such as chopping wood or going to market up to the most important, such as scheduling a wedding or making an offering to the gods. So complicated is the calendar that professional readers are consulted to determine which dates are the most propitious for an event. Daily newspapers combine the Gregorian with the Balinese calendars.

One important example is the three-day week on a calendar. In this example, *Pasah* is Day 1 of the week (on a Sunday, say), *Beteng* is Day 2 (Monday), and *Kajeng* is Day 3 (Tuesday). The cycle begins again on *Pasah,* which falls on a Wednesday. Among other things, they regulate the timing of markets. Thus, itinerant marketers time their visits of each site; they visit three different villages on the corresponding day. In Java, a five-day week is used for the same purpose.

There are even one-day weeks, and by definition their name is the same: *Luang.* In one instance, they are combined with days from the eight-week *Astawara* calendar and together they indicate the child's birthday and what he or she was in a prior life. Certain conjunctions of three-day and five-day weeks serve to determine the best day for holding a temple ceremony. Other personal events include tooth filing, weddings, and funerary cremations. Some combinations are auspicious for each event; others are not.

Beside the *pakuwon,* the other important calendar is called the *saka,* which is a lunar calendar, whose year is made up of 12 months each of 30 days. Each month begins with the new moon. The moon waxes during the first 15 days and wanes during the second 15 days of each month. Similar to the Gregorian calendar, the *saka* calendar numbers the years sequentially. The calendar is used to schedule such important events as the Eka Desa Rudra ceremonies, which are held every 100 years; the last Eka Desa Rudra was held on March 29, 1979. This series of rituals seek to cast out the demons who have increased their numbers over the past century, and to recombine the elements for a perfect order.

Eka Desa Rudra: Using the Calendar.

Eka Desa Rudra is a period in which Rudra, the embodiment of evil, must be transformed into the god Shiva (Siwa in Balinese). Offerings include blood sacrifices of every species of animal to satisfy the craving for blood of the demons. Other offerings, those for the gods, stream into Besakih Temple, the mother temple of all Bali, located on the slopes of Mount Agung, the home of the gods. The final ceremonies ensure that the forces of good and evil are held in balance.

One of the most noteworthy of recent events was the eruption of Mount Agung in 1963. This was the year that an Eka Desa Rudra event was held under pressure from the Sukarno government that was facing an economic and political crisis; these events led to the downfall of that government in 1965, accompanied by the massacre of at least half a million Indonesians. The eruption destroyed many temples, covered much of the cropland in ash and lava, and killed hundreds of

Image © Binio, 2012. Used under license from Shutterstock, Inc.

FIGURE 17.4
Besakih Temple, main temple of Bali and site of Eka Desa Rudra in 1979—and at the "wrong time" in 1963.

Balinese, if not thousands. Yet miraculously Besakih Temple was spared, the lava flowing within a few meters from the site. To many Balinese, the eruption occurred because Eka Desa Rudra was held "at the wrong time." To them, this eruption was a graphic illustration showing the importance of timing events by the calendar.

Subaks and the Irrigation System

The temples direct the allocation of water in irrigation. When a temple starts its festival, the farmers of the *subak,* or water management unit to which the temple belongs, opens its water gates. The blue algae releases nitrogen into the soil, and ducks eat the pests and fertilize the paddy with their droppings. These and other ecological practices have maintained the fertility of the soils for over a thousand years.

Subaks are units whose members manage the water, the ducks, and other functions related to the paddy under its care. They own individual plots of the land which the *subaks* service. *Subaks*

Image © Dudarev Mikhail, 2012. Used under license from Shutterstock, Inc.

FIGURE 17.5

Typical rice field in Bali. The field is irrigated from Lake Batur and three other lakes. Note the terraced slopes, requiring upstream and downstream *subaks* to negotiate the allocation of water.

number into the hundreds; for Lansing's study *Perfect Order*, 172 were included in the survey. Members of the *subaks* meet regularly to discuss water allocation, what to plant, how to maintain the dams and canals, and plan for the religious ritual associated with their tasks. They also manage pest control and water conservation.

Fertility and pest control is maintained by natural means without the use of pesticides and fertilizer. Coming from volcanic rock, the water itself provides such nutrients as potassium and phosphates from the ash. Nitrogen-fixing blue-green algae contribute to the soil's fertility, as do the droppings from ducks herded into the paddy. When it comes to pest control, ducks and frogs eat the insects; at the end of the harvest season, farmers may burn the stalks or flood them for decomposition under water.

Tropical regions have two seasons: rainy and dry. Too much water causes erosion and leaching. The dry season creates risks of drought and alteration of soil pH, causing acidity. The system serves to even out the distribution of water, which is stored behind dams and weirs during the rainy season and allocated during the dry season. The water should remain at the same level, rainy or dry.

Two deities dominate Balinese religion. The first is Dewa Agung, the god of Mount Agung. Besakih temple, located on the slopes of Mount Agung, represents this god. His consort, Dewi Danu, dominates Mt. Batur and its lake, Lake Batur. Lake Batur flows from beneath Mount Batur and is the source of most of the fresh water used for irrigation. Water is the gift of this goddess and, thereby, the focus of worship among all who benefit from this gift.

The rice paddies supported by this irrigation system produces two crops per year, and has done so for more than a thousand years. Every year, representatives of each subak meet at the master temple at Lake Batur and bring down containers of holy water from the lake to sprinkle into their own paddies. Dewi Danu is, according to myth, the provider of water for the entire part of Central Bali.

Subak administrative structure is egalitarian entities. Caste differences are disregarded at the meetings that determine how the water is to be allocated and in the election of *subak* head, secretary/treasurer, and heads of *subak* subunits. The head of the entire irrigation system is a priest, known as the Gero Gde. The Gero Gde is not a paid administrator; he makes a living from his own occupation in addition to this role. Even at the top, the organization is an egalitarian entity.

As stated, 24 priests based in the Temple of the Crater oversee the allocation of water that originates at Lake Batur. The director of the entire process, the Gero Gde, is selected as a boy by Dewi Danu herself, in a dream. In a state of trance, he receives his instructions. Thus, his decision of water allocation is thought to be divinely ordered. More likely, the decision is a product of negotiation and consensus among the *subaks*.

When a temple holds a ceremony, its *subak* opens the water supply to the fields of its owners. The supply is cut off at the end of the ceremony, and as other temples hold their ceremony, their *subaks* open their own water supply. By this staggered system, every field is watered. At each stage, the water also fertilizes the soil with the nutrients leached through the volcanic ash, and the ducks eat the insects and fertilize the soil with their droppings.

Besides the equitable distribution of water through timing of the ceremonial cycle, there is also the problem created by the better access to water that *subaks* upstream enjoy; they could allow the water to pass through the downstream—or not. There is a balance of power, however; without water, downstream *subaks* generate the insect pests who would then invade the upstream *subaks*. These form the bargaining chips in water supply negotiations between the *subaks*. Every *subak* meeting involves negotiation over water distribution.

Several sources of conflict over water supply are controlled by ritual. By the act of taking holy water from the master temple at Lake Batur, each representative participates in a ritual, as if to remind them of their dependence on Dewi Danu, the Goddess of the Lake. If the irrigation system "works," and has done so for a thousand years, it is because of this ceremonial reinforcement.

One limitation of the *subak* system is its productivity in light of the increase in population by one million between 1979 and the year 2000. This is what motivated the Indonesian government to introduce the so-called Green Revolution. Higher-producing rice varieties were introduced, and the government mandated a continuous yearlong production cycle rather than the temple-based two-year crop cycle. Fertilizer and pesticides were introduced.

Although there was an initial increase of rice production, problems soon surfaced. "Miracle rice," Steven Lansing wrote, "produced miracle pests." In the first year, the brown leaf hopper decimated much of the crop. New pest-resistant pesticides were applied, only for plant disease to destroy the second crop. During the 1980s, cycles of production and crop damage proved self-defeating. There were longer term impacts. For example, applications of even more fertilizer to an already-phosphate rich water supply encouraged the growth of algae on the reefs of the southern shore, leading to the death of these reefs. Eventually the temple system was restored, but as of 2003, only 5% to 10% were using this system of production (Pringle 2004).

Balinese Life Cycle

In the life-cycle analysis of most cultures, the ethnography starts with birth, and then addresses growth, adulthood, elderhood, and finally death. For Bali, Lansing and other ethnographers find that death and ritual is a more appropriate starting point, because the death is the culmination of the events concerning the deeds of the person who has just died. These impact the birth of the person when he or she enters the next life.

No Balinese begins life with a clean slate (would we?). There may be problems from the prior life—or lives. They may have debts. They may have committed one sin or another. Hence the process begins with the funeral: first the burial then, possibly years later, the cremation and burial of ashes at the ocean shoreline. All of these rituals are conducted with the anticipation of a rebirth.

Consulting the *tika* calendar—the one with the most important dates extracted from the 210-day *wuku* calendar—the *Ida Bagus,* or high priest, determines the proper ritual. When a person dies, the entire neighborhood, or banjar, pitches in to help the family of the victim. Since this is the period of the greatest danger for the family, the banjar is helping that family through the period. Cremation then follows, often many years after death. On the date of cremation, which usually involves several corpses, the deceased are carried to the site in a procession that may involve erratic routes to confuse the spirit so that it does not return to the village. After cremation, the ashes are taken to the seashore and scattered over the water.

At this point, the diviner who will determine the name of the child and predict its life course turns to the *tika* calendar, which retrodicts (opposite of predicts) the past life—and lives—of the newborn. The *tika* covers the most important days and weeks of the larger *wuku* calendar. It links a concept of cyclical patterns to a map of the inner world. For example, several 35-day calendars provide additional information about the child's debts from a previous life. All of these readings determine the ritual that is to be followed at the child's birth.

Both before and after birth, the child remains part of the inner world and is subjected to its dangers: sorcery and witches can cast their spells on both mother and child. Every child is born with four sibling spirits whose 27 vices (*bujang*)—108 all told—can influence the child's behavior; other spirits are beneficial. The sibling spirits may be forgotten in a lifetime, but they reappear shortly before death. Thus, a 42-day ritual during the first year of a child's life is performed to urge the 108 *bujang*—malevolent spirits—to depart.

During its first year, the child is never allowed to touch the ground. At three months, the child undergoes a ritual to strengthen their bonds with the spirit siblings, in order to confuse the demons. Finally, the child is given its first haircut and allowed to touch the ground. At this time, she or he is given a real name, based on what the diviners have determined. Several names are written on a lontar leaf, which is then burned. The name least damaged on the burnt leaf is the name assigned the child. The last obligation is for the parents to pay the debt that the child incurred it its previous life.

At puberty, both girls and boys must take part in a ritual supervised by the female and male gods of love. They then have their upper teeth filed, namely the four upper incisors and the canines. The belief holds that the "fangs" (especially the canines) are filed even, so as to make them look less animal-like. The filings are then buried in the ground near the family shrine; the house compound is decorated for the occasion.

Marriage, the Family, and the Clan

The next stage in life is marriage. The least honorable marriage is elopement (*ngerorod*), entailing the capture of the wife. A more neutral arrangement is patrilateral parallel cousin marriage. The third option is arranged marriage, called *mapadik,* performed among the aristocrats.

The most common and cheapest type of marriage, but the least desirable, is elopement. There are two kinds. The first one is the "mock capturing" of the woman, and one with the full knowledge of the family. The second is one in which the husband-to-be forces the elopement without consent of the woman's family. In either event, the father goes to the groom's family. If the woman wishes to marry, the wife's family proceeds with purification and the wedding ceremonies. However, the woman can no longer participate in the ancestral worship with her own family.

The second type of marriage involves aristocratic families; this involves an arranged marriage. This is not necessarily a desirable arrangement, because the loss of a daughter implies the loss of reproductive power within a family and therefore an increased risk of its very survival. No bridewealth or exchange of female partners is involved. But this arrangement is preferred to elopement and the public embarrassment it would entail. Though it has the potential of creating an alliance, this is not seen as a positive development because of the survival risk to the family. Elsewhere in Indonesia, marriage with partner exchange or bridewealth is the norm, and does not entail survival risk of the daughter's family.

The preferred type of marriage keeps both daughter and familial assets within the clan, or *dadia* (more below). This is patrilateral parallel cousin marriage, in which the groom marries his father's brothers daughter (FaBrDa is the notation used here; Fa is father, Br is brother, and Da is daughter). In this case, the daughter stays and reproduces, increasing the size of the clan. Male heirs will retain the clan's property—land, house, furnishings, domesticated animals. If there are no suitable males, a non-kin male might be "adopted" to become the next heir. The main drawback is that the clan does not develop an alliance with another clan.

Residence is patrilocal by default, since the parallel cousins who marry often reside in the same compound before marriage. Ideally, women who marry would leave the residence, but in this instance, they do not. One major fear is that one or more daughters may leave the residence, either through arranged marriages between *dadia* or through elopement. Patrilateral parallel cousin marriage thus modifies the patrilocal residential ideal.

Dadia are landholding (and thus corporate) clans. They consist of several extended families that have grown over time. As noted, they include male and female cousins united by the fathers and their brothers—parallel cousins, in other words.

Although Bali households tend to be made up of patrilocal extended families, the kinship terminology is Hawaiian, with all sibling terms merged with cousin terms and parent terms merged with aunts and uncles. Why marriage with parallel cousins is not regarded as incestuous when they should be is not explained.

Stratification in Bali

Although, as shown below, *subak* and *banjar* (neighborhood group) members treat each other as equals, there is an underlying stratification system in Bali, based on their adaptation of a caste system found in India. The ideal definition is that a small elite controls all or most of the resources that sustain life—water in irrigation societies, land in patrimonial (or feudal) societies, or productive assets in capitalist societies. Nevertheless, as already shown, subaks modify this form of control; water is essential to human life in Bali.

By definition, castes are endogamous categories of people that are stratified. Once a person is born as a peasant or a Brahmin, he or she remains within that class; boundaries between one caste and another remain rigid. Caste exogamy is strictly forbidden.

Four major "pure" (*varna*) divide society in India: the *Brahmins* (priests), *Kshtryas* (warrior, who may also be police), *Vaishyas* (merchants and artisans or craftpersons), and the *Sudras* (peasants). In addition, there is a vast majority of so-called untouchables called variously *Harijans* or *Dalit,* who handle such impure jobs as removing dead animals, tanning hides for leather, or cremating the dead. There are several hundred occupational subcastes in each of these castes, also endogamous.

So extreme are these castes that if the shadow of an untouchable falls on a Brahmin, the latter immediately has to take a bath. Many such castes come out only at night for that reason. The occupational subcastes are called *jati,* and one remains in his/her occupation throughout life. Providers of services (*jajman*) is permanently tied to the person for whom he provides the services (*kamin*). If you are a barber, you cut the hair of your kamin for life; and that means that your father cuts the hair of the *kamin's* father. The bond lasts throughout the generations.

Samsara, sometimes known as *maya,* and *karma* serve to justify the caste system in India. If one has done good deeds in a lifetime—or several lifetimes—that person will be reborn in a higher caste. If one's behavior has been less than ideal, he or she will be reborn in a lower caste, or an even lower station in existence.

In one sense, the Balinese caste system replicates that of India: the priestly (*Brahmana*), the officials and business persons (formerly warriors—*Satriya*), and the *Wesya* (merchants, now mostly petty bureaucrats). The *Sudras* (peasants) form the vast majority of the population.

However, there are important differences between the Indian and Balinese castes. First, there is no untouchable status in Bali. Strict intercaste avoidance is less strict in Bali than in India. In fact, the work-related aspects in *subaks* and *banjars* dissolve the barriers for the tasks at hand. Terms recognizing caste differences are dropped in these sets of circumstances.

Maya or *samsara* remain the illusory life cycle in which humans live; *wayang,* as noted above, reflects this belief on in illusory existence, *karma* also bears on the naming of a child; diviners want to determine "who" the child was in a previous life—hence the consultation with *tika* calendars. However, the nature of rebirth is different in the expectation that the dead will sooner or later return to their village, an assumption contrary to Indian Hindu belief.

The differences between caste systems are played out in Balinese government, past and present. Prior to the Dutch invasion, Klungkung was the foremost of several kingdoms in Bali, which were parallel to city-states of the Classic Maya, pre-Babylon Mesopotamia, or Hellenic Greece. They became puppet kingdoms under the Dutch, but today comprise eight administrative subunits of the Province of Bali. Today, the *subaks, banjars,* and temples are the effective units of Bali, all emphasizing participatory democracy. The Aga Bali, a unit of metalworkers, lack castes and the other units are modeled after this one.

Temples play a central role in Balinese society and are no respecter of persons or social status. There are three types of temples in each village. The one closest to the peak of Mount Agung is the one for ancestral worship. To the opposite end is the death temple, which involves the correct handling of the forces of evil and of death. The third is the water temple, the center of subak activity and matters of irrigation management.

Membership to the village origin temple is restricted to the villagers and other individuals with special privileges. Each temple has a charter that spells out the rights and obligations of the membership. The temple has the power to impose fines for the violation of any rules. There are other types of temples around Bali, such as the state temple. Besakih temple, the highest ranking temple of the province, is the best known.

Banjars, as neighborhood governance units, are models of participatory democracy. Everyone must participate at meetings; fines are imposed for absenteeism. All community projects, old or new, are addressed at these meetings. Everyone has an equal say, and caste-based constraints are suspended at the meeting and the tasks mandated by the *banjar. Banjar* functions are numerous: road upkeep, funerals, cleaning ditches, and others that maintain the physical neighborhood.

Changes in Bali

Like other countries and cultures, Bali has been subjected to pressures that are global in scale. The most evident of these influences is tourism, which has at least minimized poverty on Bali with the jobs they create and the demand for services and products generated. But population has increased astronomically, and the demand for crafts has put a strain on the forest resources. Agriculture also faces pressure, inasmuch as tourist resorts have competed with the *subaks* for both land and water. Social tensions also exist. Bombings occurred in 2002 and 2005, possibly the product of Muslim fundamentalist activity. Hindus of different stripes are themselves divided, and there is xenophobia toward Indonesians outside Bali. Finally, attempts have been made to decentralize the national government while also promoting regional level planning.

Although tourism dates back to the 1920s or even before, systematic tourism began with a master plan drawn up by the World Bank in 1971. There was much to see—the temples, the dancing, the Balinese arts, and then there were surfing and sport fishing. The primary centers of tourism were Sanur and a 325 hectare enclave south of the airport. Initially, the plan was to attract wealthy tourists, but budget travelers soon discovered Bali, and entrepreneurs built hotels, diners, and souvenir shops. Nasa Dua became a neon-lit strip and a range of hotels from luxury complexes to budget motels dotted the landscape. Thousands of Balinese became trained in the hospitality industry—and that saved them from the abject poverty and fly-by-night *maquiladoras* that have affected other Third World countries.

The 1920s Hollywood legend Mae West once said, "Too much of a good thing is wonderful." Wonderful or not, other parts of Bali got into the act. Two Australians, not able to find a cheap place to stay, became the first customers of homestay rooms, and soon others offered up rooms and, later, cheap hotels. Kuta in north Bali became a barely planned, "anything goes" resort area. Public nudity was tolerated and commercial outlets entered the town in droves. Male prostitutes set up shop to service "single office ladies," principally women from Japan off on a holiday. Ubud, somewhat classier, set up more luxury hotels. Eventually, there were 16 tourist centers everywhere on the island. The hope the World Bank had of confining the tourist area to the southern shore was dashed.

There have been two recent trends in tourism. First, other Indonesians flocked to Bali to create a robust growth in domestic tourism. The main beneficiaries of this trend were small hotels and roadside stalls for food and souvenirs. Second, wealthy Balinese and Indonesian capitalists formed an alliance for high-end investment, principally in and around the provincial capital city of Despasar. Smaller entrepreneurs were often pushed out of the market. Average Balinese found they had no control over decisions taken at Denpasar or at Jakarta.

Balinese readily and willingly participated in the tourist industry. There were service-sector jobs at hotels and restaurants. They provided the wood carvings, the dances, the stage performances that tourists were eager to partake. As of 1998, tourist financial contributions comprised 51.8% of the economy, and 38% of Balinese were directly employed in the tourist sector. In addition, furniture and women's garments (including lingerie for which Bali is well-known) formed an important part of the trade derived from tourism. One can say that Bali would be much worse off if there were no tourism.

With increased prosperity has come increased population. From an estimated 750 thousand population in 1908, the figures climbed past 2.1 million in 1971 and over 3.1 million in 2001. Faced with this population increase, Balinese planners have adopted measures to control these increases. Planned Parenthood International has set up shop in Bali and numerous *banjars* have agreed to encourage their neighborhoods to adopt contraceptive practices, principally IUD use.

In light of this population growth, Bali has become an overcrowded island. The main highways endure traffic jams, and it takes the entire day to get around a very small island. Housing is scarce, and the *banjars* and the *dadia* (clans) can no longer accommodate their members. Urban sprawl takes its toll on the attractiveness of Bali as a tourist site, so the very industry that maintained Bali is now threatened with decline.

One solution to the overpopulation crisis has been several schemes to move settlers to the less populated areas, such as Central Sulawesi in East Indonesia and other low population areas, such as Western New Guinea, Borneo, Sumatra, and others. *Banjars* have resettled entire populations in these regions. Push factors for migration besides overcrowding have been the 1963 Mount Agung eruptions, whose lava destroyed thousands of farmland, incentives for cultivating new rice, and upward mobility in caste marriages. Although this policy has been declared a success, there have been criticisms of the move: land disputes with local populations in those areas, disease in areas not immune to them, and political unrest in Indonesian areas such as Aceh and Western New Guinea.

Bali itself has not been without political unrest. In 1965, President Sukarno was overthrown in a nationwide massacre that involved Bali. Then in 2002, the Sari café in Kuta, Bali, was bombed with the loss of 202 lives, including 88 Australians. The impact on tourism was immediate: bookings were cancelled and hotel occupancy dropped to near single digits; many small businesses entered, or were close to, bankruptcy. A second bombing occurred in 2005, exacerbating both religious tensions and the decline in tourism. Although some of the terrorists were captured and executed in 2008, Bali remains in a state of uncertainty.

Balinese have developed a dislike, not toward foreign tourists, but toward Indonesians. The drug trade has expanded as well, and Balinese youth are among the participants. Small wonder, then, that Bali First, a movement for Balinese autonomy in Indonesia, has surfaced and grown. The advocates call for autonomy of the province, though not complete independence, from Indonesia.

Traditionally, Muslim enclaves have been accommodated by the Hindus of Balinese, but the bombings drove a wedge between the two religions in Bali. Furthermore, the national assembly, motivated by fundamentalist morality in Islam, has attempted to legislate against public nudity, which would include wearing bikinis among female tourists. Such a measure would further damage the tourist trade, given Bali's heavy dependence on its beachcombers and surfers. Landownership among "foreign" Indonesians add to the tension. Evangelical Christians have not been welcome either, inasmuch as their proselytization is offensive to the Balinese. Balinese converts neglect their traditional duties. Thus, in 2001, Hindus attacked a Christian neighborhood in upland Kintamani and destroyed several houses.

Religious tension is evident among the Hindu Balinese themselves. Ogoh-Ogoh, a monster in Balinese lore, has come under attack from the tradition-bound Hindus, evident when a parade carrying the papier mache monster was attacked at a New Year's celebration. Anti-caste Hindus are also criticizing the caste system, claiming that old Hindu writings say nothing about caste. The precedent of the casteless Aga Bali metalworkers association adds fuel to this movement. The matter remains unresolved to this day.

Not least among Bali's problems is that the island is running out of forests; indeed, old-growth forests were depleted years ago. Wood is essential to Bali's economy for carvings (both ceremonial and for tourists) and furniture. Low income producers are unwilling to give up this source of income. In addition, the coral reefs, already damaged by the excessive algae caused by overfertilization of the irrigation, have been overexploited to make lime for cement. Sea turtles are also at risk of extinction because of the demand for turtle soup among the tourists. And as resorts take over land and water resources for housing and swimming pools, Bali is running out of water and cropland.

Conclusion

Bali is idealized, not only by popular culture, but by anthropologists who may think Bali is, rightly to some extent, a well-integrated culture. Yet the traditions themselves may be over-romanticized. The *kaja-kelod* dichotomy can lead to extremes—why do the Polynesian Balinese avoid the ocean beyond the shoreline because, to them, it is the abode of the demons? The *subak* system works well; computer simulations have established that point. But can overpopulation finally make temple irrigation unworkable? Bali has escaped the ravages of underdevelopment that plague Third World countries—at least for now. Yet the recession, exacerbated by the bombings, have thrown hundreds of Balinese out of work, including hotel workers and shopkeepers. We can conclude that overpopulation, a foreign-dominant tourist industry, central government interference regulating what tourists shall and shall not wear, and resource depletion all remain threats to Bali as a nation and a culture.

Selected Films

The Goddess and the Computer. 1988. 59 minutes. Stephan Lansing and Andre Singer. Cambridge, MA: Documentary Educational Resources.

Perfect Order: A Thousand Years in Bali. 2006. 79 minutes. Stephen Lansing. Whole Earth Films.

Three Worlds of Bali. 1979. 59 minutes. Odyssey Series. Ira Abrams. Cambridge, MA: Documentary Educational Resources.

Selected Literature

Lansing, Stephen. 1994. *The Balinese.* Belmont, CA: Wadsworth.

Lansing, Stephen. 2006. *Perfect Order: Recognizing Complexity in Bali.* Princeton, NJ: Princeton University Press.

Pringle, Robert. 2004. *A Short History of Bali: Indonesia's Hindu Realm.* Crow's Nest, NSW Australia: Allen and Unwin.

PART VI

Melanesia

CHAPTER 18

Papua New Guinea: Last of the World's Tribal Peoples

New Guinea is one of the last large areas with tribal societies. Read on.

Papua New Guinea is (or increasingly was) the land of pristine tribes. Undiscovered by foreigners until the 1930s, the main island was one of the largest areas of uncontacted tribes—uncontacted by Europeans that is—in the world. Two brothers in search for gold happened upon them while flying into the region—and the rest became history. Anthropologists have come in droves to the island—and so have the logging and mining corporations. They are isolated no more.

Geography of Papua New Guinea

New Guinea is located 100 miles north of Australia. It comprises a large island plus a chain of small islands off the eastern coast of the mainland. Together with Australia and New Zealand, New Guinea has always been isolated from Southeast Asia, even during the Ice Ages when the sea level was at its lowest. This is one of the most interesting demographic oddities of the world. New Guinea, along with Australia, was populated from the Asian mainland long before North America: 40,000 to 50,000 BP (before the present). The Americas, in contrast, was not populated until 15,000 BP at most.

The island of New Guinea is divided into two parts. The eastern half, together with the islands you see eastward, constitutes the independent nation known as Papua New Guinea. The western half is Irian Jaya, now known as Papua, an Indonesian province. Though one is a nation-state and the other a part of one, the more than 1,200 tribes have been independent societies—until now. (There is an independence movement in Papua, the western half.)

The nation of Papua New Guinea comprises not only the eastern end of the large islands, but smaller islands off its east coast. The most famous islands in anthropology are the Trobriand Islands, noted for the Kula Ring, a system of trade involving white armshells and red necklaces. Larger islands included New Britain, Bougainville, and Bismarck Islands.

Papua New Guinea comprises three broad tribal groups. The best known and researched are the highland tribes surrounding Mount Hagan and other areas. Tribal warfare was endemic; though fighting has been suppressed, there have been recent outbreaks of violence. The staple crop is yams, and pigs are highly valued as wealth. A man gains prestige by sponsoring major pig feasts.

238

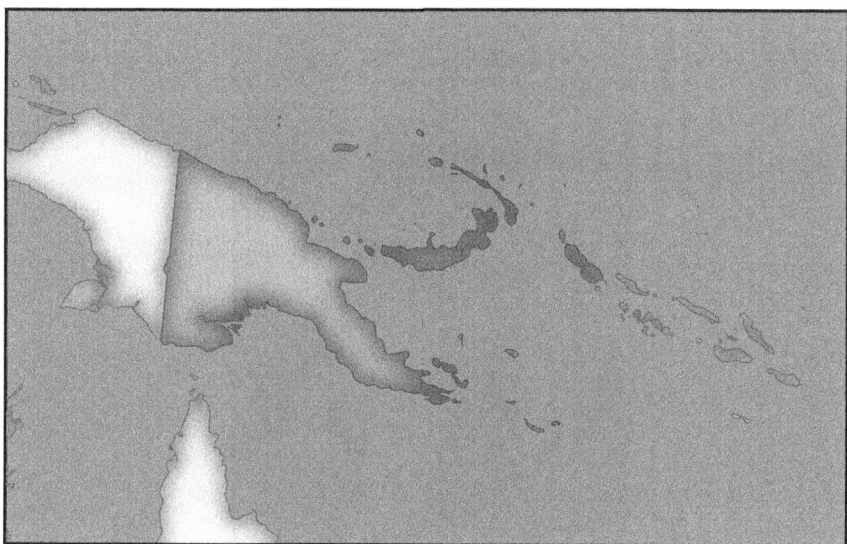

Image © AridOcean, 2012. Used under license from Shutterstock, Inc.

FIGURE 18.1

Island of New Guinea. The eastern part (darker shade) comprises the independent nation-state of New Guinea; the western part (lighter shade), is Papua, sometimes known as Irian Jaya to reflect that it is part of Indonesia.

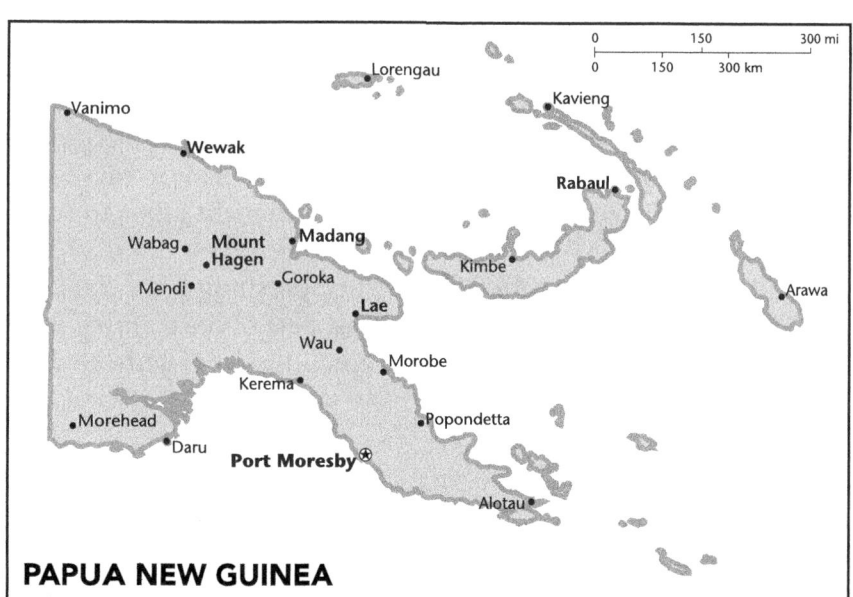

Image © Globe Turner, LLC., 2012. Used under license from Shutterstock, Inc.

FIGURE 18.2

Papua New Guinea. The nation includes several islands known collectively as Melanesia, or black island chain. This includes the Trobriand Islands, which is too small to be identified here.

Image © Byelikova Oksana, 2012. Used under license from Shutterstock, Inc.

FIGURE 18.3

Tribesman from Papua. Note penis sheath called a *namba*. As shown here, modesty varies from one culture to another; he would feel naked without his *namba*. A partygoer in the United States would probably be arrested for wearing the same "clothing."

Then there is the western side of the Island of New Guinea. Irian Jaya, also known as Papua, West Papua, and West New Guinea, covers that side of the island. It forms the northeastern part of Indonesia, of which it is a province. Recent attempts have been made to carve a second province, West Papua, with results far from clear. There is also a movement afoot to seek independence from Indonesia.

About 600 more tribal societies inhabit Papua. The best studied are the Dani, who inhabit the Grand Valley along the Balaam river in the southeast part of the country. Men are noted for wearing penis sheaths, called *namba*, made of gourd and little else (Figure 18.3).

Warfare among the Dani

Like their eastern counterparts, Dani grows yams and sponsors pig feasts. Until 1963, they engaged in longstanding feuds. Their persistent warfare is documented in the film *Dead Birds*, a classic firm directed by Robert Gardner, which portrays the feuds between two tribes that has gone back to unknown generations.

War is endemic, possibly as old as humankind itself. Tribes seem to have a long record of warfare, and New Guinea tribes have more than their share. In *Dead Birds*, one learns that revenge was mandatory among the Dani, and in fact among all New Guinea tribes. The spirit of revenge would hound the victimized tribe until they murdered someone—man, woman, child—from the offending tribe. War does not appear to be a thing of the past, as outbreaks elsewhere suggest. In Dani mythology, a bird and a snake run a race. The bird is mortal. The snake, because it sheds its skin, is immortal. In the myth, the bird wins, and so man is mortal. This myth introduces *Dead Birds.* This tit-for-tat warfare lasts as long as memory permits.

For the Dani, Henry Bagish, a locally revered anthropology professor who spent his sabbaticals recording with film more than 35 cultures in his 50-year career, revealed a practice among women when their close male relatives were killed in battle. Women and girls were taken to the funeral site and two of their fingers were chopped off with a stone adze. He took their photos at the time, in 1961, and when the Bagishes visited the same village 18 years later, there were still women with two or more digits missing. Tribal war was outlawed by the Indonesian government in 1963.

Pig Feasts among the Kawelka

One way to curtail warfare was to hold intertribal feasts. Besides enjoying the festivities, the tribes found this a good way to minimize chances of warfare. Warfare was eliminated by government intervention—or so it was thought for a long time. One way to compensate for a death was to provide bloodwealth, or compensation for the murder of a kinsman in a rival tribe.

There are two central features of New Guinean tribes (both east and west): big men and pig feasts. Big men are the chiefs of New Guinea, though ones that lack effective authority. Pig feasts are held once every ten years, both to promote solidarity within the tribe and keep the peace between them. Ongka, the big man of the Kawelka tribe portrayed in *Ongka's Big Moka,* brings a pig as a peace offering after the big man of a rival tribe has died unexpectedly and in which witchcraft is the suspected cause. His father-in-law describes a similar practice when war dominated the region. For both big men and pig feasts, there is much more than meets the eye.

The big man of the tribe directs the activities of a tribe, from warfare to pig feasts. The term means "man of influence." That does not mean he is a man of power. He is not the chief we usually think of. He cannot boss people around. He can only persuade. If men don't like their big men, they can go to support another one—or none at all. There is always more than one big man competing for influence. As *Ongka's Big Moka* shows, Ongka always has to keep an eye on his rivals. And a man does not pass his position down to his son.

Pig feasts are not everyday occurrences. They usually occur only once every ten years. It takes a lot of work, and especially coordination, to put a pig feast together. Much can go wrong, and often does. Among the Kawelka, the feast is called *moka.* Moka means many things, and it is the focus of the tribe's being and cohesion.

One of the rules of all tribal societies governs gift exchange. If you receive a gift from one group, you—or most likely your group—has to repay that gift. If you can take your time to repay it, then it is generalized reciprocity. However, if you have to repay it within a limited time frame, and repay it with a gift of the same or greater value, then you have balanced reciprocity. That involves distant kin or even two tribes.

Ongka's Big Moka depicts Ongka, a big man of the Kawelka tribe who owes the big man (Peruwa) of a rival tribe a major feast. Ten years ago, Peruwa sponsored a feast in which he gave Ongka 400 pigs. In the film, Ongka hopes to repay Peruwa with 600 pigs and a little extra, such as cassowaries (midsize flightless birds), cattle, and a truck. The film shows what he had to do to pull it off. His greatest fear is to break the rope of Moka by failing to sponsor the return feast, clearly feeling the need to return the feast.

As shown in *Ongka's Big Moka*, tribal warfare was mitigated, but the death of the big man of a rival tribe brought the two to the brink of war, and Ongka's rival, Raima, could still exploit this intertribal tension by claiming that someone among the Kawelka killed the big man in the rival tribe. That was how the moka was postponed. But has tribal warfare been eliminated everywhere in New Guinea?

Papua New Guinea, Present and Future: Two Scenarios

As a matter of fact, tribal warfare has not disappeared in recent years. If anything, warfare among many tribes has become deadlier. As a YouTube clip titled "Tribal Fighting-Papua New Guinea" points out, the mortality rate from tribal wars have increased because of the ease that guns can be obtained: from theft or from purchases from gunrunners, who may themselves be governmental officials. You may access this link by entering the title in the YouTube search box or by pasting this link to your browser: http://www.youtube.com/watch?v=hPM-gJA62Rs.

Another phenomenon afflicting New Guinea is deforestation. New Guinean tribes are making deals with logging companies to extract trees from their lands. Figure 18.4 shows the extent of deforestation as of the present, and it is expected to increase substantially by the year 2020. The forests are usually clear-cut, leaving exposed soil to be eroded or leached by rainfall. Sometimes oil palms or monoculture trees replace them. The deforestation issue can be seen in a YouTube clip titled "Rapid Deforestation—Papua New Guinea." Enter the title into the search box in YouTube or paste *http://www.youtube.com/watch?v=9aJZB2jNHRY* on your browser.

Image © Byelikova Oksana, 2012. Used under license from Shutterstock, Inc.

FIGURE 18.4
Deforested region in Papua New Guinea.

This is a common scene after logging: The stumps are left behind, and as far as the eye can see, there is not a tree left standing. Nor is it likely that trees will be planted to replace the ones that have been felled. The same video provides an extended portrait of logging in New Guinea, how loggers access tribal lands, and the destruction left behind.

Two portraits of Papua New Guineans, leaders in their own right, dramatically contrast the two cultures that still coexist in New Guinea. One is a government official in charge of environmental affairs; the other is a big man worried about his tribe's future as the forests continue to be clean-cut. With the environmental crisis escalating and the price of energy now going into the stratosphere, it is uncertain which of these two leaders represent the wave of the future. The future of Papua New Guinea is problematical. There is much to worry about. The government itself represents many tribes.

Conclusion

Papua New Guinea faces a dilemma. Can the tribes put a brake on development that will destroy tribal lands? Are the tribes themselves part of the problem by signing agreements with lumber companies to continue harvesting the forest for financial gain or by trafficking in marijuana and guns? At this point in time, there is little cause for optimism.

Selected Films

Dead Birds. 1963. 84 minutes. Robert Gardner. Cambridge, MA: Documentary Educational Resources.

Man Without Pigs. 1990. 60 minutes. Chris Owens. Cambridge, MA. Documentary Educational Resources.

Ongka's Big Moka. 2003. 60 minutes. Disappearing World Series. Odyssey. New York: Shanachie.

Selected Literature

Heider, Karl. 2000. *The Dugum Dani. A Papuan Culture in the Highlands of West New Guinea.* New York: Aldine Transaction.

Heider, Karl. *The Grand Valley Dani: Peaceful Warriors.* Belmont, CA: Wadsworth.

Strathern, Anthony. 2000. *Inequality in New Guinea Highlands.* Cambridge, UK: Cambridge University Press.

Strathern, Anthony, and Pamela J. Stewart. 1996. *Collaborations and Conflict: A Leader Through Time.* Belmont, CA: Wadsworth.

CHAPTER 19

Trobriand Islands: Archipelago of the Kula Ring

Introduction: The Trobriands and the First Ethnographer

The Trobriand Islands are a small chain of islands located off the east coast of New Guinea. One of the founding anthropologists, Bronislaw Malinowski, became known for several ethnographies of these islands, principally the kula ring that involved the exchange of two types of shell trinkets: white armshells and red necklaces. This is a description of the Trobriand Islands.

Bronislaw Malinowski, an anthropologist of Polish nationality, landed in the Trobriand Islands, also called by its native name of the main island Kiriwina, almost by accident. Receiving a doctorate in philosophy (in mathematics and physics) from Jagiellonian University in Poland, he decided to switch to ethnology after reading James Frazer's work *The Golden Bough* while recovering from an illness. He entered the London School of Economics in 1910, and in 1914 he was exploring Papua (now Papua New Guinea) and the outlying islands to the east when World War I broke out. Being a citizen of the Austria-Hungarian Empire, which included Poland, and therefore classified as an enemy alien, he was given a choice between internment or exile in the Trobriands; he chose the latter. Over the four years he lived there, he perfected the technique of participant observation and generated several books, the best known of which is *Argonauts of the Western Pacific*. He also became known as a functionalist, who argues that cultures serve the individual rather than, as structural-functionalism would have it, the individual serving the maintenance of society.

Ethnography of the Trobrianders

The Trobriand Islanders call their land Kiriwina; the name applies to both the large island and the island chain as a whole. The French first applied the name in honor of Lieutenant Denis de Trobriand, whose ship *Esperance* landed at the islands in 1793. Apart from the exchange system known as the kula, the Trobrianders are known for the open sexual behavior of their youths prior to marriage, their belief that pregnancy is caused by ancestral water spirits, and for their chieftains occupying permanent offices inherited matrilineally rather than as big men in Papua New Guinea,

Image © VIPDesignUSA, 2012. Used under license from Shutterstock, Inc.

FIGURE 19.1

Bronislaw Malinowski in a commemorative postage stamp issued in his native Poland in 1973, depicting the Trobriand (Kiriwinan) peoples whom he researched from 1914 to 1918. He laid the foundations of participant observation.

who remain heads only so long as they can maintain a following of fellow tribesmen. Their clans are linked by marriage, consolidated by yam exchanges. According to Malinowski, magic among the Trobriand Island is associated with danger. Because long distance journeys are dangerous because of storms and possible attacks by rival tribes, Trobriand canoe builders perform magic at every stage of their construction. Atoll-plying canoes are given no such magical treatment.

The Trobriand Islands (or Kiriwinas) are located 120 miles east of Papua New Guinea. It is largely a featureless chain of islands about 12 miles, including Kiriwina, a flat island. Other large islands are Kalileuna, Vakuta, and Kitava. Except for Kiriwina, the islands are atolls, small islets that face a volcanic lagoon.

The islands have the dry and wet monsoon seasons typical of New Guinea and the southern and southeastern regions of Asia. Because of their flat terrain, there are few areas of water storage of streams. The only sources of water are wells and ponds. Although drought is rare, it does occur often enough to cause concern among the Trobriand islanders.

Making a Living

Like other regions of Melanesia and Papua New Guinea, yams are the most important food in the Trobriands. Overproduction of yams is practiced, in quantities far greater than the entire population could consume. Partly, the overproduction is intended to compensate for any year of drought in which yams cannot grow, but mainly it serves to make a display of wealth, particularly among the chiefs. As will be seen from the *kula* ring below, competition for prestige both within

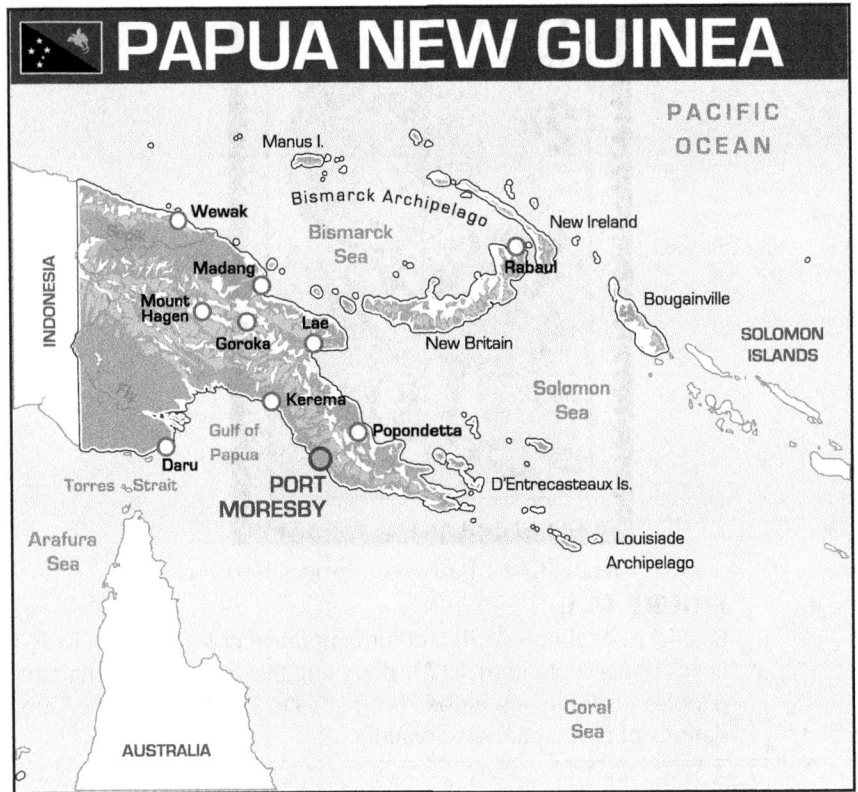

Image © Pjasha, 2012. Used under license from Shutterstock, Inc.

FIGURE 19.2
Melanesia, the islands east of Papua New Guinea, which includes the Trobriand Islands.

and between the islands is intense. Yams are grown with the use of slash and burn agriculture in which the brush is cut down at the beginning of the dry season, and then burned toward the end. Fallow season is short; usually between three and five years.

Gender division of labor is sharply defined. Men clear and burn the brush and cultivate the soils. Until the Australians occupied the islands and outlawed the practice, men engaged in tribal warfare. They still fish and engage in long-distance trading, including exchange of *kula* valuables. Women plant and weed the garden and harvest the yams. Women also engage in other crafts, including making grass skirts.

Fishing is a common task among coastal people, and they often trade fish for yams with people living in the interior. Women gather shellfish in addition to their other tasks. In addition, the Trobriand islanders lack the stone for axes and clay for pottery; therefore, it is not surprising that they obtain polished stone axes and pottery from other islands. They do grow specialty foods; one example is sago from Dobu. Trade on the islands is unorganized; external trade is directed by the chiefs.

Sex, Marriage, and the Family

Traditionally, Trobriand Islanders believed that pregnancy occurs, not by copulation between men and women, but by the infusion of women's bodies from their ancestral spirits, who live in the water, especially in Tuma, an island where it is believed they dwell after death. One hypothesis for this explanation relates to the large quantities of yams Trobrianders consume; one chemical, known as phytoestrogen, is thought to inhibit conception, so that connection between copulation and childbirth may not be made.

From prepubescent age, girls and boys engage in sexual play and games. One game involves a tug of war between female and male adolescents, held during one of the yam festivals. Here, female teenagers are performing a dance, a prelude to the night-long fertility rite. The tug of war lasts into the night, then the girls and boys pair off. This is one occasion in which all sex tabus are ignored. The stereotype that south sea islanders engage in sex play and unrestrained copulation may be attributed in part to the Trobriander adolescents.

Marriage is informal to the point where one may question whether there is such a thing as marriage at all. Typically, a couple show up at the groom's residence and announce that they are married. Alternative, a couple may simply eat together. The longer they do so, the more likely that others will considered them married. Wedding feasts do occur on occasion. Another indication of marriages involves massive gifts of yams.

When a woman marries, large quantities of yams are given to her father-in-law or brother-in-law. This gift compensates for the land she and her kin will surrender for their own clan. A chief with many wives gains numerous stores of yams, which puts him in a position of prestige as he gives his yams to potential allies. In a food-insecure environment, this gives him leverage over many households.

Image © Bobkeenan Photography, 2012. Used under license from Shutterstock, Inc.

FIGURE 19.3
Yams represent a symbol of a chief's prestige and part of a transfer of gifts to a woman's father-in-law or brother-in-law upon marriage.

From Family to Kin Group

The basic unit of Trobriand society is the household. The household unit is one of a series that form part of a matrilineal group known as the *dala,* which own all plots of land. Since this land forms part of the estate of this *dala,* it may be considered a corporate estate whose members have both rights and obligation. Inasmuch as the chieftainship is permanent, it must require a successor. Among the Trobrianders, the *dala* headship goes from a man to his sister's son. At age six, the young man as a boy leaves his parents' home and joins his mother's brother, who will train him in the practice of leadership, warfare, and trading. Later, he will marry his wife and bring her to his uncle's residence. This is an instance of avunculocal postmarital residence.

From the household grows the cluster, which is an endogamous unit: only men and women from within that cluster marry, and warfare is disallowed. Villages are ranked. The chief of the highest ranked village coordinates the cluster as a whole.

The Kula Ring

The Kula ring involves the exchange of two kinds of shell ornaments: white armshells and red necklaces. The exchange incorporates three obligations implicit in an exchange as theorized in his book *The Gift* (in French: *Essai sur le Don*). In his introduction, Mauss argues that in a society lacking a centralized state, the gift creates a series of relationships that has the force of law in the absence of codified law. The first is the obligation to give, and in so doing, to offer a relationship implicit in the gift. The second is the obligation to receive or accept the gift, and so accept the relationship as well; refusal to accept is tantamount to hostilities. The third is the obligation to pay, and so to consolidate the relationship. Failure to repay amounts to becoming indebted to the giver and, in effect, become a beggar. The system of kula exchange is consistent with these obligations.

The system of *kula* exchange is centered around white armshells, called *mwali,* which are exchanged for red necklaces called *soulava* or *bagi,* made up of spondylus shells. One trader gives his partner an armshell that has been owned by other men in the past; the more it has been traded, the greater the value of the shell. His partner must now give him a red necklace of equal or higher value, one thatalso has passed through many hands. In and of themselves, the shells are valueless. What matters is their history, of stories of all the figures that once owned the armshell or the necklace.

Nor do the shells travel in an arbitrary direction. If one man gives a *mwali,* he must always receive a *bagi* or *soulava.* From a bird's eye perspective, the *mwali* always travel in a counter-clockwise direction; the *soulava,* in a clockwise direction. They thus create a network of 12 islands covering 200 or so square miles. Danger accompanies every travel. The canoes, always small, face a treacherous journey. A canoe could sink in a storm or be smashed against rocks or reefs. Even trading partners could turn against them. Or a canoe might land on a shore of cannibalistic tribes.

When the partners do meet, the gifts are given amid feasting and elaborate ceremonies. In and of themselves, the shells have little or no value; their value is derived on their possession by chiefs and other men of prestige in the past. Therefore, if one receives a white armshell with a long history of ownership by many chiefs, he must repay with a red necklace with a history equally as

Image © Aspen Photo, 2012. Used under license from Shutterstock, Inc.

FIGURE 19.4
Woman wearing a sun dress not unlike one worn by Rebecca Camilleri-Gorman in her stay as a "sister" in Kitava. Sun dresses are unacceptable to Kitavan women, who think nothing of participation in rituals bare-breasted—in which Ms. Gorman was reluctant to participate. To be sure, this is a study in contrastive modesty.

long—or longer—by men of high prestige. If he cannot make such a repayment at the next visit, he will give a small gift as a promise to make such a repayment in the future.

Economic anthropologists often cite the kula ring as part of a system of exchange that incorporate several spheres, the most prestigious of which is the *kula*. Another sphere, which may occur at the same time as *kula* exchange, comprises trade of ordinary goods called *gimwali*. An example is a polished stone axe. Unlike kula, *gimwali* items may involve haggling for the best "price," based on a system of barter (direct trade of goods rather than through the medium of money). In another island in the Melanesian chain, Rossel Islanders have twenty-one spheres of exchange that do involve the use of shells as exchange media. Two or three involve prestige goods; the remainder is of everyday goods that vary in value.

British Colonization and Acculturation

The Trobriand Islands were soon colonized by Great Britain followed by Australia after World War II. Even the name itself reflects European influence; as noted earlier, the islands were named after Denis de Trobriand, a French naval officer. European influence is evident in many ways, from the British game of cricket to a religion founded by John Wesley known as Methodism to women's dress styles.

Cricket was introduced to the Trobriand Islands by the British Methodist missionary William Gillmore in an effort to control tribal warfare on the island. The Trobrianders first played by the rules, then immediately changed them to fit in their warlike traditions, where warfare was now banned. Any number of players may participate, and may include as many as 40 or 50 players. Chants and dancing precedes the game and rules are modified to ensure that the home team always wins. Bat styles were changed, and underarm rather than overhead pitching of the ball was adopted. The game is followed by a feast held by the home team. This is a classic example of syncretism that is not religious.

In the BBC series *Tribal Wives,* which records the experience of six women in different tribal societies around the world, the story follows the adventures of Rebecca (Becky) Camilleri-Gorman in her five-week visit of Kitava, one of the Trobriand Islands, as a "sister" given the name Ibogwa in an adopted family. She has several adjustments to make: pants are not allowed for women, she must sit in the Kitavan manner, and she must perform domestic chores in the house and garden. One adjustment she balks at is decking out in topless ceremonial dress in one of the rituals—despite the sun dresses she usually wears in hot weather. (Bare-breasted ceremonial participation is routine for Kitavan women, despite their Methodist affiliation.) She finally gives in at the final ceremony held in her honor before her departure at the end of the five weeks. When she leaves, her adopted kin mourns for "Ibogwa (Becky)," as if hers were a death in the family.

Conclusion

Unlike cultures on Papua New Guinea and other islands of Melanesia, the Trobriand Islanders are governed by chiefs, who occupy a permanent position with a rule of succession, from a chief to his sister's son. The rule of avunculocal residence reflects this rule of succession. The chief is the head of a cluster of villages comprising *dala,* or clan-based households. Premarital sex and marriage are casual affairs, and childbirth is attributed to infusions of the woman's body by ancestral water spirits rather than to copulation. The best known feature of the Trobriand Islands is the *kula* ring, made famous in the anthropological literature by the work of Bronislaw Malinowski as reported in *Argonauts of the Pacific.* The functionalist model he derived from this work provides an explanation of religion as a quest for security and the sexual behavior of the peoples, both drawing from his work in the Trobriands. In this model, society serves to satisfy the needs of the people themselves, as opposed to structural functionalism, in which individuals serve to maintain the needs of society. Thus began one of the earliest debates in social anthropology.

Selected Films

Tales from the Jungle: Malinowski. 60 minutes. London: BBC. Available on YouTube in 6 parts.

Selected Literature

Malinowski, Bronislaw. 2010 (1922). *Argonauts of the Western Pacific.* London: Benetiction Classics.

Malinowski, Bronislaw. 1978 (1935). *Coral Gardens and Their Magic.* New York: Dover.

Malinowski, Bronislaw. 1985. *Sex and Repression in Savage Society.* Chicago: University of Chicago Press.

Malinowski, Bronislaw. 1987. *Sexual Life of Savages.* Boston: Beacon Press.

Weiner, Annette. 1988. *The Trobrianders of Papua New Guinea.* New York: Holt, Rinehart and Winston.

PART VII

Africa

CHAPTER 20

West Africa: The Homeland of Afro-Americans

Introduction

West Africa is the original homeland of most people of African descent who live in the Americas, from the United States and Canada through the Caribbean islands to Brazil and other parts of South America. They are descendants of the slaves, most of whom were captured at or near the coast of West Africa and shipped as human cargo to the New World.

West Africa comprises one of the most civilized regions of Africa. Names such as Ghana, the Ashanti, the Yoruba, and many others were monarchies with advanced technology such as iron making and intensive cultivation. It was through the wars they waged that the defeated were rounded up and sold to European and American entrepreneurs who dealt with human traffic. Today, countries such as Nigeria and Ghana constitute the leading powers in the continent.

West Africa: A Geography

The definition of West Africa varies among the geographers. In this map, the countries listed along the Atlantic coast from Angola northward to Mauritania are included in this region. Some geographers might exclude both countries. In any case, countries such as Nigeria, Ghana, the Ivory Coast, Sierra Leone, and such interior countries as Burkino Faso and Mali, would be included and are the best known. Most typologies list 16 countries as comprising West Africa. (See Figure 20.1.)

When the Europeans defined the boundaries of West Africa, they ignored all the ethnic boundaries of the Africans themselves. One tribe may cross two or more states as now defined. The Fulani cross all of interior West Africa.

West Africa has a diverse climate. Tropical rain forest and woodlands border the coast, savanna (tropical grasslands) covers the intermediate strips, and desert and semi-desert that make up the Sahara cover the northern part. In recent years, the desert has crept southward, raising many concerns about the effects of climate change that concern not only Africa, but also the world at large.

Image © charobnica, 2012. Used under license from Shutterstock, Inc.

FIGURE 20.1

Africa. Countries comprising West Africa vary by geographer, but almost all include Nigeria (the largest), Ghana, Sierra Leone, and other coastal states. Interior states include Mali, Niger, and Burkina Faso.

For one thing, the pastoralists in the northern region are facing an unprecedented drought and, further to the south, desertification is a worry.

Ethnicity of West Africa: An Overview

Although the cultures are diverse, several features set the region apart from other African regions. They include long, flowing robes called *boubous* or *agbadas* that both men and women wear, national sports such as soccer, musical styles such as the High Life, and cuisine that may include yams, plantains, and sorghum.

Religions vary. There are several indigenous religions, some of which are incorporated in *Santeria* in Cuba and *Vodou* in Haiti. Major religions have also filtered in: Islam in the north of West Africa and various Christian denominations in the south. Monotheism seems to be an integral belief among West Africans, even the so-called Pagan.

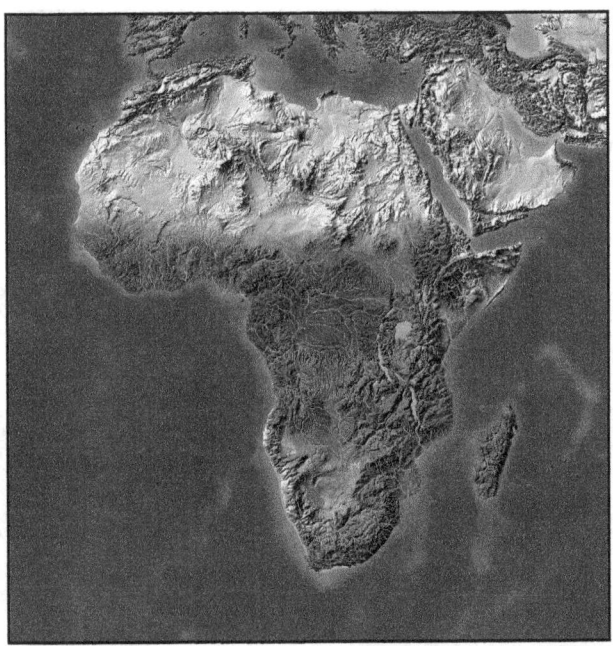

Image © AridOcean, 2012. Used under license from Shutterstock, Inc.

FIGURE 20.2
Extent of Sahara desert (light) compared with tropical rain forest (dark).

Image © iofoto, 2012. Used under license from Shutterstock, Inc.

FIGURE 20.3
Afro-American man wearing traditional West African robe of his ancestors.

West Africa: A Sequence of Cultures

Prehistory

West Africa can be divided into five broad phases of culture: prehistory, African empire, slavery, European imperialist, and African post-independence. Although many paleoanthropologists (anthropologists specializing in fossil hominins) place the first modern human species in Africa (eastern and southern); the first West African humans in the prehistorical era are in evidence by 12,000 BP (before the present). Agriculture and iron implements first appear in the fifth millennium BC. Trade and formative states begin plying the Sahara between West Africa and the principal cities and tribes of North Africa as soon as domesticated camels make their appearance.

African Empires

Early empires began with the Nok Empire in Mauritania in the eighth century. One of the most notable empires was Mali, especially during the reign of Mansa Musa, who was said to ruin the economies in his path to Mecca by his opulent gifts of gold. Timbuktu was a major center with salt, gold, and slaves forming the bulk of the trade.

Slavery Era

Slavery was not new; it flourished under the Arab traders. Europe began its Atlantic slave trade with the Portuguese in 1445; the English, Spanish, French, and later the Americans followed suit, as did the Belgians further south in the Congo.

The routes of the slave trade developed into a triangular system. Slaves went from West Africa to the southern United States, the Caribbean, and Latin America. Raw materials, namely tobacco, molasses, and sugar, went from the New World to Europe. Manufactured products, such as rum, went to West Africa and elsewhere.

Image © Georgios Kollidas, 2012. Used under license from Shutterstock, Inc.

FIGURE 20.4
Slave trade, probably in Guinea Bissau. Captives about to be loaded on slave ships.

Slavery was abolished in the nineteenth century, starting with England in 1808 and ending with Brazil in 1888. Slavery was not without its legacy. In 2009, shortly after assuming office, President Obama visited the dungeon in Ghana during his goodwill tour of that country. Ships with slaves packed like sardines were typical. If the ships' design was cruel, it was also profitable. Who says that capitalism is merciful?

European Imperialism

If slavery came to an end in the late nineteenth century, colonialism was at its height. It began not with Europeans, but with the Fulani, who in a series of so-called reformist jihads, swept the northern regions of West Africa. The European "scramble for Africa" began in the late nineteenth century, with Britain and France the principal contenders in West Africa.

By international treaty, European nations divided the entire continent among themselves. The map identifies the principal contestants in the "scramble," which also included Belgium, Portugal, Italy, and even Denmark. Liberia and Ethiopia (in East Africa) alone remained independent as of 1914.

Several factors attempt to explain this scramble for colonies: creating markets for European manufacture, of which there was a surplus at home; control of primary resources, including those that could not be obtained in Europe, such as rubber, copper, and tin; and political rivalry among the European powers.

Post-Independence Africa

Running colonies comes at a price, however, and Europeans came at a better bargain: imperialism. After World War II, country after country launched nationalist movements. Ghana under Kwame Nkrumah became the first to achieve independence in 1957, followed by Guinea in 1958 and Nigeria in 1960. It was Nkrumah who identified indirect control by economic means, calling it neocolonialism.

Independence did not bring nationalist paradise. Corruption was rampant in all but a few countries, few countries escaped military dictatorship (Sani Abacha of Nigeria was a classic example), civil war persists to this day (made famous by the movie *Blood Diamonds* for Sierra Leone, with its child soldiers), AIDS epidemics throughout Africa, and a long-term desertification of Africa from the Sahara Desert that has moved southward for the past 30 years.

Ethnicity of Africans: A Comparative Review

Here are some examples of West African cultures. The **Yoruba** are among the best known ethnic groups in Nigeria, and are also found in Togo and Benin. The two principal Western religions, Islam and Christianity, that roughly divide the population and the Indigenous religions are still present. They have been ruled by monarchs organized into royal patrilineages. Twins are a dominant theme in Yoruba values.

The **Ashanti** are a matrilineal society—kin reckoning is mediated by a line of females. Men also play a role, from provider to contributing to the life force of the infant. They are also a state society, with the Golden Stool forming a sacred symbol for royal authority. When a British administrator sat on the stool in 1900, the Ashanti rose in revolt. Nevertheless, the Ashanti and other ethnic groups see themselves as Ghanaians first and their ethnicity second.

The **Hausa** are a herding and farming people in northern Nigeria and eastern Niger. They are strictly devout Muslims and strong adherents of Shari'a law. Their language, also called Hausa, is a *lingua franca* among northern ethnicities and, as a written language, much literature has flowed from their pens.

The Igbo are, like the Yoruba, based in Nigeria, yet for the most part lack monarchs and monarchies. Traditionally, they are a stateless society organized into patrilineal clans, villages, and dialects. Traditionally they are polygynous (one man married to two or more wives) and had a systematic belief system called Odinani; in modern times they are both monogamous and strongly Christian. Their war of independence from Nigeria ended in failure.

The **Mende** comprise several cultures scattered across West Africa. Largely Muslim, their beliefs include a syncretic mixture of Islam and local belief. They are known for their secret societies, the *poro* for the men and *sande* for the women. They are also known for their griots, bards serving at the pleasure of their monarchs and with a strong oral tradition passed down over the centuries.

The *poro* and *sande* secret societies referred to here are found in the Mende-speaking peoples living in Liberia, Sierra Leone, the Ivory Coast, and Guinea. Though illegal under national law in Guinea, they are not only legal elsewhere, but membership is universally mandatory under local law. They play roles both in the political and religious sectors of society. One may legitimately ask as to how they can possibly be secret if all men and women have to join? For the Kpelle of Liberia, according to Beryl Bellman, himself a member of a *poro* association, the standard is an *ability* to keep secrets; only when members learn to do so can they be entrusted with the political and religious responsibilities associated with that society (1984).

There are two political structures in both societies: the "secular" and the "sacred." The secular structure consists of the town chief, the neighborhood and kin group headmen, and elders. The sacred structure (the *zo*) comprises a hierarchy of "priests" of both *poro* and *sande* in the neighborhood. Among the Kpelle of Liberia, the *poro* and *sande zo* take turns in dealing with in-town fighting, rape, homicide, incest, and land disputes. Not unlike the leopard-skin chief, the *zo* play important roles in mediation.

The *zo* of both the *poro* and *sande* are held in great respect, even fear. Some authors suggest that both secret societies strengthen the hands of secular political authority because chiefs and landowners occupy the most powerful positions in the associations. This suggests the formative elements of a stratified society and a state.

Conclusion

Like all underdeveloped countries around the world, West Africa has become a victim of the corporate globalization and neoliberal ideology that spans the world. The movie *Bamako* is an allegory of this process. It depicts a tribunal, seated in the courtyard of a private home and trying the World Bank for its financial crimes against humanity. Among the crimes are privatization of public assets, pollution such as that of Shell Oil in Nigeria and aversive terms of trade that developed countries impose on the underdeveloped world.

Not that the countries themselves are left blameless. The widespread practice of clitoridectomy is an issue, not only that it suppresses women's sexuality by removal of the clitoris, but also entails severe health issues. The film *Moolaade* is a graphic dramatization of this practice and the resistance of six girls to it. And corruption is everywhere present, and has played a part in Africa's status as a Fourth World region.

William Bascom, an anthropologist specializing on Yoruba culture, concluded a speech with a pun: "The future of Africa is black." With the periodical oil spills from Shell Oil within Ngoni territory in southern Nigeria, this figure of speech has come to be very real.

Selected Films

Abloni. 2005. 58 minutes. Alexandre Oktan. Cambridge, MA: Documentary Educational Resources. Consequences of charities that provide used clothing overseas, with focus on Togo and the local clothing industries damaged by the influx of second-hand clothes.

Bamako. 2008. 117 minutes. A. Sissako. French with English subtitles. New York: New Yorker Studio. Mock trial in private residential courtyard brings World Bank to task for the harm caused by its policies.

Deep Hearts. 1981. 58 minutes. Robert Gardner. Cambridge, MA: Documentary Educational Resources. Study of Bororo Fulani of Niger.

Liberia: America's Stepchild. 2002. 90 minutes. Nancee Oku Bright. Cambridge, MA: Documentary Educational Resources.

Moolaade. 2007. 124 minutes. Ousmane Sembene. New York: New Yorker Studios. Six girls refuse clitoridectomy with severe consequences on the village.

Tubali: Hausa Architecture in Northern Nigeria. 1994. 45 minutes. Sabine Jell-Ballsen. Cambridge, MA: Documentary Educational Resources.

Xala. 2005. 125 minutes. Ousmane Sembene. French and Wolof with English subtitles. New York: New Yorker Studios. Polygynous bureaucrat of a newly independent country takes on a third wife only to discover his impotence on his wedding night—because of a curse called *Xala*.

Selected Literature

Bascom, William. 1964. *The Yoruba of Southwestern Nigeria*. Prospect Heights, IL: Waveland Press.

Davidson, Basil. 1998. *West Africa before the Colonial Era: A History to 1850*. London: Longman.

McDermott, Gerald. 1987. *Anansi the Spider: A Tale from the Ashanti*. New York: Holt. A children's tale that stresses the wisdom of cooperation.

Mendonsa, Eugene. 2002. *West Africa: An Introduction to Its History, Civilization and Contemporary Situation*. Chapel Hill, NC. Carolina Academic Press.

Schwab, Peter. 2004. *Designing West Africa: Prelude to 21st Century Calamity*. London: Palgrave MacMillan.

Uchendu, Victor. 1965. *The Igbo of Southeast Nigeria*. Prospect Heights, IL: Waveland Press.

CHAPTER 21

East African Pastoralists: The Case of the Turkana and Masai

Introduction

Kenya is home to two tribes that represent the typical pastoralist peoples of East Africa. These are the Turkana and the Masai. We will focus on these two tribal societies.

Geography of Africa

Africa is one of the seven continents of the world. It was called "darkest Africa" about a century ago simply because no one outside of the region knew much about it. Geographically, Africa is located south of Europe and southwest of the Middle East.

Africa comprises more than 30 countries, most of them south of the Sahara. West African countries were traditionally kingdoms relying on horticulture or, to the north, cattle herders. East Africa is largely grassland, and most peoples there were, until recently, herders as well. To the south are a mix of hunters and gatherers (of which the !Kung San [now Ju/'hoansi] are the most studied), herders (such as the Herero), and agriculturalists (such as the states of Swazi and Lesotho). The primary focus of this lecture is Kenya in East Africa.

This map shows the regions of Kenya, including the cities and the geographical highlights, such as the Rift Valley. In this lecture, we will focus on the Turkana and the Masai, both herding or pastoralist societies. They are both located in the grasslands of western Kenya. The two societies together comprise less than three percent of all tribal societies in Kenya. The Turkana are located in the northwestern part of Kenya; the Masai live in the southwestern part.

East African pastoralists are found throughout East Africa. In addition to the Turkana and Masai, the Nuer (made famous by the renowned British anthropologist Edward E. Evans-Pritchard), the Jie, the Afar, and the Tiriki are well known in the anthropological literature. Cattle is to these peoples what money is to us—a symbol of wealth. Generally, they are patrilineal and very patriarchal—men run the show in these tribes. Tribal warfare and cattle theft are their other dubious claims to fame—dubious to us Westerners, that is. Warfare and cattle theft are as normal to them as commuting to work is to us.

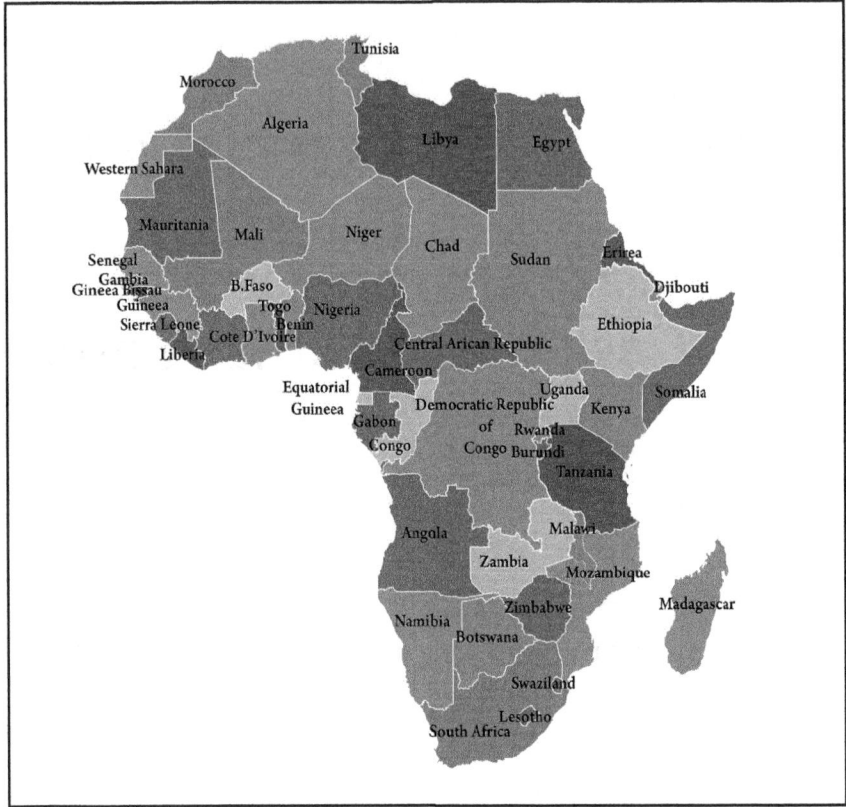

Image © Richard Laschon, 2012. Used under license from Shutterstock, Inc.

FIGURE 21.1
Political map of Africa. Because the boundaries were formed with European purpose in mind, the tribal societies are not coterminous with the nation-states and their boundaries.

The Turkana

The Turkana live in a harsher environment than the Masai, and so herd a variety of animals. Cattle are the main animals herded, but Turkana also handle other animals that thrive in dry climate, such as camels and goats. Sheep and donkeys are also herded. The animals are divided during the dry season—cattle go to the most watered valleys, whereas camels and goats go to more arid territory.

They live in villages, preferably by a water source such as Lake Turkana. When the dry season arrives, the villages will split up into smaller segments and migrate to areas appropriate for their animals.

Family and Kin Relations

The Turkana have a relatively simple social organization. They reckon their kin by patrilineal descent but have little formal social organization beyond the extended family. Nevertheless, they

Image © Olinchuk, 2012. Used under license from Shutterstock, Inc.

FIGURE 21.2
Kenya, the Turkana and the Masai are both located in the western part of the country.

Image © Piotr Gatlik, 2012. Used under license from Shutterstock, Inc.

FIGURE 21.3
A village during the rainy season, which allows greater density as seen here. Note proximity to Lake Turkana, the namesake of the tribe.

use extensive social networks to provide mutual support in times of need. Their ties include close relatives, kin related by marriage called affines, and friendship. Reciprocity is extremely important for the Turkana to survive.

Despite these extensive ties, Turkana have not found it necessary to extend ties of kinship beyond the level of the household. There are no lineages or clans that one finds among the Masai and many other East African herders. They have no age grades or age sets, unlike other pastoralists in East Africa.

Turkana social and cultural patterns reflect their adaptation to uncertain areas—it could be rainy one year and dry the next. During drought, it is better to move in small groups and to separate the herds. In rainy years, it is better to take advantage of the cooperation that larger groupings would provide—and animals do not have to be separated.

The Masai

Unlike the Turkana, who depend on a variety of animals, the Masai are mostly cattle herders. Generally they enjoy better rainfall, but drought does occur. The movie *Rain Warriors,* whose actors and producers were Masai themselves, is set in a year of drought. The Masai practice transhumance, moving their herds according to season. They seek the more moist lowlands during the dry season but the cooler highlands during the rainy season. Cattle is used for milk and blood, dung for building material and fuel, bone for various implements, horn for drinking, hides for clothing, and of course meat. Even so, cattle are more useful as food sources when alive than when slaughtered.

Masai Social Organization

Masai social organization is more complex than that of the Turkana. They have large extended families, made even larger by polygyny. The household, actually a village, of the laibon (prophet, but more accurately a rich man) depicted in the video *Masai Woman,* was made up of 12 wives and more than 60 grandchildren. You can see that large herds will be divided 12 ways if all the co-wives have sons. So although the wealth differences are great, how long will it last when it is inherited 12 ways?

Marriage is reminiscent of the odd couple. Women marry young, shortly after a ritual that involves clitoridectomy. Men, on the other hand, cannot marry, form households, or even inherit cattle until they have passed warrior status and become elder warriors around age 30. Thus, the husbands are much older than wives. Partly for that reason, women may often have illicit sexual relations with the much younger warriors—hoping to escape detection from their own husbands.

Age Grades and Age Sets

Masai are typical East African pastoralists in that they have age set and age grades. In an age set, men of the same age range move as a unit across age grades—first uninitiated males, then warriors, then junior elders. They cannot marry until they become junior elders, at an age range around 30 years. Later, they become senior elders and will direct the judicial and ritual affairs of the community.

Image © Anna Omelchenko, 2012. Used under license from Shutterstock, Inc.

FIGURE 21.4
A Masai warrior at a ritual of his age set. Warriors are not free to marry until they reach around age 30 and so are much older than their wives.

Age Grades and Age Sets

In one sense, all societies are divided into age categories. In the U.S. educational system, the age of every child is matched with the grade he or she is placed—or should be placed according to plan. If a child is six years of age, she or he should be in grade 1.

However, the herders of most East African cultures support a more or less dual age-based structure: permanent **age grades,** to which all males are assigned, and **age sets,** movable categories to which men of a certain age grade are assigned. The age grades often have duties and age-related assigns to them, and as age sets advance, the men assume these roles.

One tribal society whose age grades and sets conform closely to the ideal type is the Tiriki of Kenya, as described by Walter Sangree (1965). There are seven named age sets that move along seven age grades. These are compiled over four years in 15-year intervals.

TABLE 21.1
Idealized Age Sets and Age Grade among the Tiriki

Traditional Duties of Age Grade	Age Sets 1939	Age Sets 1954	Age Sets 1979	Age Sets 1994
Retired or Deceased: 91–105	Kabalach	Golongolo	Jiminigayi	Nyonje
Ritual Elders: 76–90	Golongolo	Jiminigayi	Nyonje	Mayina
Judicial Elders: 61–75	Jiminigayi	Nyonje	Mayina	Juma
Elder Warriors : 46–60	Nyonje	Mayina	Juma	Sawe
Warriors: 31–45	Mayina	Juma	Sawe	Kabalach
Initiated and Uninitiated Youths: 16–30	Juma	Sawe	Kabalach	Golongolo
Boys: 0–15	Sawe	Kabalach	Golongolo	Jiminigayi

In 1939, the youths and men of the Juma age set in 1939 had become warriors by 1954. The Mayima who were warriors became elder warriors during that period. In precolonial times, the men of the warrior age grade defended the herds of the Tiriki and conducted raids. In fact, by 1954, they were most likely wage or salaried workers, if they worked at all.

Though the Masai differ in detail, the rules of advancement and role-taking are similar. Warriors among both the Tiriki and the Masai cannot marry, form households, or own cattle. Only after reaching age 30 or so may they assume these roles.

Gender Inequality

If Masai men have the restrictions of an age grade and set, Masai women have it much rougher. They are owned by the men. They do not have cattle or other property of their own. They have to join their husbands at his household and deal with unrelated co-wives. Because men marry late, a woman may be much younger than their husband. And they have to bear sons. If they bear sons, they are secure for life. If not, these women will be expelled from their husband's household and depend on whoever will take them in.

Masai women describe the situation of these women. On top of all the other hardships they endure, they also undergo circumcision, really a sanitized name for clitoridectomy. Consider watching most YouTube presentations of this practice listed under "clitoridectomy" or "female circumcision." The women whose son passes the level of Elder Warriors can rest assured they will be watched after for the rest of their live; those who have no sons cannot, as the Masai say, eat their own bread. Few will want to support an old, childless woman.

Rain Warriors: A Prophecy Come to Pass?

The men among the Masai live the proverbial life of Riley, now that tribal war has been outlawed and they no longer fight. Nevertheless, they still retain their affiliation as warriors. This is the setting for *Rain Warriors.* Their star warrior has been killed by Wachuva, the lion who has the power to induce drought. And induce drought, he does. A group of teenaged warriors set out to kill this animal.

Many subplots go into *Rain Warriors.* What is unusual about sending out teenage boys, barely men, to hunt the lion? Why is this seen as necessary? A goat herder tries to prevent his son Merono to join the hunt. Why? How is the father shamed at the end? And in a society of cattle herders, what is the social standing of a man who herds only goats—not unlike their hated Turkana neighbors? There is much to think about from this video.

A drought has indeed come to pass. Over the years, the Sahara desert has moved further south, not only in Kenya, but throughout Sub-Saharan Africa at large. Clearly, this is a reflection of the climate change that is impinging on the entire world. Even the snows of Mount Kilimanjaro in Africa, which inspired the title of one novel and movie, are no more. Masai have fewer cattle than before and they are hard put to water them as the years progress.

Conclusion

What, then, have we learned about East African societies? We do see different levels of complexity even within tribal society, from the barely surviving Turkana to the well-integrated Masai, the latter an incipient chiefdom. Cattle are the mainstay of existence, though other animals may be present—camels, goats, sheep. Women are second-class citizens—if not property rather than citizens. Clitoridectomy remains a constant female rite of passage, not only the Masai (or Maasai), but throughout Africa as a whole. And as elsewhere across Africa, barrenness or infertility of women is a major problem, a cause for divorce. Finally, a drought is becoming permanent, a new normal ecological across Africa as a whole.

Selected Films

Diary of a Maasai Village Series. 1985. 5 videos of an hour each. Melissa Llewellyn-Davies. Cambridge, MA: Documentary Educational Resources.

Kenyan Boran, Parts 1 and 2. Two parts of 33 minutes each. David MacDougall and James Blue. Cambridge, MA: Documentary Educational Resources. Herding peoples face consequences of a road being constructed in their herding territory.

Maasai Women. 1980. 60 minutes. Melanie Wallace and Sanford Low. Cambridge, MA: Documentary Educational Resources. Describes the status of women as inferior.

Selected Literature

Anderson, David. 2005. *Histories of the Hanged: The Dirty War in Kenya and the End of Empire.* New York: Norton.

Cooper, Frederick. 2002. *Africa since 1940: The Past of the Present.* Cambridge, UK.

Elkins, Caroline. 2005. *Imperial Reckoning: The Untold Story of Britain's Gulag in Kenya.* New York: Owl Books.

Hornsby, Charles. 2012. *Kenya: A History Since Independence.* London: I.B. Tauris.

Kenyatta, Jomo. 1962. *Facing Mount Kenya.* New York: Vintage.

Santoti, Tepillitr Ole. 1988. *The Worlds of a Maasai Warrior: An Autobiography.* Berkeley: University of California Press.

CHAPTER 22

Peoples of the Kalahari and Their Neighbors: The Ju/'hoansi or !Kung San of Southern Africa

Southwest Africa (traditional spelling: South West Africa) has a more compelling history than it is given credit for. Of course, it is the home of the fabled hunting and gathering Bushmen (now known under various names: the !Kung, the !Kung San, the San, and the now politically correct Ju/'hoansi [pronounced ju-wa-si], their own name). The region also encompasses the cattle-herding Herero, the Tswana, and the Nama or Namaqua (also known as their archaic term Hottentots).

More important, the region has a grim history; this was the site of the genocide of the Herero and the Nama in and around Windhoek, the capital of what is now Namibia. A former German colony called German West Africa at the time, Namibia was the testing ground of the German concentration and death camps under the Second Reich of Kaiser Wilhelm II that formed the model of Germany's concentration camps under the Third Reich. Theories of eugenics and racism were formed using the Herero and the Nama as examples. The Nyae Nyae Ju/'hoansi also went through a period of internment under apartheid South Africa.

This section provides a review of the Ju/'hoansi or !Kung (as this culture will be called interchangeably) and the Herero in their respective ethnographic presence, then will trace the changes during their phases of transition to modern societies. Following an overview of the regions, the Ju/'hoansi will first be discussed in the three-stage framework as suggested in John Marshall's *A Kalahari Family* and in Lee's recent update on the Dobe (and Nyae Nyae) Ju/'hoansi, then the pastoralists will be reviewed, primarily the Herero who were forced into the Kalahari during their uprising against the German colonizers from 1903 to 1907.

Southwest Africa: A Geography

Southwest Africa is a location that seems to lack history. The region starts with a coastal area with the inland consisting of grassland and mountain. As one moves further inland, the landscape

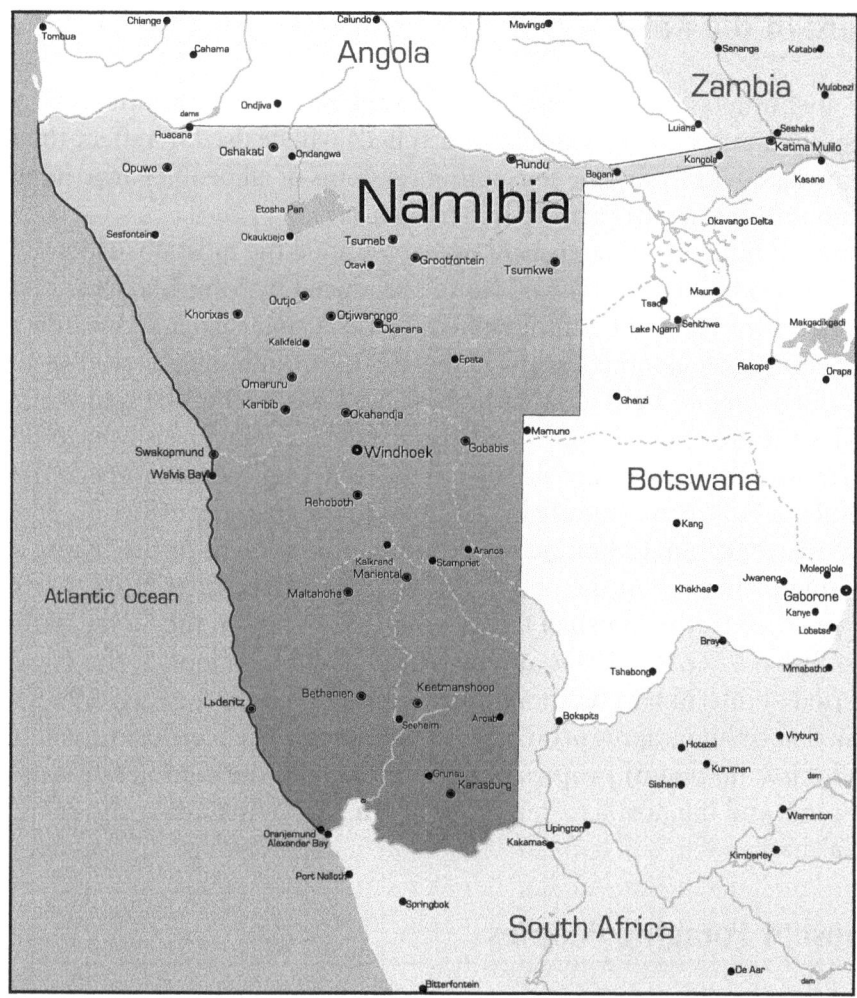

Image © Olinchuk, 2012. Used under license from Shutterstock, Inc.

FIGURE 22.1
Map of South West Africa, with Namibia to the west, Botswana to the center, South Africa to the south and northward to southern Angola. The Ju/'hoansi ranged from west Namibia into Botwana to the east, northwestern South Africa to the south, and southern portions of Angola to the north.

becomes desert, with the typical rainy and dry seasons of tropical areas, but without the rain forest. The area is too arid to consistently support cattle herding, although some cultures did raise cattle. As a marginal area, the regions could at best support hunting and gathering. The Dobe Ju/'hoansi enjoyed relatively well watered areas—enough to sustain the indigenous pastoralist Tswana, from which the nation-state of Botswana derived its name. However, the Nyae Nyae area in neighboring Namibia is extremely dry. To force the pastoralist Herero into the desert, as the Germans did in 1903, would spell certain death from lack of water.

The Ju/'hoansi of the Kalahari

The Ju/'hoansi are hunters and gatherers located in the Kalahari Desert in southern Africa. The term Ju/'hoansi (the shortened version Ju is often cited) will be used to reflect the terms the people refer to themselves. Like the ethnic self-naming systems of all peoples around the world, these are approximations of the actual terms of self-reference.

When it comes to film, the Ju/'hoansi are perhaps among the most documented culture in the world's cultures. A series titled *A Kalahari Family* produced by John Marshall, filmmaker of the Nyae Nyae !Kung for his family of ethnographers, traces a single extended family of !Kung from their days as a hunting and gathering band in the 1950s through their period of internment in a South African camp with hundreds of other Ju from the 1960s to the 1990s, to their current cattle-ranching period of the present in the independent state of Namibia. The most recent edition of *The Dobe Ju/'hoansi* by Richard Borshay Lee also brings the reader up-to-date for both the Dobe (mostly in Botswana) and the Nyae Nyae (mostly in Namibia) Ju/'hoansi (Lee 2012).

In this chapter, we will first examine the ethnographic present of the !Kung as hunters and gatherers, focusing primarily on the peoples of the Nyae Nyae district of South West Africa/Namibia as represented by the Marshall family (the 1950s) and on the Dobe !Kung of Botswana as portrayed by Richard Lee (the 1980s and before). We will then look at the Nyae Nyae peoples during their period of internment (ethnographic present, 1960s to the early 1990s) and their current ranching period (ethnographic present since the 1990s). The conclusion will cover the Dobe, Nyae Nyae, and other Ju/'hoansi peoples of the present, and the complexities of their status in Namibia, Botswana, and the northern region of South Africa, including the increased desertification of the Kalahari.

The Ju/'hoansi: A Foraging Peoples

The Ju/'hoansi constitute a culture area of nomadic hunters and gatherers dependent primarily on wild plant foods and game. They are nomadic because both their food sources game and plant foods vary by season, and their population is small from band to band. They number between 40 to 100 people in related families. As stated above, the Ju/'hoansi range throughout much of southern Africa, which covers primarily the southern one-fifth of the continent of Africa. As true in other parts of Africa, modern political boundaries overlap with culture areas, and the Ju/'hoansi range into other countries, such as Angola and Zambia (see Figure 22.1).

Foraging Technology and Economy

From a Western perspective, the technology of hunting and gathering is simple. The !Kung use bows and poison-tipped arrows to hunt large game such as giraffes (as portrayed in John Marshall's classic film *The Hunters*), wildebeest, zebras, and a variety of African antelope such as the eland and springbok. They stalk their game and penetrate their quarry with the arrows. The poison works through the bloodstream of the animal until it dies. The hunters then either track their game until the animal dies or waits and retrieves their game three or four days later. Hunting is men's work, although they may use an arrow provided by a non-hunter: an elder, a woman, or even a child. The owner whose arrow is the first to penetrate an animal "owns" that animal—but with qualification: they share their portion with other Ju in the band. The hunters then butcher the animal and summon the other villagers to bring the meat back to camp.

Gathering is less exciting but more rewarding, and it is the work of women and their children. Food sources range from roots and tubers to berries and melons (a valuable water source in a hot and dry climate) to seeds and the much favored mongongo (also called mangetti) nuts. Among the !Kung, mongongo nuts is the most popular and among the most plentiful. They also can be stored for a period up to 18 months. Estimates of the portion of plant foods in the total diet range from 75% to 85%, thus making women the most important food providers and also the more influential gender of the nomadic bands. They are the ones who best know the location of plant foods and so have a great deal of say to where the band should migrate next.

Property is nonexistent or, more accurately, communalistic. Hunters and gatherers both can go anywhere to find food. Although bands are based in particular territories, they do not exclude other bands. Often an itinerant band may ask the headman of the home territory permission to use its water hole, which is always granted. The request is a matter of etiquette. Foragers own the plant foods they gather, but unlike game, they are not hard to come by.

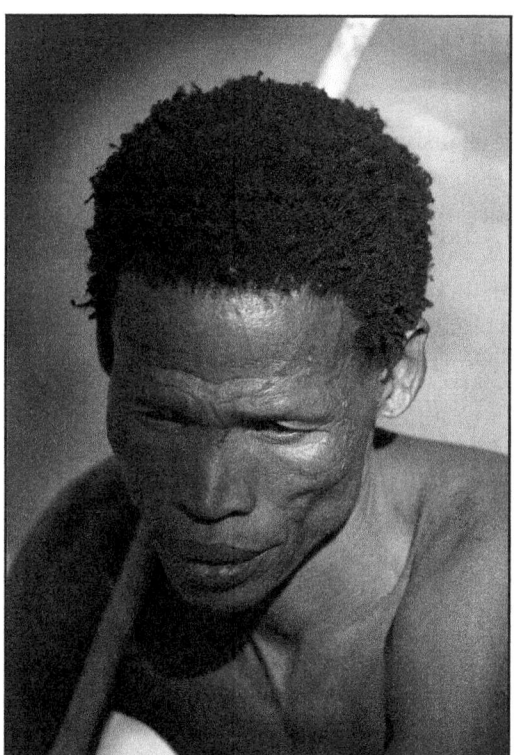

Image © Pichugin Dmitry, 2012. Used under license from Shutterstock, Inc.

FIGURE 22.2

A Ju/'hoansi or !Kung hunter. Men do the actual hunting of large game, although the owner of the arrow (the hunters themselves or a non-hunter) takes possession of the animal, only later to distribute the meat back at the camp.

Large game is always shared, and it is the owner's responsibility to share his portion of the game with his kin of specified status; rules govern the distribution. The owner of the arrow that first penetrated the animal has the same responsibility with his (or her) portion. This distribution is an example of generalized reciprocity. Not everyone bags an animal at any one time, and a hunter may go for months without a single kill. Nonetheless, others provision him with meat. When he does kill an animal, he will then repay others for their favor. But no one will keep accounts of how many kudus or elands he owes other hunters. Nevertheless, the man who has not contributed for a long time is known by all and will lose status, even thought he will not be left to starve. Marcel Mauss, a sociologist and nephew of the eminent French sociologist Emile Durkheim, developed a three-fold model of gift giving to explain how relationships are maintained in nonstate societies like the !Kung. There is the obligation to give, and thereby extend a relationship. There is the obligation to accept, and thereby accept the relationship along with the gift. There is, finally, the obligation to repay, and so validate the relationship. Failure to repay is to be reduced to the status of a beggar. If a man fails to bag and distribute an animal for months or years on end, he will be regarded as "poor, and without people."

Because of the relative scarcity of the environment, the !Kung's band is highly adaptive. Bands are made up of related families. They may be bonded together by a pair of siblings, parents, and children, or even unrelated persons who happened to be friends. Families live in small, temporary huts called *scherms.* Usually, huts are arranged in a line and dismantled when the band moves on to the next gathering site.

The upper limit of group size is established by the carrying capacity of the environment. Game could be limited, there may be a shortage of the much-favored mongongo nuts, but the efficient limit is the scarcest resource, namely water. According to Liebig's Law of the Minimum, the population may not increase beyond the level of that resource, which in a desert like the Kalahari is water.

The !Kung have been the focus of another issue: they lack social stratification. No one is superior to another, or regarded as such. Richard Lee stumbled on an explanation as to how the Dobe Ju/'hoansi, whom he had been studying for the first time in 1975, prevented social inequality in their band. This is how it went:

> Toward Christmas, when he was about to leave for the holidays, he gave a fattened ox as a gift to his Ju/'hoansi hosts. It was his way of thanking them for their cooperation during the year. Unexpectedly, the !Kung hosts ridiculed his gift. The ox was "a bag of bones" (though it was fat). He was shocked and saddened by the reaction. Only later did he learn that the Dobe likewise ridiculed all their successful hunters. The practice is called "insulting the meat."

Later, a Dobe called Tomazo, as much philosopher as hunter, explained that the insults suppressed the arrogance a hunter might have in making a big kill. "When a young man kills much meat," he said, "he thinks himself as a chief or big man, and the rest of us as servants. We cannot accept this. Someday his price will make him kill somebody. So we always speak of his meat as worthless. That way, we cool his heart and make him gentle." (Lee, Richard. *The Dobe Ju/'hoansi.* 2012)

So, Lee reports, every bandsman knows about inequality, and that is their greatest fear. Unusual gifts always involve some ulterior motive. Therefore, they denigrate his gifts. Christopher Boehm in his *Hierarchy in the Forest* (2001) reports this behavior among other peoples of the world and those with more complex and more populous societies. He calls the pattern **reverse dominance hierarchy.** This entails the active suppression of any social inequality that may arise. Though beyond the scope of this module, it had implications in understanding why states and kingdoms are recent—about 5,000 years—in the more than 100,000 to 200,000 years of humankind's evolution.

Marriage, Family, and Kinship

The Ju/'hoansi experience sexuality early in life, and children often copulate with their opposite-sex siblings. Nevertheless, the incest tabu kicks in at puberty, and by age of marriage, sibling and first cousin relationships are avoided. Indeed, given that Ju/'hoansi bands are so close, a parent may reject a prospective suitor on any of a variety of pretexts. Marriage is arranged by parents of the partners and often the man captures his bride and moves her to a marriage hut; relationships are often stormy and the tension may remain for months. Women often resist the advances of their first husbands, and more than once, the marriage is called off. This is one piece of evidence that women have a strong sense of independence from both parents and husbands. Once the stormy period is past, the spouses settle in a relationship that may last 20 years to life. Once a marriage is contracted, the groom works for the bride's parents for several months before bringing her back to his own family.

Divorce is infrequent, and marriages usually last for five years or more. Divorce, if it occurs, is usually initiated by the wife. Inasmuch as no property is involved, the spouses' divorce is amicable and the former spouses may often live nearby, each with their new husband and wife. Conflict, when it occurs, arises between two men over the same woman or the discovery of an extramarital affair by either the wife or husband.

Also as important are the alliances the marriage creates. This is a form of social security, and a band with many in-laws has ready access to many waterholes and frequent gift exchanges. In some instances, the couple may move in with the parents of either spouse, followed by other kin. Such co-residence may last for decades. However, larger groups beyond the extended family do not exist.

In the absence of states, how do the !Kung keep from each others' throats? Warfare among !Kung and other bands are rare. This is not to say that the !Kung do not argue, or fight, or even kill each other. Often disputes arise over women; sexual jealousy is not absent. Nevertheless, with so few people in the band, the rest of the people recognize the potential arguments have for disrupting the band. Most individuals, therefore, take no sides and usually the argument cools down. The dissatisfied person often leaves the band.

The Stages of !Kung Transition

The ethnographic present, as stated, is in the past. In the case of Nyae Nyae studied by the Marshalls, the ethnographic present was 1951–1957; with Richard Lee, it was the 1970s and 1980s. Since then, both the South African government under apartheid and the independent new nations of Botswana and Namibia have forced !Kung hunters to abandon hunting. Some, like Botswana, have cleared the !Kung to make way for the diamond mines; others, like those in Namibia, have been forced to make way for cattle ranches or game reserves, as shown here. Several videos have been produced to emphasize these themes. As mentioned above, Marshall's five-part series *A Kalahari Family* traces these themes through four generations. Journeyman pictures provides two DVDs tracing the forced location of Dobe !Kung to make way for corporate diamond mining operations, namely The Kalahari Bushmen–Botswana (available from YouTube).

During the period of South African internment starting in 1959, the Ju/'hoansi of Nyae Nyae were forced to abandon their hunting sites and herded into a barbed wired settlement at a place called Tsumkwe. They lived in houses and were obliged to handle chores under the South African whites. Rather than being allowed to hunt—they were forbidden to do so under the pretext of wildlife conservation—they were supplied weekly rations that included the insipid "mealie meal," a concoction that included whatever grains were available. It was there that the film *The Gods Must Be Crazy* was filmed and released as a blockbuster in Hollywood parlance. The stereotyped innocent savages who fight over a Coke bottle was countered by John Marshall's film *N!ai: A !Kung Woman,* which is an indictment of actual life of a people living in overcrowded conditions for which they had not been accustomed to before.

As the war of independence conducted by the South West African People's Organization (SWAPO) intensified, the residents of Tsumkwe were recruited to fight for the South African Defence Force (SADF). The draftees were less than effective or enthusiastic in waging the war, but the pay was relatively good. In later years, some of the Ju/'hoansi were allowed to live in model villages and dress—loincloth and all—as "real Bushmen" to attract the tourist trade to what John Marshall called "The Plastic Stone Age."

In 1990, independence came to Namibia and the Ju/'hoansi were allowed to return to their former sites. Under the auspices of the Nyae Nyae Development of Namibia (NNDFN), based in the Namibian capital of Windhoek, consultants John Marshall and Claire Ritchie, both anthropologists and filmmakers, advocated for the Ju/'hoansi. Even before independence, several Ju/'hoansi, fearing their abandoned lands would fall under control of the Nature Conservancy, left on their own and returned to their former homelands. A Farmer's Co-operative was formed, and with legal aid provided by the NNDFN and other international groups, their ownership of the land was restored. The Ju/'hoansi, former foragers, now became ranchers.

The events affecting the Nyae Nyae Ju/'hoansi did not extend to the Dobe, who lived in an independent state; Botswana foraging would continue as a lifeway for the next 20 years. Nevertheless, they were soon affected by pressures of the global economy in the form of the diamond trade, and the government was later to induce many Dobe to leave their hunting grounds for settlements established for them. Varied programs in both countries have sought to improve the lives of the Ju/'hoansi, including education, employability, and the protection against a new scourge affecting all of Africa, AID/HIV. The changes continue.

The Cattle Herders of Namibia and Botswana

Discussion of the Ju/'hoansi would be incomplete without a review of their cattle-herding neighbors, namely the Herero, the Tswana, and Nama. The Herero are pastoralists (cattle herders) concentrated predominantly in Namibia but also found in Botswana and Angola. The Tswana, who gave Botswana their name, are cattle herders in their namesake country but the majority of them live in northern South Africa. Both are descendants of Bantu people who migrated southward from regions now known as Angola, Zimbabwe, and Zambia. A third culture, known as Nama or

Namaqua, are an indigenous southwestern culture of the same Khoisan linguistic family as the several !Kung subgroups, but are, like the Herero and Tswana, pastoralists. All three are chiefdoms. Primary focus will be on the Herero because of space limitations, but the other two will be briefly described as appropriate.

Although the Tswana had coexisted with the Ju/'hoansi for generations before the twentieth century, the migration of Herero into Botwana became important only during the first decade of the twentieth century. The story begins with the migration of German colonists into what would soon become German South West Africa. From 1873 onward, Germans took increasing amounts of land and cattle from the Africans. Despite revolts against these takeovers, the Herero lost these skirmishes.

Then in 1903, the Herero people learned that they were to be placed in reservations, leaving more room for colonists to own land and prosper. In 1904, the Herero and Nama began a great rebellion that lasted until 1907. The war against the Herero (and Nama) was the first in which German imperialism resorted to methods of genocide. In 1903, an estimated 80,000 Herero lived in German South West Africa at the beginning of Germany's colonial rule over the area. After their revolt was suppressed by 1907, they numbered approximately 15,000. In a period of four years, approximately 65,000 Herero people had perished.

General Lothar Von Trotta, who took over the administration of the colony in 1904, devised a plan to annihilate the Herero nation. The plan was to surround the area where the Herero were, leaving but one route for them to escape, into the desert. The Herero battled the Germans, and the losses were minor. It was when they had escaped through the only passage made available by the Germans, and had been chased away from the last watering hole into the Kalahari Desert that casualties grew to substantial amounts. It was then that the Herero uprising changed, in 1907, from war to genocide.

There is evidence to indicate the genocide was systematically planned and laid a precedent for the better known genocidal policies in the Third Reich. Surviving Herero not executed under Von Trotta's strict orders were put into forced labor camps; the Nama caught in German West Africa were executed in death camps set up in the outskirts of Windhoek.

The Germans also laid the foundation for medical experiments that would be conducted in the Third Reich three decades later. Eugen Fischer, a German scientist who subscribed to the ideology of eugenics, came to the concentration camps in Windhoek to conduct medical experiments on race, using children of Herero people and mulatto children of Herero women and German men as test subjects. Together with Theodor Mollison, he also experimented on Herero prisoners. Those experiments included sterilization, injection of smallpox, typhus, as well as tuberculosis. Fischer also ran numerous racial tests on his subjects such as head and body measurements, eye and hair examinations. From his studies, he called for the genocide of alleged "inferior races." Thus, the precedent for what was to become Hitler's final solution toward the European Jews was set.

It with this sordid background that large numbers of Herero pastoralists migrated to Bechuanaland, where the British authorities allowed them to stay, and where their descendants would become citizens of an independent Botswana. As was probably the case in German West Africa, the Herero remained chiefdoms in their adopted country. They were organized in accordance with the rule of double unilineal descent, whereby each person is affiliated with a group of patrilineal kin (*otuzo*) and one of matrilineal kin (*omaanda* or *eanda*). This twofold rule of descent applied both to clans or sibs and to the smaller lineages.

One change that was evident was their value orientations regarding cattle. When they first arrived into the Botswana region, cattle were sacred animals. Over time, the proscription against the sale of cattle came to be relaxed.

Some ethnographers have argued that the !Kung (Ju/'hoansi) traditionally were servants or serfs of the three chiefdoms since their first contact in probably the twelfth century CE (Common Era). According to this argument, the !Kung were not independent egalitarian hunters and gatherers but were cattle-keeping serfs of the pastoralists. Lee, a long-term ethnographer of the Dobe and more recently of the Nyae Nyae !Kung, questions the argument that they occupied the lowest rung of the pastoralist hierarchy. Whatever their relationship might have been to the Tswana, or the Nama, it seems less likely the case with those Herero who migrated from the Namibia region.

Conclusion

The Ju/'hoansi or !Kung are one of the most studied foraging societies in the world. They are classic examples of foragers, of stateless societies, and they raise this question: How can societies without central government or legal code or police forces manage their affairs? The answer is simple, yet complex: very well, with the sanctions they impose on deviant individuals. Conflicts erupt, but they seldom explode into all-out war. This way of life is disappearing as the Kalahari Desert attracts mining and cattle industries, tourist trophy hunters, game preserves—the list goes on.

Finally, there is a little known history about the Namibia region: how the Herero were forced out of the then-colony of German West Africa and into the British colony of Bechuanaland. Even deeper questions are raised by this history: how did the colonial power elite of German West Africa develop the death camp of Stark Island, which would serve as the prototype of Auschwitz and Dachau? Further, what role did their scientists play in establishing the medical experiments using live subjects that would be replicated in the German Third Reich only a few decades later?

Selected Films

A Kalahari Family. 2000. John Marshall. 5 vols. Cambridge, MA: Documentary Resources Center.

The Hunters. 1957. 72 minutes. John Marshall and Robert Gardner. Cambridge, MA: Documentary Resources Center.

N!ai: A !Kung Woman. 1980. 59 minutes. John Marshall. Cambridge, MA: Documentary Resources Center.

Namibia: Genocide and the Second Reich. 2007. London: BBC Documentaries.

Selected Literature

Lee, Richard B. 2012. *The Dobe Ju/'hoansi.* Belmont, CA: Wadsworth.

Madley, Benjamin. 2005. "From Africa to Auschwitz: How German South West Africa Incubated Ideas and Methods Adopted and Developed by the Nazis in Eastern Europe." *European History Quarterly* 35: 429 ff.